LIGHT

AND

SHADOWS

$8.95

LIGHT

AND

SHADOWS

A HISTORY OF MOTION PICTURES

THOMAS W. BOHN, University of Evansville
and
RICHARD L. STROMGREN, University of Massachusetts
with the assistance of
DANIEL H. JOHNSON, University of Minnesota—Duluth

ALFRED PUBLISHING CO., INC.

Printed in the United States of America

Library of Congress Cataloging in Publication Data

Bohn, Thomas W.
  Light and shadows: a history of motion pictures.

  Bibliography: p.
  Filmography: p.
  Includes index.
    1. Moving-pictures. I. Stromgren, Richard, 1932-   joint
author. II. Johnson, Daniel, 1940-   joint author. III. Title.
PN1994.B564   791.43   75-640
ISBN 0-88284-024-X

Alfred Publishing Co., Inc.
75 Channel Drive, Port Washington, N.Y. 11050

Contents

Illustrations

Preface

The scope, design, and direction of this book are strongly influenced by the factors that characterize film's uniqueness. No other art is so interdependent with the worlds of commerce and technology. No other medium so completely fulfills the functions of both high art and popular culture. Film is clearly a form which reflects contemporary social thought—the fears, joys, obsessions, taboos—of its time; and it is just as surely responsible for reinforcing and modifying our understanding, attitudes and beliefs about the world around us. In addition, for all this interaction, film is often a strongly personal medium reflecting the dreams, ideas, and inspirations of producers, directors, screenwriters, set designers, costumers, editors, actors as well as the audiences themselves.

The history of motion pictures, then, is necessarily industrial, technological, social, aesthetic, and personal. Furthermore, it reflects not simply independent parallel events within these categories, but strongly interdependent activities as well.

With film's unique properties in mind, this book presents a history which is more than a chronology of films and personalities. Instead, it tells an integrated story of those experiences which influenced artistic expression (cultural, economic, political) and those which influenced the advancement of an industry (technological, management, distribution).

Although not rigidly defined, the book is divided into three parts. Chapters 1 through 6 present the earliest beginnings of film and continue through the technological improvements and the artistic development that began an industry. The second part (chapters 7 through 11) begins with sound. In this part, the reader is engaged by the problems, frustrations, and inspirations which came from the addition of the new dimension. The final section begins with an international renaissance, the simultaneous arrival of television, a crucial court decision, political pressures, and the beginning of the "new realism" directly after World War II. The concluding chapters in the three sections are intended to serve as an overview of the period, pulling together the evolution of form and function up to those pivotal periods.

Finally, in the belief that a history of this young and exciting medium should be more than an accounting of titles, synopses, and production notations, the authors bring with them all of their biases and other forms of prejudice, favoritism and discrimination that have been and remain a part of their movie experience.

Acknowledgments

The authors would like to thank the following people for their generous help and cooperation in the preparation of this book: John Kuiper, Rita Horowitz and staff at The Library of Congress, Colin McArthur, Nicky North and the staff of the Education Department at The British Film Institute and Mary Corliss at the Museum of Modern Art. A special word of thanks must go to Ron Shelly who encouraged us to start and John Stout of Alfred Publishing who prodded us to finish.

A final word of appreciation must also go to the many students in film who by their enthusiasm and curiosity have pushed us to search for new meanings in films' past and present.

An early slide used to welcome
audiences into theaters.

Prehistory
and Beginnings

Introduction

Most historians face the question of where to begin their narrative and so does the historian of film. The issue should be clear, since motion pictures are less than 100 years old. However, it is only the accumulation of technology known as cinematography which has not quite reached its centennial; the *concept* of reality in motion is as old as man. The search for a beginning, then, can lead in many directions: to cave paintings showing a boar with eight legs, Chinese shadow plays, Aristotle's "dark room," or Ptolemy's writing on optics, *ad infinitum.* However, most film historians agree that the nineteenth century, with its tremendous scientific and technical achievements, marks the true beginning of motion pictures. Here, for the first time, events and discoveries were·connected in meaningful fashion.

However, beginning at this time would mean denying the entire experience of man's fascination with reality and motion and his attempts to duplicate them in art and science. We would be focusing our attention almost exclusively on the technological apparatus and overlooking the human need and desire behind the apparatus.

The Substrata

In looking at the maze of ideas and discoveries concerned with the reproduction of physical reality that occurred before the nineteenth century, it is pointless to try to construct a single evolutionary line. Not one but several lines exist. In addition, the lines are broken, diffused, and at times contradictory.

Cave paintings represent the most primitive example of man's attempts to recreate motion. However, the earliest conscious attempt of a culture to both recreate reality and present an interpreted event in motion occurs in Chinese and Japanese shadow plays using silhouette figures to depict various stories and legends.

Around 340 B.C. Aristotle noted that sunlight passing through a square hole cast a round image on the wall. This "dark room" was in reality a camera, with the square hole acting as an aperture. As Martin Quigley notes in his book *Magic Shadows*, this was the first important contribution to the art/science of reproducing reality by a single individual.

From this point on the twin lines of art and science moved forward as hundreds of individuals noted, studied, experimented with, and wrote on various phenomena regarding light and motion. Choosing what is important or significant among this maze is like throwing darts blindfolded, but at least six men and their efforts stand out.

Leon Battista Alberti

In 1450 this Italian architect constructed the *camera lucida,* a device similar to a large box camera which was used by artists to copy life and nature.

Leonardo da Vinci

In 1500 da Vinci, through his analysis of the human eye, set forth a theory of the *camera obscura* or "dark room." He was one of the first to explain accurately how the eye functioned and used this explanation as the basis for his scientific description of the *camera obscura*. This phenomenon was achieved by cutting a hole in one wall of a dark room so that light from it fell on the opposite wall. If the scene outside were bright enough, an image would be visible on the wall, upside down and right for left. Whereas Aristotle regarded the phenomenon as a scientific oddity, da Vinci's work formed the theoretical basis for photography. Da Vinci, however, was interested in many areas of scientific inquiry and did little to develop and popularize his findings.

Giambattista della Porta

It remained for this entrepreneur to popularize and refine both Alberti's and da Vinci's work. Della Porta borrowed freely and usually without credit from many previous works. However, his significant contribution came in the way he used the *camera obscura*. Della Porta did not confine himself to scientific descriptions, but created illustrations of hunting and battle scenes, thereby substituting artificial objects and painted scenes for reality. Della Porta even refers to presenting "little shows" for important people.

The real importance of the developments so far is that man had advanced to the point where he could accurately *duplicate* reality and did not have to depend solely on his eye and mind to *remember* reality. For the first time the artist began to use the tools of science for public presentations of reality.

Athanasius Kircher

Perhaps the most significant pre-nineteenth century discovery is Kircher's magic lantern. Its significance is that of all the "substratum" discoveries and inventions the magic lantern is the only direct ancestor of a modern device—the projector. Indeed, magic lanterns similar to those used in the 1600's were still used

Two illustrations from Athanasius Kircher's
Ars Magna Lucis et Umbrae show the properties of the lens and a projection of a slide in addition to a portrait of Kircher.

by traveling showmen into the twentieth century. Although somewhat obscured by conflicting claims, the development of the magic lantern most likely dates from Kircher's 1646 publication *Ars Magna Lucis et Umbrae* ("The Great Art of Light and Shadow"). In this work Kircher described, among other things, the *Magia Catoptrica,* a device using mirrors and a light source capable of projecting objects. Kircher developed the lantern to the point where he and others were using a series of slides to tell simple stories. Throughout the seventeenth, eighteenth, and nineteenth centuries the magic lantern remained popular, as both elaborate theaters and traveling showmen used Kircher's invention for the amusement of rich and poor alike. This represented a significant step in the evolution of the motion picture process as the *masses* were now being entertained rather than simply the rich and well educated.

Johannes Zahn

The first step in linking projection with motion was taken by Zahn at the end of the seventeenth century. He used glass slides mounted on a circular disk which revolved in front of a magic lantern. This was only a crude form of motion, since there was no shutter, a candle was the only light source, and the pictures were simple phase drawings (illustrations of an object or person in various stages of animated motion).

E. G. Robertson

Following Zahn's innovations, the magic lantern was soon being used for increasingly elaborate productions. Perhaps the ultimate theatrical "experience" was E. G. Robertson's *Phantasmagoria.* Using a rear projection method coupled with a complex system of lenses and reflectors, Robertson told macabre stories as witches, ghosts, and other apparitions appeared before startled audiences assembled in old ruins and deserted mansions. This late eighteenth century use of the magic lantern was the natural predecessor of Georges Méliès, who used motion pictures for the same purposes a century later.

This brief exploration of cinematic substrata saw basic developments in optics and projection reach the point where elaborate and complex amusements were presented to a paying public. However, the images presented were drawn pictures of still life. There was no photography and no motion.

It seems proper at this time to ask a basic question: Why are we concerned with events and discoveries which occurred before motion pictures actually came into existence? Why don't we simply start in 1895? A good question, and the answer is just as basic. The motion picture is a medium which communicates with the help of machines. Without the actual apparatus of cameras, film, and projectors there would be no communication. No one is denying the importance of people in creating and designing messages and in operating the machines. A camera only photographs what it is "told" to by someone. And yet, only a camera can reproduce reality in the form of a photograph or motion picture. Two primary ingredients of the motion pictures go hand in hand—people and machines. Orson Welles "saw" certain scenes in *Citizen Kane* in deep focus, but only a camera could reproduce them. Therefore, we have to give more than a casual nod to technology. It must take its legitimate place alongside aesthetic development, industrial expansion, and audience analysis as a basis for understanding motion pictures. Of all these, technology comes first. The motion picture is the child of science. Cinematography is technical apparatus reproducing reality in motion. Cinematography is our first concern, because only when the technical reality exists can the artistic and industrial possibilities take form and grow.

The Age of Discovery

Any attempt to construct an overview of the major discoveries leading up to the development of cinematography must begin with a debt of acknowledgment to C. W. Ceram's book *Archeology of the Cinema*. This is quite simply the key source for any student wanting a detailed exposition of the 19th century development of cinematography.

It was Ceram who stated that the basic change occurring in the 19th century was a shift from mechanical to technical thinking. Mechanics are static, according to Ceram, technology is dynamic. He might even have used the word "explosive" in describing the tremendous technological advances of this "age of invention." The dynamic explosion of ideas, discoveries, and inventions again makes this historical chronicle difficult, as there are few unbroken lines. Although it represents only 70 years of development, independent parallel movements exist which do not automatically link up in a preset plan. For example, once Daguerre and others developed photography they did not proceed to work on motion photography. Eastman was not particularly interested in motion picture film. Edison was not concerned at first with projection. What was happening in the 19th century was an overwhelming, driving need to discover. The urge to solve the problem of recreating life in motion was tremendous. As such, the actual development of various phases of the process took place in many locations and often at the same time. The motion picture was truly a child of its time. It was one of many problems solved, concepts realized, and inventions perfected. Those who worked on the many stages in motion picture development were usually individuals working alone, pursuing their particular field of research out of a sense of discovery and personal interest. As a result, the inventions were developed and adopted very quickly. Researchers were quite willing to share the fruits of their labor; in fact, most of them eagerly accepted any opportunity to "show off" the results of their often anonymous efforts. It was only when these inventions became the basis for financial gain that the inventive process slowed down in a concern over patents and control.

Five Essential Steps

Although cinematography is a mix of many discoveries and ideas, there are five major developments which form its essential technological and theoretical base.

1. Persistence of Vision
2. Photography
3. Motion Picture Camera
4. Film
5. Motion Picture Projector

Persistence of Vision

With all this talk of machines and technology it probably seems strange and somewhat contradictory to begin this review with an explanation of a physical phenomenon. However, it is only because of this phenomenon of the human eye that the machines are able to function at all. Motion pictures do not actually move. What you see is simply the illusion of motion created by the projection of individual still photographs (frames). The frames are held in place for a fraction of a second and it is the quality of the eye known as persistence of vision which helps create the illusion of motion by retaining the image of the projected frame a fraction of a second longer than it actually appears on the screen. With a shutter mechanism masking the actual movement of the still frames into place, the projector and the eye work in tandem to create the illusion of motion. The same effect occurs when a burning stick is whirled around in a circle. If whirled fast enough, an unbroken circle of fire results. Although this phenomenon has been observed and commented on for centuries, it was not until the early 1800's that a concrete theory of how and why the phenomenon worked was presented.

No less than three people set down this theory, beginning with an anonymous contributor known only as "J.M." in 1820. Four years later Peter Mark Roget, known primarily for his *Thesaurus*, read a paper developing the same theory. At about the same time Dr. John Paris described a toy he constructed called a Thaumatrope which worked on the principle of persistence of vision. Paris quickly realized the commercial value of the theory and arranged to have various motion devices made and sold in London.

Following Paris' exploitation, a great many toys and devices sprang up. The most important and popular were Joseph Plateau's Phenakistoscope (1832), Simon von Stampfer's Stroboscopic Disk (1832), George Horner's Zoetrope (1834), and Emil Reynaud's Praxinoscope (1877). These were the first devices based on a realized theory of the persistence of vision; they formed the core of many commercial enterprises and an industry soon grew up to build and sell them.

Dr. John Paris invented the little spinning discs he called the Thaumatrope. When spun, the pictures on either side of the disk merged and became one picture.

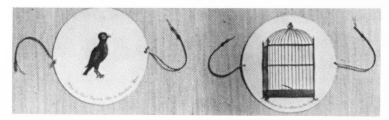

Photography

As motion toys were becoming popular parlor entertain-
ments, developments in the permanent recording of reality were
reaching fruition. Once again, experiments dating back several
centuries preceded the actual invention of photography. However, it was not until 1813, when Joseph Nicéphore Niepce
began to experiment with transferring lithographic drawings by
the aid of light, that photography as we know it appeared. Niepce
soon teamed up with Louis Jacque Mandé Daguerre and together they worked to perfect a photographic process. Niepce died
in 1833, but Daguerre continued the research and in 1839
produced a workable system of photography, but one in which
each photograph taken was unique and not reproducible. For the
first time, man had the technological capability to duplicate
reality in its natural form. Improvements in the process by
William Henry Fox Talbot in England soon made it possible for
any number of positive prints to be made. Photography became
not only a method of duplication, but multiplication as well.
Exposure time was soon reduced to three minutes, but it was not
until the development of a dry plate process in 1871 that any type
of instantaneous photography was possible.

The importance of photography to the development of
motion pictures is obvious. Even with sophisticated motion toys
the phenomenon of motion was still being illustrated by drawings. Now for the first time photographs were substituted for
phase drawings and reality in motion was possible.

Motion Picture Camera

Despite the increasing use of photographs in motion toys,
the best impressions of motion were fairly crude, since individual "frames" consisted of posed stills. A method of taking
photographs of a subject in a natural state of motion was
necessary.

The solution to this problem was lengthy and involved. It
begins with a man named Eadweard Muybridge, a wager on a
horse, and a former governor of California. The former governor
was Leland Stanford and the bet concerned whether or not a
galloping horse ever had all four legs off the ground at the same
time. In order to settle the question, Stanford hired Muybridge,
a photographer of some note. Muybridge immediately realized

These phase pictures illustrate the type of motion study work produced by Eadweard Muybridge in the late 1880's.
LIBRARY OF CONGRESS

that no single camera could do the job, so he stationed 24 cameras side by side along a track. Twenty-four strings were stretched across the track and as the horse galloped down the track it broke the strings and tripped the cameras' shutters. The result was a series of twenty-four phase pictures which, when put together, formed a series picture. Muybridge continued to use this method to conduct motion studies of animals and humans, although he later perfected a timing device which automatically tripped the shutter.

Muybridge's method, however, was obviously not the solution to moving picture photography. A single camera was needed and a number of people began working in this direction. The most significant development occurred in France in 1882, when a French physiologist, Dr. E. J. Marey, developed a photographic gun capable of taking twelve pictures a second. He soon began to work with rolls of paper film, then celluloid, and ultimately increased the capacity of his camera to 100 pictures a second. Marey, however, was concerned primarily with animal locomotion for scientific study and did little to develop the commercial potential of his work.

Film

We have reached a point with Marey's camera where another line of scientific development intersects. One of the major obstacles confronting anyone working on instantaneous photography was the necessity to use glass plates. Plates were bulky and incapable of reproducing long sequences of action. This problem was solved in 1887 when an American preacher and amateur inventor named Hannibal Goodwin developed celluloid film. However, it was George Eastman who in 1888, with his famous Kodak camera, perfected and promoted film.

Eastman, however, was not concerned with cinematography. The idea of using Eastman's film for taking motion pictures was established by Thomas Edison and his associate William L. Dickson. A good deal of controversy surrounds Edison and his work on motion pictures. Some claim he is the inventor of motion pictures. Others state that he left most of the work to Dickson and then "borrowed" ideas from others. There is probably truth on both sides. However, Edison's importance should not be weighed on the basis of pinning down his exact ideas and working methods. His work was a combination of both invention and consolidation. That he employed associates or

Thomas Edison's Kinetoscope.
MUSEUM OF MODERN ART/FILM STILLS ARCHIV\

developed others' preliminary ideas should not detract from his deserved reputation as one of the key individuals responsible for the invention of motion pictures.

Using celluloid film, Edison and Dickson worked on the motion picture camera, developing their first workable model in 1888. By October, 1889, Dickson had taken and projected motion pictures in Edison's studio in West Orange, New Jersey. Soon, part of the laboratory was turned into a studio for shooting brief film clips. In 1891 Edison applied for patents on the Kinetograph as a motion picture camera and the Kinetoscope as a viewing device. This viewing device, however, was not a projector, but simply a cabinet containing a 50' loop of film which could be seen by only one individual at a time looking into the top of the machine.

By 1894, the Kinetoscope was being marketed on an international basis. As the demand for Kinetoscope films grew, Edison was forced to build a motion picture studio. Dubbed the "Black Maria," the "studio" was simply a tar paper shack with openings in the roof to let in the sun. It was hung on a pivot so it could be turned to catch the sun, but even so, most of Edison's films were apparently shot around noon.

Edison filmed a great variety of subjects, including a barbershop scene, a Chinese laundry scene, and such celebrities as Buffalo Bill, Annie Oakley, Annabelle the dancer, and a strong man. By 1894 Edison's catalog listed sixty subjects, most of them determined by what could most easily be filmed in the cramped studio space of the Black Maria and not put too great a strain on the heavy, immobile camera.

The Kinetoscope was a great success, but Edison soon

The Black Maria, Edison's first motion picture studio.

turned his attention to other scientific inquiries, failing to develop a projection system. By the time he got back to the idea, several others had beaten him to the punch.

Projection

Kircher's magic lantern had been around for more than 200 years when an Austrian military officer named Baron Franz von Uchatius combined it with the Plateau disks to achieve moving images on a screen. However, the Uchatius machine used phase drawings rather than photographs and the light source moved past the pictures, achieving a dissolve rather than a shutter effect. The idea of using photographs on disks and projecting them was developed by several people, including Jules Duboscq in France and Charles Wheatstone in England. Around 1870, an American, Henry Heyl, developed a projector using posed motion photographs and gave public showings before large audiences in Philadelphia.

All of this early experimentation was limited, however, by the lack of true motion pictures. As soon as film became available and motion picture cameras began their recording of life in motion, projection as the last step in the development of cinematography became a reality.

As we have seen, many of the inventions associated with cinematography were developed in simultaneous fashion. This was no less true of projection, and as a result there are many conflicting claims of authorship. William-Friese Greene of England patented a camera in 1889, but apparently did little with projection even though there is a plaque perpetuating his name and memory as "the inventor of commercial Kinematography." Louis-Aimé-Augustin Leprince holds a more substantial claim, as it has been documented that between 1888 and 1890 he was taking and projecting motion pictures. However, Leprince boarded a train to Paris in 1890 and disappeared without a trace.

This brings us to two brothers, Auguste and Louis Lumière, who perfected a camera and projector which they called a Cinématographe and exhibited films before a paying public in Paris on December 28, 1895. Their important contribution was a claw device which moved the film strip in front of the light source. This was soon replaced by the so-called Maltese Cross developed by Oskar Messter, which created the intermittent movement effect basic to modern projectors. The Lumière brothers began producing films at a rapid rate and published their first large catalog in 1897, listing 358 different films. By 1898 they had several catalogs, listing over 1,000 films. These short films reflected an amazing range, including documentaries, short stories, and trick films. The most dominant form, however, was the simple recording of reality, such as workers leaving a factory, a train entering the Paris station, or one of the Lumière children eating breakfast.

All this activity soon made it apparent to Edison that he had been mistaken in his decision not to develop a system of projection. His Kinetoscope would soon be obsolete and his embryonic motion picture empire was in danger of crumbling. Subsequently, Edison's agents, Raff and Gammon, came to him with a projection system based on the work of Thomas Armat and C. Francis Jenkins. Edison incorporated a loop in the film lead apparatus developed by Woodville Latham which helped ease the strain on the film strip and used the projector for the first time on April 23, 1896, at Koster and Bial's Music Hall in New York. This was the first public projection of motion pictures in the United States. Dubbed the Vitascope, Edison's name was used in promoting the multi-developed projector since he had more prestige and had the facilities to produce films.

> The effect of these enlarged pictures in motion on the screen is very pleasing and novel, those we have seen illustrating marching soldiers, railway trains approaching a station, street episodes, ocean surf, Niagara Falls, bathing scenes, dancing girls, and the life in aquariums being remarkably natural and effective.

B. F. Keith's Union Square Theater in New York where the Lumière Cinematographe opened on June 29, 1896.
MUSEUM OF MODERN ART/FILM STILLS ARCHIVE

With the development of projection a long, complicated, and often confusing process came to an end. On the other hand, a process equally as complex, almost as confusing, and much more interesting was just beginning. Film history moved from the sometimes arid world of science and technology to the exciting arena of the artist and businessman.

Industrial Development

As the first films of Edison, Lumière and others began to attract large audiences the economic potential of this revolutionary new medium soon became apparent. The various cinematic devices soon became the basis of thriving industries and the first years of development were dominated by a concern over patents and a jockeying for position in the new get-rich-quick world of motion picture production and exhibition.

An Industry Emerges: 1895–1900

The first five years of industrial development were clearly tied to technological development. No manufacturer anywhere was able to supply a complete equipment package for motion picture photography and exhibition. Edison could not make enough projectors, Biograph (an early rival) would not sell them, and neither Edison nor Biograph would rent or sell cameras. With equipment in short supply and the public clamoring for more films, the fledgling industry was in a state of chaos. Most of the early developers did not anticipate the tremendous popularity of motion pictures, and when the explosion came they were caught unprepared.

Edison is a good example of this "only a novelty" thinking. He ignored projection until others had already entered the field and in perhaps one of the greatest financial blunders of all time failed to spend the extra $150.00 for a worldwide patent on his Kinetoscope in 1891. The industrial and technological advance of the motion picture in these first years was literally forced by the public's acceptance of the product.

Although the incredible popularity of motion pictures could not really be foreseen, the hindsight of history illustrates that, as Nicholas Vardac has so brilliantly demonstrated in his book *From Stage to Screen*, society was ready for the new medium.

As Vardac points out, 19th century theater had, by its stress on realism, unwittingly provided a "climate of acceptance" for motion pictures. Theatrical realism could only go so far, even with such elaborate spectacles as actual chariot races, real forests, and live animals, including camels and elephants. All of this was only possible, of course, in large theaters in major cities. Audiences in small towns heard about these performances, but never saw them. Motion pictures arrived and immediately addressed themselves to both issues. They not only replaced elaborate stage realism in large cities, but more importantly brought new dimensions of realism to the towns of rural America.

For the first time, but most certainly not the last, motion pictures met the needs of society. Certainly, motion pictures were a novelty. But forces more far-reaching and deeper than simply novelty helped motion pictures gain acceptance. Urbanization, industrialization, immigration, growth of a strong middle class, and increased leisure time all helped to create this climate of acceptance. America had large cities filled with an immigrant working class which had the time and the money to enjoy itself.

Basing their position on patent holdings and financial backing, Edison and Biograph were the two dominant companies until Vitagraph appeared in 1897. Biograph was initially a competitor of Edison in the peep show business with its Mutoscope. Edison's former key associate, William Dickson, helped to found Biograph by building a camera and projector designed to circumvent Edison's patents. Vitagraph came into existence through the efforts of J. Stuart Blackton and Albert E. Smith, who also designed apparatus which got around Edison's patents. However, Smith and Blackton based their system more closely on Edison's and therefore Vitagraph films could be used in Edison projectors, greatly expanding their potential market.

Industrial development was not confined to the United States. In Germany, Oskar Messter invented an "independent projector," substituting the Maltese Cross for the Lumière claw movement. He soon began producing films and by 1897 published his first cinema catalog containing 84 films. Even more significant was the Frenchman Charles Pathé, who has been referred to as "the first international film czar." He founded Pathé Frères in 1896 with a total capital of 24,000 francs and by 1913 had a capital of over 20,000,000 francs. Pathé soon became the dominant company in Europe and was strongly established in Russia and the United States as well.

At first none of the producers needed experience or training.

They did not use actors, writers, editors; there was no organized film distribution system. Companies simply set up their cameras, shot a street scene, printed the film, and sold it themselves. There were no middlemen and no professionals. Despite this chaotic amateurish state, the industry was conscious of the commercial potential in the medium and was rapidly moving toward a more professional status. However, one of the factors holding back commercial, technical, and artistic development was the lack of film stock. The manufacturers of raw film stock, most notably Eastman, made most of their film for amateur still cameras and did not immediately set up production systems for motion picture film. As a result, the fifty-foot length of film set by Edison's Kinetoscope became a standard. In order to create longer programs, exhibitors had to splice together fifty-foot films. Since it is difficult to produce complex stories in fifty feet, narrative development became closely tied to the development of longer film stock. It was not until 1900 that 250-foot lengths (3–4 minutes) became available.

Refinement and Progress: 1900–1907

By 1900, primarily as a result of audience dissatisfaction with simple snapshots of reality, production quality began to improve. Certain talented cameramen, such as Edwin S. Porter, became directors, and professional actors were sought for more demanding roles. Henry Marvin of Biograph began training photographers and actors and organized scenario writing as a separate phase of production. Although production was still haphazard, the exhibition of motion pictures was developing quickly. At first, motion pictures fit into the existing entertainment structure and became part of vaudeville presentations. However, it was not long before public demand signaled to certain showmen that the motion picture could be exhibited as a separate attraction. The 1904 World's Fair brought motion pictures to St. Louis, but in less than grand fashion. The theater consisted of 94 camp chairs and a bed sheet for a screen. The World's Dream opened in St. Louis two years later with 140 folding chairs and room for 200 more. Operating costs amounted to slightly over $50.00 a week, including $25.00 for films, $12.00 for the projectionist, and $15.00 for a barker.

Black top tents were among the first theaters as motion

pictures moved out of the large cities into rural areas. These were generally crude affairs with coal stove heat and boards laid in the aisles. However, their large seating capacity, in some cases up to 3,000 people, compensated for their primitive state. Soon, however, permanent buildings were being converted into crude theaters. There was little concern for quality in these early years, as the largely lower-class audiences were not accustomed to the luxury associated with legitimate theater or even vaudeville. As the *Architectural Record* notes:

> The decoration of the hall is usually simple. No great elaboration is necessary as the waits between reels are usually short and the audience has little time to admire the auditorium.

Motion pictures were fascinating by themselves. The experience of three young men in New Orleans is typical. William Rock, R. J. Wainright, and William Reed opened up Vitascope Hall on Canal Street in 1896, charging 10¢ admission, another 10¢ if the audience wanted to see the projection booth, and yet another 10¢ for a single frame of film.

Soon other theaters were opened. Thomas Tally, a pioneer exhibitor on the West Coast, opened his first theater in 1897. However, it was not until 1902 that he announced the motion picture was ready to make its debut as an independent entertainer.

> Electric Theater 262 S. Main, opp. 3rd. St.
> New Place of Amusement
> Up to date high class moving picture entertainment especially for ladies and children. See the Capture of the Biddle Bros., New York in a Blizzard, and many other interesting and exciting scenes. An hour's amusement and genuine fun for 10 cents admission.
> Evenings: 7:30–10:30

Herbert Miles opened up one of the first specially adapted motion picture theaters in New York in 1898 and soon people all over the country were busy converting stores into theaters. Even this development was limited, however, by the availability of films. It was not until after the Edison-Biograph stranglehold on equipment was broken around 1900 that exhibition emerged as a truly separate, independent branch of the industry. This was possible primarily because of Edison's mistakes. His failure to develop projection and take out an international patent allowed several companies to enter the field of both exhibition and production, mainly with the help of foreign equipment.

A motion picture theater of 1903
in Tacoma, Washington.
LIBRARY OF CONGRESS

The quality of production was limited by the somewhat haphazard operations of many corporations. Most producers made little conscious effort to create a quality product. The concern of most companies was quantity, as exhibitors were constantly clamoring for more films to fill what seemed like an insatiable public appetite. Films were sold by the foot, so production was geared to manufacturing so many feet per week.

Motion pictures were an expensive product and producers were reluctant to try anything new. It was not until 1903 that films longer than 400 feet were produced. With production geared to a linear philosophy, longer films meant more money, and if the public was satisfied with short films, why rock the boat? However, 1903 saw the appearance of perhaps the most significant film in motion picture history, *The Great Train Robbery.* This *was* something new and the industry reacted to it with incredible speed. The film's 740 foot length, outdoor location, cinematic structure, and sense of realism spurred the industry into the age of longer story films. By 1905, 1,000 feet or "one reel" (fourteen minutes) became the standard length of most films.

By 1907 the motion picture industry was alive with surging new business. New companies were springing up daily and theaters were spreading across the country. *The Motion Picture World's Buyers Guide* (an early trade journal) listed ten major manufacturers of equipment and films. Almost all of them achieved their prominence because of original patent holdings.

However, these preeminent firms were being pressed to maintain their position by companies producing nothing but exciting films.

As production and facilities expanded, many companies began issuing two or three films (reels) a week. Well-known writers, such as Rex Beach and Richard Harding Davis, began writing film scenarios. Sigmund Lubin built a new glass studio in Philadelphia in which four companies could work simultaneously. Edison built a new studio in 1907 at the cost of more than $100,000. It was even equipped with underground water tanks to create everything from a brook to an ocean. Edison, however, had by this time slipped in popularity and the top spots in the industry were taken over by Biograph and Vitagraph, primarily because these two companies concentrated on attracting talented artists, such as D. W. Griffith at Biograph.

Production was limited almost exclusively to the East Coast, although several companies, including Selig and Essanay, operated out of Chicago. West Coast production was limited to occasional sporadic trips to shoot a location Western or aquatic adventure. William Selig supposedly shot the first film in California in 1908 when he photographed the water scenes for *The Count of Monte Cristo*. However, it was not until the Motion Picture Patents Company made it necessary for certain companies to move west that California production assumed any significance. Hundreds of small companies appeared in many different

The first home of
Famous Players Film Co.,
the forerunner of Paramount.
MUSEUM OF MODERN ART/FILM
STILLS ARCHIVE

locales, including San Antonio, Texas, Ogden, Utah, and Jacksonville, Florida. However, it was the East Coast and especially the
areas around New York that saw production companies spring up
almost overnight. At first, the major studios, such as Edison,
Vitagraph, and Biograph, set up their studios in brownstones
with outdoor sets located on the roof. However, these companies
soon outgrew these locations and moved to the suburbs.

Many small companies set up shop throughout the East,
including Providence, Rhode Island, Ithaca and Saranac Lake,
New York. Kathleen Karr writes about some of these studios and
relates a fascinating history of tiny independent companies
struggling to survive in isolated locations such as "Caribou Bill"
Copper's Arctic Film Company in Saranac Lake, New York. These
companies did not last long, but their history remains an
unexplored and fascinating footnote to the development of
motion pictures in the United States.

With production increasing in both quantity and quality,
exhibition began to improve as well. Progress was slow, however, because as with production, the criterion of cost dominated every aspect of exhibition. The cheaper the theater the
better. Any structure that could be darkened and hold 100 people
was "converted" into a theater. Converted is in quotation marks
because this usually meant renting 100 folding chairs, throwing
a sheet across a wire, begging, borrowing, or stealing a projector,
and projecting films for a paying public. The following announce-
ment in *The Moving Picture World* gives some indication of the
state of exhibition around 1905–1907.

> Housewives of Knoxville, Mt. Oliver and Carrick boroughs Pa. are
> mourning the abandonment of the garden truck stands and the meat
> stalls at the Knoxville market house in Bausman street. The space
> formerly occupied by the stands is now being used for a moving
> picture show on the first floor and a roller skating rink on the
> second floor.

Even lower-class audiences, however, ultimately tired of
dirty, airless rooms and grainy prints. Something else was
needed to attract audiences and several people began to experiment in new exhibition patterns. One of the most unusual
attempts was that of George C. Hale, who first exhibited
something he called "Hales Tours" at the St. Louis Exposition
of 1904. "Hales Tours" consisted of travel pictures projected in
tiny theaters built to resemble railway coaches. A conductor took
tickets inside and the car rumbled and swayed as the awed and

sometimes frightened spectators watched Yellowstone Park's "Old Faithful" erupt before their very eyes.

By far the most significant development took place in Pittsburgh in 1905 when two brothers, Harry and John Harris, opened their "Nickelodeon." Reprinted below is a short essay on the subject from *The Moving Picture World* of May 4, 1907 which sums up the essence of this new phenomenon better than any contemporary description.

THE NICKELODEON

There is a new thing under the sun—at least new within a short period of time—and entirely new in the sense that the public is waking up to what it means.

It is the 5-cent theater.

The nickel place of amusement made its appearance with no greater blare of trumpets than the noise of its phonograph horn and the throaty persuasions of its barker. It came unobtrusively, in the still of night. It is multiplying faster than guinea pigs, and within a few months has attained to that importance where we may no longer snub it as one of the catch-pennies of the street.

One day a Pittsburg man hit on the 5-cent theater idea. He equipped a building at a cost of $40,000, bought a phonograph with a big horn, hired a leather-lunged barker and threw his doors open.

The theater was such an unqualified go in Pittsburg that the men who started in competition with the originator of the scheme decided that a new popular chord had been struck in the amusement line. They hiked to Chicago and opened a theater near State and Van Buren streets. The theater prospered from the moment the barker first opened his mobile face to extol the wonders of the show "upon the inside." That was the beginning in Chicago.

One of its chief attractions is the knowledge that if you are stung it is for "only a nickel, five pennies, a half a dime," as the barker says, and that if you don't like the show they can inflict only fifteen minutes of it on you.

Here are the ingredients of a 5-cent theater:
One storeroom, seating from 200 to 500 persons.
One phonograph with extra large horn.
One young woman cashier.
One electric sign.
One cinematograph, with operator.
One canvas on which to throw the pictures.
One piano.
One barker.
One manager.
As many chairs as the store will hold.
A few brains and a little tact. Mix pepper and salt to taste.

After that all you have to do is to open the doors, start the phonograph and carry the money to the bank. The public does the rest.

It makes little difference what time of day you go to a 5-cent theater. The doors are opened as early in the forenoon as there is a chance of gathering in a few nickels, the downtown theaters opening earlier than those in the outlying districts to accommodate the visitors. Each "performance" lasts fifteen minutes. At the end of each a sign is thrown from the cinematograph on the canvas announcing that those who came late may stay for the next "performance."

Often they stay for several. After they find out that nobody cares and that they can stay all day and far into the night and bring their lunch if they want to, they leave, disappointed because nobody tried to get the best of them.

They are great places for the foot-sore shopper, who is not used to cement sidewalks, to rest; and it took the aforesaid foot-sore shoppers about one minute to find this out. It is much more comfortable than to take streetcar rides to rest, and they don't have to pay the return nickels.

The name of the play is flashed on the canvas, so that it may be identified if ever seen again. Understand that the young men who sing the "illustrated songs" are the only live performers in these theaters. The rest is moving pictures; and that is the startling part of the great favor with which these theaters have been received by the public.

The plays that are put on at the 5-cent theaters are for the most part manufactured abroad. Paris is a great producing center. London has numerous factories that grind them out. They are bought by the foot.

This system of buying drama and comedy by the foot has its distinct advantages. If the piece grows dull at any point the manager can take a pair of shears and carve out a few yards or rods, thereby enlivening the whole performance.

The worst charge that has been made against the 5-cent theaters is that some of them put on pieces of the blood-and-thunder type, depicting murders, hold-ups, train robberies and other crimes. This charge has led the managers of the new style theaters into a hot discussion with the uplifters of the public morals.

Few people realize the important part these theaters are beginning to play in city life. They have been looked upon largely as places of trivial amusement, not calling for any serious consideration. They seem, however, to be something that may become one of the greatest forces for good or for evil in the city.

On the other hand, in the congested districts the 5-cent theaters are proving a source of much innocent entertainment. The mothers do not have to "dress" to attend them, and they take the children and spend many restful hours in them at very small expense.

The exterior of a typical Nickelodeon
of the period 1905–1910.
LIBRARY OF CONGRESS

The interior of a typical Nickelodeon
of the period 1905–1910.
LIBRARY OF CONGRESS

The possibilities of them in an educational way are unlimited. The tuberculosis society already has seen them and has under way a plan for having the cinematograph theaters show pictures which will instruct the public of and precautions to be taken against consumption. A great many educational lines might be developed among the people in this way.

The idea of a theater caught on immediately. Soon the Harris brothers had fourteen nickelodeons in Pittsburgh open from 8:00 AM to midnight six days a week. Since the program would change every fifteen minutes audiences of seven to eight thousand people were possible every day. Attendance in Chicago's nickelodeons averaged 100,000 a day in 1907. By 1910 there were over 10,000 nickelodeons in the United States.

The nickelodeon was the first permanent home of motion pictures. Its importance should not be underestimated, because its development had as much to do with keeping the industry vital and alive as Griffith's contributions at Biograph. Theaters began expanding beyond the nickelodeon phase and by 1910 there were elaborate new theaters like the marble and glass front theater built in Louisville, Kentucky, for $35,000. This theater contained 700 upholstered tip-up chairs, a mechanical piano and barrel organ, and uniformed ushers with syringes used to kill germs and sweeten the air. By 1910 national attendance figures were being estimated at four million people daily and twenty-five million per week.

All of this development in production and exhibition was an indication of the industry's growing professionalism and maturity. By 1910 many future patterns of production and exhibition had already been set in motion. The last area of industrial development to emerge as a separate phase was distribution. In the early years exhibitors simply bought films by ordering from a catalog. Prices were listed by cost per foot; the going rate was usually 10¢ a foot. Films were bought and exhibitors would then informally exchange them among their various theaters.

This was an expensive practice for exhibitors and soon many of them developed the practice of exchanging or "bicycling" prints between various theaters. Producers did not care for this practice and as a result a new industrial pattern involving the distribution of motion pictures evolved. The first step involved setting up an organization where someone rented an office and invited exhibitors to come and trade films. Soon, the idea of a more formal method of distribution emerged. Harry Miles, a San Francisco exhibitor, bought films from producers and rented them to exhibitors for a week at a time for about one-half the original price. Soon other men caught on to yet another big money scheme and "exchanges," as they were called, began opening up across the country. By 1907 there were 125 to 150 exchanges. This method of getting films from producer to exhibitor would remain the same throughout the history of the motion picture, although later the production studios would assume distribution as an automatic arm of production and change certain policies and practices which will be discussed later.

The Trust and the Independents: 1908–1912

Up to this point industrial development was essentially a haphazard accumulation of technology and industrial experimentation. There was little real organization. A few companies were dominant, but many more were going into business every day. It was at this time in the medium's history that several of the industry's major figures got together to try to bring some order out of chaos. The chaos was primarily a result of patent disputes. The early companies did not try to control the industry by making the best films or hiring the most famous stars. They dominated by controlling patents. However, with the tremendous financial potential recognized by many entrepreneurs, the patent holding companies soon found themselves turning out as many lawsuits as films. In late 1908 one of the major company heads, George Kleine, suggested a solution—a patent pool. In January, 1909, the Motion Picture Patents Company was formed by ten companies which pooled sixteen patents controlling film, cameras, and projectors.

THE MPPC

1. Edison	6. Selig
2. Biograph	7. Lubin
3. Vitagraph	8. Pathé Frères
4. Essanay	9. George Kleine
5. Kalem	10. Méliès

The patents pool granted uniform licenses to the ten member companies to manufacture and use cameras and to manufacture and lease motion pictures. They agreed to lease their films only to exchanges and exhibitors using licensed machines, to lease films only to those exchanges that dealt exclusively in the films of the ten manufacturers and at prices not lower than those stipulated in the agreement. The "trust," as it came to be called, collected royalties of $2.00 a week from all exhibitors using projection machines based on its patents. It issued licenses to make and sell such machines upon condition that they be used solely for exhibiting films leased by one of the ten manufacturers and it charged a royalty of $5.00 on every machine manufactured.

Quite obviously, this was a restrictive monopoly. Between 1908 and 1914 open warfare existed in the industry as independent producers, exchanges, and exhibitors engaged the trust in a battle for the American audience. Much to the amazement of the trust these "independents" found a ready market for their films. The following letter from an exhibitor points to some reasons why.

Pittsfield, Mass., January 22, 1910.

Editors Moving Picture World:

Gentlemen—Having been a subscriber to your valuable publication for many months I have been very much interested in reading the letters from exhibitors regarding the Patents Company and the Independent movement.

At one time I paid a license fee to the Patents Company for three theaters. I mention this to show that I think I was entitled to some consideration from the Patents Company. There are at the present time two picture houses in this city of 35,000 people. My competitor changed his service from nine reels per week to eighteen. I had to do the same in order to get first and second run pictures. Of course we began to show repeaters and very often both houses would show the same pictures the same day. I wrote the Patents Company asking them if they did not think this was one of the evils they had promised to regulate, especially as I had tried to have my competitor agree to nine reels per week. The film exchanges supplying us both had also advised him to change, but he did not care to.

The Patents Company answered my letters after a lapse of a couple of weeks saying that they did not care to interfere with exhibitors especially if the exhibitor was willing to pay a reasonable rental for his service. In other words the Patents Company refused to do anything to relieve a situation that was demoralizing the moving picture public in this city, as the people became disgusted at seeing repeaters at every show.

Seven weeks ago I changed to Independent service and never in my years of experience in the theatrical and moving picture business have I seen such a continuous run of beautiful and interesting pictures as I have shown during that time.

Result: My business has increased 40 per cent, and I am charging ten cents on Saturday nights, against my competitor's five cents, and am "packing them in."

My advice to exhibitors who wish to increase their receipts and decrease their worries, "Find a good Independent film exchange" and watch the results. The Association has never put out the unbroken line of good pictures that the Independents are renting to-day.

Trusting these lines may help some exhibitor who has been paying the $2 weekly and receiving no benefit from the same, I am,

Very truly yours,

A. H. Sawyer

Subsequently, consolidation and control of the distribution-exchanges was the only method by which complete control could be maintained. In 1910 the trust organized the General Film Company as a distribution subsidiary.

Despite this atmosphere of control, several independents kept fighting the trust, legally in the courts, and illegally by making motion pictures with "borrowed" equipment. Distribution became the key to fighting the system and as the General Film Company was the distributor source for most exhibitors, either willingly or unwillingly the independents had to work hard to get their films accepted.

The exhibitors themselves did not like the trust because of the weekly $2.00 license fee and other restrictive practices, and so the independents took heart and continued to produce films. They had several important advantages, the most important one being the attitude of the trust. The MPPC looked at films as a commodity sold by the foot, regardless of star, story, or size of theater. For the most part, the men who controlled the Patents Company were inventors and businessmen out of touch with the growing demand for better and longer films. The independents included men such as William Fox, Carl Laemmle, and Adolph Zukor. Most of them were uneducated immigrants who got their start operating local theaters. However, they knew what the public wanted. Between 1909 and 1914 the independents fought savagely for survival. Labeled "outlaws," they were not restricted in any way, and so a second great advantage was the freedom to experiment. This does not mean that the trust studios were not progressive—remember, Griffith was at Biograph—but they were locked into the concept of film as product sold by the foot. The independents subsequently raided the trust for their best talent and soon began developing films based on length, story, and stars.

Although the trust was legally dissolved in 1915, it had died almost three years earlier. There were a number of reasons for this, but three main factors stand out: (1) establishment of a star system; (2) development of the feature-length film; and (3) a move west.

The first two factors were innovations which enabled the independents, especially Carl Laemmle and Adolph Zukor, to successfully market their films; the third factor allowed the independents the freedom to make film far away from the Eastern-based trust.

The trust refused to identify actors and actresses in order to avoid any "unreasonable" salary demands from suddenly established "stars." The independents capitalized on this by signing the best-known players and publicizing their names. Carl Laemmle's IMP Company, one of the first to base films around a star, created a huge publicity campaign around a young actress named Florence Lawrence. Bison, another independent, began to feature a young English comedian named Charles Chaplin. Adolph Zukor started Famous Players in Famous Plays in 1912 with Sarah Bernhardt starring in *Queen Elizabeth*. Mary Pickford soon moved from Biograph to IMP and the star system began to mushroom beyond all expectations.

Feature films were another innovation used by the independents to fight the trust. The standard two-reel length imposed by the cost-per-foot conscious trust began to limit severely commercial and artistic development. One of the reasons Griffith left Biograph was that he and other filmmakers felt film's potential was being unnecessarily restricted. With the successful United States showing of the nine-reel Italian production *Quo Vadis* (1913), the opportunities for innovation and experimentation in length suddenly became real. The independents, especially Adolph Zukor, seized upon this as another way to compete with the trust and by 1914 several other independents had joined Zukor in the rush toward feature-length production.

All of this activity in stars and longer films was taking place against the backdrop of a new and unfamiliar name to most Americans—Hollywood. The move west began around 1908 and by 1910 several companies had established studios in California. However, the big rush occurred around 1913 when the independents began to look for locations where production could continue without trust harassment. San Francisco seemed to be the logical spot, as it was an established community with many advantages, but the "frontier" town of Los Angeles and its sleepy suburb Hollywood were chosen primarily because they were close to the Mexican border. The move west, begun in fear and flight by a few independent companies, soon reached avalanche proportions as more and more production companies found both the Eastern climate and geography too confining. Simple inexpensive outdoor sets were a clear advantage over elaborate glassed-in studios and the 365-day shooting schedule further lowered production expenses.

The trust continued the fight on the nation's screens and in the courts, but ultimately lost both battles. Most of the original trust studios either quietly faded away or were absorbed by the stronger independent companies. By 1920 not one of the original trust companies was a major force in the industry. The efforts of Carl Laemmle, Adolph Zukor, William Fox, and others formed the base of a new system, one based not on patents and

An early outdoor set of the Selig Company. Note how many films could be shot side by side and the gauze covering the set which acted as a filter for the intense California sunshine.
MUSEUM OF MODERN ART/FILM STILLS ARCHIVE

equipment, but on stars and popular stories. As Benjamin Hampton notes: "The story of the patents company and of General Film deserves to be remembered as a perfect illustration of the futility of laws that lack the support and sympathy of the populace." The independents gambled on the public's taste and won. They created a new system based on this single great intangible, a system which ultimately surpassed the trust in its domination of the motion picture industry.

The history of motion pictures up to this time has centered around the development of a technological reality and an industrial empire. The first eighty years were years of groping and grasping, years filled with new ideas and rapid development. Motion pictures were kicked screaming into the 20th century by an enthusiastic public who wanted, *demanded* new forms of entertainment.

2
Beginnings of Form

The Single-Shot Film

In focusing on the beginnings of film history in terms of the form itself and its function, a perfectly logical starting point, and one which many historians prefer, is the first experimental clips by the pioneers Edison and Lumière from 1888 to 1895, or the first public showings in Paris and New York in 1895 and 1896. The survey of various technological apparatus related to projection and graphic motion which led up to the invention of cinematography extends the "prehistory" period back to the 16th century. But the desire to illustrate the kind of appeal the earliest film had for audiences, citing man's drive since the dawn of civilization to bring motion to the graphic arts, tempts the historian to extend this prehistory period as far back as the 20,000-year-old Lascaux cave drawings of animals in suspended motion. From such a perspective, then, the function of the original films can be seen as satisfying the age-old desire to combine the essence of theatre and graphic arts by preserving images of events without stilling the action.

As the earliest films were strictly recordings of what came before the camera lens, there is little to be said of form, but the function of these pioneer works was clearly to exploit early viewers' fascination with the medium's ability to provide images of both real and dramatized activities. One need only look at a few of the earliest Edison and Lumière efforts to appreciate their

31

commonality of purpose. *The Black Diamond Express*, a brief clip made by the Edison Company in 1896, records the hurtling movement of an oncoming train, while *Fatima*, produced by Edison the following year, captures the gyrations of an exotic dancer. At the same time the Lumière brothers in Paris were using their Cinématographe camera to record *Workers Leaving the Lumière Factory*, *Boat Leaving the Harbor*, and *Fish Market at Marseilles*.

The natural extension of these clips was to expand upon brief glimpses of activities, real or staged, to somewhat more elaborate routines and historical events. The Edison studios in the 1890's captured *Gold Rush Scenes in the Klondike*, and in 1901 recorded *The Funeral of Queen Victoria*, which, along with countless other special event clips by both American and French studios, form the beginning in newsreel film. Although staged films were usually of brief vaudeville routines, the attempt to recreate actual events is illustrated by such clips as Edison's *Execution of Mary Queen of Scots* (1895) and the *McGovern-Corbett Fight* staged in the Biograph Studios in 1903.

At the turn of the century, with films still limited to clips running less than a minute, it is questionable that audiences would have continued to woo the infant industry had not several of the men pioneering the field extended the medium beyond its original function of peep show of fact and fancy. The rudiments of narrative construction gradually developed through the middle years of the first decade; movie men were discovering that film could be used to tell a story.

Although it is the Frenchman, Georges Méliès, and the American, Edwin S. Porter, who are generally given the lion's share of credit for the beginnings of screen storytelling, it was actually the several anonymous "idea men" and directors working in the Edison and Lumière studios in the late 1890's that began to explore film's narrative potential. Still no more than a minute in length and limited to a series of actions that could be recorded from a fixed camera position through a single running of the camera, some of these early clips revealed definite progression and causal relationship between actions. *Washday Troubles* (1895) was a short routine by Edison involving a prankster upsetting a washtub and being chased by the irate washerwoman. In the same year the Lumière company produced *Teasing the Gardener*, which, in a similar vein, shows a gardener becoming the victim of a boy who crimps a garden hose and then releases it when the gardener brings the nozzle closer for inspection. The limitations to narrative development of the film composed of a single shot or one "take" of the camera go without saying.

Georges Méliès

The next important step to narrative construction was the linking together of a series of such shots so that actions requiring more than a single location or time period could be recorded. It was Georges Méliès, theatre producer, actor, designer, and professional magician who, in 1896, became fascinated with the Lumière camera and its possibilities and led motion pictures into the true beginnings of storytelling. At first it was in his role as conjurer that Méliès explored the medium. His early films reveal a wide range of trick effects used to produce imaginative fantasies involving miraculous appearances and disappearances, transformations, and the bringing to life of inanimate objects. All the tricks of his magical trade were explored and given cinematic

Teasing the Gardener (1895). The Lumière comic skit which reveals the rudiments of narrative within the single shot.
MUSEUM OF MODERN ART/FILM STILLS ARCHIVE

dimension through the use of such devices as double exposure or superimposition of two images; fast and slow motion of screen action, accomplished by slowing down or speeding up the cranking of the camera; and optical effects which were soon to become basic transitional devices in film narrative—the fading an image to black and dissolving one image into another. Méliès quickly outdistanced his fellow filmmakers on both sides of the Atlantic with his carefully planned and fancifully executed bits of film magic, and his richly inventive fantasies were being enjoyed by American as well as European audiences by the turn of the century. But it was in his films produced after 1900 that Méliès began to reveal what became a most significant step in the development of narrative construction. Until this time his films were also limited to action that could be developed within a single setting and uninterrupted time period. What he now began to explore was the camera's ability to record, through multiple scenes, a series of events which combined to tell a unified story. Using both original narratives and those adapted from literature, Méliès, through a series of action tableaux which he himself labeled "artificially arranged scenes," fashioned in sequence and *linked* together the several units of action required to spin the tale. Primitive though these films were at first, they illustrated the fundamental techniques of narrative cinema and marked the beginning of a creative use of the medium. As "screenwriter" Méliès planned, before shooting, the tableaux sequence which would provide continuity and progression; as "scenic designer" he produced the setting appropriate to each unit of action; and as "director" he orchestrated movement and business within each of the scenes. It goes without saying that Méliès was also his own special effects man. The result is a style which is distinctive and identifiable.

Cinderella, the first of Méliès' "motion tableaux" films, made in 1899, was composed of twenty scenes and well illustrates not only Méliès' firsts in cinematic construction, but also the rich, elaborate, theatrical style which he brought to the screen. More inventive and elaborate films followed, with Méliès' imaginative wit, along with his growing technical control, reaching a peak in *A Trip to the Moon* (1902). Here, in thirty scenes, Méliès created a wildly fanciful version of a Jules Verne story which followed scientists from the astronomic club through planning, construction, flight, a bizarre series of lunar experiences including an encounter with the Selenites, and finally return to earth and triumphal reception. The film is a completely absurdist romp and its charm is in its imaginative visual render-

ing of settings and action. But Méliès had also taken the opportunity to weave into the simple narrative a good-natured spoof of scientific and technological interests of the day. Méliès has been credited with being the screen's first satirist, and he does indeed in several subsequent films exploit contemporary social foibles and preoccupations, but these remain in the service of fantasy, and Méliès in the service of dream building, not preachment.

For the next few years, Méliès continued to delight audiences with his fairy tales and fantasies, occasionally turning his hand to realistic recreation of historical events. By the close of the decade, however, he was declining in popularity, a victim of innovations in both production and distribution methods, but in a real sense a victim of his own limitations in the use of the medium that he had so enthusiastically adopted in 1896. For all his inventiveness and imagination in planning and execution, and ultimately the linking of scenes for storytelling, Méliès was never able to use the camera itself as more than an instrument to record staged business. Though he had seen very quickly the many trick possibilities of the camera, its fundamental use as a creative and fashioning tool had apparently escaped him. With camera set up at one end of his studio, entire scenes would be played in typical theatrical fashion, with actors entering and leaving the scene from left and right, occasionally bowing to the camera audience with no change in perspective or break in action until the scene had run its course. To put it simply, Méliès had created a richly inventive style of storytelling, but left unexplored the unique properties of the medium for plastic expression—the control of time and space.

35

The Impossible Voyage (1905). Méliès further
explores the world of science fiction and reveals
again his talents as scenic designer.

Though this limitation explains Méliès' decline and eventual obscurity by the early Teens, it does not alter the fact that he had, for the first time, brought planning, selection, and control to moviemaking, had begun the medium on its way to storytelling, and been an inspiration to filmmakers that followed. The most obvious influence is seen in the French chase and trick films, which had become a staple of the industry by 1910. But one need only look at Edwin S. Porter's *Dream of a Rarebit Fiend* (1906), to say nothing of the countless lesser efforts by outright imitators, both in Europe and America, to appreciate how infectious was Méliès' fanciful style. It has often been reported by historians that Griffith said of Méliès, "I owe him everything." In view of Griffith's own revolutionary approach to the medium, this may seem indulgent, but it is perhaps recognition of that important first step that begins any long journey, in this case the linking of scenes to give visual life to a story.

Edwin S. Porter

The person more responsible than any other for development in film narrative technique that began to overshadow the works of Méliès by the middle of the first decade was the American Edwin S. Porter. Unlike Méliès, whose background had been in theater, Porter was a machinist whose expertise in electrical apparatus drew him to a series of jobs related to the motion picture industry. Through the 1890's, Porter worked intermittently as projectionist, inventor of motion picture equipment, and free lance newsreel photographer, much of it for Edison. Porter was hired full time by the Edison Company in 1899, initially to work as a mechanic, but soon began to direct. By 1902 he had become a key director for the company, with an impressive list of films behind him. But there was little to distinguish this early work. In addition to continuing his work in newsreel, Porter became increasingly involved in the production of the short single-situation comic routines which had become a staple of the industry. Though uninspired in terms of dramatic quality, the films did exhibit some technical advances. Under the influence of Méliès, whose trick films fascinated him, and stimulated by his own love of machines, Porter began to experiment with such devices as double exposure, split screen (two images projected side by side), panoramic shooting, a primitive form of animation, and shooting film at night with incandes-

Edwin S. Porter.
MUSEUM OF MODERN ART/FILM STILLS ARCHIVE

cent light. His *Uncle Josh at the Moving Picture Show* employs
double exposure to combine the antics of a country hick's reaction to his first movie with an image representing the action on
the screen. The earlier Edison film of *The Black Diamond
Express* was among the inserts used in the film within a film.
Porter employed both night shooting and a complete 360° pan of
the camera in a film shot at the Pan-American Exposition at
Buffalo, New York, in 1901.

It was toward the end of the following year that Porter
produced *The Life of an American Fireman*, which, along with
his *Great Train Robbery* (1903), established the foundation of
cinematic narrative construction and earned for Porter the title
of "father of the story film." *The Life of an American Fireman*
seems a crude film by contemporary standards. It is the simple
story of an alarm sounding, the fire department's race to the fire,
and the rescue of mother and child—all told in seven scenes and
less than two minutes' running time. With the exception of the
final scene depicting the arrival at the fire and the rescue, the
scenes are all composed of single shots from a fixed camera
position. Some of these were actually stock shots of real fire
department activities taken by Porter from Edison files, though
the extent of such borrowed footage is still debated. But what
made the film a significant breakthrough in narrative construction was the arrangement of scenes to follow traditional dramatic
progression to include exposition, development of action, suspense, crisis, climax and denouement or resolution. Porter, like
Méliès, was demonstrating that the action of a film need not be

38

completed within a single scene. He discovered that he could establish progression and draw meaning from a combination of scenes, and represent a longer period of time than it takes to tell in film. As in Méliès' *Cinderella*, the basic principles of structural editing were employed for story building.

Though its potential was probably not fully understood by Porter at the time, the final scene of the film reveals another basic tool of cinematic construction, the breaking down of a scene into individual shots. Here, Porter dissolves from the arrival of fire apparatus to the fate of mother and child within the burning building, and dissolves again to the exterior for the rescue. But in subsequent films, Porter was to revert to single-shot scenes, and the use of the shot as the basic building block in narrative construction was to await Griffith's work of nearly a decade later.

Porter's revolutionary use of the medium in *The Life of an American Fireman* might be seen as more of an incidental experiment than some sudden awakening to the true method of film construction in view of the inferior quality of his next several films, which reverted to single-situation gags. But these were simply Edison assignments, which Porter had been given to fill the heavy production schedule, and in which Porter had no particular interest. Even *Uncle Tom's Cabin*, which was the longest and most ambitious film to come from the Edison studio to date, was a photographed stage play, much in the Méliès tradition. The story is told by linking heavily theatrical tableaux which represent key action. Despite a certain charm of dressing and decor, it lacks any real development in narrative construction.

Among his other assignments, Porter was given the promotional film, *A Romance of the Rails*, commissioned by the Delaware, Lackawanna and Western Railroad, and intended to sell the joys—services and cleanliness in particular—of train travel. This project, coupled with the dramatic potential he saw in a currently popular road show entitled "The Great Train Robbery," spurred Porter on to produce what was to become a legendary contribution to the development of screen narrative as well as a pioneer classic of the American Western.

Released late in 1903, *The Great Train Robbery* quickly became a sensation and helped assure the success of the nickelodeons which were soon springing up across the country. What made the film a new experience for movie audiences, and a critical influence on the development of the medium, was its closely knit construction and momentum or narrative flow. Composed of fourteen scenes and running nearly twelve minutes, the film builds a simple, closely knit narrative concerning a train hijacking by outlaws, who, after robbing both mail bags and passengers, flee the train and are pursued and killed by a posse in a desperate gun battle. The film, of course, has the intrinsic drama of railroading and the built-in momentum of the chase. But what Porter was able to do with this material was to develop the action within each scene so as to create a natural association and flow when these were combined. Freeing himself of the limitation of the single situation and real time, he introduced three distinct units of action—the interior of a telegraph office, the dance hall where the posse is alerted, both fixed locations, and the third, which changes in location as it follows the fleeing bandits. The result of linking the several scenes together now is a natural progression of action in time and space. In itself this was not new, having been accomplished by Méliès in *A Trip to the Moon* and by Porter himself in his earlier *The Life of an American Fireman*. What made the construction unique was the cross-cutting among the three units of action that were going on simultaneously until the climactic gun battle, when two of these —bandits and posse—are brought together within a single scene. The effect of the cross-cutting, in addition to moving the action forward, was to create tension by leaving momentarily unresolved each phase of the action. The fate of such a key formative work, of course, is to attract accolades which make it a veritable catalogue of film firsts. Mention is often made, for example, of camera movement—a short tilt of the camera to follow the fleeing bandits—and the close-up of the outlaw leader firing directly at the audience; it could be used, according to Edison catalogue suggestion, to either begin or end the film. But camera movement here is so minimal as to be negligible, and the close-up, though perhaps startling in its effect on early audiences, is not an integral part of the narrative. The designation of the film as the first Western is also misleading, as short single-scene vignettes, such as *Cripple Creek Barroom*, made by the Edison Company in 1898, and Porter's own *The Life of An American Cowboy* (1902) preceded it.

The importance of basic structural editing to the film also tends to lead to the assumption that Porter utilizes shot breakdown; that is, that the action of scenes is made up of a series of shots of that same action taken from varying angles and distances from the action. This is not the case, and it in fact illustrates the key limitation of the film. The camera, from a fixed medium shot, eye-level position, simply records the activities designed for the scene. Though intercutting of scenes does help to build suspense, the added pull of pace or tempo created by controlling shot length is lost here. With the release of *The Great Train Robbery*, Porter's reputation as a leader in moviemaking was secure. The rapidly expanding nickelodeon circuit brought ever increasing demands for film, and short narrative films began to flood the market. Porter's own rigorous production schedule, and his continued fascination with the technological end of the industry, left him with little time or inclination for further experimentation in narrative technique.

A further contribution to narrative instruction, however, is found in his use of contrast editing in *The Ex-Convict* (1904) and *The Kleptomaniac* (1905). Extending the simple cross-cutting of separate but related actions of *The Great Train Robbery*, he now provides for direct comparative study of two parallel events. In *The Ex-Convict* it involves a comparison of life styles between rich industrialist and poverty-stricken ex-convict; in *Kleptomaniac* it is on how justice serves the rich and the poor that Porter draws his comparison. Probably more significant than the editing device itself was the fact that movies were now being used to reflect social values and conditions. The message movie had arrived.

By 1907, the year that D. W. Griffith joined the Edison studio to begin his own impressive rise to director stardom, Porter was becoming more of a supervisor than director. His remaining career, though distinguishing him oddly enough as both executive and inventor, has little to do directly with the course of film form and function.

Griffith: The Formative Years

When David Wark Griffith was hired by the American Mutoscope and Biograph Company in the spring of 1908, the single-reel narrative film, running from five to twelve minutes in length, had been established as standard fare. In addition to the continued production of filmed records of actual topical events, the films of this period were generally of two types: comedies, which were made up of a single comic routine or incident and usually ran for about five to six minutes, and stock melodramas, which were further developed in terms of story and ran for about

David Wark Griffith.
MUSEUM OF MODERN ART/FILM STILLS ARCHIVE

twelve minutes. The comedy films, shown in pairs or "split reels" because of their length, were slapstick affairs which had not gone much beyond recording of vaudeville routines, with perhaps an occasional shift in location. The melodramas were designed in traditional format with hero and villain in battle or chase over the heroine, with the inevitable rescue providing climax and resolution. Though subject material came from a variety of sources, both original and borrowed from literature and stage, the plots were remarkably similar, with costumes and settings providing the major variation.

Films were still being sold outright at this point, on a per foot basis, and with nickelodeons and storefront theatres now spreading well into the hinterlands, the market for films was increasing sharply. Biograph was struggling to keep pace with the other major companies in output while at the same time trying to freeze out the upstart independents. To meet the demands of competition, Biograph found it necessary to hold to a production schedule calling for two to three films per week.

It was under such "bullish" market conditions that D. W. Griffith came to Biograph in 1908. With a background in stock company acting, and aspirations as a playwright, he came to New York with his actress wife, Linda Arvidson, in hopes of selling some of his stories to the film companies. The idea of acting in films was for Griffith, as for most self-respecting theatre people, demeaning; but after an unsuccessful attempt to sell a synopsis

Rescued from an Eagle's Nest (1907). A tale of abduction and rescue which features Griffith in his first acting assignment, and shows Porter's command of special-effects cinematography.

of *La Tosca* to the Edison studio, he acquiesced, and accepted the offer of Edwin S. Porter to play the lead role in *Rescued From an Eagle's Nest*. This led to acting assignments for Biograph, and when the call went out for someone to help Biograph's only director, Wallace McCutcheon, to meet the two-a-week schedule, it was the energetic young actor Griffith, that the studio turned to.

Griffith's first assignment as director was *The Adventures of Dollie*, which he shot in two days. It consisted of about twelve scenes, all single-shot affairs taken from a fixed, full-shot position. The melodramatic action involves a child afloat in a barrel drifting toward a waterfall. There may have been little in the film to suggest the revolutionary effect its director was soon to have on the medium, but it impressed Biograph's front office and Griffith was quickly assigned to another picture. It was after directing some eighteen films that Griffith, two months after his directorial debut, signed his first contract. His films to this point showed no real breakthrough in technique, but were respectably crafted within the limits of the two-a-week schedule that Griffith was obliged to meet. They showed more care perhaps in the staging of action, as Griffith resisted the rather extemporaneous

43

fashion of shooting scenes that was customary and began to insist on adequate rehearsal time for run-throughs. Better acting, and more attention to detail generally, was the result.

Once under contract to Biograph, Griffith, like other film-makers of the period, set about the business of providing visual representation of literary narrative. Following the patterns set down by Porter, he began to produce single-reel melodramas and comedies consisting of from two or three up to twenty or more scenes, carefully selected and arranged to provide for natural association and forward flow. But within his first year of directing for Biograph, Griffith began to sense the need for an approach to the use of the motion picture medium which exploited those characteristics and affinities which were fundamental and peculiar to film.

Recognizing the dramatic impact that cross-cutting between actions of a story could produce, he began to extend and refine this device which Porter had brought to film in *The Great Train Robbery*. Concerning himself not only with the selection and relationship of shots, but with controlling the length of shots themselves, he began to provide films with a kind of visual rhythm which was consonant with the emotional quality of the scene. The device, which became a trademark of the Griffith style, was particularly well suited to the concluding scenes of melodramas, which usually involved the chase, rescue, or both. Increasing the rate of cross-cutting towards the climactic point of the story could greatly intensify the suspense and general thrust of the film. Referred to as the "Griffith last-minute rescue," it became the hallmark of screen melodrama and a key ingredient of the serial film some years later. So we see in the stock melodrama situation of *The Lonely Villa* (1909)—mother and children being threatened by robbers while alerted father and police race to the scene—the twofold use Griffith makes of the cross-cut or "cutback," as it was called then. The separate but converging story elements could be brought into closer proximity, while at the same time reinforcing the emotional tone through the rhythmic cutting.

A more fundamental of Griffith's contributions to screen narrative, and a distinct departure from anything that had gone before, was the conscious control and change of visual perspective within the scene. Mention has already been made of Porter's use of a three-shot scene at the conclusion of *The Life of an American Fireman* and his close-up of the gunman in *The Great Train Robbery*. But the former was more a primitive form of cross-cutting than shot-breakdown, since technically there was a change in location from exterior to interior, and the latter, as already mentioned, was not an integral part of the action. What Griffith gradually began to explore was the possibility of changing the perspective of the camera from the fixed, eye-level, middle-distance position that had been a holdover from theatrical tradition and the belief that the camera was simply an instrument for recording action.

The implications of such an approach to narrative construction were probably not realized even by Griffith at the time. There is no evidence that he theorized to any extent over the true nature of screen storytelling, but rather solved individual problems in exposition, dramatic reinforcement, transition, etc., as they came along. The result, however, as revealed through the more than 450 films he made for Biograph, was a fundamentally original approach to film narrative. The camera, not the actor, became the key to exposition and dramatic development. No longer treated as simply an instrument for recording staged business, it became instead the interpretive eye of the storyteller. As such it had to be free to choose its own perspective, to change its angle and distance from the central action, to be selective and search out significant detail, and then step back and survey all elements of the action as they related to one another. Consonant with this approach, and indeed a necessary realization of it, was the breaking down of scenes into a series of individual shots. Using the shot as the basic building block in construction, it became possible to shift perspective instantaneously a number of times within the scene, so that action could be observed always from the best vantage point. With the camera free to move into the scene, into a close-up position, details of the scene began to take on greater significance. Not only could more subtle nuances of gesture and movement of actors help convey the meaning of a scene, but inanimate props and details of the setting itself could be used to both develop the narrative line and enhance the mood of the scene. The setting for a particular action, which, until this time, had been treated mostly as "scenery" to fill the frame, now became a functional part of the action and an integral and supportive part of the narrative.

The implication of shot breakdown, however, extended beyond manipulation of the camera and opened up for Griffith and his heirs the whole field of constructive or creative editing, which was to become the foundation of the Soviet school of montage almost two decades later. Just as the camera had become the key creative instrument for the filmmaker, so the unity of theme and the natural association of images rather than slavish adherence to unities of time and place became central to building the drama. Though application of the principle is best illustrated in Griffith's feature films made after his apprenticeship years with Biograph, his introduction of the cut-away for a momentary shift in action in *After Many Years* (1908), and his subsequent use of the flash-back for past tense exposition, illustrate his early determination to extend screen storytelling beyond the single-setting, single-time-period scene. In *After Many Years*, which Griffith based on Tennyson's Enoch Arden, a close-up of Annie Lee waiting for her husband to return is followed by a cut-away scene of Enoch cast away on a desert island. Like his use of crosscutting for parallel action, Griffith's original use of such creative editing devices was to solve the practical problem of providing necessary exposition and building suspense.

Of the many other innovations which Griffith brought to film during his years with Biograph, the most significant, in terms of their influence on the development of the medium, continued to be those directly related to his conception of basic narrative design. Two which represented a further break with theatrical tradition was his movement of actors toward and away from the camera on entrances and exits from the scene, and, as an outgrowth of his crosscutting technique, allowing the scene to begin with action already in progress. Other devices, for which at least part credit should go to Griffith's cameraman Billy Bitzer, include moving camera and optical devices such as the freezing of action within the frame, a device which seems to have its origins in theatrical tableaux, and which today is a stock-in-trade of television comedy. Others include the fade-out to conclude a scene and the iris or circular masking of part of the frame, which Griffith used both as a means of focusing attention and as a transitional device.

Though perhaps less directly a part of basic narrative construction, yet important contributions to the total dramatic effect of a scene, were Griffith's use of lighting, tinting, soft focus photography, and the attention given to such details as costuming, make-up, and set design. His use of lighting to establish mood and reinforce the emotional tone of a scene was particularly significant, as lighting until this time had been thought of as a technical problem—getting enough light upon the action for adequate exposure of film—rather than a dramatic tool. With the help of improved incandescent lighting, Griffith was able to

A Corner in Wheat (1909). Frank Powell is the unscrupulous wheat trader who brings despair to farmers and poor consumers, and meets a just and ironic end when he trips into a grain elevator pit.

fashion light and shadow both for general composition and special effects.

Unlike other film pioneers, whose contributions are associated with one or a few particular films, Griffith developed and refined his art of screen storytelling through such a large number of single-reel films that it is difficult and misleading to point to a handful as representing milestones in the development of screen narrative. Many techniques, in fact, were not original with Griffith but adopted and fashioned by him to become an integral part of the film's fabric, and not simply as a gimmick or addendum. Certain films from his Biograph years do, however, represent peaks of his creative energy and have become something of minor classics of his early period. In addition to the already mentioned *The Lonely Villa* and *After Many Years*, these include *Pippa Passes* (1907), which Griffith based on the Robert Browning poem and was heralded for its significant content and dramatic use of lighting, and *A Corner in Wheat* (1909), which employs a combination of freeze frame and contrast editing, and includes social commentary worked out to ironic

47

The Lonedale Operator (1911). Blanche Sweet uses the telegraph key in a desperate attempt to signal her plight at the hands of railroad bandits.
MUSEUM OF MODERN ART/ FILM STILLS ARCHIVE

conclusion when the villainous wheat tycoon is buried in one of his own grain elevators. *Pippa Passes* also illustrates Griffith's interest in more complex structures for film narrative, with its four separate sections and linking motif foreshadowing the design Griffith was to use later in *Intolerance*.

Although Griffith began to find the single-reel film length restrictive by 1910, the Patents Company practice of limiting films to one reel checked his ambition. Two films which have the distinction of being the first, and in fact among the few, two-reelers that Griffith made for Biograph were *His Trust* and *His Trust Fulfilled* (1910) and *Enoch Arden* (1911). Although each reel of *His Trust* was a complete story, Griffith had intended both parts to be shown together. Studio pressure resulted in their being released separately. *Enoch Arden*, a remake of his earlier *After Many Years*, was even more clearly a single entity, and despite studio attempts to release one reel at a time, exhibitor and audience pressure won out, and the film became one of the first multi-reel films to be exhibited as a single unit.

The Lonedale Operator, produced in 1911, is a single-reel melodrama, but is among Griffith's best-crafted and most popular short films. In addition to its carefully edited cross-cuts, it utilizes both camera movement and movement within the frame to provide a kind of visual orchestration that was to become the key to the movie chase and rescue. A train engineer's race to save a telegraph operator from robbers sets the pace for cuts between hurtling train and telegraph office, where the frantic heroine vainly tries to barricade the door. It was a pattern often repeated in Griffith films.

Of the sixty-odd films Griffith made in 1912 (all but three were single reelers), the two which stand out, more for their stories and social themes than particular techniques, are *The Musketeers of Pig Alley* and *The New York Hat*. The first is especially effective in its representation of New York slum life and is considered a vintage gangster film. *The New York Hat* combines the talents of Griffith with those of the film's sixteen-year-old scenarist, Anita Loos, and the stars—Mary Pickford, Lionel Barrymore, Mae Marsh and the Gish sisters.

By 1913, the Patents Company pressure against multi-reel film had fallen away under the rush of "feature films" from independent producers and foreign exchanges, particularly the Italian historical pieces. Stimulated once again by the challenge of the longer film, particularly the nine-reel *Quo Vadis* from Italy, Griffith produced his own first feature and last film for the Biograph Studio, the four-reel biblical epic *Judith of Bethulia*. By the time Griffith began production of *Judith*, he had mastered most of the narrative tools of film; what this film provided was the training ground in large cast and multi-scene scope and spectacle that were to follow.

Judith of Bethulia (1913). The biblical epic casts Blanche Sweet as Judith and Henry Walthall as the Assyrian general she is supposed to assassinate.
MUSEUM OF MODERN ART/FILM STILLS ARCHIVE

The release of *Judith of Bethulia* marked the end of Griffith's association with Biograph and the close of his apprenticeship years of filmmaking. Although the films for which he was to be best known were yet to come, it was Biograph one-reelers that had provided Griffith with the training ground for development of an approach to visual expression, and given the art of screen narrative its foundation and early direction. These contributions to film form have probably been best summed up by Lewis Jacobs, who says,

> Griffith had hit upon a truth with implications that all motion picture directors since then have been trying to command. It is that the primary tools of the screen medium are the camera and the film rather than the actor; that the subject matter must be conceived in terms of the camera's eye and film cutting; that the unit of the film art is the shot; that manipulation of the shots builds the scene; that the continuity of scenes builds the sequences; and that the progression of sequences composes the totality of the production. Upon the composition of this interplay of shots, scenes, and sequences depends the clarity and vigor of the story. Here Griffith saw the epitome of motion picture method.*

Other Pioneers

Although their work is less easily documented as helping to shape the development of screen narrative, a number of other early directors were making popular and even influential contributions to the form. By 1907 in France, Méliès was joined by several filmmakers who pioneered the fields of documentary, animation, melodrama, and, most significantly, comic fantasy. Like Méliès, Ferdinand Zecca, Emile Cohl, Louis Feuillade, and Jean Durand were exploring the trick potential of the camera and finding a basic narrative framework—usually a chase sequence—upon which to hang their handiwork. Both French and American schools of silent screen comedy, particularly the early works of René Clair and the original Sennett Keystone films, show evidence of their influence. Both the pursuit of runaway pumpkins in Cohl's *The Pumpkin Race* (1907) and runaway time in Durand's *Onésime Horloger* (1910) illustrate how central the manipulation of time and motion through trick effects was to even these pioneer directors of screen slapstick and farce. In the

*Lewis Jacobs, "D. W. Griffith: New Discoveries," in *The Rise of the American Film* (New York, 1939), and *The Emergence of Film Art* (New York, 1969).

latter work a young man, who is to inherit a fortune from an uncle in twenty years, shortens the waiting time by tampering with a clock and thereby speeding up his life.

In England, Cecil Hepworth as early as 1904 was extending Porter's basic blueprint for narrative and providing a preview of Griffith's own rescue formula in *Rescued by Rover*. This film, made up of twenty individual shots, relates the abduction of a child from its pram by a gypsy. Progression of the drama follows the family dog, who, alerted to the crisis, takes up the trail of the infant. Following the scent across a stream and into an attic room, he discovers the babe and then races back to the family home to alert the master and lead him to the hideout of the kidnapper. Although not a chase in the strict sense of the word, the feats of the canine hero, together with Hepworth's own accomplishments in building the story from a collection of shots, makes the film an original in dramatic rescue. *Daylight Burglary,* produced by the Sheffield Photo Company in 1903, and *The Pickpocket,* produced the same year by Gaumont, further illustrate the early use of multiple camera position by British filmmakers and the beginnings of the movie chase. The former work was imported by the Edison Company and is thought to be influential in the development of this cinematic device.

In both France and Italy the stage was being set, before the end of the first decade, for the costume spectacles, which, though ponderous and basically uncinematic, were extending Méliès' early attention to scenic design and providing films like Italy's *The Fall of Troy* and *The Sack of Rome* with settings and décor both decorative and appropriate to their historical period. Similarly, by 1907 the French Film d'Art Company was bringing to the screen a series of classic plays performed by the French National Theatre. Though straight recordings of stage pieces, they helped to push films beyond the single-reel length and introduced more prestigious dramatic material to the screen.

But it was finally the works of Méliès, Porter, and Griffith that stand out as being exploratory and setting the direction of narrative form. It is these pioneer works that also earned for their makers the respective titles of "Dean of Motion Picture Directors," "Father of the Story Film," and "Father of Film Technique."

3
Refinement in Form

Griffith—The Art of Filmic Representation

By 1913, when Griffith left Biograph to begin work on his monumental *The Birth of a Nation*, the American film industry was about to launch an important new phase in its growth and development. The formative years had passed and the Teens were to become years of refinement in form, years in which the term "art" could legitimately be associated with the medium, and years of preparation for what would come to be called the Golden Age of American Cinema—the Twenties.

With the Teens came the multi-reel film, and with the push past the single-reel length, more intricate, more fully developed stories could be told. The "photoplay" had established itself as a popular form with audiences and a lucrative one for producing companies. The challenge now was the refinement in visual storytelling, the tailoring of screenplays which went beyond the bare bones of narrative and provided some sense of mood, emotional tone and characterization. If indeed film had any claim to artistry at this point it was in the successful visualization or filmic representation of dramatic incidents, both historical and contemporary and both originally conceived and adapted from literature and the stage. And it was Griffith who once again led the way.

Griffith brought his ace cameraman, Billy Bitzer, and the best of Biograph's talent with him when he joined the Mutual

Film Corporation in 1913 as head of production. Here he rushed production of four films while occupied with the planning of his next spectacle film—a story of the American Civil War and the Reconstruction period, based on the Thomas Dixon novel, *The Clansman*, with additional inspiration coming from another Dixon work, *The Leopard's Spots*. Even while absorbed in this project, however, Griffith was able to break new ground in such films as *The Avenging Conscience* (1914). Here he developed a psychological theme in a story adapted from Edgar Allan Poe's "The Telltale Heart" and "Annabel Lee," foreshadowing the style of Jean Epstein and others of the avant-garde who were to explore expressionist and other non-naturalistic modes.

The Birth of a Nation

Griffith's Civil War epic went into production in 1914. Unable to find studio support, he had to finance the film independently, a sum which turned out to be five times the expenditure of any film to date. Once again, working without a shooting script, he produced and edited the film virtually single-handedly,* save the invaluable aid of his cameraman, Bitzer. The result was the twelve-reel *The Birth of a Nation*, which had its premier showing in Los Angeles in February, 1915.

The film's reception, both critical and popular, can only be described as monumental, not just the immediate reception, but in terms of the accumulated praise and financial returns over the years. It brought to the screen a consolidation and refinement of Griffith's storehouse of techniques in cinematic construction and dramatic representation tried and refined over the years at Biograph. It was something more than a spectacle film—Griffith had already introduced spectacle to the screen with *Judith of Bethulia*, as had the Italian filmmakers. But by comparison these remained limited in scope. Here was super-spectacle—a kind of cataract flow of history blended with an emotionally charged, intimate story which provided the grand sweep of great legend.

The setting is the South during and after the Civil War. The first half of the film portrays incidents of the war itself, while the second half is devoted to post-war reconstruction, during which political power is given to former Negro slaves and the Southern whites become the victims of Negro terrorists and their Northern

*Griffith continued to edit the film after its New York showing, and followed its opening in other major cities, still adjusting the print.

sympathizers (carpetbaggers). The final sequences portray the formation of the Ku Klux Klan as an instrument of self-protection.

Onto this historical panorama is superimposed the personal story of the film. It concerns two families—the Stonemans of Pennsylvania and the Camerons of South Carolina. Growing friendship and romance among the Stoneman and Cameron sons and daughters lead to the conflicts of war. Phil Stoneman and Ben Cameron actually come face to face on the battlefield. It is in the post-war period, however, that conflicts deepen. Ben, in love with Elsie Stoneman, finds that her father, a powerful figure in Washington politics, is plotting with Negro terrorists to ravage the Southern whites. Ben finally provides the inspiration and leadership for the formation of the Ku Klux Klan, which rides, in the best tradition of the Griffith last-minute rescue, to save the Cameron family from the marauding blacks who are breaking into a hut where the family has taken refuge.

It is the film's over-all design—the blending of the historical events with the personal drama—that is first most impressive. Neither Griffith nor any other filmmaker had ever attempted to recreate history, such recent and, for Griffith, such personal history, on such a grand scale, and the director obviously took pride in his role as historian. In the title which introduces the fateful Ford Theatre sequence where Lincoln is shot, Griffith states:

> An historical facsimile of Ford's Theatre as on that night, exact in size and detail with the recorded incidents, after Nicolay and Hay in *Lincoln, a History*.

Griffith provided similar notes in introducing other key historical scenes, such as Lee and Grant at Appomattox.

Beyond the general construction, what is impressive even today is the composition, the camera work, and the editing of individual scenes. It is here that Griffith proves himself the master craftsman: his cross-cutting between units of action while varying shot length to create rhythm; his integration of long, medium, and close shots to build a scene; the cutting away from an action before it is completed to build suspense and increase tempo. This mastery of editing together with Griffith's handling of actors is what gives individual scenes such dramatic force and makes them individually famous—battlefield struggles, Ben Cameron's return to Piedmont, the Lincoln assassination, and, of course, the ride of the Klan.

But, beneath these intense scenes, masterfully conceived and executed, was a sentiment and theme that many viewers found repugnant. As the son of a Confederate colonel, Griffith had grown up on romantic tales of the Old South and he saw in the Dixon novel and other accounts of the period what he believed to be a true picture of things—the "Black stranglehold" on the South after the war and the benevolent crusades of the Klan. This theme, together with the stereotypes that Griffith either consciously or unconsciously produced—the black Mammy and faithful darkies on the one hand and a wide assortment of lust-crazed, arrogant, whiskey-drinking "blacks" who terrorized the white community on the other—made the film immediately explosive. It was barred from exhibition in a dozen states and where it was shown in the North protests and demonstrations followed. In at least one instance, at the film's opening at the Tremont Theatre in Boston, the showing led to a full-scale riot. Years after its initial release controversy continued to surround the film. Charges and countercharges of racism filled the press and periodicals, some written by Griffith himself. Subsequent releases of *The Birth of a Nation* continued to bring protests, and as late as 1931, it was banned in Philadelphia.

Sensitivity to the film's inflammatory subject is evident even today. The Introductory Notes to a pamphlet issued by the Museum of Modern Art in New York in connection with its series

The Birth of a Nation (1915). Depiction of Klan activities provided one of the film's most controversial ingredients.
MUSEUM OF MODERN ART/
FILM STILLS ARCHIVE

several years ago on "The History of the Motion Pictures, 1895–
1946" reads:

> It is by our decision that D. W. Griffith's *The Birth of a Nation* will
> not appear in this cycle. Fully aware of the greatness of the film
> and its artistic and historic importance, we have also had sufficient
> and repeated evidence of the potency of the anti-Negro bias and
> believe that exhibiting it at this time of heightened social tensions
> cannot be justified.

Intolerance – Grand Fugue or Visual Babel

Before the release of *The Birth of a Nation*, Griffith was
already hard at work on a film centering on modern industrial
strife and miscarriage of justice which he called *The Mother and
the Law*. The project, however, lacked the spectacle and epic
proportions of *Birth* and the rival Italian films, so Griffith conceived and added to the original project two period pieces which
had more of the epic quality—the fall of the ancient city of
Babylon and the events surrounding the Huguenot slaughter in
Paris which has come to be known as the St. Bartholomew's Day
Massacre. The result was his monumental 1916 release, *Intolerance*.

In the modern story, the focus is on a boy and girl who, as
the result of a factory strike, are forced to leave their home for
the city. Their marriage is followed by false imprisonment of the
boy and the arrival of a baby which is taken from the young
mother by the "do-gooders" of the community. No sooner released from prison, the boy once again becomes innocently
implicated in a crime—this time murder—and is convicted and
sentenced to death. The climax to this episode follows the
Griffith chase formula as desperate wife and friends rush to
overtake the governor's train to secure a pardon as the boy is
being led to the gallows.

This story of *The Mother and the Law* is reminiscent of
Griffith's earlier one- and two-reel melodramas for Biograph. Its
distinguishing features, in addition to its place in the over-all
design of the film, is its pointed social commentary. The plight
of the young couple illustrates the suffering which results from
legal injustice, industrial turmoil, and hypocritical philanthropy.
The story is also notable for its composition and the internal
construction of scenes which, like those of *The Birth of a Nation*,
have become revered as classic Griffith: Mae Marsh wandering

Intolerance (1916). Spectacle unsurpassed—the court of Belshazzar in the city of Babylon.

the streets in search of the child that has been taken from her; the frantic attempt to secure a pardon as the boy is being administered the last rites.

The Babylonian sequence is more in the tradition of *Judith of Bethulia*. It traces the attacks of Cyrus and his Persian horde on the city of Babylon (circa 539 B.C.), which is ruled by the benevolent monarch Belshazzar. Betrayal by the city's priests brings about the invasion of Belshazzar's court, despite the valiant efforts of the loyal mountain girl to warn her king.

The style here most closely resembles the Italian spectacles of the period, with its overpowering settings, elaborate costuming, and huge cast of men and beasts. And though Griffith may well have been inspired by the Italian product in conceiving his spectacle, he shunned the traditions and limitations of the stage. He showed here that spectacle need not be weighted down by the slow solemnity of the triumphal march. The camera was free to roam (and with the aid of editing to cut) from detail to detail and characters, both principals and supernumeraries, were part of the action rather than of some theatrical design.

58

Considerably less developed, but no doubt of particular interest to Griffith as a historical document, was the French segment, which deals with Catherine de Medici's instigation of the massacre of the Huguenots in Paris in 1572. Here the intrigue within the court of Charles IX gives way to the personal story of two lovers, Prosper and Brown Eyes, who become victims of the slaughter. Though undistinguished in structure and lacking dramatic force, the segment is of interest for Griffith's conception of the French court and the Paris streets of the period.

There is a fourth motif which Griffith added to the three stories to further expand the theme of intolerance through the ages; it is a series of scenes depicting key events in the life of Christ. Although generally referred to as the "Judean Story," it hardly constitutes a narrative. It is rather a series of vignettes, (often just single shots) showing Christ with his disciples, his entrance into Jerusalem, the way of the cross, and finally the crucifixion. It gave Griffith an opportunity to introduce a great and familiar theme which could serve as both parallel and counterpoint to the other three tales.

What made *Intolerance* revolutionary was the complex interweaving of the four units. Griffith, still smarting from the "racist" criticism of *The Birth of a Nation*, wanted to show intolerance through the ages and attempted to isolate the theme and at the same time weld together the separate period pieces by introducing at key transitions a scene of a woman rocking a cradle accompanied by the Walt Whitman line "endlessly rocks the cradle, uniter of here and hereafter." The effect was for the viewer to be swept from life in a present-day city to ancient Babylon and then back to the Christian era and on to 16th century France. And so the cross-cutting continued throughout the four-and-a-half hour film, sometimes with, but often without the cradle motif, until the four come rushing together in final resolution. An epilogue provided a vision of a future world of love and harmony where prison walls are replaced by flowering fields and heavenly angels look down upon a world of peace and tranquility.

It was this complex structure that brought Griffith under the gun of some critics who found the work heavy-handed and difficult to follow. Others obviously saw the liberating potential in the new design. A critic for the Boston *Transcript* expressed the hope that "American producers take the technical freedom of *Intolerance* to heart and get away from many of the stiff conventions of the present-day method of telling a story on the screen."

The film appears to have been overwhelming, if not confusing, for most audiences and it failed to do business. It was shortly recut by Griffith and released as two separate films—*The Fall of Babylon* and *The Mother and the Law*. Catherine de Medici and Christ were left by the wayside.

Though a financial failure, the film proved to be an inspiration and guide for the young Soviet filmmakers who were soon to make their own mark on the film world. In spite of its poor public showing and some adverse criticism, it became the second great monument to its creator's genius. If *The Birth of a Nation* was "like writing history with lightning," as Woodrow Wilson is supposed to have said, then *Intolerance* was a moral tract in the manner of a grand fugue. Its spectacle and structural bravado perhaps overshadow the mastery which Griffith was once more able to display in visualization and cinematic rendering of individual scenes.

The Other Side of the Peak

By 1916, eight years after joining Biograph as an actor in single-reel "potboilers," Griffith was the world's foremost director. Besides producing the medium's first two masterworks, he had set down an entire system of narrative technique which has served as the foundation for screen storytelling ever since. His films in the years which followed proved to be an odd mixture of brilliance (*Broken Blossoms,* 1919), strained competence (*Way Down East,* 1920 and *Orphans of the Storm,* 1921) and pedestrian romantic larks (*Hearts of the World,* 1918 and *True Heart Susie,* 1919).

Broken Blossoms, the first film to be released through United Artists, effectively illustrated Griffith's ability to return to the simple story of intimate relationships after the scope and complexity of *Intolerance.* Here Lillian Gish plays the London waif who is befriended by a Chinese boy (Richard Barthelmess) and as a result becomes the victim of her own cruel father's wrath. In place of action reinforced by editing techniques and spectacle, the film is bathed in a poetic atmosphere created through soft-focus photography, an intimate and searching camera, and exceptionally sensitive acting. Like *Intolerance,* the photography was embellished by use of tinted film stock and carefully worked out lighting designs, with the final touch being the pervasive London fog. The film, though not unique in this respect, also demonstrated the potential for realism and atmospheric effects within the confines of the studio. The film inspired one writer for an exhibitors' trade review to suggest that Griffith "paints the lily. He adds another hue to the rainbow."

Orphans of the Storm gave Griffith the opportunity to return to the historical spectacle, this time the French Revolution, as a backdrop for personal drama. It is in the orchestration of historical pageantry while examining intimate detail of personal conflict that Griffith continued to show his dedication and control—surging crowds, the storming of the Bastille, and the rescue of Lillian Gish from the guillotine. Though a popular and profitable addition to Griffith's "big pictures," *Way Down East,* an adaptation from a popular stage work, never quite reached the levels of artistry of Griffith's other major works. The turgid plot and Victorian morality made it almost a caricature of the stage "mellerdrama." What sustains the film as a more than routine contribution to silent cinema is the portrayal of the heroine by Lillian Gish, Griffith's use of natural settings, and a particularly fine example of the last-minute rescue accomplished by Richard Barthelmess on the ice floes at the brink of a waterfall.

Gish also managed to add some lustre to the uneven *Hearts of the World,* which was Griffith's contribution to the war effort. The film once again displayed his special skill in blending the personal story with the spectacular background. It is a propaganda piece, which dramatizes the plight of a woman and her children in a French village who become victims of the hated "Huns." Gish's anguish at the death of her mother is unsurpassed and perhaps even more to her credit is the ability to carry off the film's rather contrived scene in which she wanders through the battlefield in a state of shock searching for her love, while clutching the wedding dress she was to have worn that very day. Finding him and presuming him dead, she lies down beside the "body" as a title reads, "and so they spent their wedding night." Initial enthusiasm for this first panoramic treatment of the great war quickly waned with the signing of the armistice and it has since been generally ignored.

True Heart Susie, which was released as the war in Europe came to an end, was a return to the Victorian morality play of Griffith's Biograph years. It even more clearly illustrates how out of touch he was with the worldly wise and sophisticated attitudes of the postwar audience. Dedicated to women who must wait patiently for the one man who is to be the only one in their life, the film shows the pain and sacrifice that such a "true heart" must endure. There is never the least concession to the impulsive act contrary to Victorian precepts. The extent of Susie's indiscretions are when she uses corn starch as makeup in order to "do battle against the paint and powder brigade," or when she is chided as "reckless Susie" for having two plates of ice cream at the church social. It is a world of comely virtues in which the true heart's sacrifice wins out over the painted lady of easy virtue (she dies for her transgressions) and wins the hand of one whose "great and simple heart cannot believe that all are not like himself."

Griffith had come under fire earlier for his maudlin sentimentality, particularly in *Intolerance*, but in the postwar era it was even more out of tune with what was to be the "Roaring Twenties." By 1925 he no longer commanded the singular reputation of master director. Younger men with new ideas for film (if not new techniques) were arriving on the scene. Griffith by this time was also becoming a victim of the system he helped to create—the big studio operation. Under the unit system of production he no longer had control over all stages of production. His innovations, however, continued to influence a host of directors both at home and abroad. Von Stroheim, De Mille, Rex Ingram, Henry King and King Vidor all show the Griffith influence in their early work. European directors who acknowledged his influence include Carl Dreyer and Sergei Eisenstein, who years later said of Griffith:

> I wish to recall what David Wark Griffith himself represented to us, the young Soviet film-makers of the twenties. To say it simply and without equivocation: a revelation.

The Aesop of Inceville

The formation of the Triangle Film Corporation in July of 1915 represented an important consolidation within the American industry. The name was intended to reflect the three production units which would be responsible for producing what had by this time become the three staples of the American silents: the regular dramas and melodramas which were pushing beyond the single-reel length, the specials or large-budget showcase

Thomas Ince.
MUSEUM OF MODERN ART/FILM
STILLS ARCHIVE

films which ran several reels, and the comedy shorts. The new company also brought together the three men who were each establishing a reputation as master of the particular form. Griffith, of course, was the champion of the specials, and in charge of the bread and butter genres—regular dramas and comedies—were Thomas Ince and Mack Sennett.

Thomas Ince, like Griffith, had come to film initially as an actor with a background in theatre. He starred in a Griffith-directed film in November, 1910, wrote and directed his first film the following month, and by 1915 was a major creative force in the industry. His rise as a star director was actually the result of his combined talents as creative filmmaker and studio ruler.

When hired by the New York Motion Picture Company in 1911 to produce that company's first two-reel film, Ince was already studio building as well as filmmaking. It was at his suggestion that an 18,000 acre tract of diverse topography along the Pacific was leased by the company for the filming of *War on the Plains* (1912). Under Ince's direction the film became a prototype of the many epic Westerns which were to follow; the California real estate on which it was shot was soon to become known as Inceville, the largest back lot in Hollywood history. It had separate villages constructed to provide Spanish, Dutch, Japanese, Irish and Canadian locations; for *War on the Plains* Ince hired his own Wild West Show and a Sioux tribe was also in residence.

Ince followed *War on the Plains* with more than two dozen double-reel films the same year. With studio operations of modest size, and Ince able to devote his attention to personal supervision of both planning and execution of film projects, he entered into his most creative period between 1912 and 1916. Major films of the period included *Custer's Last Fight* (1912), *The Battle of Gettysburg* (1913), *The Wrath of the Gods* (1914), *The Italian* (1915), *The Coward* (1915), and *Hell's Hinges* (1916).

63

Ince's reputation as a director came to be linked strongly with the Western film, but the prior-mentioned works serve to illustrate how diversified his films were in subject and stylistic approach. In addition to the Westerns are found an ambitious historical piece, a saga of the South Pacific, and a caustic and heart-rending social document on the fate of the American immigrant (the Italian).

But it was in the Western that Ince's special talents for direct story approach and tight dramatic structure were best displayed. The Western was a natural for film because action was its stock-in-trade: riding, roping, jumping, brawling, the chase of runaway gunman, the overland stage, and stampeding cattle. It was the rough and tumble action of the opening up of the frontier which had a romantic quality about it while providing for realistic detail and lean and direct progression. In the hands of Ince, and with the help of Western star William S. Hart, the genre was on its way to becoming a national institution.

What is impressive, even today, about the Ince two-reel westerns is how remarkably simple and direct they are. Every incident, every action, is directly related to the basic plot struc-

The Toll Gate (1920). William S. Hart makes a significant contribution to the mystique of the Western hero in this and other Ince films.
MUSEUM OF MODERN ART/FILM STILLS ARCHIVE

ture, with exposition both in action itself and by way of titles uncluttered and unambiguous. Ince, in fact, carries this almost to a fault and his works seem simplistic at times.

Even the longer films display this spartan approach. *Hell's Hinges,* made by Ince and Hart for the Triangle Company in 1916, is a model of straight-from-the-hip storytelling. The romantic image of the West has brought the weak-willed Reverend Henley and his sister Faith to Placer Center—"Hell's Hinges" it is affectionately called by its inhabitants. Blaze Tracey, local gunslinger, is turned from his job of intimidating the new arrivals by the sweet innocence of Faith. "A different kind of smile—sweet, honest, and trustful, and seeming to say, 'How do you do, Friend?'" is the title. The weak parson becomes a victim of the mob and is shot in the struggle that develops between the "Petticoat Brigade" and the saloon mob bent on setting fire to the church. In the closing scenes, daybreak finds Blaze and Faith by the simple grave of the parson, while smoke drifts over the ruined town of Hell's Hinges. Blaze's final words: "Over yonder hills is the future—both yours and mine. It's callin' and I reckon we'd better go."

The titles, which today may seem stilted, have a simplicity and directness about them that is consistent with the Ince style. Also well represented here is the simple, uncluttered setting, which also fits and has an interesting textural appeal. Another important feature of the film is the restrained acting of Hart coupled with Ince's carefully worked out close camera. The only suggestion of complexity comes in the characterization of Blaze Tracey himself. There is an enigma about the personality that is summed up in another title: "An embodiment of the best and worst in the West." Blaze resolves to keep law and religion out of Hell's Hinges, but dissolves in the face of kindness and purity. The Ince plot may have been kept simple, but in the characterization, particularly in the Western hero as portrayed by Hart, there was some suggestion of depth. It was an enormously popular characterization, which became a model for many other heroes of both the East and West: clean living, rough riding, kind to animals and old folk, shy with women, often preoccupied with a troublesome past or some personality quirk (akin to character flaw in classic tragedy), and living according to some personal code which we might not understand but are perfectly willing to accept.

As Inceville developed as a major production center with an increasingly heavy schedule, Ince began to share more of the directorial chores with others in order to devote his time to overseeing the number of films being produced simultaneously on the lot. To maintain control of each production, the brief synopsis with marginal notations from which he had customarily worked gave way to the detailed shooting script with shot and scene breakdowns, camera positions, descriptions of action, and even lines for the actors to speak. Ince was thus able to make the shift from director to producer and still administer quality control and keep films, though directed by others, very much in the Ince image.

Under this new system, the greatest part of the work of producing a picture was now completed once the continuity had been finished and put in the hands of a director. From the continuity writers the scenario would come under Ince's careful scrutiny and go back to the scenario department for changes, sometimes several times, before being given to the director with the instructions to "shoot as is."

The system was not one which encouraged creative contributions on the part of directors. Many working under these ties argued that such a procedure produced a mechanical effect which was devoid of any distinctive style. The Ince film, however, provided the best evidence that in the case of this creative producer at least, the argument would not hold. In actuality it was Ince directing all films on the lot, but from his office and in his mind's eye rather than from behind the camera lens. It was the combined talents of knowing thoroughly every aspect of production, a keen visual sense, and his ability to give orders without giving offense that made Ince's method work for him. Though others tried to adopt it, few realized the same success.

With the formation of the Triangle Company in 1915, Ince became increasingly involved in production supervision and did little of his own directing thereafter. William S. Hart was still under contract to Ince and went with the producer when he broke with Triangle in 1918 and joined Adolph Zukor at Paramount. Hart was to make some of his best films for Paramount, but Ince, increasingly involved with general supervision, had little to do with their production.

Screenwriting—The Anonymous Legion

As studios grew in size and more elaborate and expensive films went into production, planning and scripting of films became an increasingly important phase of production. This brought with it increasing animosity on the part of many directors, who saw their role diminished to that of stage manager. With big production companies in particular, heavy production schedules did not allow directors time to collaborate on scenarios, even if a producer was so inclined. Ince had helped to make the producer the man who called the shots and the director was relegated to the position of glorified cameraman. The directors who were to make their names as creative artists were those who could summon the independence and creative energy to be a part of the planning and scripting process as well as being the man behind the camera.

And if Ince's role as producer showed that creativity in film could be centered elsewhere than in the imagination of the director, it also helped indirectly to encourage the talent of the legions of scenarists or screen writers who labored in obscurity for each of the major companies. The film writer became a fixture of studio operations several years before the big studio assembly line techniques were developing in the mid Teens. Ince, as already mentioned, was employing scenarists to hammer out scripts for him, albeit under close supervision. Sennett at the same time had his stable of "idea men" who brainstormed the early Keystone antics. Even earlier, Griffith collaborated with several scenarists, such as Frank Woods, Gerrit J. Lloyd, and Anita Loos, the teenage girl who provided him with his script for *The New York Hat*. Most Griffith works, however, were shot "off the cuff" and he seldom used a continuity or shooting script once involved in production.

By the late Teens, with the exception of these few master directors (or "producers" as each was to become), most films had their beginnings with scenario writers or continuity writers, whether the story was an original idea or adapted from another medium. Where the director worked in the scripting and continuity stage himself, it was a collaborative effort; where not, it was likely to be some unnamed or hardly noted scenarist who became the key creative mind in the production of a film.

Such a scenario writer, destined to remain a footnote to the history of film form, is Anita Loos, who began her writing career at the age of fourteen and had two hundred scenarios and countless film title assignments to her credit by the close of the silent era. With a ferocious appetite for literature and aspirations for becoming a writer, Loos began submitting scenarios to the major film companies when she found it was lucrative and could provide her the financial independence desirable for a literary career. By 1916, barely in her twenties, she had an impressive

Anita Loos—1923.
MUSEUM OF MODERN ART/FILM STILLS ARCHIVE

list of film credits for Biograph, Reliance, Lubin and Metro behind her. She was creating dramas of people and places around the world though she herself had never been out of California.

But Loos' special gift proved to be in a wry comic vein. Douglas Fairbanks found himself on his way to stardom with the Loos script for *His Picture in the Paper,* and most of his screenplays after that, as well as several of Pickford's, were written by her. She also wrote several films for Constance Talmadge between 1919 and 1925, and when she joined Irving Thalberg in 1929 she began writing screenplays for Jean Harlow. For M.G.M. she took on the added job of "film doctor," working over faltering scripts by other scenarists. *San Francisco, The Women,* and *I Married An Angel* are among her more prominent feature film credits, but it is her novel *Gentlemen Prefer Blondes,* that brought her the cheers and admiration of world statesmen and the literary elite. It also proved to be one of the most durable properties in the history of the arts, having gone from novel to Broadway play (1926) to movie (1928) to stage musical (1949) to movie musical (1953) with Loos writing or collaborating on each version.*

In addition to her role as scenarist, Loos also made important contributions to film by way of title writing. In addition to titles

*A new stage musical version, *Lorelei,* opened on Broadway in early 1974.

for most of her own screenplays, she supplied titles for many films she didn't script, including *Intolerance*. Through titles Loos found it possible to introduce verbal humor to the silent screen and though difficult to document, one wonders if the florid style of titles in many of the early silents was not Loos having some private fun with the melodramatic form and Victorian sentiment.

Loos, of course, was only one of the many unsung creative spirits who gave birth to film stories. Sonya Levien began writing screenplays in 1919 and later produced scripts for *State Fair*, *In Old Chicago*, *Drums Along the Mohawk*, *Cass Timberlane* and *Hit the Deck*. Frances Marion, who scripted some of the best of the Valentino and Pickford films went on to writing the screenplays for *Anna Christie*, *Stella Dallas* and *The Big House*.* Jeanie MacPherson wrote many of the DeMille scenarios, while Jane Murfin, who began writing for film in 1917, went on later to create screenplays for Hawks, Wyler and Cukor. Screenwriting in the Teens was a training ground for many who were to labor, virtually unnoticed by filmgoers, on films large and small, sound and silent—and they were virtually all women.

Silent Comedy and the Art of Mime

With Griffith and Ince leading the way, the dramatic film reigned supreme by 1913. Major trust and independent companies had all experimented with comedy, but with few exceptions, these remained little more than an extension of vaudeville and circus routines. Vitagraph, Lubin, and Essanay in particular were producing comic skits in fair number, but American screen comedy had not yet found a true form and was still a minor genre.

It is curious in a way that the form was slow to flower, because film, as a purely visual medium, was perfectly suited to comic mime and the visual gag. And with less reliance on titles to convey meaning than in dramatic films, it was a visual experience with universal understanding and appeal. It was perhaps the continued preoccupation with trick possibilities that the French pioneers had introduced that retarded the realization

*By 1931, having won Academy Awards for screenplays for two consecutive years (*The Big House* and *The Champ*), this former war correspondent had become the dean of Hollywood screenwriters.

that, although comedy could be endowed with a host of camera
and editing devices, it is finally movement and visual expression
that is the essence of screen comedy. Like drama, it is dependent
on the human element, and although cinematic devices may help
to get a laugh, they can never make a screen comedian.

Within the next few years there were to be changes that
would produce what may well stand even today as the American
film's great renaissance—that of silent screen comedy. It was the
coming together of major comic talents in Hollywood, along with
the production personnel that knew how to exploit it, that made
American comedy in the Teens and early Twenties unrivaled.

The inspiration was largely European, however. Both comics and filmmakers (Chaplin, Stan Laurel, and later Lubitsch
among others came from abroad) had been strongly influenced
by the pioneer works in England, Germany, and France. Of
particular importance were the early French chase and trick
films of Lumière, Méliès, Zecca, and Durand, and the singular
reputation of Max Linder, who by the early Teens had become
an international favorite and Pathé's star attraction. Few of Linder's films have survived and he is almost forgotten today, but his
presence in evening dress or morning coat, with mustache and
cane, was both a joy to audiences and an inspiration to later
comic stars. Both Sennett and Chaplin acknowledge their debt
to Linder, Chaplin calling him his teacher. Like Chaplin's, his
routines were in clear contrast to the frantic style of other comedians, and his invention of bits of business with the most ordinary of props was a preview of Chaplin's own special comic
approach.

Sennett—The Fastest Fun on Earth

The man who became the catalyst for the development of
silent screen comedy and gave it an identifiable style was the
Canadian-born Mack Sennett. Sennett began his career in film
in 1908 after an unsuccessful stint in musical comedy, appearing
in many Griffith-directed films. Biograph was doing little in the
comedy field when Sennett first arrived, but the young actor
could not look at the tragedies and melodramas being turned out
without seeing the potential for pure farce. Gradually, Sennett
began directing comedies for Biograph and it is here that he
began to develop his frenetic comic style—a combination of
vaudeville, circus, pantomime, and commedia dell'arte. By the

time he became head of the Keystone Company in 1912 he had a wealth of experience in comic forms both in and outside of film.

But if Sennett had been conditioned by a number of comic forms, the film critics by this time were showing the kind of conditioning that screen narrative was having on them. A review of Sennett's first Keystone film, *Cohen Collects a Debt*, appeared in the *New York Dramatic Mirror* in September of 1912. It reads:

> As one sits through this eight or ten minutes of senseless, idiotic horseplay he wonders what it is all about. Never once is the spectator allowed to grasp the thread of the story, if there is a thread . . .*

If lacking in continuity in the usual story sense, what Sennett's films did exhibit was an incredible economy of film time in working out various bits of action. Cutting was central to the Sennett style, but cutting which tightened up the *action* (a more appropriate word than narrative) and propelled it forward.

The immediate popularity of the Sennett comedies with "low-brow" audiences is understandable. It was screen comedy in the simplest and purest form: completely visual, depending on neither narrative nor characterization, but simply on visual incongruity and surprise. Although creating a world in which conventional logic must be suspended, it dealt with people, objects and conventions of the real world rather than the fantasy and illusion of the French pioneers. It was a distorting lens that grossly exaggerated perhaps, but was a reflection of the real policeman and tramp and dowager rather than a complete fabrication. Sennett ingeniously converted men into character types and these in turn were transformed into machines.

Unlike Ince and Griffith, who, each in his own way, carefully planned a film's action in advance, Sennett was a master of improvisation, allowing many gag routines to develop out of basic situations which were often the barest suggestion of a location or bits of business. What was at the heart of the formula was *pace*. Often with meager indication of what motivated it, a chase would begin: an automobile careening through busy city traffic would miraculously escape demolition though continuing with little more than wheels and frame, leaving behind a nightmare of confusion and sometimes wreckage. Passing within inches of an oncoming locomotive, it would charge through pond

*"Reviews of Supply Company Films," *The New York Dramatic Mirror*, Vol. 68, No. 1762, September 25, 1912, p. 29.

and brush, demolish at least one frame building along the way
before taking to the air at cliffside or dockside and landing in the
Pacific Ocean. The occupants would then regain their compo-
sure for the next phase of the chase; they might be bruised and
shaken but were seldom badly injured.

There were, of course, many variations to the chase or rapid-
action sequences. One that became a trademark of Keystone
slapstick was the pie-throwing battle. A key ingredient here, as
with many routines, was exploring every angle or variation on
the basic gag, and when these had been exhausted, finding one
more, with the whole thing occurring in about two-thirds the
time physically possible.

Keystone films were usually group efforts. Sennett's idea
men would come together to discuss possible routines for a film;
suggestions would be passed around, modified, embellished,
and gradually a general "plot" outline would evolve. But it was
an outline that Keystone directors worked from, not a script.
Thus, much of the action could be worked out and even invented
on the set. Often a production unit would be sent out to take
advantage of some scheduled community activity, and once
there would work out comic routines that the event itself

Mack Sennett.

suggested—a street parade, a beauty contest, a carnival. It was a children's soap box derby being held at Venice, California, that prompted Sennett to develop a single-reel comedy around that event. The result was Charlie Chaplin's second film for Keystone, *The Kids' Auto Race at Venice* (1914).

If gag routines and pace were at the heart of Keystone comedy, it was the preposterous characterizations that provided the finishing touch. And so it was that Sennett, through the Keystone years, groomed an entire stable of comic stars. Top among these in the early years were Ford Sterling and Mabel Normand, whose mimic abilities were the central focus of many single-reel romps for the studio. In a sense, Sterling and Normand were among the straightest of the Keystone comics. Many were endowed with physical characteristics that could be exploited to serve the slapstick formula. Mack Swain, with imposing frame, bushy mustache and eyebrows, and withering stare, was the perfect foil. Chester Conklin, who could rival Keaton for use of deadpan expression, had a quality of movement that might be described as mechanical rag doll. With Ben Turpin it was all in the eyes, and with Roscoe (Fatty) Arbuckle all in the size. If, individually, in ordinary dress they had comic potential, then together, as a befuddled police force the possibilities were even greater. So reasoned Sennett, and so were born the Keystone Kops. And as the Kops became famous, Sennett found that even greater attraction could be provided by the introduction of sex appeal. His equally famous bathing beauties were the result.

Altogether what Keystone created was a surreal world of characters and situations with the special qualities of the incongruous, of surprise and of spatial and temporal license that film could so effectively provide. It was a form that was uniquely cinema, but at the same time borrowing from other comedic arts as well as pioneer screen works. Sennett had been schooled by Griffith, Max Linder, Méliès and other early French directors. Like Méliès he used camera tricks to exploit the absurd; from Linder he learned how to develop plot or situation to suit the personality and bearing of his actors; and Griffith had taught him pacing so that a scene could be more effectively built up through shot selection and arrangement. He also learned how much fun could be extracted from the same basic melodramatic situation that was the hallmark of so many Griffith works.

Just as Sennett had been a pupil of Griffith, Méliès and Linder, so his Keystone studio became the schoolroom for both comic stars and directors to follow. In addition to Chaplin,

Keystone Comedies—Charlie Murray makes his entrance
into a dress shop in a variation of the Sennett chase.
MUSEUM OF MODERN ART/FILM STILLS ARCHIVE

Langdon, Keaton, and Lloyd, who all worked under Sennett at
some point in their careers, other members of the company to
eventually reach stardom were Marie Dressler, Wallace Beery,
W. C. Fields, Gloria Swanson, Bebe Daniels, and Carole Lombard. Directors such as Frank Capra and George Stevens also
had their basic training under Sennett.

By 1915, when Sennett joined the Triangle Company, he
had established himself as the top producer of screen comedy,
with an unrivaled stable of comic talent. As independent production companies increased and the market for comedy continued
bullish, production expanded under an array of banners, with a
host of performers. By this time, however, routines were being
repeated many times over and little was being added to the form.
In addition to the borrowing of ideas and situations, some comedians adopted the style of comic stars who had found a formula
for success. Imitation Chaplin was naturally the most prevalent.
With the market remaining strong, earlier comedies were recut,
regrouped or simply retitled to play along with successors and
imitators.

With the idea men and gag writers unable to provide much

that was original, it was the stars themselves who through the late Teens and Twenties brought new vigor and artistry to silent comedy. But not all screen comedians were able to make the grade. Those who were to survive through the Twenties were essentially those who could develop a personality or characterization revealing some emotional make-up. Pure slapstick, physical incongruity, and mechanical gag would no longer suffice; conveying visually some reflection of internal conflicts and aspirations was now required.

Chaplin—The Mob God*

Of the comics that were to reign during the golden age, the names of Keaton, Langdon, and Lloyd are prominent in terms of popularity and artistry, but Chaplin was the undisputed champion. Chaplin's contributions to the art of mime have been so often, and sometimes so eloquently, described that it has established its own art of superlatives. (Even George Bernard Shaw has ranked Chaplin as "the only genius developed in the motion pictures.") Most of the accolades have been earned. What Chaplin brought to the screen, in addition to the adored characterization of the little tramp—wistful underdog and foil of pomposity—was a rare gift of mime and seemingly boundless imagination in exploring the comic and pathetic possibilities of each situation, each object, each shade of human reaction.

It was while touring the United States with the English vaudeville troupe, the Karno Pantomime Company, that Chaplin was called by Keystone to replace Ford Sterling, who was threatening to quit the company. Chaplin's first film for Keystone, *Making a Living*, was released in February, 1914. The film is in the true spirit of most Keystone films, with Charlie here dressed as something of an English dandy complete with monocle and cane, a dashing way with the ladies, but without a job. He finds employment with a newspaper and manages to make the big scoop on an auto accident by stealing the story from another reporter. Even in this earliest of Chaplin films there is an occasional gesture or expression and a way of embarking on the inevitable chase that sets him apart from the other stars of the Keystone lot.

*Title of an article on Chaplin published in 1915, just a year after his start in films.

Making a Living (1914). Chaplin as an English dandy
in his first film appearance. Henry Lehrman, with Chaplin
here, also directed the film.
MUSEUM OF MODERN ART/FILM STILLS ARCHIVE

But Chaplin's own tradition in comic mime was almost immediately at odds with the frenetic and slap-dash style of the Sennett studio. After a dozen films directed by others, he began to write and direct his own material. He began adopting the costume of the little tramp in his second Keystone film and as he took over more completely the control of his films, a slower, more studied, and disciplined style began to develop. But Chaplin was still obliged to meet a production schedule of nearly one film a week, which gave him little time for reflection and refinement. His Keystone films were mostly improvised, dependent on fast-paced action, with little attention to characterization. Several of them were collaborative efforts with Mabel Normand, which gave her equal billing. In his one year with Keystone, Chaplin made thirty-four shorts and one six-reel feature, *Tillie's Punctured Romance* (1914), in which he co-starred with Marie Dressler, who had created the role of Tillie on the stage.

The lure of a less demanding production schedule and a handsome increase in salary brought Chaplin to the Essanay Company, a chief rival of Keystone in the production of comedies. It was in his sixteen films for Essanay that Chaplin began to develop the distinctive style of tragi-comedy that was to make the term "pathos" forever linked with his screen characterization. *The Tramp* (1915), his sixth film for Essanay, clearly shows the development of the sad clown. Here Charlie, a tramp, comes to the rescue of Edna Purviance (the female lead in most of his subsequent shorts), who is being robbed. He is rewarded by a job on her father's farm, where he once more routs the robbers, but loses the girl to her handsome lover. The film's sad ending shows Charlie walking down the road away from the camera, with a shrug of the shoulders, as the frame is gradually masked out with an iris. This closing action was used in other of his shorts and became a Chaplin trademark.

Another outstanding and favorite work of his Essanay period was *The Bank* (1915). Here Chaplin illustrates perfectly how the simple action which relates to characterization can be the most rewarding. Charlie enters a bank looking for all the world like the manager, with calm self-assurance and cocky gait. He walks over to the huge bank vault, deftly twirls the combination, swings open the door, enters, and emerges with mop and pail, ready to start the day's work. Chaplin himself became quickly aware of the importance of small bits of by-play to his screen personality. Just a year after his first film he reflected in an interview with *Motion Picture* magazine that "to pull off an unexpected trick, which the audience sees is a logical sequence, brings down the house. It is always the little things that bring the laughs. It's the little actions suited to the situation, that makes the hit."

By the time Chaplin joined the Mutual Company in 1916, his films were becoming increasingly rich in such little actions. As a confirmed alcoholic in *The Cure* (1917), his almost catatonic reaction to a drink of "health water" offered him by Edna Purviance is inspired. In *The Rink* (1916), the invention is equally rewarding. Here Charlie plays a waiter who finds traces of various dinner courses a customer has spilled on his person, a helpful reminder in preparing the bill. In *The Immigrant* (1917), Chaplin takes advantage of camera angle to gain surprise. Charlie, presumably seasick, is seen heaving at the rail. It is not until he straightens up and the camera comes around to a new vantage point that we realize Charlie is enthusiastically engaged in hauling in a big fish.

Although it was the basic tramp characterization that Chaplin was in the process of refining, he did not allow himself to become completely restricted to the familiar costume and social status it represented. Many variations were slight and simply adapted Charlie to the professional role in which he was engaged—waiter, clerk, even policeman were still unmistakeably the little tramp. Occasionally, however, Chaplin's social status would be noticeably improved and the costume showed more marked modification. In *One A.M.* (1916), Charlie is in evening dress when he does battle with a revolving table and a Murphy bed. In *Carmen*, he dons the costume of a toreador for his role as Don Hosierey. The most pronounced transformation comes in *The Woman*, in which he plays the title role in appropriate finery. Though roles shifted at times, basic attitude and invention remained undisturbed. Adopting a professional air, Charlie could charm a man in the post office into sticking out his tongue under the pretext of checking his health. The motive was actually to get a stamp licked for posting a letter.

The Mutual films still showed vestiges of slapstick humor, but a slower, more controlled pace began to evolve. Routines were more carefully worked out and a subtler style of mime came into play. This marked the extension and refinement of bits of business into what came to be regarded as classic routines which themselves became famous, even when the particular film in which they appeared might be forgotten. *Easy Street* (1917) and *The Pawn Shop* (1916), which became the most popular of the twelve Mutual films, illustrate how far Chaplin had come in perfecting his style. In *Easy Street*, Charlie, a policeman now, has his big confrontation with Eric Campbell, the strong-man bully who has been terrorizing the neighborhood. To demonstrate his strength, Campbell bends the post of a gas street lamp so the globe is nearly to the ground. This provides Charlie with his weapon. Maneuvering the bully's head into the globe, he turns on the gas and Campbell is efficiently put to sleep. Each time he begins to revive, Charlie lowers the globe over his head with the calm self-assurance of an anesthetist. The same deft and "professional" handling of the situation marks his famous clock routine in *The Pawn Shop*. Here Chaplin undertakes the examination of an old-fashioned alarm clock that has been handed him by a customer. Charlie begins his examination with a stethoscope, followed by the tapping of the ailing instrument with all the expertise of a crack diagnostician. For the operation on the timepiece which follows directly, he turns to hammer, brace and bit and finally a can opener. Peeling back the cover he judiciously sniffs at the innards and begins his extraction using a pair of pliers. He periodically squirts the interior with oil, removes the mainspring, which he carefully measures from nose to extended fingers like a piece of yardgoods, and finishes the operation by squirting and hitting the moving parts until all have been stilled. He then shovels the remains into the owner's hat and completes the routine by hitting the already stunned customer on the head with a rubber mallet.

In addition to the refinement of such visual routines, the Mutual films also show more attention to the character of Charlie himself. No longer simply the initiator or victim of visual gags, the little tramp emerges as an emotional being. He aspires to some role in life that will afford some particle of prestige (which Charlie can usually find, no matter how lowly the job). He falls in love and suffers the anxiety of the quest and the heartbreak of rebuff or disillusionment. In *The Vagabond* (1916), Charlie is once again seen walking the lonely road, but now he is a personality whose actions reflect the inner state rather than the physical resolution to mechanical routines.

With the link between character and action thus established, there is a unity and cohesiveness not present in earlier films. But Chaplin was not primarily a storyteller, and narrative provides a basic framework or setting which might reasonably accommodate Charlie's various trials and aspirations. In fact, even with the polish of the Mutual films, many routines—his bit as a waiter in *The Rink*, the superb ballet sequence with a masseur in *The Cure*, and his drying of dishes in a clothes ringer in *The Pawn Shop*—might easily be interchangeable. Unity is one of character motivation rather than smooth narrative progression.

By the time Chaplin completed his twelve films for Mutual, his tramp had become an international star and even a household word. Virtually all of these films have become mini-classics and serve the bulk of the retrospectives of Chaplin's short films today. In addition to the more elaborate routines he had begun to develop, the films were still enriched by rare moments of seemingly spontaneous byplay. Much of this involved a precision in gesture and movement that makes Chaplin a master of ballet in addition to his other talents. His stand-off with the masseur in *The Cure* is a masterpiece in choreography and shows the discipline of his style. But planning had not robbed the films of the freshness and vigor of earlier works.

With his style perfected, Chaplin's association with the First National Company between 1918 and 1923 marked a transitional period in terms of format. Until now, with the exception of the Sennett directed adaptation of *Tillie's Punctured Romance* and Chaplin's four-reel spoof of *Carmen*, all his films had been either one or two reels long. With *A Dog's Life* (1918), *Shoulder Arms* (1918), and *Sunnyside* (1919), Chaplin expanded films to three reels; with *The Pilgrim* (1923) to four; and with *The Kid* (1921), a short feature length of six reels. The increase in length was not in itself much of an innovation. What it did provide, however, was an extended study of Chaplin's characterization of the wistful and lonely but always resourceful and outgoing little fellow. It continued to be the individual routine which made films like *Shoulder Arms* and *The Pilgrim* memorable rather than the narrative itself. In *Shoulder Arms*, Charlie in the front line trenches, finds he is the only soldier who does not receive a letter at mail call. But pathos turns to glee and then a mixture of the tragi-comic as a package arrives for Charlie—a cheese so overripe that he needs to put on his gas mask before hurling it into the enemy lines. In *The Pilgrim*, Chaplin provides another treasured sampling of mimic artistry when, masquerading as a minister, he delivers a sermon on the story of David and Goliath, all in pantomime.

By the time Chaplin joined Mary Pickford, Douglas Fairbanks and D. W. Griffith in 1923 to form United Artists, he was devoting himself exclusively to feature films produced at an average rate of only one in four years. In fact after seventy films

The Gold Rush (1925). Chaplin's shoulders could be as expressive as his face. He looks on admiringly as Georgia Hale entertains.
MUSEUM OF MODERN ART/FILM STILLS ARCHIVE

made between 1914 and 1923, he would make only three more before the sound era burst upon the screen, and only ten more before his retirement.

A Woman of Paris (1923), Chaplin's first film for United Artists, was an abrupt change of pace for the director. Abandoning his tramp character (and role as actor except for a minor walk-on), he produced what he called "a drama of fate," in fact an ironic and sophisticated tragi-comedy which was to help spawn a whole series of suave and sparkling comedies of manners which were to thrive in the coming years. Though a disappointment to audiences who wanted more of Charlie, the film foreshadowed the sardonic social commentary which was to become a central element of most of Chaplin's later works. It also suggested that Chaplin the screenwriter and director could make it alone, without the help of the little tramp.

The film which Chaplin himself says he wants to be remembered by is his 1925 *The Gold Rush*. Here was his princely gift to Hollywood's golden age, a compendium of his now polished style and a showcase of comedic poetry. The film is a treasure house of classic mime: Charlie's Thanksgiving dinner, when near starvation in a snowbound cabin forces him to cook and serve up one of his boots, which he proceeds to tackle with all the dexterity and relish of a true gourmet; Charlie's New Year's Eve party, when Charlie, anxiously awaiting the arrival of Georgia, with whom he has fallen in love, sits at the festive table he has prepared and dreamily creates a dance with the "oceana rolls" on the end of two forks. At the heart of his mime is the precise and painstaking attention to detail of an action and applying these to some incongruous and unexpected situation. We are delighted with the surprise, impressed with the invention, but what finally enriches and caps the experience is the satisfaction that the action is somehow wholly consistent with the characterization itself.

Although the carefully crafted screenplay was not a key feature of most Chaplin works, *The Gold Rush* and *City Lights* (1931) both demonstrate that he could work effectively within the feature-length format. More attention was given to narrative links, and routines and byplay were allowed to grow more naturally out of basic situations. But it was finally the details in human behavior, the consistency of mimic style that satisfied the sense of unity.

The sound era had arrived by the time Chaplin released *The Circus* in 1928 and the silent era was already a memory by the time *City Lights* appeared in 1931. The fact that Chaplin dared to remain silent—except for background music and sound effects —not only in *City Lights,* but even in *Modern Times* (1936), made nearly a decade after the arrival of sound, shows the strength of his convictions about silent comedy. And the public enthusiasm over these films is perhaps the best testament to the durability of Chaplin's art. As screenwriter, director, and even composer of film music, he was to continue his work in film on a less frequent but regular basis right into the Sixties, but with the coming of sound, the little tramp's days were numbered.

What finally is most significant about Chaplin's legacy of film is the things it eschews or simply ignores. With the greater narrative potential of the multi-reel film, Chaplin never really concerned himself with plot; with the coming of sound he continued successfully in silence; and even the storehouse of cinematic technique—camera composition, editing, set design—which Griffith had bequeathed and others had anxiously adopted, were put to work in a functional and unassuming manner. It would be difficult to find another filmmaker of either his time or since that shows as much independence in the approach to his art.

Buster Keaton

If Chaplin was the undisputed king of comedy in the late
Teens, by the Twenties he at least had contenders for the crown.
Chief among these was Buster Keaton, who, like Chaplin, was
his own "auteur" of silent comedy, writing and directing his own
material. He too had started in vaudeville, but had the edge on
others with similar background by having been initiated to the
stage when less than a year old by his parents, who toured the
circuit with an acrobatic routine. His screen career began in 1917
with several shorts made for Joseph Schenk, followed by several
years' association with Metro, first in shorts and eventually in
feature-length films. By 1921, while still making two-reel shorts,
Keaton was establishing himself as one of the industry's top
comic artists, even though the number of films to his credit was
much smaller than either Chaplin's or Harold Lloyd's, the third
of the major comic stars.

Like Chaplin, Keaton's dramatization was that of the unassuming fellow who struggles against the big and unpredictable
world; unlike the little tramp, it was essentially an unsentimen-
tal role with greater pessimism toward unending adversities.
And yet, the earnestness, calm assurance, and lonely detachment
of his character has a strange comic appeal, though the term
clown hardly seems to apply.

His careful, methodical approach seems the antithesis of
Keystone slapstick, yet like the Sennett comedies, Keaton's ad-
versaries were often from the mechanical world: a runaway train,
a balloon, a foundering boat or thrashing paddlewheel. In *Cops*
(1922), Keaton was already displaying virtuosity in his portrayal
of the well-meaning young man who becomes the victim of his
own contrivance. He has equipped a wagon being used to de-
liver a load of furniture with a directional signal fashioned out
of a retractable clothes rack fitted with a boxing glove. His
ingenuity produces a sense of pride which is subtly revealed in
the way he operates the mechanism, until he unknowingly
knocks down a policeman directing traffic. In *The Boat* (1921),
it is once again Keaton's pride in workmanship that produces a solemn posture of self-esteem as he stands at the
helm of the boat he made as it slips down the skids into the
water, slowly sinking out of sight until only his hat floats on the
surface. The situations are funny in themselves, but what provides for more than the superficial laugh, what makes it a richer
experience, is the humanity that even the mask that Keaton

wears—that frozen expression that came to be known as "the Great Stone Face"—can hide. A complete range of expression reflecting emotional tone is present; it is simply all concentrated in the eyes and subtle shades of gesture and movement.

By 1923 Keaton had launched into feature films and it was in these that his special talents as "auteur" as well as mimic artist are best revealed. In *The General* (1926), his most impressive work, is found a unity and tightness in narrative structure not present in any other silent comedy. Keaton based the film on an actual Civil War episode in which a Confederate train engineer gave chase and recovered a locomotive named "The General" which Union spies had stolen. In the film Keaton plays the role of Johnny Gray, a loyal Confederate son who has been rejected for military service because of his vital job as engineer. Undaunted, he accomplishes the great train rescue and in the process wins his lovely if dim-witted Southern sweetheart.

An important feature of the film is the strength of the story itself. Unlike Chaplin, who, in even his most polished works, used the film narrative as a framework for his routines, Keaton was interested in telling a story. It is being drawn into *events* and not simply being surprised by gags that provides added delight. *The General* is more than a showcase for Keaton the comic star, it is a splendidly conceived screenplay. Rarely, if ever, has an entire film been devoted to the chase with such rewarding results.

Within his basic framework is found a flawless arrangement and pacing of visual gags to exploit the fortuitous. If we are amused at one moment by Keaton unknowingly sending a pursuing engine off onto a siding, we are delighted by the unexpected ingenuity he shows in clearing railroad ties off the tracks at another. It is the constant shifting from active to passive roles, whereby Keaton is at one moment the victim and at the next the master of the situation, that satisfies our love of surprises and makes the character seem more human. What makes it even more difficult to anticipate the direction of the next routine is that as often as not Keaton's active role will prove hopeless. When he tries to load a tender with firewood, the trees teeter on the edge of the car and bounce to the ground. In *Sherlock Jr.* (1924), his struggle with a piece of paper which has become stuck to his shoe is equally frustrated. On the other hand, when he is unaware of the nature of a situation, or unable to respond, the fateful link of circumstances often wins the day. In *The General*, he accidentally knocks out a Union soldier when he turns around with a piece of firewood in his hand, and in *Sherlock Jr.*, he man-

The Navigator (1924)/*The General* (1926).
Classic Keaton poses revealing solemn
dedication to the task at hand.
MUSEUM OF MODERN ART/FILM STILLS ARCHIVE

ages to miss the several booby traps that have been planted for him in a billiard room.

This careful plotting of routines in order to keep an audience constantly off guard is certainly not unique with Keaton. It is at the heart of much of Chaplin and is found even in the broader style of slapstick comedians. What makes Keaton's use of the device so rewarding is the fact that it fits so smoothly into the general design of the film and of the characterization being portrayed.

An added bonus to be found in Keaton's films is an interest in humanity that goes beyond the central character and provides a gentle spoof of character types and institutions. In *The General*, Keaton is having fun with military ritual and heroism. The Union troops fall like dominoes each time the train comes to a stop; the officers scratch their heads in bewilderment over a railroad siding switch that has been jammed; and the General orders a train over a burning trestle which collapses, sending the train hurtling into the ravine below. The honors of the Confederate victory do not escape spoofing. Johnny draws his sword only to have the blade fall off, and when he finally embraces his girl for a kiss, he carries on the romance while saluting an entire battalion passing by. Even Annabelle Lee is depicted as a hare-brained young thing who retrieves a splinter to help feed the fire box of the train. Nothing is sacred, but all is carefully designed to fit not just the moment but the narrative and the theme.

By the middle of the decade Keaton had become one of Metro's biggest attractions and was being ranked second only to Chaplin among the comic stars of the golden age. But like many others, Keaton found the transition to sound a difficult hurdle. Silent suffering and solitary wonder were too much a part of the character he had developed. After several sound shorts and features he became a gagman and script doctor for MGM. The last years of his career were filled out with cameo appearances in several films which provided little opportunity for any further extension of his creative spirit and disciplined style. But his contributions to the great comedic renaissance of the silent period had been considerable.

Harold Lloyd

Though never enjoying the acclaim that Sennett had been afforded, another pioneer producer of silent screen comedies was Hal Roach, who by the early Twenties was giving Sennett stiff competition in the production of two-reelers. A major part of Roach's success came from launching Harold Lloyd on a screen career which itself was to complement and rival those of the top stars, Chaplin and Keaton. The Roach-Lloyd association began with a series of shorts in which Lloyd portrayed his own version of the little fellow, Willie Work. After a brief stint with Keystone, Lloyd was signed by the American Pathé Company, which was interested in promoting a new comic star to compete with Chaplin. The result was nearly a hundred *Lonesome Luke* single-reel films between 1915 and 1917 under the supervision of Roach.

In *Lonesome Luke* could be found at least part of the Chaplin formula for comic suspense and ingenuity in handling of props. Some early criticism that Lloyd was mock Chaplin gave way to adulation as Lloyd found his own screen personality. In oversized glasses with tortoise-shell rims, he portrays the innocent and mild-mannered young man who, despite the initially bland appearance, reveals a zest for life and a tenacity to succeed. Still, he was the straightest of the major comics. With the exception of the glasses, there was no distinctive visual characteristic to identify him; he could easily have been lost in a crowd. But when that blandness of character was put into the bizarre and hair-raising circumstances in which Lloyd was inevitably found, the result was an incomparable comic style.

Safety Last (1923) and *The Freshman* (1925), two of his most popular films, illustrate the essence of this juxtaposition of character and situation. In *Safety Last*, Harold is employed by a store to climb the outside wall of the building as a publicity stunt. Nearly half of the film is taken up with the climbing sequence, which had been central to his earlier *High and Dizzy* (1921) as well as other shorts, and had become something of a Lloyd trademark. The controlled frenzy that he displayed while hanging from an awning, a flagpole, or the hand of a gigantic clock proved far more hilarious than the hysteria of a cross-eyed cop or other slapstick antics. In *The Freshman*, it is shy innocence in the face of adversity that proves to be the magic formula. Here Harold has come to a school dance in a tuxedo that has been only temporarily stitched together. Absent-mindedly twirling a loose thread around his finger, he unravels the stitching so that the suit begins to fall apart as he stands on the dance floor. Entanglement in a dance partner's dress and a table-cloth complete the destruction and humiliation in spite of the efforts of an on-the-spot tailor to sew him back together.

If somewhat trusting in the kind intervention of fate, Lloyd's reaction to the calamities that befell him was not one of resignation or blind faith. He was continually aggressive in the most unpredictable and seemingly insoluble of problems. What his characterization may have lacked in emotional depth was made up for by his unflagging determination to succeed. And though seriously determined to make a go of it in society, his aggressive behavior was never rebellious or even questioning of social values as the works of Chaplin and Keaton are. He simply adopted a role that would place him most comfortably and advantageously within the social order.

Harry Langdon/Laurel and Hardy

In terms of both critical and popular reception at the time, and the historical perspective by which they are seen today, Chaplin, Keaton and Lloyd are secure in their positions as

The Freshman (1925). Shy innocence in the face of adversity proves once again to be Harold Lloyd's magic formula.
MUSEUM OF MODERN ART/FILM STILLS ARCHIVE

leading comics of the period. Because of their personal control over their material, they may also be considered the most influential in the direction of silent screen comedy. Yet there were others who enjoyed a tremendous following, and though less directly in control of total production, remain major contributors to the form.

Sennett's own choice of the greatest comedian of them all was Harry Langdon, who had also come via the vaudeville route to film shorts for Sennett in 1924. In a film career that was to end in virtual obscurity barely five years after its beginning, Langdon was able to develop a characterization that brought him close to, if not within, the circle of the major comic stars. Langdon's style comes closest to that of Chaplin in its suggestion of innocence and pathos, but he was not a mimic of Chaplin. With large dark eyes and pretty face, he invariably played the part of a child who had never grown up. His innocence was trusting—an unalterable faith in people and a humble belief in finding his way in the sometimes hostile world.

Yet the depth of emotional sensitivity present in Chaplin's tramp and even the wooden stare of Keaton was never revealed in Langdon's characterization. More the child than the man, there was a passivity that prevented strong empathy.

Like Lloyd, Langdon was a performer who did his best work when guided by another director. His best films, *The Strong Man* and *Long Pants,* were produced in 1926 and 1927 under the direction of Frank Capra. His eclipse came with his attempt to write and direct his own material and to move into feature-length films which could not effectively support his simple, low-key style.

Along with Harold Lloyd, the biggest comic stars to come from the Roach lot was the comedy team of Stan Laurel and Oliver Hardy. Laurel had arrived from England with Chaplin on the Karno Pantomime Company tour where he occasionally worked as an understudy for Chaplin roles. After a stint with American vaudeville, he worked for Universal, Vitagraph, and finally Hal Roach. Oliver Hardy joined Roach in 1927. His earlier film career had included a portrayal of a Mack Swain type of character as foil for Billy West, one of the more successful imitators of Chaplin. The first films in which the two appeared did not use them as a team. Once working together, however, they began a relationship which was to span twenty-five years and make them the first and probably the most durable of the screen's many comedy teams.

There is little that is refined or emotionally endearing about the comic style of Laurel and Hardy. Earlier shorts such as *Big Business* (1929) resemble a Sennett romp with its zany physical (often destructive) antics. Here the pair are attempting to sell a Christmas tree to an uninterested homeowner—Jimmy Finlayson, who is a favorite heavy in many of their films. Their persistent ringing of the doorbell to release a branch which is caught in the door just slammed on them, brings Finlayson back with hedgeclippers, which he uses to top the tree. This brings instant retaliation from Stan and Ollie, who begin to dismantle the house, which in turn prompts the demolition of their car. Where Laurel and Hardy surpass the Sennett free-wheeling patchwork of gags is in the progression that develops from the building upon the basic routine.

Unlike the other major comics, characterization is thin and more reflective of types rather than individuals—Stan the delicate, nervous, whimpering and uncoordinated mouse and Ollie the fat, pompous bully who is just as easily cowed and equally clumsy. Both are characterized, like Langdon, as outsized children. What did grow through the association, however, and what helped to assure the team success well into the sound era was a sense of balance in the way each became the perfect foil for the other. It was teamwork *par excellence*, in which the unity of structure was revealed in the continued interplay between Stan and Ollie keeping one another in line while together conquering their frightfully disordered world.

There were other notable contributors to American silent screen comedy. Ben Turpin, Chester Conklin, Snub Pollard, Larry Semon and Al St. John were among the many who seldom enjoyed center ring status, but were creators of screen characterizations that greatly enriched the genre. What enabled the first magnitude stars to stand out among the multitude of lesser comics was their individual identity, the dimension and resulting unity of their films, especially when comedy began to push toward feature length.

With Sennett the individual gag was the basic unit of construction. As each was developed it was strung together with as many others as could be created from the basic situation, and even then extended, repeated, modified, and repeated again to fill out the single- or double-reel length. With the major talent that Sennett helped to groom, the basic unit or central element in design became the characterization itself. Even here narrative development remained a framework upon which comic incidents could be hung. Even feature-length silent comedies, when used to illustrate refinement in form, must be looked at in terms of discipline and consistency in style rather than the dovetailing of plot lines.

The Other Auteurs*

With the industrialization of Hollywood filmmaking in the Twenties came control and standardization. This brought on a plethora of undistinguished films by company directors who, under assembly-line methods, had little opportunity to break new ground in the use of the medium or to otherwise distinguish themselves as screen artists. With Chaplin now joined by Keaton, Lloyd, and other popular comics, silent screen comedy was enjoying its golden age. The genre was to be further enriched in the course of the decade by a new sophisticated style fashioned by Ernst Lubitsch, Douglas Fairbanks and Chaplin himself. In the dramatic film, where there was less likely to be consolidation of creative energy in the single writer-star-director, the films which distinguished themselves and influenced the course of screen drama were those by a few directors who could manage to break stride, pull themselves out of the assembly-line routine, and, while fighting off constant studio pressures, follow their own creative instincts.

Hollywood's Prussian Prodigy—von Stroheim

Eric von Stroheim, as both actor and director, was possessed of the kind of individuality and determination that enabled him to make his mark, and in so doing draw himself into a critical crossfire of both producers and public. His own real-life role as an Austrian army officer became a recurring role for him when he began acting in early Hollywood films. His American screen acting debut actually began with several minor roles in *The Birth of a Nation* (appearing in blackface) and *Intolerance,* where, in addition to assisting Griffith in directing, he appeared as the Pharisee. But it was his image of suave and seductive count,

---

*The controversial term, which is generally applied to later directors and which has no generally accepted definition, is used here to identify filmmakers of sufficient stature, independence, and creative spirit to stand out among the ever increasing number of hack directors.

Eric von Stroheim.
MUSEUM OF MODERN ART/FILM STILLS ARCHIVE

prince, and Prussian officer in his own early directorial efforts that made him known to audiences, and which helped earn him a reputation of panderer and corrupter of morals. Even in his later works, in which he does not appear, there is a pervasive erotic quality which is at times sophisticated and elegant and at times sordid, but which always seems a bit perverse. It was his earliest films that brought him under fire, however. *Photoplay,* in reviewing *Foolish Wives* (1922), called it "an insult to American ideals and womanhood." The reviewer goes on to give von Stroheim his due, however, when he speaks of his "genius for detail and artistic talents nothing short of incredible."

It was his "genius for detail" that made von Stroheim's relations with producers strained at best. His career provides a case study of the independent and uncompromising director who found himself continually at odds with an industry increasingly concerned with production schedules and cost accounting. The first film he directed in Hollywood, *Blind Husbands* (1919), had been undertaken by von Stroheim with the promise to Carl Laemmle, president of Universal Pictures, to make it for no more than $25,000; the final cost was more than three times that figure. The success of the film, however, convinced Laemmle to give the director another assignment, *The Devil's Passkey* (1920). He was also given a $75,000 ceiling, which he exceeded by $100,000. The film also took an unprecedented nine months to produce. In spite of his continued extravagance in both time and money, von Stroheim somehow prevailed upon Laemmle once again and the result was *Foolish Wives* (1922), in thirty-two reels

92

(about seven hours running time), and costing over $1 million to produce. In spite of the commercial success of these films, Universal finally lost patience with von Stroheim's extravagance and he was fired.

Within the industry von Stroheim's reputation was being well established, both as an accomplished screen artist and reckless squanderer of time and money. His films were long, expensive and slow to produce, but they were also popular and had helped to keep Universal solvent. So Metro, willing to risk the excesses of Hollywood's *enfant terrible,* hired him to direct an adaptation of the popular Frank Norris novel *McTeague.* The grisly image of human avarice and seamy life style of the novel, though the antithesis of the Viennese gloss of both earlier and later works, was well suited to von Stroheim's developing sense of naturalism, and in *Greed,* released in 1924, he produced his longest, costliest, and clearly most impressive work. Following closely the Norris story, von Stroheim once again so magnified and extended details that the film ran over forty reels in length (nearly nine hours). It brought to life the adventures of Mc-Teague, the brutish self-styled San Francisco dentist who marries the miserly Trina. Doting on her lottery fortune, and grasping for odd change from her struggling husband, she is finally murdered by McTeague. The setting shifts in the final scenes from the squalid San Francisco interiors to the scorching expanse of Death Valley, where McTeague, with his wife's gold coins in hand, is stalked by Trina's former sweetheart.

The emasculation of the original, in order to bring it down to a viewable ten reels, makes any analysis of over-all structure of the film impossible. What does survive among the fragments are masterful moments of action in a total atmosphere that is as much tactile as visual. Von Stroheim's dedication to detail is seen in the grimy walls, drab furnishings, and unmade beds that are so much a part of *Greed:* it is the kind of mise-en-scène which forty years later came to be known as "kitchen sink" realism. As a result of such painstaking care over detail, *Greed* is virtually a document of social realism in America at the turn of the century. This is not self-indulgent, but rather a means of revealing the total environment of characters—here the sordid and drab existence of Trina and McTeague. Von Stroheim had said that "a shot of an inanimate object accentuates its dramatic importance." It is a lesson which he had learned from Griffith and had now become the essence of his own style.

Social realism became a trademark of von Stroheim's later

Greed (1924). Trina and McTeague's wedding feast, like many scenes in the film, is a treasure of symbolic visual detail.
MUSEUM OF MODERN ART/FILM STILLS ARCHIVE

work as well. *The Wedding March* (1927) and the unfinished *Queen Kelly* (1928) were both drawn from the director's impressions of Vienna royalty, and although fantasy at times became mingled with realistic themes (the common girl in love with the prince), the films were a reflection of the gradual dissolution of the Hapsburg Empire. Even *The Merry Widow* (1925), based on the operetta, became in von Stroheim's hands a sardonic satire on the Austrian royal family.

It was this blending of naturalistic detail with ironic imagery that gave von Stroheim's work an added power. In *Greed*, it was represented by the spilling of life-sustaining water and useless gold, as McTeague and adversary die in the desert; the glimpse of a funeral procession during Trina and McTeague's wedding reception; and the murder of Trina taking place beneath the branches of a Christmas tree. Some of von Stroheim's most grotesque, ironic images are found in *The Wedding March*, which he made for Paramount in 1927. The attempted rape of Mitzi takes place in a slaughterhouse, with a boar's head gazing from the wall and carcasses hanging from the ceiling. The cruelest of von Stroheim's imagery is revealed in the scene in which the crippled princess limps down the aisle on her wedding day

94

for a forced marriage to the unwilling prince. Here gay Vienna is turned into a place of misery and want for the poor, and decay born of excessive wealth and privilege. As with *Greed*, the extravagance and length of *The Wedding March* forced Paramount to turn the project over to professional film cutters to piece together and it is the impact of individual scenes rather than the work as a whole that remains impressive.

Von Stroheim's virtues and shortcomings as a director both seem to be bound to the same spirit of extravagance for which all of his work became known. At its best it showed uncompromising detail which was the essence of screen realism and created scenes incredibly rich in meaning. At its worst it revealed the kind of excess which resulted in films of staggering length and complexity, and, once the film doctors were finished with them, of questionable unity.

The seamier variety of realism and lower-class milieu which was so much a part of von Stroheim's work was further explored by another Viennese born director, Joseph Stern, who later adopted the more imposing name of von Sternberg. His first film, *The Salvation Hunters* (1925), brought critical plaudits for its dreary, realistic settings and sordid story of a couple who exchange their river scow home for a room and the wife's services as a prostitute. In this and two other silent films—*Underworld* (1927) and *Docks of New York* (1928)—von Sternberg revealed a special talent for creating a darkly poetic mood and sordid atmosphere to complement his stories of degradation, disillusionment, and despair.

DeMille—The Bath and the Bible

Although von Stroheim's films added something of the realistic (and often erotic) to screen drama, his works, in spite of length and budget excesses, could never be classified as spectacle films. The distinction for carrying on the tradition of screen spectacle as well as furthering the cause of sophisticated sex goes to Cecil B. DeMille, whose film career spanned forty-six years and included seventy feature films. He became Hollywood's supershowman, known especially for the biblical spectacle and the exotic bedroom or bathroom drama.

DeMille, with some experience as bit actor and playwright, joined Jesse Lasky (ex-cornet player and vaudeville producer) and Sam Goldwyn (ex-glove salesman) to form the Lasky Feature Play Company in 1913. DeMille's first film, *The Squaw Man* (1913), made the young company a profit, in spite of the fact that the original print was destroyed by sabotage—a victim of the continued patent war. *The Virginian* (1914) and *Call of the North* (1914), which followed, proved to be even more successful and with *The Cheat* (1915), which won a particularly warm reception in France, DeMille was gaining international recognition. Even his early films covered a broad range of subjects and styles, ranging from the amours of a sheik in *The Arab* (1915) to the exploits of a Bowery tough in *Chimie Fadden* (1915). It was the frontier of the American West that provided his favorite early setting, however.

With *Joan The Woman* (1917) DeMille moved into historical spectacle with a dual story structure he was to use again in *The Ten Commandments* (1923). Here the story of Joan of Arc was introduced as a vision of a World War I officer about to go into battle. Even the otherwise acerbic Alexander Woollcott, in reviewing *Joan* for the *New York Times* speaks glowingly of "the beautiful and exalted pageantry of the coronation [which] is the sort of spectacle that takes the breath away and lingers always in the memory."

Cecil B. DeMille directing a camera crew in the filming of *The Ten Commandments* (1923).
MUSEUM OF MODERN ART/FILM STILLS ARCHIVE

By 1918 the bucolic setting of the frontier and the sweet innocence of Mary Pickford's *The Little American* (1917) were being traded for the drawing room, boudoir, and ultimately the bathroom in a succession of sophisticated and intimate dramas the titles of which themselves suggest DeMille's ever watchful eye on popular appeal: *Old Wives for New, Don't Change Your Husband, For Better, For Worse* (1919), *Male and Female* (1919), *Why Change Your Wife?* (1919), *Forbidden Fruit* (1920), *Fool's Paradise* (1921), and *Saturday Night* (1922). Burns Mantle, in reviewing *Why Change Your Wife?*, speaks of "a rare concoction —the most gorgeously sensual film of the month; in decoration the most costly; in physical allure the most fascinating; in effect the most immoral." *Male and Female* (1919), though titled to fit the new image of its director's films, is actually a more moral and substantial work, based on the James Barrie play *Admirable Crichton*.

Bringing DeMille to the forefront as a director was *The Ten Commandments* (1923), which, like Griffith's *Intolerance*, brought together historical spectacle and contemporary conflict. Receiving of the tablets, the pillar of fire, the parting of the Red Sea were here coupled with a modern parable of good and evil in a turgid tale about an evil son who cuts costs in the building of a cathedral, which results in the death of his mother when she wanders into the crumbling structure. In spite of melodrama which borders on self-parody, the piety and pomp of the film won the favor of audiences and even critical superlatives. *Photoplay* Magazine called it "the greatest theatrical spectacle in history." And with obvious allusions to the central action of the biblical segment goes on to say, "it will last as long as the film on which it is recorded. It wipes the slate clean of charges of an immoral influence against the screen." Keeping within the guidelines of the industry's code of morality, DeMille had found the formula for showing the erotic and otherwise sinful pleasures, while, with appropriate condemnation, keeping the film clean. The formula worked for DeMille again in *The King of Kings* (1927), which was his second big spectacle and next to last silent film. This time the New Testament was the source, and after paying deference to the sinning woman in the person of Mary Magdalene, the film followed the major events of the life of Christ. Mordaunt Hall, *New York Times* film critic, called it the most impressive of all motion pictures.

Such excesses on the part of critics notwithstanding, DeMille's silent films suffer by comparison with the other major works of key American and foreign directors and he is today either ignored or attacked by critics for "puerile" and "pretentious" works that catered to mass appeal of the moment and have worn badly over the years. Though such charges are probably deserved, DeMille's prominence and final influence on film's development is undeniable. He was clearly a master technician in the building of spectacle, and in the organization and visualization of historical material in a way that could be understood and enjoyed. No other director, save Griffith and Chaplin, was able to draw audiences on the strength of his own direction. His stardom as director is supported by the number of times he has appeared on screen playing himself. But more significant in terms of long-range influence than his own stardom is the important role he played in launching many important screen actors on their careers. The list includes Gloria Swanson, Bebe Daniels, Wallace Reid, Fredric March, Claudette Colbert, Gary Cooper, Barbara Stanwyck and Loretta Young, all of whom came under DeMille's tutelage. DeMille's instruction of the screen itself is best observed by Bardéche and Brasillach in their *History of the Motion Pictures,* in which they suggest that it was DeMille who brought Park Avenue to the screen and

> taught Babbitt how to kiss a countess' hand, how to peel a peach, use finger bowls and keep his hands out of his pockets. Cinema attitudes, cinema drawing rooms, cinema society women, cinema sentiments, cinema adulteries and forgivenesses were established.

The Velvet Touch — Ernst Lubitsch

When Chaplin made *A Woman of Paris* in 1923, he set the tone for a new era of sophistication in American film which, together with von Stroheim's own continental contribution, established a new film genre before the silent era ended. A director who joined the ranks of star directors and made important contributions to screen elegance and sophistication was the German, Ernst Lubitsch. Lubitsch is better known today for his comedy/romances of the Thirties, but was becoming a major creative force in the industry, first in his native land and subsequently in Hollywood, before the movies learned to speak.

With cabaret and music hall acting, as well as classical training under the guidance of Max Reinhardt behind him, he began his film career in 1913. Appearing first as a Jewish comic in a popular series which he finally began to write and direct for

Ernst Lubitsch and Mary Pickford during a break in the filming of *Rosita* (1923), the director's first Hollywood film.
MUSEUM OF MODERN ART/FILM STILLS ARCHIVE

himself, he continued his role as writer, director, and actor in short comedies through the war years until his first big picture assignment—*Carmen* (1918)—which, with his *Madam Dubarry* of the following year, put him into the international spotlight.

Although the foreign invasion of screen talent was not to peak in Hollywood until the close of the silent era, Lubitsch marked the beginning of the European exodus when he went to Hollywood in 1923 to direct Mary Pickford in *Rosita*. The enthusiastic reception of his early Hollywood films, first as director and later as producer, won him a place among the industry's top film creators. Turning from period costume pieces, he began to make his own contributions to sophisticated comedy in 1924 with *The Marriage Circle,* and continued to explore the more intimate and "tasteful" approaches to the genre with *Kiss Me Again* (1925), *Lady Windermere's Fan* (1925), and *So This is Paris* (1926). By 1935 he had become production chief for Paramount and as such supervised every film to come off the lot. But he still believed that a director must be allowed to direct: "There are two kinds of directors, one type follows his shooting script religiously, the other creates as he goes, but both must be left alone once production has started."

Lubitsch himself had been the kind of director that could not be bound by the script, and his films reveal his talents as set designer and choreographer as well as in his handling of camera. The charm and sophistication which became the hallmark of his work was to be found as much in the decor, and in the dress and movement of actors, as in the handling of the story itself, perhaps more so. Sets were uncluttered and functional and stage business

99

was laced with subtle insight into human relationships. The racetrack sequence from *Lady Windermere's Fan* and the wedding procession in *The Love Parade* (1929) provide particularly extravagant examples. Precision and elegance (no matter how inane the plot), these were at the heart of what came to be known as "the Lubitsch touch."

As with von Stroheim and DeMille, sex was a major ingredient of a Lubitsch film. He believed that "you cannot ignore one of the most important and profound relations in life." His delicate handling of the subject was in clear contrast to the works of the other directors, however. Where DeMille and von Stroheim's films have an underlying hint of the naughty and perverse, Lubitsch dealt with the subject as delightful, healthy fun and revealed most American attitudes toward the subject as rather silly hang-ups. He was able to carry this off by a special attitude or style of production that exuded a sense of the good-natured, well-mannered and well-bred. The result was glittering images with more romantic than erotic appeal.

Lubitsch resisted the use of titles in silent film and was thus able to become a master of innuendo. His control of both actors and camera enabled him to convey ideas with subtlety and wit in perfect harmony with the era of sophisticated sex. Though he went on to an equally distinguished career in sound film, his place in the silent cinema is undiminished and earns him a position among the handful of directors in Hollywood who had the independence and creative energy to bring the art of silent film to full flower.

Fairbanks in Adventureland—The Original One-Man Genre

Though major refinements in silent screen art are usually attributable to insightful and independent directors, the actor himself was often the source of creative energy which not only strongly influenced the success of individual films, but helped set the direction of styles and genres. Some, like Chaplin and Keaton, quickly took over the direction of their own films and their contributions as director vs. actor became indistinguishable. Many others, like Mary Pickford, Richard Barthelmess, Emil Jannings, and Pola Negri, were groomed by the masters, and the extent of their influence often depended upon their handling by the director with whom they happened to be work-

The Black Pirate (1926). The stage is set here for another flash of grace, dexterity, and derring-do by Douglas Fairbanks, the screen's original "swashbuckler."
MUSEUM OF MODERN ART/
FILM STILLS ARCHIVE

ing at the time. A third class was the actor whose personality and style was so pervasive and so much his own that directorial credit became incidental to the star's own dynamic influence over virtually every aspect of production.

With perhaps the exception of Fred Astaire, who was, in the following decade, to dance his way through a series of films without the least fear of competition, no screen personality had such exclusive control as well as universal appeal in his own brand of screen entertainment as Douglas Fairbanks. Fairbanks brought a new type of hero to the silent screen—the suave, dashing idol whose charm was exceeded only by his acrobatic derring-do. It established the screen's first one-man genre.

Fairbanks was working under Griffith as early as 1915 in a variety of comedies and period pieces and later in the decade began to settle into light, good-natured comedies of American manners like *His Majesty, The American* (1919) and *Mollycoddle* (1920)—more spoof than satire. It was the comic-romantic adventure films of the Twenties, however, that enabled Fairbanks to excel as combination superhero and clown in the guise of Zorro, Robin Hood, The Thief of Bagdad and Dumas' D'Artagnan.

Fairbanks became unique among romantic heroes because of the incredible array of athletic skills he mustered for his various roles. For his characterization as D'Artagnan, "the best swordsman in France," in *The Three Musketeers* (1921), he spent months in training with the foil. Balletic movement and whip

101

handling are dazzling in his dual role of father and son in *Don Q, Son of Zorro* (1925). And for general athletic prowess, his aerial antics in *Robin Hood* (1922) and *The Black Pirate* (1926) set a standard which was challenged, but never beaten, by the later "swashbucklers," Tyrone Power and Errol Flynn. The major appeal was in physical attractiveness rather than any real depth of character, but a bonus to the display of grace and dexterity was a *joie de vivre* and a hint of self-parody that audiences found irresistible.

What made the Fairbanks films of the Twenties more than popular oddities, and justifies their inclusion here, under refinements in form, is the overall flow and tempo they displayed. Sparked by the star's own exuberant and exacting flight, films like *The Three Musketeers* (1921) and *The Mark of Zorro* (1921), both directed by the otherwise undistinguished Fred Niblo, show overall command in the building of action sequence and a dynamic quality in editing.

The Second String

The overpowering presence of stars like Pickford and Fairbanks tended to obscure the names of directors like Allan Dwan, Fred Niblo, Rex Ingram and Raoul Walsh, who, in addition to the constant pressures of the studio front offices, were faced with accommodating the temperaments and creative inspirations of their actors. Though compromise was undoubtedly the result of many such associations, the contributions of these "second-string" directors is still significant. They represented a new breed of filmmakers whose talents were often more closely associated with the successful handling or display of the stars than in story invention or camera and editing technique. Nonetheless, some became more than star-handlers and stand above the array of hack directors under contract to the major studios.

Several notable films mark the career of Henry King in silent features, including *Romola* (1924), *Stella Dallas* (1925), but *Tol'able David* (1921), which came early in his career, would alone place him among the decade's distinguished directors. This David and Goliath tale of a country boy who sees his family shattered by a hateful clan of distant relatives shows how well-schooled King had been by both Ince and Griffith. The general story line and attitude of the film are clearly in the Griffith mold, though free of the cloying sentimentality of that director's work. The quality of gentle and loving rural life is accentuated through both the sensitivity of the characterizations and the extraordinary visual appeal of the settings. Coupled with this is a tight, lean narrative design which displays all the momentum (and often brutality) of the Ince Westerns.

Like King, James Cruze's reputation in silent films rests primarily on a single film. *The Covered Wagon* (1923), which lifted the Western melodrama to epic stature and helped establish its form, showed the director's facility for using the frontier setting to infuse the drama with a sense of national (and natural) history. Cruze's subsequent films, *Ruggles of Red Gap* (1923), *Old Ironsides* (1926), and several sound features, showed his ability to work with at least moderate success in a variety of styles and genres, avoiding the single-track syndrome of many of his contemporaries.

The Big Parade (1925) and *The Crowd* (1928) were two films of sufficient technical stature and strong enough social conscience to place their director, King Vidor, into the ranks of major directors of the late silent era. In *The Big Parade*, Vidor created a panorama of war's imprint on life styles without the overinflated look of the spectacle. *The Crowd* provided Vidor with a more intimate focus and became a human interest study of its central character and his struggle against the unfeeling masses. In terms of continued success through the sound era, Vidor ranks at the top of the second-string directors.

Allan Dwan and Frank Borzage were among the others to show sufficient versatility and control to assure themselves film careers extending through the Fifties. Rex Ingram, who did not fare as well in longevity, did escape obscurity and enjoyed some critical tributes for such spectacles as *The Four Horsemen of the Apocalypse* (1921) and *The Prisoner of Zenda* (1922). He believed that along with narrative techniques and characterization, an important part of screen storytelling was in creating an atmosphere consistent with and complementary to the mood of the film. He was less interested in slavish attention to realistic detail than in what could be suggested by a bit of set decoration or gesture by an actor. But this flair in direction seems to have been more in the service of popular appeal than true exploration and he is best known today for making an international hero of Rudolph Valentino. Ingram retired from film shortly after the coming of sound.

Silent Beginnings

A number of filmmakers whose major legacy in film was to come after the arrival of sound had their basic training in the silents. William Wellman began making films in 1923 and won the distinction of an Academy Award for his 1927 *Wings*, the first Oscar ever to be awarded for best picture. An important phase of Frank Capra's training had come in directing Harry Langdon in his impressive if short career. And Howard Hawks, whose prolific and versatile career in sound features was to range from *Bringing Up Baby* (1938) to *Rio Bravo* (1958), had his start as scriptwriter and editor in the late Teens.

John Ford, whose work was to become synonymous in the sound era with rugged individualism and virility, was in the process of learning the fundamentals of filmmaking and developing his style through the late silent era. His directing started in 1917 with two-reel Westerns for Universal, and although his silent film credits span a decade and include, in addition to early shorts, fifty features of at least five reels, his reputation as a major American director was not established until the advent of the sound film. His early works did, however, receive favorable reaction from public and critics and gave the Western a new hero in Harry Carey, who appeared in most of Ford's early features. The sole silent film for which Ford is remembered today is his 1924 *The Iron Horse*, which, along with James Cruze's *The Covered Wagon*, made the year before, helped to usher in the panoramic Western. Where Cruze had dramatized the crossing of the continent by the wagon train, Ford showed the crossing of the first transcontinental railroad. The film was an important boost for Ford toward director stardom, but his day was yet to come.

If Griffith was the "father of film technique," and Ince the first "creative producer," it was the legion of creative spirits, the anonymous as well as the internationally acclaimed, who gave film its form and direction between the mid Teens and the mid Twenties. It included, in addition to the screenwriters, directors, actors, and actor-directors mentioned here, the hundreds of production personnel who, in increasingly discrete areas of specialization, were learning to master a new medium and a new art.

4

An Industry Emerges

Introduction

The first fifteen years of industrial and technical development had been a time of sporadic, amateurish testing, searching for the elusive handle by which to gain control of this new medium. The MPPC's early attempt at control had failed. The reasons were many, but ultimately the MPPC did not succeed for the simple reason that motion pictures had grown too big too fast. The trust's attempt to dominate film was like trying to keep a teenage child in a playpen. The child was simply too large and too strong to be controlled in this way any longer. The parents suffered from a generation gap and imposed rules which the child would not accept, especially when it was being nurtured and weaned by peers who had in a sense grown up with it.

The changes in the industry from 1912 to 1927 were in some ways not changes at all. The desire to control and monopolize was still present and in some ways even stronger. The real change was in the men who tried to gain control and the means by which they made the attempt. Unlike the trust, which regarded motion pictures as a product manufactured like cars or shoes, the independents gambled their ideas and money on public attitude. The *concept* of control remained intact. The patterns this control took would dominate motion pictures for the next forty years.

The Independents Take Over

The important men and organizations in this immediate post-trust period were Adolph Zukor's Famous Players Company (later incorporated into Paramount), Jesse Lasky Productions (also incorporated into Paramount), The Mutual Film Company, Carl Laemmle's Universal Company, Lewis J. Selznick, William Fox, Richard Rowland's Metro (later incorporated into MGM), and VLSE (a combination of four former Trust companies, Vitagraph, Lubin, Selig, and Essanay). In addition, hundreds of smaller organizations and production companies jumped in to fill the void caused by the trust's decline, so that by 1916 there were well over 150 production companies manufacturing between 1200 and 1500 films a year. Most of these early post-trust companies developed out of their own financial resources, were fiercely independent, and fought savagely for survival. Most of them failed, but those that survived ultimately formed the backbone of the studio structure of American film for the next forty years.

Adolph Zukor and his Famous Players Company were dominant in this early stage of development. The formation of Paramount in 1914 by Zukor, Lasky, and W. W. Hodkinson is a good example of how power in the industry had quickly shifted. Only a few years before, Hodkinson had been an employee of General Film. Zukor had sat for hours in the reception room of the same company trying to get permission to exhibit his film *Queen Elizabeth* (1912). Zukor had originally come to the United States in 1888 from Hungary with, as the legend goes, $40.00 sewn into the lining of his coat. After achieving some success manufacturing furs, he became interested in penny arcades and after "observing the interests of the customers" he and two partners opened up their own arcade in New York in 1902. He opened his first motion picture theater, The Crystal Palace, in 1904 and "finding the show business very much to my liking" began what is perhaps the longest career in film history. (He celebrated his 100th birthday in 1973 at a Hollywood gala.)

Zukor's history is typical of the men who would soon come to dominate the industry. William Fox was a garment worker who became a partner in a theater which he developed into a major production organization. Carl Laemmle was managing a clothing store in Oshkosh, Wisconsin. He went to Chicago and was given a vacant theater, which he expanded into a chain and ultimately Universal studios. Marcus Loew was a fur dealer who bought a penny arcade which he expanded into the most powerful studio (MGM) in the industry. It is not accidental that most of the men who emerged victorious in this early struggle for control got their start in exhibition. Running penny arcades and store theaters gave them a knowledge of the public and what it wanted. Adolph Zukor stated in his autobiography, *The Public Is Never Wrong*:

> In The Crystal Hall it was my custom to take a seat about six rows from the front. . . . I spent a good deal of time watching the faces of the audience, even turning around to do so. . . . With a little experience I could see, hear, and "feel" the reaction to each melodrama and comedy.

When Zukor and others turned to production, it followed quite logically that they would use the same criterion of public taste in determining the course their films should take.

The failures were many, of course, and included both the powerful and the weak. Two of the strongest were the Mutual Company, destroyed by internal dissension and timidity concerning the feature-length film, and the Triangle Company, destroyed because its corporate heads were not in touch with public taste. Triangle had great initial promise. Its name was derived from its three premier directors, D. W. Griffith, Mack Sennett, and Thomas Ince. Triangle wanted to bring the stories and stars of the legitimate stage to the screen. However, the public did not want Sarah Bernhardt, Lily Langtry, or James O'Neil when it could see Mary Pickford, Bronco Billy Anderson, and Charlie Chaplin.

On the eve of World War I, Zukor, Fox, Laemmle, and others were poised and ready to take control of, and create a new structure for, the rapidly expanding motion picture industry. Their methods, unlike the trust's before them, were not restrictive or negative. Instead, they achieved control by promoting new ideas: feature-length films, actors and actresses publicized as "stars," and better quality motion pictures. As Terry Ramsaye said of the new breed: "They bettered the art to better their own business. Pictures improved to improve the power of the box office."

The Feature Film

One of the most important methods used by the independents to break the trust monopoly was the production of longer films. However, since the trust restriction simply meant films of one reel, at first longer films meant only longer than one reel. The true feature-length film had not yet arrived. In 1913, however, the Italian spectacle *Quo Vadis* was imported into the United States. It was a huge success, running twenty-two weeks in New York at $1.00 a ticket. As the *New York Times* said in its review of April 22, 1912, ". . . if a feature moving picture production can fill a Broadway theatre, *Quo Vadis* ought to be able to do it." The film wielded enormous influence as its eight-reel length (slightly over two hours), spectacular content, and $1.00 admission price prompted some of the bolder independents to begin experimenting with a feature-length format. Although employed by the trust studio Biograph, D. W. Griffith was eager to attempt the new format. Partially inspired by *Quo Vadis*, but more importantly compelled by a need to develop his style and content, he made *Judith of Bethulia* in 1914. Its $36,000 cost proved to be too much for the conservative Biograph owners, however, and Griffith soon departed to begin preparations for his next film, *The Birth of a Nation.*

The most important figure in beginning a regular system of feature production, however, was not a director, but producer Adolph Zukor. By 1914 he and Jesse Lasky were releasing three to four features a week through Paramount. This was a significant step. The mass production of feature films stimulated tremendous growth in the size of the industry. Entire new departments were established, employing thousands of new people. Huge studios and backlots were constructed. The specialization of skills became more important than ever. One person simply could not do everything anymore. Quite obviously, costs rose as well. Prior to 1910 a one-reel film cost approximately $2,000 to produce. By 1915 the average feature-length film (three to four reels) cost between $20,000 and $40,000. However, the rise in cost was more than compensated for by higher gross earnings and an average net profit of $10,000–$20,000 per picture. These profits spurred even further expansion of the feature format, so that by 1920, with the exception of serials and comedy shorts, the entire industry had switched to feature production. Of course, it was ultimately the public's acceptance of both the format *and* the increased admission price that made the transition possible.

Also, the motion picture was beginning to attract a higher-class audience, one that was accustomed to long plays and literature. One-reel shorts were simply an inadequate form for treating more complex and sophisticated stories.

The Star System

Even more important to the independents' rise to power was selling motion pictures through the appeal of certain men or women who "starred" in them. If there is a beginning, it might well be April 2, 1910, when a young woman named Florence Lawrence left Biograph and joined Carl Laemmle's Independent Motion Picture Company (IMP). She had been earning $25.00 a week at Biograph and like many other "faces" was beginning to accumulate a large public following. Biograph and other trust companies clearly recognized that if these "faces" acquired "names" they might start to demand more money. Since the trust sold films by the foot, regardless of who appeared in them, paying a higher salary to a more popular face would disrupt the entire system. The independents, Carl Laemmle in particular, perceived this restrictive philosophy as a way to create dissension and desertion among the actors and actresses working for trust studios. In 1910, therefore, Laemmle offered Miss Lawrence $1,000 a week to "star" in his IMP productions. He followed this up with an extensive publicity campaign and soon audiences were clamoring for more of Miss Lawrence.

Even more significant than Laemmle and Lawrence was another producer-star team by the name of Zukor and Pickford. Together with Charlie Chaplin they created a revolution in the industry and established some new rules for making motion pictures.

In his climb up the competitive ladder Zukor did not follow the usual method of dominating by corporate consolidation and merger. Rather, he gained power by absorbing the strength of his competitors, most importantly star actors and actresses. Zukor's primary asset in this struggle was Mary Pickford, who along with Chaplin was the most popular screen personality up to 1920.

Dubbed "America's Sweetheart," Pickford presented the image of youthful womanhood with golden curls. She started her career with D. W. Griffith in 1909; however, because Griffith was the "star" of most of his pictures, she soon moved on to Paramount.

Mary Pickford in a typical
"girl with the golden curls" pose.
MUSEUM OF MODERN ART/FILM STILLS ARCHIVE

Between 1914 and 1919 she made more than twenty films, ranging from low comedy to high drama. What is often lost in the stereotyped historical image of her as a pre-1920 Shirley Temple is her remarkable versatility and range as an actress. She did play cute little girl roles, but she usually played these with amazing strength and vitality. There was cloying sentimentality in her films, but there was also a freshness and exuberance that is often overlooked. Even today, her character is appealing and believable.

However, both "Little Mary" and America grew up and the jazz-age Twenties were not the proper climate for her continued growth. She did make several fairly successful films in the Twenties, but American audiences identified her with another age and after one early talking film she retired.

With Zukor and Laemmle showing the way, most of the major film producers quickly jumped on the star bandwagon, so that by 1914 nearly all feature films were sold on the basis of specific personalities. The feature film was of great benefit to the star system, since the longer a popular star was on the screen the better the audience liked it. It also allowed certain stars time to develop and demonstrate their talents. Stars became the pegs upon which producers hung the whole system of mass feature production. Within three years a profound shift in the balance of power had occurred in the industry. Not only had a new breed of independent producers replaced the old conservative trust leaders, but perhaps just as importantly control had shifted from employer to employee. The children had taken over the nursery.

Chaplin and Pickford led the revolution. Their careers closely paralleled each other's. In fact, Pickford, with the help and guidance of her mother Charlotte, seemed to base her increasing salary demands on what Chaplin was earning. The following chart indicates the meteoric rise of these two young people, and at the same time indicates the growing strength of the industry, which was quite able, although not always willing, to pay these fantastic salaries.

A Rise to the Top

Charles Chaplin

1913—Keystone: $150.00 per week
1915—Essanay: $1,250 per week
1916—Mutual: $10,000 per week
1917—First National: $1,075,000 for eight pictures
1919—United Artists: Has own production company

Mary Pickford

1913—Famous Players: $1,000 per week
1915—Famous Players: $2,000 per week
1916—Famous Players: $10,000 per week plus 50% of film profits
1918—First National: $15–20,000 per week plus 50% of film profits
1919—United Artists: Has own production company

By 1915 there were not enough stars to go around and the Hollywood "talent hunt" was on. Soon, audiences were seeing new discoveries, such as Theda Bara, Tom Mix, Norma Talmadge, William S. Hart, Lillian and Dorothy Gish, among many others. Although Chaplin and Pickford led the parade, they were never really part of it in the first place. They were a natural phenomena, as much cause of the whole system as symbols of it.

More interesting in terms of what the star system finally came to mean for the American motion picture are the stars created and nurtured by the studios. The story of Theodosia Goodman is a case in point. She first appeared in a 1915 production called *A Fool There Was*. She played a "siren" role and

Theda Bara, the first screen
"vamp" and one of the
most popular stars of the
pre-World War I period.
MUSEUM OF MODERN ART/
FILM STILLS ARCHIVE

attracted strong public attention. The studio publicity machine swung into full gear and ultimately produced one Theda Bara, who emerged as one of the most popular stars of the time. She starred in more than forty pictures for Fox in three years and made "Vamp" a household word. The production system had created a star and then built its structure around her. Her appeal was carefully nurtured and ultimately she became the prototype/stereotype of a certain type of female. As the *New York Times* remarked in 1916: "Since Miss Bara is so well fitted by looks to act this sort of creater [vampire] before the camera, it would be squandering her resources to cast her in a Mary Pickford sort of role."

There were hundreds of others with similar manufactured personalities. In 1926, *Photoplay* published the following lineup of stars with a description of their public image.

Ramon Novarro	The perfect troubadour, lyric charm and the beauty of a Greek boy.
Lewis Stone	The man of the world, the aristocrat, the diplomat, the seigneur.
John Gilbert	The fiery Slav—that stirs your pulses with the wanderlust.
George O'Brien	The most irresistible thing that walks the globe—a black Irishman.
Ben Lyon	The way football heroes should look in their street clothes.
Reginald Denny	The perfect athlete—the Roman gladiator of our century.

Richard Barthelmess   The way every man looks to the woman who loves him.

Richard Dix   The typical young American, as story-tellers sing of him.

Ronald Colman   Soldier-man, explorer adventurer, he draws you against your will.

John Barrymore   Classic simplicity—an old Greek God in a museum.

Female stars were typed just as religiously. Lillian Gish was the sweet fragile heroine, Clara Bow the wild reckless flapper, Vilma Banky the regal, ethereal aristocrat, Greta Garbo the femme fatale, Laura La Plante the girl next door, and so on ad infinitum. There were clowns, vamps, flappers, villains, Latin lovers, and almost anything the audience and the times permitted. Perhaps equally indicative of the system and how it worked were "the next" stars. These included such personalities as Betty Brown, who was the next Mary Pickford, Bessie Love, the next Lillian Gish, etc.

Perhaps the most publicized aspect of the star system was the salaries paid to various stars every week. Studio publicity departments were quick to capitalize on the public's desire to know such details, and stories were soon circulating concerning such salaries as Pickford's and Chaplin's $10,000 a week. These figures, although accurate, were not really representative, since, according to Benjamin Hampton, prior to 1920 most stars earned between $500 and $1,000 a week. Lead players earned $150.00 to $500.00 and character actors $75.00 to $250.00. Even these salaries were not universal or perhaps even typical. Mae Marsh, a major star in the silent period, remarked in a recent interview that when she appeared in *Birth of a Nation* in 1915 she was still making $35.00 a week and was grateful. As she stated: "I wasn't supporting myself, so I was having a grand time. I was living at home and 'I had $35.00 a week to spend on candy and other things I wanted." (She was 16 at the time.) Rod La Rocque, also to become a major silent star in the 20's, stated: "In those years 1914, '15, '16, '17 I hung on, finally getting up to five bucks a day because I had a wardrobe." However, these figures increased dramatically following the end of World War I. As the industry expanded in order to keep up with public demand, more and more stars began sensing their own importance and asked for and received huge salaries. Indeed, the well publicized weekly salaries of Tom Mix ($10,000), Geraldine Farrar ($10,000), Alla Nazimova ($13,000) serve to illustrate that the star system reigned supreme.

The inevitable outcome of this "people power" was the formation of personal production companies by certain major stars. It represented the formalization of a vague process in which motion pictures were sold on the basis of the stars. These stars demanded more and more money as their films grew more popular. The studios found it increasingly difficult to pay these huge salaries, despite increased profits. However, the public seemed willing to pay almost any price to see them and so the stars went into business for themselves. This was, of course, possible only for those few whose power matched that of the studios themselves. "Ordinary" stars did not have this type of strength.

Some of the major personalities who went into production for themselves included Harold Lloyd, Norma Talmadge, Buster Keaton, Gloria Swanson, and Harry Langdon. A few, such as Lloyd and Keaton were successful. However, the majority failed, because production had become too large and complex and most stars didn't possess adequate or even minimal knowledge of what made a film successful. Harry Langdon is a good example of this, as Frank Capra relates in his autobiography, *The Name Above the Title:* "The tragedy of this supreme talent is that he never knew what made him great, nor why the world forgot him. Quick fame, and the consequent barnacles of conceit that clogged his ego, made him impervious to help from those who *knew* the secret of his magic." The most successful personal production organization was formed by Mary Pickford, Charles Chaplin, Douglas Fairbanks, D. W. Griffith, and William S. Hart. In 1919, with the advice and consultation of B. P. Schulberg, they formed United Artists. Hart soon dropped out, but was very successful producing films on his own. The remaining four worked out a system where they financed everything themselves, but earned producer profits along with a share from distribution. Fairbanks and Pickford, soon to become partners in marriage as well as business, bought their own studio, as did Chaplin. Among the three of them they made around eight films a year. Griffith was kept busy satisfying other contracts and his production for the company was limited.

United Artists represented the zenith of the star system. By 1920 the system had reached a proportion entirely out of scale with reality as stars became more important than the studios

Charlie Chaplin, with pen in hand along with D. W.
Griffith and Mary Pickford, signs the papers
incorporating the stars into United Artists in 1919.
MUSEUM OF MODERN ART/FILM STILLS ARCHIVE

which employed them. This changed very quickly, however, as
film costs rose rapidly and the industry expanded. The studios
could no longer afford to pay astronomical salaries when other
costs were rising as well. Outside financial backing was required
and as conservative businessmen entered the scene stars were
forced out of their dominant position. In 1919, *The Miracle Man*
was made starring a group of relatively unknown actors and
actresses, including Betty Compson, Joseph Dowling, Thomas
Meigham, and Lon Chaney. The film cost $120,000 and grossed
over $3,000,000. This proved to be somewhat of a watershed film
in that it convinced the studios that competent players under
solid direction in a well-scripted film could make a profit. Soon,
producers and directors were making films without stars. Cecil
B. DeMille, for one, emphasized elaborate sets and sexual
themes. His films were a success and the system began to
produce films based on content, theme, and production value as
well as stars.

    Once again the balance of power had shifted. The result was
the death of a *star dominated* system, but not the star system

itself. Stars were still powerful and would remain one of the major criteria by which films were made and sold. However, once again they were employees working under lucrative but very tight and at times restrictive contracts. It was not until the 1960's, when the studio system had crumbled under its own weight, that the employer-employee relationship would turn around again.

Chaplin and Pickford, however, as pioneers, never really dropped back into the system. They continued to produce their own films along with a few others, such as Buster Keaton and Harold Lloyd. For the remaining 99% life was not uncomfortable, as salaries for top stars went as high as $7,000 a week, with $2,000–5,000 an average. However, stars would no longer dominate and rule the system. Again, as with the trust, the industry had grown too quickly and too large to be controlled by one part of it. A new system emerged, one which defined itself more in terms of the latest stock market quotations than the salaries paid to a young man with a mustache and baggy pants or a little girl with blonde curls.

The Establishment of Hollywood

Emerging alongside the shift in industrial power was a shift in geography as well. The move west was initially a result of the independents' conflict with the trust, but soon the appeal of year-round production in inexpensive outdoor sets began to attract more companies. As Kevin Brownlow has pointed out, the arrival of motion pictures to the west coast in general and Hollywood in particular took more the form of a gradual infiltration than a direct invasion. The industry was once again displaying its natural reluctance to depart from established procedure.

The years 1908–1914 were the pioneer period in which many companies went west, some to succeed, most to fail. By 1914 Hollywood began to take on the appearance of a major industrial center. By 1919 approximately 80% of the world's motion pictures were being made there. Gertrude Jobes in her book *Motion Picture Empire* describes this geographical transition well:

> Well paved boulevards extended for miles where for generations muddy paths had been the only roads. Building after building

covered what had been pasture land fifteen years before. Palatial studios replaced tottering shacks. Millionaires Lane supplanted Poverty Row. The world's glamorous city emerged on the site of an unknown sleepy village.

By 1921–22 there were 49 studios in and around Los Angeles and about 175 production units. In 1920 studio payrolls reached almost $40,000,000.

The shift was mental as well as geographical. The West Coast, with its air of newness, of enthusiasm, of unfulfilled growth and size, fit the rapidly expanding industry ideally. The East was staid, conservative, heavy, and old. There was no preset mental concept of Hollywood and as a result the industry created its own image. The sense and feel of the West in American heritage and tradition has been a powerful one. There was always new land, new opportunity, and new life in the West and for the motion picture industry this "newness" was just as much a reality as it had been for those coming in wagon trains 50 years earlier. Hollywood became motion pictures. The city symbolized the appeal and glamor of motion pictures for the public as much as the films themselves. As Richard Griffith and Arthur Mayer state in *The Movies*: "Hollywood in the Twenties was garish, extravagant, ludicrous, acquisitive, ambitious, ruthless, beautiful—which was just what its world public wanted it to be."

Changing Exhibition Patterns

"The nickel is dead" became the cry of motion picture exhibitors as $10,000-a-week salaries and two-hour films soon brought the age of the nickelodeon to an end. At first many producers and exhibitors felt that audiences would pay only a nickel, or at the most a dime, to see motion pictures. However, the success of charging $1.00 and more for films such as *Quo Vadis* and *The Birth of a Nation* convinced theater owners that the public would pay higher admission prices. Even if the public had not seemed willing to pay higher prices, they would have been forced to sooner or later because of increasing production costs. However, a necessary improvement in exhibition quality also had to occur before the public would accept increased prices.

In 1912, there were approximately 13,000 motion picture

theaters in the United States, most of them nickelodeons. However, in 1914, Mitchell Mark opened the Strand Theater in New York and the age of the motion picture palace began. Designed for motion pictures exclusively, the Strand occupied an entire block and seated 3,500 people. It was equipped with a huge pipe organ and could accommodate a symphony orchestra. The Strand was not simply another new theater. It symbolized a turning point in motion picture history. The following article from the *New York Times* (April 22, 1916) reporting the opening of another theater says it beautifully:

RIALTO THEATRE OPENS ITS DOORS

Luxurious Motion Picture House Begins Business in Times Square

WITH FAIRBANKS AS STAR

Stageless Theatre, Handsomely Appointed and Seating 2,000 Has Replaced the Old Victoria

The Rialto Theatre, which for nearly a year has been building on the spot in Times Square where Hammerstein's old Victoria used to stand, opened its doors last evening to a specially invited and very imposing audience. Today and daily hereafter the clamorous public will be admitted, and so another motion picture house has been added to the thousands which dot the map of the United States. But the difference between the queer, jiggly films that used to serve as chasers on the Keith programs fifteen years ago and the elaborate photoplays of 1916 is no greater than the difference between the evilly ventilated little nickelodeons and the luxurious theatre which was opened last night.

A handsomely appointed house dedicated entirely to the movies is thus established on one of the finest theatrical sites in the world. At every turn you found some grounds for the enthusiasm of the laureate of the occasion, who in the program burst forth as follows:

"With the peal of the grand organ, the fanfare of the orchestra, and the flash of thousands of iridescent lights, a new palace of polite pleasure for thousands is born tonight."

The interior is done in ivory and gray with hangings of red. The dome over the balcony is lovely in coloring, a playground for innumerable lights of every hue. The very ushers are elegantly upholstered, each carrying an electric flash and a swaggerstick. There was some speculation last night as to whether these were to be used for prodding a sleepy patron or for hitting the critics over the knuckles, but a part of the Rialto Review showed the ushers in action. It seems they are trained in first aid work, and the swaggersticks are used in making tourniquets. The Review also transports you to the Rialto in Venice with Nevin's lovely Venetian music as the appropriate accompaniment.

Like the Strand, which preceded it and has served to some

degree as the model for all of the finer motion picture theatres in America, the Rialto expressed the taste and ideas of Roxy Rothapfel, its managing director. Here is a goodly auditorium, with seats downstairs and in the steep cantilever balcony to the number of 2,000. Here is a big orchestra, a program that includes some singing and then no end of movies, with two photoplays and a topical review of the sort that shows a Governor dedicating something somewhere and some children doing something somewhere else, and so on.

The Knickerbocker is a fine old theatre temporarily made over into a movie house, and even the Strand is so built that at very short notice it could be converted to the uses of opera or drama, but the Rialto is a motion picture house, pure and simple. It is stageless, the screen being placed boldly against the back wall of the theatre. It is built in the conviction that the American passion for the movies is here to stay.

By 1916 film occupied a position of strength, size, grandeur, and sophistication. It was no longer simply a vaudeville "chaser" or the working man's amusement.

Two events helped create this change in exhibition. One was the feature film. Audiences were now viewing films for two hours at a time, and the wooden chairs and cramped conditions of the nickelodeon were uncomfortable and inadequate. The quality of a theater became important, therefore, simply in order to increase audience comfort. However, perhaps the greatest cause for change was the audience itself. In 1914, almost $300,000,000 were spent on motion picture tickets. Middle-class America had discovered motion pictures and was able and willing to pay for them. However, this new audience exercised greater care and discretion and demanded better quality in both films and theaters. *The Great Train Robbery* was fine in a store theater filled with wooden benches. However, with such people as President Wilson making up part of the audience for *The Birth of a Nation,* wooden benches were no longer adequate. Sophisticated musical scores required more than a piano. Theaters were soon equipped with elaborate organs and in large cities symphony orchestras played original scores for important productions. By 1916 there were more than 21,000 new or remodeled theaters. The Riviera Theater, opened in New York in 1917, had a playroom equipped with all the latest innovations, including a sandbox, slides, seesaws, and attendants. In 1919, the $2,000,000 Capitol Theater opened in New York with a seating capacity of 5,300 (compared to the capacity of the Metropolitan Opera—3,000, and Carnegie Hall—2,632). The motion picture had overtaken established culture, at least in terms of seating capacity. Hundreds of new motion picture theaters were being constructed with interiors designed to match the sets of the motion pictures being shown in them. All types of design were being incorporated in theater construction. *Architectural Record* began to note some of the more unusual designs, such as the all redwood theater in Scotia, California, with an entrance vestibule supported by eight redwood trunks two feet in diameter.

Atmospheric houses became the rage in the Twenties, with such exotic environments as a rural French village in Rochester, Minnesota, a $500,000 Egyptian theater in Milwaukee, Wisconsin, or Portland, Oregon's Indian temple. These new homes included crystal chandeliers, oriental rugs, original paintings, statuary, and elaborately uniformed attendants.

The peak was reached in 1927, when Roxy Rothapfel opened the Roxy Theater in New York. This was the ultimate in exhibition exhibition. The "cathedral of motion pictures" with its 6,200 seats and elaborate facilities was a perfect illustration of Rothapfel's philosophy as stated by Benjamin Hampton.

> He wanted a great orchestra and fine music, great singers, a great ballet; if a picture was good, these additional features brought more people to the box-office, and if a picture was not good, the orchestra, the singing and the dancing, flowers and paintings in the lobby, and ushers trained to meticulous politeness, made patrons comfortable and happy and induced them to come again.

A New System

The result of all this change in production and exhibition was a new system of making, distributing, and exhibiting motion pictures. In fact, what emerged was a new style and form of film which took on the characteristics of an industrial product. Standardization was a goal eagerly sought by the new system and motion pictures had to be brought into line. One of the key individuals in establishing this new system was Thomas Ince. Accomplished as a director, especially of Westerns, he made his real contribution as the industry's first production supervisor. Ince's contribution is discussed in detail in Chapter 3, but his importance in standardizing the production of motion pictures cannot be overemphasized. Some have felt that Ince's contribution was ultimately a negative one in that he took motion pictures

This artist's drawing gives some indication of the grandeur of the Roxy theater, built by S. L. "Roxy" Rothapfel in 1927.

away from individual directors. However, his contribution, whether negative or positive, was above all else a necessary one. The number of motion pictures produced by Ince and others had grown tremendously, to the point where a more efficient system was required. Ince devised a system that served as the model for the studio producers who came later.

Up until 1915–16 financial practices were fairly sane and businesslike despite the war with the trust, the rise of the star system, and the conversion to feature films. Costs were kept at a reasonable level, primarily because most companies were self-sufficient, requiring no outside capital. However, the influence of Chaplin and Pickford and the feature film made financial sanity not only difficult, but risky. While conservative companies pondered new salary demands and looked hesitatingly at feature production, bold competitors rushed in and gambled their resources on stars and stories.

Adolph Zukor continued to lead the parade. By 1916–17, through consolidation, merger, and acquisition of competing companies' stars, he had become the largest producer and distributor of motion pictures in the world. His most significant accomplishment and one of the most important developments in this early period was the consolidation of distribution and production under one corporate structure. The rest of the industry soon followed in his footsteps, so that by 1917 the profits made from distribution were financing production.

This consolidation left the exhibitor in an extremely vulnerable position. Zukor, especially, made life difficult for exhibitors by instituting and promoting a policy known as block booking. This procedure forced exhibitors to rent their films in blocks from certain companies and in effect required that they accept both good and bad films. Zukor's studio, Paramount, was especially secure in this practice, because it employed most of the major stars of the period. As the plan went, in order for an exhibitor to get a Mary Pickford film, he might have to take three or four other films of less quality. The scheme was of tremendous value to industrial standardization, because a production company was guaranteed exhibition for virtually all its products, regardless of quality.

Exhibitors complained bitterly about the practice, but were powerless until Thomas Tally and other exhibitors formed the First National Company in 1917. First National was an independent production company which, at least in the beginning, did not employ actors or own a studio but allowed players and directors to act as their own producers. First National would then distribute and exhibit their films. Charlie Chaplin was the first major star to join in 1917, followed soon by Mary Pickford. Soon, First National, by acquiring its own production facilities and signing actors and actresses to contracts, became second in power only to Paramount.

All of this activity was taking place against the background and drama of World War I. The war was an important factor in establishing the dominance of American film. In 1914, American films accounted for approximately 50% of the world's market. In 1918, they accounted for 80%. Most of Europe's major industries were decimated by the war and the American industry rushed in to fill the vacuum. As Lewis J. Selznick said in 1920: "Naturally the most important thing that has happened since the beginning of the war is the ending of the war. The reopening of the European market is the big opportunity we have been awaiting for four years." International domination now became possible without the artificial stimulus of war. American corporations began setting up foreign subsidiaries and raiding the native European industry for much of its best talent. By 1925, American films had captured 95% of the British market and 70% of French and Italian screen time.

The end of the war brought a temporary depression in the film industry caused by the reduction of the European market, a large backlog of war films, and an influenza epidemic. All of these factors combined to spell disaster for many small independent companies, but the large organizations came through relatively unscathed. The industry was simply too strong at this point to be wiped out and 1919 brought with it new prosperity.

On the heels of the Armistice came booming prosperity, which was reflected in all areas of American life, including motion pictures. The demand for motion pictures on both the foreign and domestic front was great and the industry was on the edge of skyrocketing into one of the most glorious and extravagant periods in its history.

The period was created and sustained by a new order of men and organizations, as Benjamin Hampton states:

> The movie business was no longer an infant industry in which anyone might find fame and fortune. It had passed the middle period in which men with moderate capital might establish themselves. Within a few years it had grown to maturity and had become one of America's greatest industries, subject to large capital necessities and the financing rules and regulations of big business and Wall Street. Twilight was descending on independent control of theaters, studios, and exchanges.

The industry had in a sense come full circle and was now similar in organization and structure to the trust which it had displaced only eight years earlier. Men such as Zukor, Laemmle, and Fox had worked hard to establish this new order and were not about to lose control now. Control of both distribution and exhibition became vital as merger, consolidation, and interlock became watchwords of a new system.

The big three at the beginning of the Twenties were Paramount, First National, and Fox. Second-level companies included Universal, Selznick, Metro, and Goldwyn. Bringing up the rear were thirty or forty "poverty row" companies, such as Columbia and Monogram. Universal, under the leadership of Carl Laemmle, was one of the strongest companies in the fight against the trust. However, it did not attempt to compete with the "big three" in elaborate, star-studded feature films, emphasizing instead low-cost features, comedies, Westerns, and serials. Universal became known as the "family" studio both for its emphasis on these types of motion pictures and for the nepotism which "Uncle Carl" established as the basic organizational structure for the studio.

Major Studios of the Twenties
Silent Feature Production

	Paramount	MGM	Universal	UA	Fox	First National	Warner Bros.
1921	101	—	55	9	64	—	4
1922	84	—	46	8	64	—	5
1923	55	—	60	4	52	—	11
1924	57	19	50	4	53	15	22
1925	74	27	51	10	43	52	26
1926	64	34	57	6	51	52	32
1927	67	42	64	13	49	58	43
1928	60	42	59	14	51	47	28

Industry statistics of 1919–20 reveal a gross industry income of $750,000,000, 15,000 theaters with a seating capacity of 8,000,000 people, and another 1,200 theaters under construction. These figures were only the tip of an iceberg of feverish financial activity. In addition to the money required to buy theaters, film costs were rising at an incredible rate, and the industry was turning into a monetary madhouse. The primary factors were theater acquisition, salaries, feature-length films, and an emphasis on spectacular sets, costumes, and design. As the postwar boom settled in, many companies felt there was no limit to the amount of money they could spend on production, since the public seemed willing to pay to see almost anything. In 1913–15 Griffith's *The Birth of a Nation* cost $100,000. Five years later he reportedly paid $175,000 for the rights to *Way Down East*. MGM spent $4,500,000 on Ben Hur in 1925. Other costly films of this period included *The King of Kings* (1927, $2,500,000), and *Wings* (1927, $2,000,000). According to Benjamin Hampton, there was a 1500% increase in the cost of a feature film between 1914 and 1924. In 1919–20, while at Paramount, Cecil B. DeMille devised a formula based on a combination of money and sex. With it, he produced a number of extremely successful films, some of which are indicated in the chart below.

DeMille Film Costs

Title	Cost	Gross Earning
Male and Female	$170,000	$1,250,000
Why Change Your Husband?	74,000	300,000
Forbidden Fruit	340,000	850,000
Adam's Rib	400,000	880,000
Manslaughter	385,000	1,200,000
The Golden Bed	440,000	800,000

The industry quickly took notice of these figures, especially the cost-to-profit ratios. However, whereas *Male and Female* grossed almost eight times its cost, for *Ben Hur* (1926), *Thief of Bagdad* (1924), or *The King of Kings* (1927) to do so would mean that each of these films would have to set box-office records. Overproduction was a problem as well, as the industry was making 600 to 800 features a year. In 1922, there were over 200 production units and 52 studios in Hollywood, employing over 15,000 people.

1922 was something of a high-water mark in terms of industry excess, aptly symbolized by Douglas Fairbanks' $2,000,000+ spectacle, *The Thief of Bagdad*. Following the diminished returns from this and other films, producers began to realize that increased cost did not automatically result in increased profits in the same ratio as lower-cost pictures.

The 1923 *Film Daily Yearbook* signaled the end to this monetary extravaganza with its headline: "Production Orgy Over." It followed with the statement: "Until 1923 the motion picture industry was the spoiled child among American industries, spending as lavishly as it pleased on more and more costly productions, knowing that the generous public would foot the bills." What the industry found out was that there was a limit to the public's ability and willingness to pay. In addition, other leisure activities, made possible by radio and the automobile, were taking increasing amounts of the public's time and money.

Hollywood's meteoric rise into prosperity and worldwide popularity was also brought up short by the impact and effect of a series of public scandals.

While motion pictures treated sex with increasing candor, the public was relatively tolerant until the sex moved off the screen and into real life. Actually, there were three related events dealing with sex, drugs, and murder that shocked the American public and brought demands for control and censorship.

The first and most famous scandal occurred in 1921 and involved Fatty Arbuckle, a major silent comedian who, at the

The castle set from Douglas Fairbank's 1925 production of *Robin Hood* gives some indication of the extravagance of Hollywood productions in the boom years of the 1920's.
MUSEUM OF MODERN ART/FILM STILLS ARCHIVE

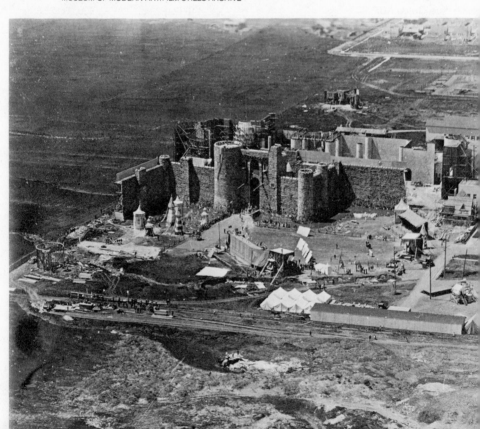

time, was probably second in popularity only to Chaplin. Arbuckle was accused of causing the death of a young actress at a party. The party soon became a "wild orgy" and Arbuckle was characterized as a sex fiend. The case was dragged through three court trials and the nation's press before Arbuckle was eventually declared innocent. By this time the publicity was so unfavorable that Arbuckle never worked in films again, except under an alias in a few cheap potboilers.

The second incident involved the murder of a well-known director, William Desmond Taylor. This time two leading actresses were implicated through their personal relationship with Taylor. One was Mary Miles Minter, hailed as the new Mary Pickford; the other was Mack Sennett's leading comedienne, Mabel Normand. Again, as in the Arbuckle case, neither woman was convicted of anything more than indiscretion. However, the public was outraged and both actresses' careers were ruined.

The final tragedy occurred in 1923 and involved popular actor Wallace Reid, who died while trying to cure himself of drug addiction. While no one else was implicated in his death, the publicity only served to fan the flames of censorship even higher.

The public outrage was enormous, primarily because the scandals confirmed what many were thinking all along, that Hollywood was a den of sin and iniquity. Pressure started to come from all quarters, including the federal government. By the end of 1921, thirty-six states were considering censorship legislation and Hollywood kept appearing in Congressional speeches filled with unfavorable adjectives.

The industry leaders got together and in desperation hired Will Hays, Postmaster General under President Harding, to head up a new industry self-regulatory agency, The Motion Picture Producers and Distributors Association of America, Inc. The Hays office, as the organization came to be known, functioned very effectively in fending off local, state, and federal censorship. It got the studios to tone down content and applied pressure on stars to avoid public scandals. Most importantly, it reviewed summaries of screenplays and passed judgment on their acceptability.

All of this activity was conducted on an informal basis until 1930, when sound films brought new problems with dialogue and studio competition for public attention grew increasingly fierce. Again, as public concern grew the industry responded by adopting The Motion Picture Production Code, which would remain the basic self-regulatory mechanism of the industry for almost forty years.

On the heels of this public outcry and increased concern over costs, several studios closed in order to stabilize costs. However, the most important result of these developments was a rigorous attempt at standardization. Among the many changes brought about was the rigid inspection of scenarios and preproduction cost analyses. Efficiency experts were brought in and, although not always successful, at least helped to bring some degree of sanity to this ephemeral world of shadows and emotions. Not everyone agreed, however, that the type of sanity introduced was good. James Morrison is quoted in Kevin Brownlow's book, *The Parades Gone By . . .*:

> I left the Vitagraph in 1918 when they brought in efficiency experts. When that happened the art of the company disappeared. Here were three people dividing two million dollars a year—and yet they brought in efficiency experts. These people limited the amount of film that directors could shoot . . . and they even had people straightening nails.

An even more significant factor was the introduction of the production supervisor. Although pioneered by Thomas Ince, it took one of its first and most dominant forms in the person of Irving Thalberg, who joined MGM in 1925 and proceeded to revolutionize the business of making motion pictures. No director, regardless of previous reputation, was safe from Thalberg's supervision and revision, and he quickly became the model for the entire industry. Fortunately for MGM, Thalberg was an intelligent, creative man; many who followed in the same path were not. Many directors and players rebelled, but with little effect. The producer was here to stay. What they did exactly was open to question. In the best sense of Thalberg's tradition they could curb artistic excess and help make a film a success. In the worst sense they were unnecessary and uncreative burdens. As Kevin Brownlow notes: "Hollywood summed up their value by calling them 'glacier watchers'—they stand around making sure the studio isn't engulfed by a glacier."

A further sign of the industry's attempt to reach some form of financial stability is found in a 1923 report by The National Bank of Commerce: "The motion picture industry is slowly getting out of the class of a game and more in the class of a business." By 1924 most studios had adopted a budget system and the average cost of a feature had stabilized at $150,000–

200,000. In addition, some studios instituted special features, such as giving a director a certain amount of money to make a picture and letting him keep what was left over. Most studios went to a diversified plan where they made a variety of films, refusing to put all their eggs in one basket. Foreign domination was a reality by this time as American films accounted for 80–90% of the world's screen time. Conversely, any attempts by foreign companies to infiltrate the United States market met with almost total defeat. In 1922, 425 foreign motion pictures were sent to the U.S. for sale and of these only six were sold and distributed.

Film Formulas

Just what type of films were produced by this new system? A good place to start might be to look at what it did not produce, and who it refused to accommodate.

The system produced a number of casualties, but three stand out above all the rest as being most significant and representative. They were D. W. Griffith, Eric von Stroheim, and Robert Flaherty. All three exercised total control over their films. More importantly, their work habits were not in the best tradition of the production line. Griffith worked on an elaborate scale, which frightened most producers out of their budgets. When he was not constructing huge sets, he was creating stories of Victorian romance which most people, including producers, simply could not relate to any more. Von Stroheim insisted on exact detail in his films right down to the underwear for Prussian Guards. He felt that this attention to realistic detail heightened and increased the meaning of his drama. Most producers felt the only thing it increased was cost. All Flaherty wanted to do was travel to some far-off island and live with the natives for a couple of years *before* he actually began making his film. Ninety-day shooting schedules on back lots did not fit in too well with this method.

Instead, the studios hired directors, writers, cameramen, editors, actors and actresses by the carload, signed them to long-term contracts, and placed them in their proper position on the assembly line.

The films produced in this manner were characterized by stars and plot formulas. Although the studios produced a variety of films, most of the films of the Twenties were what for lack of a better term could be called modern, reflecting the postwar decade with all its exuberance and spirit. This was the Jazz Age, a time of letting loose. It was also a production age. Between 1920 and 1929 industrial production increased 50%. America moved from the farm of *Tol'able David* to the city of *The Jazz Singer*. In between more than 5,000 feature films were made, most of them long forgotten.

Whether well known or forgotten, the films truly reflected the time and the system by which they were produced. There were, for example, almost 100 films on alcoholism, more than 150 on automobiles, 49 on bigamy. However, there were only six films on bigotry. Bootlegging appeared as a major theme in 87 films, chorus girls were the subject of over 100 pictures. Farming, however, was a theme in only eleven films.

Most of these were studio formula films produced in cycles and distinct patterns. For example, there were more than 60 films dealing with flappers, and about the same number emphasizing aviation. However, the pattern of their production is more interesting and revealing than the simple numbers.

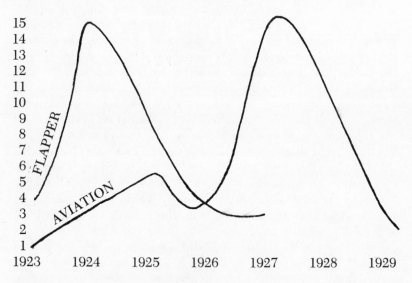

What the chart reveals is that the system was responsive to both internal and external influences. In the case of flappers, the minute one studio began to push the theme and it proved popular the other studios followed suit. With aviation, the key was Lindbergh's flight in 1927, which the studios jumped on with gleeful abandon.

The system worked very efficiently and very predictably. It produced a huge number of films on a wide variety of subjects with the absolute confidence that whatever it produced would be accepted. Part of this confidence was because the consolidation in production, distribution, and exhibition continued unabated. Exhibition control became the new key to success. Exhibitor Marcus Loew formed MGM in 1924. Paramount and Fox began acquiring first-run theaters in earnest and soon began to effect a stranglehold on the industry. Many independent producers were forced to merge with the major studios as they could not get their films shown in enough first-run screens to make costs. First-run theaters were simply large theaters in key cities, such as New York, Los Angeles, and Chicago. However, they were vital cogs in the studio system, since a majority of a film's gross earnings was usually earned in a few cities. Even today, exhibiting a film at certain theaters in New York can account for as much as 40% of a film's gross. Therefore, the major studios did not have to control a large number of theaters in order to control exhibition, since by controlling 10% of the 15,000–20,000 theaters in the country they dominated the industry.

By 1927 the motion picture industry had reached huge proportions. In the fifteen years from 1912, the investment in studios and equipment had grown to over two billion dollars. The number of theaters had doubled from 10,000 to 20,000. Just as importantly they had changed in character. Attendance figures had risen to almost 100,000,000 per week. To supply this audience with films there were almost 2,500 producer/exhibitor corporations in 1927. Southern California contained 54 studios, employing over 42,000 workers.

The motion picture industry of the silent era had been built on a foundation of ashes and dreams—the ashes of a monopoly and the dreams of ambitious men. Incredible changes had taken place and opinion was and still is divided on the value of most of them. Many felt the commercialization and industrialization of a potential art form had created irreparable damage from which the motion picture would never recover. Others felt that the necessary and useful function of entertaining a mass audience, which only a large industry could perform, was sufficient justification for what happened. Mae Marsh, a major silent-film star, stated: "Looking back, there's surely been a change in the film business over the decades. First it was a little family, then it became an industry, and then it became a match factory."

5

International
Silent Film

The most casual student of film history cannot fail to notice that great film movements germinate during periods of economic and political chaos.

—Rod Whitaker, *The Language of Film*

Inflation, deflation, unemployment, decadence, moral decay, and the disintegration of traditional values and institutions characterize the period surrounding World War I. Revolutions were forever changing governmental forms and the lives of various societies. Monarchical thrones littered the landscape of Europe by the end of the armed struggles, and people had to adjust to new forms, new leaders, and new philosophies or perish. The Four Horsemen of the Apocalypse were on the horizon. "A heap of broken images," wrote T. S. Eliot in 1922.

There were students in Russia who had provoked the police and the Czar's troops a dozen and more times before 1917; there were students throughout Europe, and disaffected intelligentsia, who were talking and plotting rebellions. Said Elmer Davis, the noted newscaster, in 1927, "That the universe is unsatisfactory is not exactly a novel discovery, but it is news to most of the earnest young people." To the German expressionists, Soviet revolutionaries and French intellectuals there was little from the past worth conserving. The world needed to be shaken upside down, the vestigial remnants of lingering institutional forms needed to be crushed and a new order built from the rubble, a

133

new world free from former conventions, behaviors, and structures. God was dead and sin was abolished. Humankind would
stumble toward the light in a state of benign anarchy (or Soviet
social regimentation), liberated from psychological hangups by
the new scientists (or Pavlovian environmental engineering). It
was a time of political, social, and artistic extremes.

It was to be from Germany, the defeated nation, that the first
few foreign film imports were to come after World War I. Just a
few years later new visions and ideas about the film medium
began to flow from the young Union of Soviet Socialist Repub-
lics, and then from France, fermenting in the juices of displaced
intellectuals and artists from other European states and from
America.

Imports, August 6, 1909 — June 20, 1910

Film Feet	Cost	Source
9,051,112	$555,603	France
1,254,813	74,001	England
1,174,738	65,806	Italy
1,084,519	65,543	Denmark
100,416	4,257	Germany
87,101	2,983	Canada
72,216	2,832	Others

—*Motion Picture News,* January 14, 1911

From the earliest days American audiences had patronized
the nickelodeon where foreign-made flicks danced upon the
screens. But the war had interrupted the product flow. While
European energies were brought to bear upon survival, and then
upon reconstruction, the American industry was evolving toward world domination. In 1922, for instance, U. S. companies
purchased more than 400 foreign-made titles, but only six were
released for exhibition.

The dream factories were in full production, having suffered
not at all from the war effort. The studio system was in the ascent,
financial resources plentiful. Feature-length films were the norm
and only in America were the resources of both capital and
personnel available in the quantity to satisfy both demand and
production values to which the world was becoming accustomed. President Coolidge represented the mood of America:
"The business of America is business." It happened that in the
case of the movies business was booming, because a product—
slick, smooth, well-made—was apparently desired by the public

not only at home, but also abroad. In contrast, the health of the European industry was so weakened by the war and by ensuing change—and the prognosis was so dim—that one American businessman suggested that embargoes be placed upon all American imports so that European industries would be *forced* to revive and find a solid base once again. When foreign audiences had a choice between seeing a movie made in their own country or one made in America, it was the American offering which all too often won at the cash register ballot box.

There had been a brief flurry of activity immediately after the war as Universal, for example, arranged trade agreements with the Italian industry, speculating on the chance that the familiar spectaculars of old might once again appear. London, Copenhagen, and Paris were initially thought to represent sources of product as before.

But feature film production was a different business from the days of short quickies, and on that score Hollywood had the upper hand. Prewar levels of foreign film imports would never again reach the levels of 1910. A two-way pattern of exchange had become a single direction of product flow, from the U. S. outward. And yet, with the few imports screened in this country after the war, an impact was to be made on the history of American film. They seldom made an impact upon the masses of moviegoers directly, but Hollywood watched them carefully; critics wrote at length; serious film buffs discussed endlessly; and the art of film was given substance.

If economic and political choas generated ideas and fostered ideological breakthroughs, the American industry weathered the storm, adapted to a few ideas, and generally reduced theories of art to useful techniques in the business of providing variations on styles already on the verge of mass audience monotony.

Germany

Actualities, Méliès-type fantasies, and Film d'Art productions characterize the early period of German film production, an industry which had joined the international pool as a source of film by 1910. In 1913, there were 28 producing companies; in 1917, 245. Oskar Messter had experimented in 1898 with intercutting a close-up within a short. German participation in the early period of experimentation also included medical authorities, who were convinced that the viewing of movies was deleterious to human vision. Thereafter, the city of Boston decreed that audiences must be treated to a neutral white screen periodically to minimize the "damage."

The early footage seen in America is now thought to be lost. What we were to see after the war, however, was to leave an indelible mark for all time.

Immediately following the war that brought Germany to bitter defeat, companies quickly moved to reestablish the industry by restaging the popular prewar spectaculars, the costume and historical dramas derived from ancient Teutonic myths and legends. The music of Wagner, *Die Walküre* or *Die Götterdämmerung*, suggests a parallel to the action and the massive emotion of these films.

Unlike prewar production, however, were sex films such as *Hyenas of Lust* (1918). Formerly taboo themes including homosexuality were featured in such titles as *A Man's Girlhood* (1919) or *Different from Others* (1919).

Government and industrial leaders had goals in mind for their national cinema other than Teutonic myths and sexploitation flicks. They saw the medium as a channel through which the German image could be redeemed, the perceived humiliation at Versailles ameliorated. Henceforth, resources would be assembled and a national industry created to promote German culture through film—not direct propaganda, but an intelligent cinema, a medium that had emerged as a universal language with universal appeal. If Hollywood could use the medium for slick profit, why not utilize the medium for more lofty goals?

Fresh talent was recruited from the established arts—literature, drama, and art. The unified production organization was known as Ufa, with facilities centered at Neubabelsberg, at the time, the most elaborate studio facility in the world.

Postwar German Films Seen In America

1918, *Gypsy Blood*
1919, *The Cabinet of Dr. Caligari*
1919, *Passion*
1920, *Deception*
1921, *Loves of Pharaoh*

Soon the first productions were being seen in America, mostly historical dramas. A few appeared to rationalize Ger-

In 1917, German film production was merged under a national
umbrella known as Ufa (Universal Film A. G.). The enormous,
efficient and technologically advanced studio center was located
at Neubabelsberg.

many's cause in the war. Others were unique to the genre
because there was a quality which set them apart from the
costume spectaculars and casts of thousands of old. The historical figures were given psychological depth; causes for actions
were suggested. Americans who saw these pictures noted the
differences between the former one-dimensional panoramas and
these new variations; the notice was reflected in the box office,
which in turn was noted by Hollywood. And Hollywood already
knew about cycles, about the one success which spawned myriad
copies until the mass audience tired of the entire cycle, waiting
only for someone else to come along with a novel twist.

Ernst Lubitsch, a man who later played a prominent role in
American film history, directed a number of the costume-histori-
cal spectaculars. Americans liked his movies even though they
came from Germany.

It was not difficult to see why. Lubitsch offered new faces,
faces with the magical "it" quality, "stars" such as Pola Negri
and Emil Jannings, who were immediately raised to the firmament by the American public.

Carmen, Madame du Barry, Anne Boleyn, and even the
ancient Egyptian pharaohs were given a new life. There was also
a style to these movies. It had to do with character, yes, but there
was also a verve, an energy, and an ensuing pleasure from the
care with which movement was planned and executed, pleasure
in movement caused by the angles of the camera, and pleasure
induced by the smooth editing and sophisticated matching action. What the camera caught was nuance, innuendo. Probably
few in the audience could name these factors. But they knew
what they liked. The studios remembered his name, Lubitsch,
and in those days of "silent" film, the names of actors and
actresses—even technicians and cinematographers.

These films were minor, however, in comparison to *The*

Cabinet of Dr. Caligari (1919). There were other forces who were to shake the foundations of the medium, radical forces coming from other art forms and from politics, whose ideas, although compromised by industrial system and conservative control, called attention to unimagined possibilities.

Hermann Warm, *Caligari* designer, believed that "films should be drawings brought to life." In France, René Clair praised the film because it made a "cheap" medium worthy of the intellect. In Moscow, Sergei Eisenstein thought it "a barbaric carnival of the destruction of the healthy human infancy of our art." But Western spokesmen for high culture agreed it was perhaps the first truly artistic film expression.

Few Germans were impressed except for the intellectuals, and in America it was not the masses who were flocking to the latest sensation either. Macabre, morbid, threatening, grotesque, it was a horror show reflecting the spirit of the times.

The idea was hatched in the minds of two young leftist artists, devotees of the radical Expressionist art movement, and embittered by their experiences in the war. It was in perfect harmony with leftists of the time, the feeling that the common man was but a tool in the hands of power-mad leaders.

Carl Mayer and Hans Janowitz had visualized an evil man,

The Cabinet of Dr. Caligari. "Life in Germany is now unbearably intense, a turmoil seemingly without beginning or end. In a world that is upside down, what is more natural than that the films, too, shall, metaphorically, stand on their heads."
—*Shadowland,*
January, 1921
THE BETTMANN ARCHIVE

Dr. Caligari, who would symbolize the power-mad leaders, a man who could cast spells over simple folks, causing them to do his dirty work. They would show poor Cesare made to commit various criminal acts under the demonic and hellishly corrupt figure of authority.

"Really something new—different," they said to Erich Pommer, powerful German producer. It proved to be that and more. Stylize. Distort. Play havoc with images. Destroy the Griffith romantic naturalism and sentiment with political intentions, set design, acting style. Unleash the gut emotion. As institutions crumble and the Lost Generation of the Jazz Age moans and whimpers, dare to look into the bottomless pit. Only then can a new order arise.

Said Pommer later, "They saw an 'experiment' in the script. I saw a comparatively cheap production."

Janowitz and Mayer were to find that in Germany, as in America, the name of the game was not revolution. They saw their "experiment" emerge as a "cheap production," its revolutionary intention demolished. Their story was framed in such a way as to comfort the audience with merely an escapist thriller. The evil doctor is revealed as simply the figment of a lunatic's imagination, who is in reality a kindly supervisor of a mental institution, not the symbol of corrupt political power which they had intended.

The political sting was removed. But the technique even at that was impressive. Never before had such visual images been seen. It seemed to scream, "Look, there are other realities than surface ones. Anyway, what is reality? We'll show you a movie nightmare, making the camera reveal hidden levels of psychological realities." To do that they transposed to the screen Expressionist forms, forms which were, after all, not abstractions but totally committed to representational communication.

Two hundred years before, Goethe had been drawn to the speculation that man finally becomes used to cruelty, and "in the end makes a law of that which he despises." There were traditions in German—and American—film which emphasized the influence of dark forces on human life, even questioning the whole notion of free choice. Selig-Polyscope had presented *Dr. Jekyll and Mr. Hyde* in 1908. Edison released *Frankenstein* in 1910. *The Golem*, from Germany in 1920, had introduced the robot, and the Faustian *Student of Prague* in the same year ended with the student's damnation for consorting with the devil. And *Life Without Soul* (1915) used the bookend device to show that the main story was a dream. The American Draculas and Frankensteins of the 1930's lacked the despair, horror, and doom so heavy in the German films.

But there was more coming, some shown to audiences throughout America, others limited to larger cities:

1920: *The Golem*, by Paul Wegener and Carl Boese, designed by Hans Poelzig (architect), who achieved remarkable effects by creating environments within which the faces of the characters created a shock attraction. The Golem was the monster robot, anti-social, uncontrollable; a terrifying representation of a side of mankind's own psychic reality.

1921: *Destiny*, directed by Fritz Lang, was designed by Expressionist Warm (who did *Caligari*). Fate looms in the distortions of settings and lighting: a girl is given a chance to save her lover from death—to challenge Fate. The harder she tries, the more events lead to the inevitable end. Individuals appear to be mere puppets of forces beyond their control.

1922: *Dr. Mabuse, the Gambler*, also by Lang. Some saw in this picture a prediction of Hitler's rise. Similar to *Caligari*, the doctor heads a gang of criminals, killers whom he controls by hypnosis. Caught, he goes mad.

Nosferatu, directed by F. W. Murnau, was based upon the Dracula novel. Murnau departed from typical German form and made this film outdoors, not on the gigantic stages of Neubabelsberg. But the camera angles, stop-action filming, and editing rendered even inanimate objects as laden with sinister potential. There were terrors even in the every-day outward levels of reality.

Warning Shadows was a psychological study illustrating Freudian preoccupation with shadows—an illusionist who permits his repressed unconscious to live in secret fantasies, the entire tempo of the film increasing as the fantasies come to gain control. The camera work was so superb that no titles were necessary. It was directed by an American, Arthur Robison, who had been drawn to the ferment of Europe.

1923: *The Street* was different from the others, the first major production to illustrate the Neue Sachlichkeit, the new realism, a new social consciousness forcing its way into German cinema. Entire sections of large urban cities were created within Ufa's stages. Breaking from the restraints of traditional values of home and security, the hero goes into the streets to vent his internal and uncontrollable passions—and is punished. By Karl Grune, *The Street* did not shock with purposefully distorted sets and acting. This genre, commonly referred to as the "street" film, found that similar terrors could be revealed in even the most common and recognizable surfaces.

The Golem applied the "futuristic" style to German medieval lore. Unrealistic architecture in set design, lighting, costume and acting style evokes a nightmare scene.

The dark and foreboding titles continued to roll out of Germany through the Twenties. Fritz Lang followed with *Siegfried* (1924), the first part of the Niebelungen trilogy in which subconscious passions run their course. *Metropolis* (1927) was his largest production effort, taking eighteen months to film with a cast of 36,000 people. Lang, denied permission to land in New York, had gazed at the panorama of the city from the ship's deck and envisioned the world in the year 2000, a world of class warfare and robots tracking about in science-fiction type sets. To him the future was but an extension of his contemporary experience.

Paul Leni's *Waxworks* (1924) presented through the mind of a starving poet the nature of absolute power gone mad using an Oriental tyrant, Ivan the Terrible, and Jack the Ripper.

F. W. Murnau, an art historian, also used the Expressionist style to conjure the supernatural in *Faust* (1926). Gerhardt Hauptmann, the poet, created the titles. It was Murnau's last film made in Germany. He left for the United States soon thereafter.

It was the street film which was to eclipse the Expressionist

141

There were few effects which could not be re-created within Ufa's studios. Fritz Lang's *Metropolis* being filmed.
MUSEUM OF MODERN·ART/FILM STILLS ARCHIVE

The Last Laugh illustrates how unreal effects created by the "futurists" could be modified to give depth to the more traditional story film. Emil Jannings' performance made an impact on American audiences.
MUSEUM OF MODERN ART/FILM STILLS ARCHIVE

style. Following Grune's work, *The Street* (1923), was Murnau's *The Last Laugh* (1924), enormously popular in the United States. Fluid camera work said everything and titles were not necessary. Emil Jannings' portrayal of the hotel doorman, so proud of his uniform and function, remains a compelling performance even today. The social realism of the time pathetically reveals the little man's despair at being reduced to a lavatory attendant. But at the end a sequence is tacked on, perhaps to make the depressing slice of life acceptable in America: a millionaire (from America) leaves Jannings his fortune, and the former doorman/lavatory attendant is now the guest to whom everyone else must bow. It was the traditional American happy ending.

Hollywood was luring German talent to America, and the drain on Germany's talent pool began to be felt. The German mark was set at a level unfavorable to German production. And Hollywood escapist fare continued to dominate the world market. Compromise in serious German work was ordered by Ufa to meet American competition.

Variety (E. A. Dupont, 1925) and *Joyless Street* (G. W. Pabst, 1925) were both seen and acclaimed in America. *Variety* extended the camera's versatility even further, capitalizing on subjective camera shots, which put the viewer in the character's situation (as had *The Last Laugh*). *Joyless Street* naturalized the social realist idea even further, perhaps suggested by the story material of postwar prostitutes caught in the chaos of the time.

Joyless Street reflected the social and economic terror of the period in a style know as the "street film." Entire city blocks were built within the Ufa studios so that complete control could be exerted over the material.
MUSEUM OF MODERN ART/FILM STILLS ARCHIVE

Asta Neilsen (pin-up girl of the First World War) and Greta Garbo were endorsed by the American public.

The street films closed out the silent period. *The Love of Jenny Ney* (Pabst, 1927), triumphed over German producing orders to avoid, in Hollywood tradition, serious social, sexual, and political themes (and at the same time to at least equal Soviet montage techniques). Natural lighting, unique traveling and panning shots, editing on action (a three-minute sequence had more than 40 cuts), and a narrative of compelling interest despite orders, caused much comment in the U. S.

It was, however, the naturalistic style that carried the German film into sound. While hundreds of German film-makers and technicians had responded to Hollywood's attractive offers, Pommer brought the American director, Josef von Sternberg, to direct the first German sound motion picture, *The Blue Angel* (1930) with Marlene Dietrich and Emil Jannings. But it was the American product that had secured its stranglehold on world markets.

The Creative Milieu

How was it that these remarkable film ideas had come to be in the first place, despite the terror of the times, despite Hollywood's vast resources and ability to purchase almost whatever and whomever it desired?

Serious and well-trained European artists and craftsmen traditionally moved between the various art forms and the film industry. Although the Film d'Art movement did not produce filmic visions, it did create an aura of respectability for the popular form. Famous stage actors, writers and artists had long been working in the medium. Saint-Saëns and others had composed scores for these "silent" pictures. Most of the names we have seen in connection with the films previously discussed came from the fine arts, a good many trained under the flamboyant and emotional theatrical designer and director Max Reinhardt. They brought, as we have seen, both their backgrounds and sometimes their radical political orientation to the movies.

Robert Wiene, the director of *Caligari*, noted the following criticisms of the American system (in 1926, a time when the drain of German talent was beginning to be felt): (1) Americans refuse to deal with problem themes, opting for the trite and mundane; (2) they insist on copying successful treatments, which finally breeds dullness; (3) they resist experimentation with new approaches and with new talent; (4) they insist on casting stars in roles for which they have no particular ability; (5) they appeal to the "weaknesses" of the American public, pandering to the perceived lowest common denominator; and finally, (6) the film industry in America was captured by cagey businessmen looking for private profit, caring little for quality and worthiness of ideas. No wonder, Wiene thought, serious artists in America continued to scorn their own country's productions.

In contrast consider cameraman Karl Freund's recollections of the milieu surrounding the creative process by which the startling filming techniques evolved in *The Last Laugh*:

> In the two and a half months of preparation on *The Last Laugh*, [scriptwriter Carl Mayer, leftist creator of *Caligari*] conferred every day with at least one of us—with Murnau, the designers Herlth and Rohrig, with Pommer, with Jannings, or with me. It was out of this team-work that all the innovations in *The Last Laugh* evolved.
>
> I remember the first words that set the camera into motion. Mayer asked me, "Karl, is there any way to film a person's head first in a medium shot and then move in to a great close-up of his eyes alone?" This was for the moment when the aunt discovers that Jannings has been demoted to a lavatory attendant—and it was Jannings' reaction to her discovery that Mayer wanted to heighten. "I guess you'd have to mount the whole camera apparatus on a wheeled platform of some sort. . . ." Actually, when we came to the shot that had started all this movement, wheels were useless, because the aunt looked down on Jannings from the top flight of steps. So we worked out a contraption for a descending approach to Jannings' face; taking a fire-ladder that was built in sections that were raised or lowered with a crank, we mounted the Debrie on its top, and chose our *smallest* camera assistant to sit by it to adjust the focus. We all began to look forward to new difficulties—as challenges that required completely original solutions. For the well-known trumpet shot, we suspended the camera in a basket from a bridge that ran the length of the courtyard, and when we found that our pulley couldn't manage the upward movement of the camera-basket, we made the shot downwards—and reversed the film in the camera. When the film had to be a drunken Jannings, I strapped the camera to my chest (with batteries on my back for balance), and played drunk! For the opening shot—down the elevator, across the lobby, and through the revolving door, my camera and I sat on a bicycle in the descending elevator, and rode out through the opened elevator-door across the lobby, and through the huge revolving-doors. Mayer's imagination convinced us that we could do anything!
>
> —Karl Freund, "A Film Artist," *The Film Till Now*

Certainly Freund's description illustrates the collective effort required of filmmaking. And certainly there is reason to temper our tendency to think of films in terms of only the director. Writers, designers, and obviously cameramen figure directly in the creative act. At the same time there appears to be the requirement of the great individual—the Griffiths, Langs, Mayers—to fire the imaginations of others so that great and memorable results flow from the collective act.

German Filmmakers in America

Films in America

Lubitsch	Lang
The Marriage Circle (1924)	*Fury* (1936)
The Love Parade (1929)	*You Only Live Once* (1937)
Ninotchka (1939)	*The Big Heat* (1953)
That Uncertain Feeling (1941)	*Human Desire* (1954)
Heaven Can Wait (1943)	*Beyond a Reasonable Doubt* (1956)

Both Lang and Lubitsch continued to work in themes and attitudes they had begun in Germany. Hollywood producers were adept at assigning suitable tasks to directors particularly skilled in certain styles and themes.

Lubitsch had no ideological ideas to bring to the masses and he certainly was not out to disparage popular institutions and values. But he did work effectively within the conventions and values of his time, affirming honesty, integrity, and happy endings. But he never stooped to the easy, trite, or leering symbols. Sentimental, yes, but with style and sensibility unusual to Hollywood. Maurice Chevalier, Jeannette MacDonald, Carole Lombard, Greta Garbo and Jack Benny, all different types, inhabited popular films under his care.

Some Germans, like Lubitsch, came to America simply for the opportunity to work at the center of the garish film capital. Others, like Lang, came because the Nazi climb to power violated their own ethical values and because of threats to their very lives. Lang's last film in Germany was *The Testament of Dr. Mabuse* (1922), which was never shown in Germany because of what some Nazis thought bore an unhealthy similarity to their own leader and methods. Indeed, the important early sound film, *M* (1931), had been given this title as a substitute for the proposed title, *The Murderer Among Us*, again uncomfortably close to political realities.

Lang had always been attracted to the issue of mankind's inability to direct its own future, characters caught in circumstances beyond their control. His American films are filled with three-time losers, characters accused of crimes they did not commit, and crusaders getting caught in the legal deficiencies they had set out to change. These figures often went down to defeat, but they fought all the way, committed to the existential struggle. Caught in the period of the Red Scare in the early Fifties, Lang remained loyal to his ideals. Uncomfortable with the trend toward gratuitous violence and the hatred still loose in the world, he said,

> [There] is nothing creative in hatred. Hatred is a lousy feeling and it's not productive. . . . Everywhere today you hear voices against the so-called Philosophy of Hate. About the Philosophy of Love no one even dares speak any more because they will be laughed off the screen. . . . [But] there are others—the Philosophy of Indifference, of Superficiality—that I think are more dangerous. . . .

Another who came to America was Freund, who filmed *Metropolis* and *Variety*, for example, where his talent came to bear upon *Camille* (1936), *The Good Earth* (1937), and *Key Largo* (1948). Still later he was cameraman for American television (including the *I Love Lucy* series). Even Erich Pommer was to do a stint on the West Coast. So did E. A. Dupont, and for a time, Jannings, Pola Negri, Lya de Putti, and many others. Mayer resisted the call, but did provide the script for the Fox production *Sunrise* (1927). His careful preplanning had always amazed the American producers, and the German approach was incorporated into our system.

Motion picture technology was deeply enriched by German inventiveness. Photographic elements, tracking rigs, and even sound technology were incorporated into our production systems. The story-board greatly facilitated Ince's production. Production terminology was stamped with the German sound: MOS refers to a shot to be filmed "mitout sound."

What are we to make of this strange period of German creativity? A new approach made a genre formerly thought sapped of its viability take new life. Expressionist visions unleashed a new look at screen realism, showing how manipulation of surface reality could reveal a deeper interior state of affairs. The street films showed how the craft of filmmaking could be perfected so that even surface realities could give up the meaning locked within—through camera angle, nuances of lighting, set design, character movement, camera pan, crane shot, and subjective point of view.

The fact of Hollywood affected the course of development as much as local and national affairs within Germany. Even though creative artists were invited into the cinema under the influence of Ufa, compromise was still demanded. Competition from Hollywood finally dictated changes in treatments, and the talent drain took its toll.

As the vital period of German invention and discovery began to wane far more radical ideas about the nature of film began to surface from a previously backward source—the Soviet Union. These ideas had been in ferment, and been tested, at about the same time as the German period; it took longer for the Soviet ideas to gain attention in this country.

A *Götterdammerung* mentality seethed throughout the German period, a filmic epoch given to explication of emotions and passions out of control, as if a prelude to the rise of Nazi power and a holocaust the nature of which was to terrorize the world.

The Soviet Union

On October 15, 1926, David O. Selznick, an MGM producer and director, dictated one of his numerous memos to his boss, Harry Rapf:

> It was my privilege a few months ago to be present at two private screenings of what is unquestionably one of the greatest motion pictures ever made, *The Armoured Cruiser Potemkin*, made in Russia under the supervision of the Soviet Government. . . . It possesses a technique entirely new to the screen, and I therefore suggest that it might be very advantageous to have the organization view it in the same way that a group of artists might view a Rubens or a Raphael.

Selznick noted that there were no individual characters in this piece of "superb craftsmanship" and no studio sets; he also noted the strength of character types, lack of make-up, "exquisite pieces of photography," and "starkly realistic dramatic scenes."

In what had become standard studio procedure, Selznick suggested that his organization "consider securing the man responsible for it, a young Russian director named Eisenstein."

Who was this Eisenstein, and what was going on in the Soviet Union that gathered comment from Hollywood moguls and American critics? New film ideas had burst forth from a defeated Deutschland. And now again from Red revolutionaries surrounded by recent civil war and devastating famine?

Until 1908 there was very little of any movie production by

Sergei M. Eisenstein (1898–1948) clowning on the
Czar's throne where events of the past were re-enacted
for the film, *October* (1928).
MUSEUM OF MODERN ART/FILM STILLS ARCHIVE

Russians and of Russian events or stories. Dominated by the
French film companies, the movies shown to Russian audiences
were imported in large scale. The crowning of Nicholas was a hit,
and soon many such actualities made their way to the screen.
Tiring of these Lumière-type bits and pieces, the first narratives
of Russian material, although made by foreigners, were immediate hits, and soon Pathé was exporting to the United States
topical dramas about Jewish life and the pogroms of the period.
Meanwhile, the Russian police kept a close watch on all story
and newsreel materials and treatments.

A few years before the Revolution indigenous Russian production was under way, but little of the material reached the
United States. The long-brewing and incipient revolutionary
zeal on the political front also included feverish experimentation
in other areas, sometimes repressed by the House of Romanov.
Wild movements in theatre included the naturalism of Stanislavsky and the structuralism of Meyerhold. Music was being
treated to atonal arrangements, and under the decay and rot of
a dying empire, there were fresh and energetic creative minds
at work. An indigenous national expression arising from the roots
of the people's experience was gathering its forces.

During the chaos of the Revolution, many in the Russian
film industry fled to Western Europe, many to Paris. One who
remained was Lev Kuleshov, a dominant figure in Soviet film
who remained active until his death in 1970. This seminal figure

149

taught most of the Soviet filmmakers, including those who were
to attain international status.

When *The Birth of a Nation* and *Intolerance* reached the
Soviet Union, smuggled in from Germany, Kuleshov and others
were amazed by the use of close-ups and parallel action (think
of the superb battle scenes of *Nation* and the four themes worked
into *Intolerance*). Already these Soviet filmmakers were getting
a good deal of experience with editing. Unable to shoot the film
they wanted because of a lack of equipment and film stock, they
set about re-editing shots of existing film, both fiction and actualities, to make them say what they wished. Already fascinated with
the possibilities and the power of the editing process, they recut
time and again those earlier American masterpieces, each time
delighted with the effects produced.

Kuleshov began to wonder if the reality of the shot's context
was at all important. To test his idea he filmed a close-up of an
old man who showed no particular emotional expression. Then
he shot a bowl of soup, a child at play, and an old woman lying
in a coffin. To each of these he attached a section of the close-up
of the old man, and when he projected the results people remarked on what a fine actor the old man was. In the viewers'
minds, the old man's face and the bowl of soup created a new
meaning: hunger. Old man plus child at play equals the pleasure
and delight of a grandfather. Old man plus woman in coffin
equals sorrow.

And so, working from Griffith's pioneering efforts, Kuleshov
concentrated on the shot itself, finding that he could greatly
intensify emotional response. It is something like what Francis
Ford Coppola did in *Patton* (1970). When the figure of Patton is
first introduced, there follows a series of extreme close-ups:
shots of the medals on the chest, the helmet, the riding crop,
holster, and other such details. Suddenly that figure takes on
heightened emotional qualities which could never have been
achieved had we been left with a long or medium shot.

Dziga Vertov was another filmmaker active in the production of those "compilation" documentaries and films—new film
statements derived from previously shot material. He was busy
creating a weekly newsreel called *Kino-Pravda*, "film truth,"
designed to help the Soviet people build the new society. Unlike
the American kind, these films were created to provide depth to
headlines, to instruct and propagandize. Said he,

> I am eye, I am a mechanical eye. I, a machine, am showing you a
> world, the likes of which only I can see. . . . My road is toward the

creation of a fresh perception of the world. Thus I decipher in a new way the world unknown to you.

Both of them, Kuleshov and Vertov, saw that to date little of the medium's potential had been tapped. By editing shots, "plastic material," new potentials were available. The cinema could find a new impulse, new purposes to be served, new functions. Vertov was to go on with his experimental editing and film theories, leaving production for the masses to others.

It should be noted, however, that even though all film production was centralized under the People's Commissariat of Propaganda and Education in 1919, there was still a great deal of freedom and inventiveness unhampered by political factors.

And then it happened, first *Strike* (1924), and *Potemkin* (1925) by Sergei Eisenstein, and *Mother* (1925) by Vsevolod Pudovkin, three films which generated the same kind of excitement as had *Caligari*. In 1923, Lenin had asked Griffith to come to the Soviet Union to head Soviet production, but soon Hollywood studios were planning to draw Soviet filmmakers to Hollywood.

Sergei Eisenstein

What Selznick saw at a private screening, New Yorkers were seeing on their downtown movie screen—despite the prevailing Red scare mongering and general distrust of things and people foreign. What they saw was shockingly different from the American or German productions. Unlike the Germans, emphasis was on real locations, not Expressionist or studio renderings. Even though the Soviets had returned to Lumière's world of surface reality, they were obviously able to penetrate to deep emotional and psychological levels. Rather than probing subterranean, Freudian depths, these were uplifting, inspiring film experiences. No cheap productions here, and because the production system was in harmony with the creative impulse, there were no sellouts to profit factors or demands of the lowest common denominator. But then these films were not catering to escapist entertainment.

Although he was never a member of the Party, Eisenstein was committed to the ideals of the Revolution. He went to the material of the collective experience, to the historical events which formed the new political experiment. And to this material he brought the thinking and techniques formulated by Kuleshov and others. With his shots—and through the editing of those shots—he produced his own documents, his own arguments much as a historian does with selected facts and selected words. When in *Strike* shots of butchers killing a bull were combined with Czarist cavalry cutting down the masses, the simile was crystal clear. This was anything but the smoothly edited matching action material, the passivity inducing Hollywood product. This editing idea agitated, shocked, and compelled the viewer into participation. Of course, it is a highly manipulative method, one which allows only for one deductive meaning: the filmmaker's.

Soon filmmakers everywhere were talking about "montage," that "technique entirely new to the screen," as Selznick had noted. And it was in *Potemkin* that Eisenstein perfected the application of montage.

He used the "fact" of a naval mutiny which had taken place aboard the battleship *Potemkin* during a period of unrest in 1905. Beyond that there may not be much else of fact. The film was constructed in five segments, each carefully worked out in advance; there is a remarkable unity within each part as well as within the whole work.

There is a mathematical progression within each sequence. In fact, Eisenstein used a metronome on location to help the characters pace themselves. And there they are, example after example of shock attraction, visual symbols juxtaposed against each other producing the shock of recognition in the minds of the viewers. An officer's sword in close-up revealing the elaborate hilt is followed by a close-up of the Orthodox chaplain holding a crucifix: and the point was made that a barrier to social change was the close relationship between the Czarist regime and the Church, which reinforced Government control over the people.

With his fascinaton for shot combinations Eisenstein achieved another technique. A crew member on mess duty is setting the tables. Fury is growing, because the meat intended for the meal is full of maggots. A critical moment in the life of the sailor comes as he picks up a plate. The moment of his radicalization occurs when he notices, perhaps for the first time in his life, the phrase "Give us this day our daily bread" painted on the edge of the dish. Eisenstein takes this moment and breaks it down into a number of separate shots as the man grabs the plate, raises it over his head, and slams it into pieces. The truth which Eisenstein was after was the psychological condition at a moment of crisis—which in retrospect *seems* to have lasted forever, similar to the dream of being caught at a moment and being able to move only in slow motion.

Griffith had done a masterful job of reducing real time so that screen time would be tolerable for the viewer. After all, most of life and experience is quite dull. Eisenstein expanded real time on the screen, finding a way visually to communicate a psychological reality everyone has experienced. This expansion of time is used again at several points, most dramatically in "The Odessa Steps Sequence," Part IV.

Eisenstein himself has effectively described the major sequence:

> First there are *close-ups* of human figures rushing chaotically. Then, *long-shots* of the same scene. The *chaotic movement* is next superseded by shots showing the feet of soldiers as they march *rhythmically* down the steps.
> Tempo increases. Rhythm accelerates.
> And then, as the *downward* movement reaches its culmination, the movement is suddenly reversed: instead of the headlong rush of the *crowd* down the steps we see the *solitary* figure of a mother carrying her dead son, *slowly* and *solemnly going up* the steps.
> *Mass.* Headlong rush. *Downward.* And all of a sudden—
> A *solitary* figure. Slow and solemn. *Going up.* But only for a moment. Then again *a leap in the reverse direction. Downward* movement.

Potemkin: Photo 1.   MUSEUM OF MODERN ART/FILM STILLS ARCHIVE

Rhythm accelerates. Tempo increases.

The shot of *the rushing crowd* is suddenly followed by one showing a perambulator [baby carriage] hurtling down the steps. This is more than just different tempos. This is *a leap in the method of representation*—from the abstract to the physical. This gives one more aspect of the downward movement.

Close-ups, accordingly, give place to *long shots*. The *chaotic* rush (of the mass) is succeeded by the *rhythmic* march of the soldiers. One aspect of movement (people running, falling, tumbling down steps) gives way to another (rolling perambulator). *Descent* gives place to *ascent*. *Many* volleys of *many* rifles give place to *one* shot from *one* of the battleship's guns.

At each step there is a leap from one dimension to another, from one quality to another, until, finally, the change affects not one individual episode (the perambulator) but the whole of the method: the risen lions mark the point where the *narrative* turns into a *presentation through images*.

The visible steps of the stairs marking the downward progress of action correspond to steps marking qualitative leaps but proceeding in the opposite direction of mounting intensity.

— Eisenstein, *Notes of a Film Director*, pp. 59–60.

That is the rationale from the mouth of the director. It is interesting to note that a similar pattern of description was used

Potemkin: Photo 2.    MUSEUM OF MODERN ART/FILM STILLS ARCHIVE

by Evelyn Gerstein, *New Republic* critic, in her review of October 20, 1926:

> A cripple moves suddenly. The armed guard press slowly, pitilessly, down the broad stone steps, abreast. Only terror now. A woman rushes down the steps with her child. She misses him. He has been shot down. She runs with the boy in her arms, chattering, pleading, into the fire from the guard. A beautiful young mother in a mantilla, wheeling a baby carriage, falls on the stones. Down, down, gathering speed in its flight, whistles the carriage.

What fascinated Eisenstein was not complicated and abstract film theory, but a quality worked into the film itself, a quality which was apparent to the viewer, however far removed from the process of its construction. The *New York Times* noted "an excellent conception of rhythm . . . a sort of purr to this picture as it is unfurled."

Even though Max Reinhardt, Douglas Fairbanks, and many critics—as well as American leftists—sang its praises, others were shocked and worried over its strong and affecting revolutionary edge. Germany and England were to avoid it, and in America there was concern that Will Hays would ban it. He did not, and *Potemkin* was shown in large cities; the *New York Times* listed it as one of its top ten for the year.

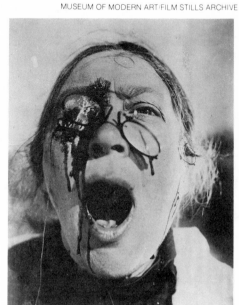

Potemkin: Photo 3.

Not only were the differences noted and the Soviet film idea successful in causing reevaluation of the medium, but so did these new films cause a closer look at the economic bases for production. Eisenstein was to write,

> Imagine a cinema which is not dominated by the dollar; a cinema industry where one man's pocket is not filled at other people's expense; which is not for the pocket of two or three people, but for the heads and hearts of 150 million people. Every motion picture affects heads and hearts, but as a rule motion pictures are not produced especially for heads and hearts. Most motion pictures are turned out for the benefit of two or three pockets; only incidentally do they affect the heads and hearts of millions. Suddenly a new system arises. A cinema is created, based not on private profit but on popular needs.

Wrote Ernestine Evans, *Potemkin* indicated "in which direction the art of the movies is to lie, if the screen is to be something more than a vehicle for exploiting the personalities of stars and a distractor of the public gaze from public and private conflicts."

It was earlier rumored that Eisenstein would be coming to America to work for United Artists. Indeed, there was a great affinity in Soviet filmmakers for Chaplin's work. But it was Lasky who succeeded in bringing Eisenstein to America for Paramount, where he produced a script for Theodore Dreiser's *An American Tragedy* that was never filmed.

Meanwhile, the infamous Fish Committee was calling Eisenstein the "international Judas of the cinema" and a Hollywood Technical Directors official used such epithets as "Red Jew" and "Jewish Bolshevik." One pamphlet of the time was titled, "Eisenstein, Hollywood's Messenger from Hell." Later he was even arrested in Mexico as the most "dangerous agent Moscow has ever sent on a mission." But the most revealing evidence illustrative of the differences between intentions of commercial exploitation of the medium and seriously intended and enduring film art is to be found in another Selznick memo to Paramount's general manager, B. P. Schulberg, for whom Selznick was now working. Having read Eisenstein's treatment for *An American Tragedy,* Selznick found it "a memorable experience; the most moving script I have ever read. It was so effective that it was positively torturing." However, he added, "As entertainment, I don't think it has one chance in a hundred."

> If we want to make *An American Tragedy* as a glorious experiment, and purely for the advancement of the art (which I certainly do not think is the business of this organization), then let's do it with a

[John] Cromwell directing, and chop three or four hundred thousand dollars off the loss. If the cry of "Courage!" be raised against this protest, I should like to suggest that we have the courage not to make the picture, but to take whatever rap is coming to us for not supporting Eisenstein (as he proves himself to be with this script), with a million or more of the stockholder's cash.

Let's try new things, by all means. But let's keep these gambles within the bounds of those that would be indulged in by rational businessmen. . . . [*An American Tragedy*] cannot possibly offer anything but a most miserable two hours to millions of happy-minded young Americans.

Pudovkin, Vertov, and Dovzhenko

When Americans finally saw Pudovkin's *Mother* (1925) in 1934, the revolutionary fervor was noted but also the major difference between Eisenstein and Pudovkin was immediately apparent. While *Potemkin* was perceived as lucky shooting of an uncontrolled event, *Mother* was seen as more traditional, particularly because it follows a narrative line, events hinging upon the mother and her son. By its array of jolting images (such as the imprisoned boy's agony reflected in close-ups of his hands; his quiet joy in anticipation of his release joined to shots of melting snow and ice representing the promise of spring and new life; the masses on their way through the streets to liberate the political prisoners joined with shots of river ice churning under spring's thaw with no power able to stop the inevitability of either; the cavalry coming from the left joined to shots of the masses coming from the right suggesting the inevitable conflict), we are forced to feel deeply with the son and exhilarate when mother finally picks up the red flag. Although both are killed, and even though events have been plotted around these two characters, we are still left with heady emotions of inevitable victory. No sniveling private agonies here, but bigger issues, ideology moving a nation toward ultimate victory.

Pudovkin was to follow with *The End of St. Petersburg* (1927), *Storm Over Asia* (1928), and the first major Soviet sound picture, *The Deserter* (1933). Vertov was to go on with his own theories and approach, denying theatrical action entirely—and also the style by which mass emotions could be stirred. Alexander Dovzhenko (*Arsenal*, 1929, and *Earth*, 1930), carved a middle ground between Eisenstein and Pudovkin by uniting the epic story lines of the former's mass hero with the latter's personal stories. While the others came from mathematical (and theatrical) backgrounds, he was more rooted in the poetic humanism of the 19th century. So his hero in *Arsenal* stands against the firing squad and poetically remains impervious to the bullets. Characters frequently did implausible acts, but he had driven home the point, and always in a style which was deeply moving and affective.

No small credit is deserved by many others in addition to the directors. In this sense the Soviet production process resembled the German (recall Freund's description of the making of *The Last Laugh*), and even as one ought to think of Griffith *and* Bitzer, so must one associate Eisenstein and Tisse, Dovzhenko and Vassily. Without these equally brilliant cinematographers, the films would not have been possible. It was truly a collective and creative process.

Never given wide distribution in America, Soviet films did leave the industry, critics, and others interested in the film's development with memorable filmgoing experiences, its history mightily enriched. Unfortunately, these exciting and positive events were now tempered by another dimension. Compromise was a way of life in Hollywood. Germans faced limits in their situations, and so did the Soviets. If it had not been for a production manager's sympathy for Eisenstein's vision, last-minute changes would not have been allowed. A studio official trusted Pudovkin enough to force cooperation out of a bureaucratic bookkeeping department. Eisenstein, returning from the abortive *Que Viva Mexico* project, undertaken through funds raised by the Upton Sinclairs (and a story in itself), found himself in a dangerous position under the repressive demands for Socialist Realism imposed by a new head of state, Josef Stalin. One did not know from one minute to the next what points of view were to be perceived as heresy or truth.

Eisenstein died in his forties, frustrated and embittered. Vertov was to say of himself, "The tragedy of Vertov is that he didn't know how to grow old." Before he died in 1956, Dovzhenko was to mourn,

> Our art is dull, humdrum, and uninspired primarily because the artists stand cold and indifferent on the same level with the facts and subjects of their work.
> The high mental plateau, the loftiness and clarity of the artist's vision, and the profundity of his world-view, formed by a thirty-year-old energy, have given way to the narrow-minded speculations in realism and indifference of petty reptiles who lack ideas and principles.
> There is no love; there is no passion.

But for a time there was, as Eisenstein said, a time for artistic expression free from the ruts of the past and intentionally avoiding the cheap and easy, a time for "the expression of new thoughts, new ideas, new feelings and new words for a new era."

The German films seemed hypnotized by their own reflections, and the innovation was crushed by goose-stepping hordes; the Soviets lifted the medium into exaltation and celebration of a new order founded on new ideals, but it atrophied in regimentation.

Both movements were born out of chaos; both flamed brightly and long enough to affect the medium fundamentally and permanently; but the conjunction of forces which fostered the movements were soon out of phase, the creative spirit hovering on in search of a new place and a new time, capriciously perhaps, to make more magic happen.

France

While the giant film combines in Germany and the Soviet Union were earning international praise for their remarkable motion pictures, the French were going their own eclectic way. Government resources were not made available. Private patrons were underwriting some unusual work, however, and a number of individuals, mostly from other art media, were picking up cameras to make their own personal explorations.

Small cinema societies and clubs were exhibiting older "classics" and stimulated independent production. There was precious little in the way of mass dreams and popular culture connected with these works. Dadaism, surrealism, impressionism, and poetic naturalism were the root sources of these ideas. These offerings were outrageous, to say the least, and frequently caused riots when shown. Some were censored entirely by the government. The masses wanted heroes and happy endings. The creations of Hollywood would satisfy the masses.

The great French comic, Max Linder, a man whom Chaplin was to refer as *the* master comic, had gone to Hollywood in 1914. And it was appreciation of Chaplin which offered a departure point for the *avant-garde* in France.

One of the trademarks of the French cinema, the chase, could not sustain interest in the years following World War I. For the most part the French industry could not locate the elements which collectively would restore production to prewar levels. In France, too, Hollywood was captivating mass dreams. Beyond the fringes of mass entertainment, however, forces were at work which offered directions for the art film never envisioned by Film d'Art.

Salvadore Dali boasted that his *Un Chien Andalou* (1928) "ruined in a single evening 10 years of pseudo-intellectual postwar advance-guardism." Cocteau referred to his work, such as *The Blood of a Poet* (1930), as "cinematographs," quite literally personal statements. Epstein rejected the popular story film, insisting that life offered no stories, but merely presented situations without a beginning, middle, or end. Dulac was not interested in human forms at all, concentrating rather upon motion studies, inanimate objects, machines. Impulse rather than discipline and analysis marks their visions.

The Paris milieu of the 1920's encouraged experimentation. An influx of writers, artists, philosophers, and hangers-on—expatriates all—provided an atmosphere conducive to revolt and discovery. One film project is said to have involved seventeen nationalities. Both functions and manipulations of the medium were challenged, and it was proven that the resources of vast studios were not essential for production, technology having made it possible for anyone to run film through a camera.

Louis Delluc was a writer who turned to the cinema. For years he had advocated a pure cinematic style free from past conventions established by Griffith. Subsequent and rampant imitation of German and Soviet styles appalled him. He and his followers returned to the life experiences of the masses, choosing romantic themes for the substance of his impressionistic camera. *Fièvre* (1921) is such an example, a film where a single flower on a bar-top signifies a beauty and sensitivity beyond the reach of a woman caught within an environment beyond her control.

In Germany, Hans Richter had rejected the human form for studies into the nature of the camera, lenses, exposures, forms, rhythms, motion, and animation. As an abstract painter he was fascinated by options offered by the medium of film which were impossible on the static canvas. *Rhythmus 21* (1921) and *Film-studie* (1926) suggest the nature of his work. Back in France, Fernand Léger applied a cubist approach to motion and light in his *Ballet Mécanique* (1925). Ballerinas dance up and down in slow motion on top of the camera lens; gears and levers are synchronized through angle and cutting to produce a cubist symphony of forms in motion.

René Clair, always with the most delightful sense of humor, took his departure point from the Dadaists. *The Crazy Ray* (1923) revels in a sense of the absurd. A mysterious ray has frozen motion and time, leaving the people of Paris caught in their various activities, from romance to picking pockets. When the crazy scientist is convinced to restore motion to life, natural pace is altered, and life picks up, first absurdly fast and then slow. Clair's *Entr'acte* (1924) makes sport of the funeral as a societal convention. The procession speeds in madcap fashion to the cemetery, the mourners wearing white and eating the decorations from the hearse; a camel and a legless man rolling along in a cart from which he leaps to run on his own legs in Laurel and Hardy style; the frenzied chase ending Méliès-fashion as the funeral director makes everyone vanish with his magic wand, including, finally, even himself.

These sight gags, sense of the ridiculous, and lofty characters reduced to common foolery all inhabit *The Italian Straw Hat* (1927). Mistaken identities, articles of clothing which will not stay in place, a wedding ceremony threatened by the loss of a woman's straw hat, revealed philanderings and the like create wonderful comedy. In much the same way as Chaplin had reduced the best laid plans of the upper classes, so had Clair delighted in the foibles common to all humanity. The fantasy, mischief and whimsy of Méliès was reaffirmed.

While the avant-gardists were at work, the French industry was continuing to supply the national market. Other experiments were also underway. Abel Gance, for instance, revived earlier attempts at 360-degree projection, but modified the idea to what he called the triptych screen, something like Montreal's split-screen exhibitions at the 1967 World's Fair. *Napoleon* (1925) might be called a precursor of Cinerama. The wide screen was sometimes a single panoramic scene, sometimes three individual scenes. The approach enabled Gance to play with images, utilizing perhaps the middle scene as a symbol for the other two.

Eisenstein had complained about being forced to employ a single frame, wishing for not only Gance's system, but also to determine aspect ratio on the basis of the visual material. Gance's screen technique was modified just a few years later by Fox, a wide-screen process called Magnascope. Hollywood was not to pursue the idea, however, until compelled by the competition from television in the early 1950's.

Meanwhile, the surrealists were taking the experimental stage as Luis Buñuel from Spain and the controversial Salvadore Dali combined forces to create *Un Chien Andalou* (1928). Once

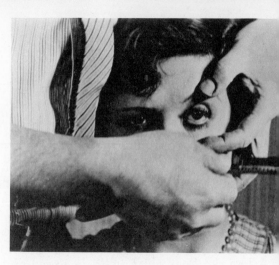

again the story film was renounced as images surfaced from the subconscious. Screams can still be heard as the knife slices across the woman's eyeball (actually a donkey's, it is rumored). Buñuel's *L'Age d'Or* (1930) lashed out in acid images at political and Roman Catholic institutions. Reaction was so strong that the government removed the film from exhibition.

Jacques Feyder drew strong reaction to some of his work, although he shared little in common with the extremists. Like Delluc, he made films closer to the mainstream of everyday life, such as his *Les Nouveaux Messieurs* (1929). His sense of comedy, similar to Clair's, infused simple vignettes of everyday life. But he was caustic when dealing with institutions. *Messieurs* was banned by the government because of his substitution in one scene of court judges with their mistresses. Looking at his films is to be reminded of Chaplin's treatments of the common man in the hands of the power structure.

Jean Cocteau was able to gain the patronage of the Vicomte and Vicomtesse de Noailles. *The Blood of a Poet* (1930) was the result. His patrons finding themselves and their friends a part of his personal mythological and aesthetic analysis, he was cut off from their resources. It remains a fascinating document of the man, Cocteau, and a model for generations of similar personal explorations in film.

What these French filmmakers did with film had little impact on either mass audiences or the mass entertainment industry. But they established a new kind of film movement, one which was to spread to other countries: the experimental, or underground, cinema. The American, Man Ray, was part of that French movement from the beginning; his *Return to Reason* (1923) spawned a riot among the French viewers. But his counterparts in America were learning from these experiments. After the Second World War the underground cinema was alive and strong even in America. They were to learn what Vertov had shown with his *Man With a Movie Camera* (1928): the potential for meaning is almost limitless. When the intention is not merely to tell a story, but to explore the meaning of images drawn either, as Vertov did, from the surfaces of reality surrounding one, or as the French did, with images conjured from the subconscious, anything can happen.

Scandinavia

Many Scandinavian films had been shown to American audiences by 1910. But by the 1920's production had declined and only a few titles were screened in the United States. An industry which had been a significant force in the days of more simple mass entertainment had been absorbed by Germany's Ufa organization. Hollywood attracted others, notably Sweden's directors Victor Sjöstrom and Mauritz Stiller, the latter bringing along two of his most famous stars, Lars Hanson and a young woman by the name of Greta Garbo.

The Danish actress Asta Neilsen performed brilliantly in her last Danish film, *Toward the Light* (1918), and then joined other Danes already at work in German studios. Hers was an acting style which was later to be identified as appropriate to the screen —simple, spare, natural. Scandinavian technicians had earlier demonstrated the functions of shadows and focus by means of lighting control, techniques which were being copied by the Germans.

One of Garbo's last films in Sweden was *The Story of Gösta Berling* (1924). As the rather innocent wife of a repressed, prudish, and emotionally stunted aristocrat, Garbo's Countess Elizabeth Dohna captured world attention. She had the star quality, the "it" presence, the mystery of gesture and facial expression which fired dreams.

In theme *Berling* fits within the Scandinavian tradition, a preoccupation with the attitudes of Kirkegaard, Ibsen and Strindberg, a tradition from which Ingmar Bergman was to develop thirty years later.

Reverend Berling is a man on fire, full of passions and emotions which conflict with society's laws and conventions. As an alcoholic he is defrocked, and he alternates between extremes of behavior, unable to find motives for a life gone sour. It is Garbo who lifts him from the abyss—and thousands who viewed the film. And yet it is not a formula film. An undercurrent of modern *angst* pervades the story. Social conventions no longer serving modern needs, barren religious puritanism, psychological ills, and primitive superstitions pervade this work through which absurd formulations lurk in the shadows. With their similar backgrounds and traditions, it was fitting perhaps that Neilsen from Denmark and Garbo from Sweden should be featured in G. W. Pabst's German *Joyless Street* (1925).

If the international co-production was to mark the 1960's, then the pattern was merely a repeat of the 1920's. In 1928, Carl Dreyer, originally from Denmark, but soon working for Ufa, made *The Passion of Joan of Arc*—in France. The picture was designed by Hermann Warm of *Caligari* fame, photographed by Poland's Rudolph Mate, and featured the Italian actress Falconetti as Joan.

International audiences were deeply affected by this work. The camera recorded probably the largest collection of remarkable compositions ever assembled in a motion picture, and the film remains lasting testament to the power of the silent screen. If actress Falconetti was so drained by the experience that she never appeared in a motion picture again, American audiences were similarly devastated. The picture was banned in Britain because of the effectiveness and pathos built into the final sequence as the flames and smoke consume the body of the French maid. Wrote Mordaunt Hall in the *New York Times,*

> When one leaves the theatre the face of that peasant girl with all its soulfulness appears to leap from one to another in the throng. Long afterward you think of the tears welling from the eyes, of the faith that seemed to stay any suggestion of attrition. . . . [As] the smoke streaks up birds are seen in the heavens.

Summary

The upheavals of the 1920's produced one of the most fascinating periods in film history. Concepts of the nature of film were shaken and potentials for artistic manipulation of the medium were forever enriched. And what a period of international cross-fertilization! Buñuel, from Spain, working in France; Feyder, born in Belgium, working in Hollywood and in France; Dreyer, from Denmark, working in Germany and France; Robison and Man Ray, from the United States, working in France; Eisenstein's abortive attempts in America and Mexico—a continuous interchange of directors, technicians, and actors throughout the filmmaking world. The serious cinema finally tapped the resources of the other arts, and intentions other than mass entertainment carved new territory on the film landscape.

Always the initial intention of the filmmaker figures in the work, sometimes unconsciously, perhaps: from the foreboding intimations from Germany, the powerful constructions from the Soviet Union, and the careful experiments and wild French abandon represented by the *avant-garde*. Unique factors were at work within these societies impelling the medium toward the diverse expressions of revelation.

Always there were the fires of passion, and sometimes of love, which poured forth from the individual and collective visions. And always there were oppressive reactions, policies and pressures which got in the way of the makers' purposes. As the intensity of the period came to a close, the new factor of sound was to cause new responses and generate new problems. But the times had changed. Not until after another world war would movements with the intensity of the 1920's emerge again from Europe. For the next decade contributions to the growth and development of the medium would come from a few individuals whose vision was able to transcend the economic collapse and political terror appearing on the horizon.

European Profile

Year	Germany	Soviet Union	France
1919	Caligari, Wiene		
1920	The Golem, Wegener, Boese		
1921	Destiny, Lang Rhythmus 21, Richter, Eggeling		Fièvre, Delluc
1922	Dr. Mabuse, Lang Nosferatu, Murnau Warning Shadows, Robison		
1923	The Street, Grune		The Crazy Ray, Clair Return to Reason, Ray
1924	Siegfried, Lang Waxworks, Leni The Last Laugh, Murnau	Strike, Eisenstein	Entr'acte, Clair Ballet Mécanique, Léger
1925	Variety, Dupont Joyless Street, Pabst	Potemkin, Eisenstein	Napoleon, Gance
1926	Faust, Murnau Filmstudie, Richter	Mother, Pudovkin	
1927	Metropolis, Lang	St. Petersburg, Pudovkin	The Italian Straw Hat, Clair
1928		October, Eisenstein Storm Over Asia, Pudovkin	Joan of Arc, Dreyer Un Chien Andalou, Dali, Buñuel
1929		Man With a Movie Camera, Vertov Arsenal, Dovzhenko The Old and the New, Eisenstein	Les Nouveaux Messieurs, Feyder Sous les Toits de Paris, Clair (sound elements integrated)
1930	Blue Angel, von Sternberg, imported from U.S. (sound elements integrated)	Earth, Dovzhenko	L'Age d'Or, Buñuel The Blood of a Poet, Cocteau Le Million, Clair
1931	M, Lang		
1932			
1933		Deserter, Pudovkin (sound technology now available)	

Evolution in Form and Function

The Many Faces of Film

The original functions of film had little to do with art. Pioneers like Edison and Lumière were interested in technological challenge. Early producers found film lucrative business and filmmakers saw that the properties of motion pictures provided them with a unique means for both story construction and dream building long before anyone bothered to question aesthetic validity.

In the history of the early years of motion pictures, so much attention has been focused on the technological aspects that the extent to which the film medium satisfied the needs and aspirations of both the artists creating films and the viewing public is often neglected.

From the beginning, films were undertaking a variety of functions which were disparate, overlapping, and at times even contradictory. With films, as with other media and art forms, function became closely bound to the properties and qualities peculiar to the particular medium. Film, it was quickly discovered, had a unique potential in the recording and representation of real and realistic events. The screen's ability to record such events, to recreate works originally produced in other arts and media, and even its potential for original storytelling with an agreeable sense of realism, had been recognized and explored by the time the medium was a decade old. The possibilities it

167

offered for fantasy and dream building were discovered even earlier.

What began to develop within the first years of film production were two major avenues or approaches to the use of the medium: the recording function, which embraced the nonnarrative forms of newsreel, instructional films, and documentary; and the creative or revealing function, associated with the narrative and experimental genres. Though such groupings may be helpful in understanding the medium and its artistic potential, they tend to affix labels to film which deny the complexity and intermingling of functions. Thus, the newsreel is seldom thought of as either creative or entertaining, an escapist romp is given little attention as significant social comment, and the "message picture," though good for the soul, provides little pleasure.

Probably the least complex type of film, in terms of function, was the newsreel. Exploiting the medium's unique affinity for photographic realism, it provided a visual record of history in the making. Queen Victoria's diamond jubilee and funeral, the San Francisco earthquake, the Spanish-American, Russo-Japanese and Boer wars, as well as the "Great War," Chaplin's homecoming in London, the death of Valentino and Lindbergh's flight— all these and many more form an historical legacy on film.

But even these straight records went beyond simple documentation and began to reveal attitudes, preoccupations, and even obsessions of the time. It was the tendency of the British newsreel to turn to activities of royalty and of the French to Paris fashions when headline events slackened. Military reviews and maneuvers became increasingly prevalent as nations braced for war, and once engaged in conflict, there followed a great outpouring of campaign films. The motivation here clearly went beyond simple documentation. Films produced by major American companies to cover the Spanish-American war were not only strongly editorial, they also consisted in part or whole of rousing battles filmed in the studio. Most involved ground skirmishes which invariably ended with American troops overrunning an enemy position and carrying the American flag to a Cuban hilltop. *Advance of Kansas Volunteers at Caloocan,* produced by the Edison Company in 1899, was a brief "news event" showing the advance of American soldiers in the Philippines. When a soldier carrying the American flag is shot, another picks up the standard. The Russo-Japanese war was likewise covered by the major studios, with the naval battle (*Attack on Port Arthur—* Selig, 1904, *Battle of Chemulpo Bay—*Edison, 1904) and ground

skirmish (*The Battle of the Yalu*—Biograph, 1904) followed by
the stock ending of Japanese flag raising. Even with the lines
between the "story film" and the "film of fact" becoming more
clearly drawn, the newsreel continued to serve as more than
historical record. By the First World War, it was becoming
recognized as an important propaganda tool.

The documentary, an offspring and elaboration of the newsreel, likewise became a multipurpose genre. Its evolution is
discussed in chapters 10 and 14, but even a cursory glance at the
genre reveals that its potential for dramatic involvement and
narrative progression was soon recognized and continually explored. As well as revealing and interpreting facts, it could
inspire, provoke, and certainly reflect the disposition of both
filmmaker and audience to events and ideas of the time.

The so-called experimental film presents an especially difficult problem in terms of identifying function. At the very heart
of the experimental tradition is the attempt to extend the possibilities and range of the medium in terms of both structure and
content, and although attention tends to be focused on form and
innovations in cinematic technique, the messages of such films
often go beyond their architecture and indeed beyond the purpose intended by the filmmaker. As mentioned earlier, the announced purpose of *Un Chien Andalou* was "to destroy in a
single evening ten years of pseudo-intellectual post-war avant-
gardism." The variety of ways in which critics have attacked this
work suggest its wider role.

But just as the narrative film has been the more dominant
form, so it presents the most complex and in many respects the
more interesting study of multiple and often conflicting functions. It is here that the influence of other arts is most clearly
at work, it is here that social concerns can be elaborated on and
given dramatic dress, and it is here that the profit motive exerts
its strongest influence. So the history of the silent photoplay, as
it was being produced by the American industry* reflects the
often conflicting motivations of producer, filmmaker, and viewing public.

The quest of the director might be to represent an original
dramatic incident or one borrowed from a stage or literary work,
striving for that elusive quality—screen realism. The producer,
conscious of both cost accounting and audience disposition, was
dedicated to efficient dreambuilding. And the audience voiced,

---

*Foreign features present a somewhat different picture but represent only 10
to 20 percent of world production during the silent era.

by means of patronage, its own satisfaction with the dream and the fulfillment of its positive values.

Much of the early realism of the screen drama was in physical detail. The use of exteriors in Porter's *The Great Train Robbery* and Griffith's faithful reconstruction of key Civil War events in *The Birth of a Nation* were major attractions of these films. Social realism, the representation of contemporary social thought, the reflection of attitudes toward human behavior, and the mores and institutions which guide and support a civilized existence, also found expression in early silent films. Méliès' spoof of scientific thought and Porter's indictment of American jurisprudence in *Kleptomaniac* are good illustrations. Even the earliest of Edison and Lumière comic routines inadvertently, if not intentionally, say something of attitudes and values. Screen realism, however one chooses to define that term, had its roots in the earliest of motion pictures.

Dreambuilding, Cinemorality, and the Formula Film

Two other motivating factors were also at work from the very beginning and became increasingly important as motion pictures became a major industry; these were production demands and the demands, or at least what were thought to be the demands, of audiences. This critical role for film might be summed up with the term *efficient dreambuilding. Efficient* meant meeting production demands of cost and time while developing an intelligible visual narrative within the prescribed single-, double- or multi-reel length. *Dreambuilding* meant satisfying audiences' appetite for formula structure in comedy and melodrama with accepted standards of moral and philosophic thought.

These combined requirements of the industry, the medium, and the viewing public quickly brought about a kind of standardization and formula method of filmmaking that was to have a profound effect not only on film structure and style, but on what film had to say about the world it represented. Throughout the first decade and on into the Teens and Twenties, the key ingredients for efficient dreambuilding were being discovered, proven, and made a permanent fixture in the majority of films. It began with motion, at first any kind of motion; then the motion of the chase proved a most durable kind of film fare. From this developed the chase with Western setting, from which sprang the Western star vehicle. By the time William S. Hart was emerging as a hero of the frontier, so was the formula of the Western hero being carefully set to fit the basic framework of the melodrama. With minor variation the Western hero was endowed with key physical and moral attributes which served both the style of drama and the expectations of fans. Agility, particularly in the handling of firearms, resourcefulness in finding water, lost cattle, or the villain, and endurance to fatigue and pain were basic requirements. In terms of personality and moral stature, the hero showed particular kindness to old people and animals, tended to be shy with women, and was unshakable in his sense of justice and loyalty. His strength of character was made the more appealing by the fact that his past was in some way blemished (reformed outlaw) or his personal code was not completely revealed. Other characteristics of the Western formula further reinforced efficient visual storytelling while providing the appeal of the open and unregimented life far removed from the convention-bound existence of the city dweller.

The evolution of the Western is used here to illustrate the way the formula film developed, because of its distinctness and popularity. Basically, the same kind of standardization occurred with non-Western melodramas and indeed with comedy as well. The comic chase provided the perfect kind of routine for the deflation or upsetting of pomposity and petty authority. Once again the affinities of the medium were being explored and audiences were being satisfied with slightly irreverent fun.

It is the melodrama, however, in both the Eastern and Western setting that best illustrates the flourishing formulas for dreambuilding and cinemorality. The prestige and popularity afforded comedy in the Teens and Twenties tends to obscure the fact that the preponderance of American films being produced were still melodramas. They had proven their durability and were still the popular art form of the masses. Mind-boggling plot complications notwithstanding, they were the essence of simplicity in terms of characterization, motivation, and general attitude. They evolved from surprisingly few key situations and could, with the simplest of modifications, be ground out easily to meet heavy production schedules. Themes which proved particularly popular could be repeated again and again with the slightest change of location, season of the year, or nationality of its characters.

Iris Barry in *Let's Go to the Pictures* provides an interesting sampling of the kind of standardization and rounding off that occurred in silent screen drama. She begins by pointing out that everybody is always doing something in films and goes on to suggest that husbands and wives, no matter the motivation for marriage, must fall in love by the end of the film; however poor a workingman hero, he will be rich by the end of the film; rich people are never seen at home except at mealtime; women are either young girls or grey-haired matrons; only wild women smoke; unchaste women are either frail or involved in a great love affair; fallen women are usually foreign.*

To keep the narrative simple (a requisite of production crews and a comfort to most viewers) meant reducing all variables to their lowest common denominator. It was a great game of rounding off fractions. East was East, West was West, heroes wore white, villains wore black, Irish women took in washing, Jews ran pawnshops, Indians were either on the warpath or if peaceable, were ultimately goaded into action by the villain's gift of firewater and firearms. It was no more possible to be a little bit good, a little bit perverse, or a little bit Italian than a woman can be a little bit pregnant. This rounding off to the nearest whole number was naturally in favor of reinforcing stereotypes and casting off unwieldy, unpopular, and taboo or otherwise uncomfortable subjects. The effects of the formula, in addition to perpetuating film's own simplistic vision of manners and morals in general, was establishing and reinforcing stereotypical patterns of thought and behavior in specific circumstances for specific character types. Thus developed not only movies' own code of morality, but a record of attitudes expressed (or as significant, omitted) on a great variety of social issues. The extent to which film began to seriously reflect social thought and examine specific social issues depended upon which of three general categories the film or part thereof fell—incidental, gratuitous, or exploratory.

Incidental social commentary was usually a passing reference to peoples, places, and times in order to give some dimension, space or time fix to the film, or to otherwise embellish or refine the setting. Thus a South Seas island, a Union Civil War camp or a Chinatown opium den during the Tong wars might provide the appropriately exotic, heroic, or sinister social milieu in which the story could thrive. Though it might appear to have

*Iris Barry, "Conventions and Morals," in *Let's Go to the Pictures*, London: Chatto and Windus, 1926.

little social reference and be simply a matter of visual backdrop, such choices of setting could, because of the need to generalize and simplify, express stereotyped impressions of people and events as well as locations. The choice of a New York tenement for a setting might well reinforce an oversimplified image of the Irish immigrant and give a film an appropriately humble setting. And the presence of a doting black servant was ultimately doing more than establishing the affluence and cozy comforts of the Southern plantation.

Gratuitous social commentary was more than social dressing. Here social conditions and conflicts were used to trigger or "enrich" the conflict of the drama, but never undertook to seriously examine the conditions or their causes directly. The social condition was simply plugged into the formula as an acceptable factor affecting the twists and turns of plot, with the focus finally being an acceptable resolution of the plot line rather than any discovery of the nature of human weakness and want. The films here are legion. The Western once again provides the perfect example of exploitation or gratuitous social comment. With the need for conflict and some means by which the Western hero could prove his gallantry, filmmakers found the menacing Redman as the natural adversary. There was little concern for motivation or characterization; it was simply accepted that when a wagon train moved West, it would be besieged by a whooping mass of painted savages who would kill and scalp all the settlers save the heroine, who was taken as hostage or to satisfy the lust of some Indian brave, until the hero (usually the wagon train guide or cavalry officer) came to the rescue. Likewise, it was the corrupt political boss who made life miserable for the aspiring statesman, the Oriental opium smoker who nearly caused the downfall of the heroine, and the lynch mob who made possible the most serviceable of all plot ingredients—the last-minute rescue.

Finally, there was exploratory commentary in which dramatic development was an integral part or outgrowth of social circumstances. Though treatment might be superficial, it involved a conscious attempt to make some realistic observations of social thought and conditions and, at times, even to reinforce or alter existing attitudes and beliefs. The "message picture," as it is popularly called, is represented by many of the classics of the silent screen. Nevertheless, the formula method of filmmaking usually discouraged social commentary that had any dimension, shading, and direction. But it was often those same "auteurs" who were able to find the independence to experiment structurally and stylistically who also could afford to experiment with an added function of film: the direct look at aspects of the real rather than the dream world. In proportion to the over-all output of films, such social documents provided a very small fraction, but where they occurred, they represented the roots of what was to be touted in later decades by many names in a variety of genres, but all of which were a part of social realism in film storytelling.

Celluloid Mirror—Silent Films and Social Issues

It has already been established that under the American system of production particularly, with the formula film generally providing an efficient and popular guide for most filmmakers, there was little opportunity for direct, conscious, and detailed treatment of social issues in the silent story films. This by no means suggests that films were not providing a mirror of the preoccupations, biases, and taboos of both filmmakers and viewers. Not only did screen stereotypes and the kind of cinemorality that evolved from melodrama reflect the prejudices of the time, the abstinence in connection with some issues itself revealed what some of the unmentionables were. The films of the period, even the most pedestrian and silly screenplays with shockingly puerile moral sentiment, were often significant not only for what they did say, but what they chose to ignore about the social order.

Institutional and Public Issues

One of the most pervasive and timeless areas of social concern, which finds expression in the arts as well as politics, regards how our social institutions function or fail to function. Issues related to law, justice, and the penal system, those concerning aid to the young, old, sick, handicapped or disadvantaged, and those dealing with man at work, particularly relations between labor, management and working conditions, were among those that had sufficiently broad application and dramatic potential to be represented in some of the earliest of silent films.

Where films went beyond the incidental or gratuitous reference and focused on the issue itself—capital punishment, prison reform, child welfare, mental illness, the plight of migratory workers—it was sometimes able to make a responsible observation and even a judgment on how the system was working and how the individual related to it. But within the American industry, the formula system favored the uninvolving and simplistic reference.

Capital punishment is a particularly good example of an issue which is both timeless and controversial on the one hand and also excellent plotting material for melodrama on the other. Its appearance on the screen dates back at least to a clip produced by Biograph in 1902 called *Career in Crime*, which shows the electrocution of a man. Throughout silent film can be found scores of crime melodramas, many of which are built around false sentencing and the last-minute rescue. The modern sequence of Griffith's *Intolerance* is the classic example, but there are many others which use such miscarriage of justice as a plot device with no pretense of examining the problem itself. Occasionally, circumstances surrounding the execution or near execution are bizarre. In DeMille's 1927 film *The Forbidden Woman*, Zita is allowed to be executed as a spy as two brothers who have both loved her look on. In *The Daring Years* (1923), it is the combination of last-minute confession and a power failure that saves the innocent; and in *The Last Hour* (1923), it is a malfunction at the gallows. There are few films that get beyond such machinations. A notable exception is a 1935 film, *Capital Punishment*, which was taken from a B. P. Schulberg story of a man who, after a vain attempt to save an innocent man from execution, plots a fictitious murder with a friend in order to discredit capital punishment. The hoax very nearly sends the friend to his death. *Legally Dead*, produced by Universal Pictures in 1923, also managed both to make its point and throw in the plot twist as well. Here a newspaper reporter gets himself arrested so that he can interview inmates to support his theory that most victims of capital punishment are innocent. He is later wrongfully convicted of a murder and is executed, declared legally dead but . . . restored to life by a shot of adrenalin.

Lynching, like the legal execution of criminals, was a popular plot device in many Westerns, in which the innocent was rescued from the rope by the timely arrival of the posse. It was very often the villain who incited the lynch mob; and the escape, when not accomplished by the posse, was aided by the efforts of the village idiot or a Mexican child. In one instance an irate Irish washwoman with rolling pin in hand, stopped the lynch mob. It was not until Paramount's *The Virginian* (1929), directed by Victor Fleming, that the subject was treated with something that suggests an emotional commitment (Gary Cooper is forced to supervise the hanging of his friend who has been caught cattle rustling), and not until *The Ox-Bow Incident* (1942) that it became a cause.

Matters of prison conditions and the need for reform likewise did not receive very serious consideration until the 1930 sound film *The Big House*, though as early as 1903, Biograph showed a prisoner being accosted, tied, and whipped by two prison guards in *A Convict's Punishment*. Cruel wardens were convenient heavies and wretched prison conditions helped to supply motivation for a dramatic escape attempt, but films which dealt with the penal system as an issue were rare. Thomas Mott Osborne, a former warden of Sing Sing Prison produced one in 1921. Titled *The Right Way*, it told the story of two boys who became members of a "Mutual Welfare League," a prisoners' organization which attempted to save prisoners from execution.

Sparrows (1926). Mary Pickford's valiant rescue of mistreated orphans in a southern swamp.
MUSEUM OF MODERN ART/FILM STILLS ARCHIVE

For its time, Porter's *The Ex-Convict* (1907) was a rare example of exploring the problems facing the person with a prison record, but serious and central focus on the issue was scant until Mervyn LeRoy's *I Am a Fugitive from a Chain Gang* in 1931.

Issues related to child labor and child welfare were represented by Mary Pickford's 1926 *Sparrows*, made for United Artists, in which a farm for unwanted children in the Southern swamps is run by a brutal family that mistreats and starves its charges. Though hardly a tough look at the issue of child abuse, it at least escapes the romantic image of many screen waifs. The assorted breeds of abandoned and orphaned children were usually depicted as tenacious street urchins (*The Heart of a Waif* [1915] and *The Gutter-Snipe* [1915]), true to the spirit of Dickens. Often they straightened out predicaments of their elders and were especially adept at sparking romance, as in DeMille's *Let 'er Go Gallegher* (1928), in which a waif helps her friend, a reporter, to capture a notorious criminal and save his romance. Chaplin's *The Kid* (1921) is, of course, the darling of the genre.

The old, like the young, fell into stereotyped patterns. Until Warner Brothers' 1930 sound feature, *Old English*, based on a John Galsworthy work, there was little direct focus on the problems of age. Comedy seems to come the closest as in the Paramount film *Welcome Home* (1925), which was based on a Kaufman and Ferber play and directed by James Cruze. This is the now oft-repeated tale of the old man who moves in with son and daughter-in-law and causes strains, until he decides to join his cronies in a home for the aged when the daughter-in-law becomes pregnant.

A 1929 comedy, *Skinner's Big Deal*, concerns a junior partner's plan to rejuvenate the elderly employees whom the senior partners have instructed him to fire. Geriatrics too was designed to satisfy the formula and the dream.

Problems of mental illness, particularly insanity, were so exploited in the earliest of silent comedies as well as dramas that the composite screen image of the disturbed individual is a well stereotyped and grotesque one. The American Mutoscope and Biograph Company, as early as 1904, in *The Escaped Lunatic*, was finding the comic chase potential in the mental institution, where an inmate thinks he is Napoleon. The topic was fair game even for such comic stars as Harold Lloyd, who in a Hal Roach film entitled *Doctor Jack* (1922), portrays a doctor who cheers up a despondent girl by acting like an escaped lunatic. In *The Lunatic at Large*, made by First National in 1927, most of the farcical action takes place on the grounds of a private sanitarium for the wealthy. This tendency toward affluence on the part of the insane seems to suggest a belief that the subject could not be offensive if the inmates were well-heeled.

In melodramas, the nervous breakdown or temporary insanity provided convenient plot devices. Causes ranged from mental cruelty to Chinese water torture, but in the case of the mad scientist no explanation seemed necessary. Halfwits were convenient for taking murder raps and otherwise helping work out the plot without risk of protestation. Insanity began to appear with some regularity in Gothic horror pieces, such as Metro's *The Monster* (1925), which starred Lon Chaney, *The Cat and the Canary* (1927), and *The House of Secrets* (1929). Some sobriety and distinction if not exploration of the subject came with Victor Sjöstrom's *The Tower of Lies* in 1926.

Poverty was a major ingredient of melodrama and even romantic fantasy, *The Prince and the Pauper* and *The Little Match Girl* having paved the way. The real-life and contemporary problems of the city poor—the slum dwellers, and the country poor—the tenant farmers and migratory workers, received little serious attention. However, Griffith's *The Musketeers of Pig Alley* (1912) was something of a pioneer work in the field. With much of its footage shot in New York city streets, it emphasized the milieu of the city slum and the effects on its people. *Means and Morals*, produced by Essanay in 1915, dramatized young people's moral lapses when faced with a life of poverty, and the same studio's *The Rose of Italy* (1916) depicted the dangers that confront an immigrant girl from Little Italy at the hands of an ex-Mafia member who is himself being hunted by members of the organization. More films on the topic tended toward *Sally in Our Alley* (1927), in which a tenement orphan who is adopted by three neighbors—a Scotsman, an Italian and a Jew—is later taken away to the home of a wealthy aunt who almost succeeds in teaching her snobbery and embarrassment toward her old friends.

The plight of the immigrant, though not seriously explored in early films, seemed to be more than a plot convenience in the 1921 film *The Land of Hope*. It deals with a Polish immigrant who is unable to continue his education and is forced to the breadlines. Even here, though, the upbeat ending is provided when he finds his dream of a home for immigrants realized through the help of a wealthy philanthropist. Thomas Ince's *The*

Italian (1915) may well remain the most honest and realistic treatment of the subject in silent film.

There seems to be virtually no recognition of the tenant farmer until King Vidor's *Hallelujah* in 1929 and the obscure 1930 musical *Georgia Rose*. Though Griffith had made something of a beginning in examining problems of the farmer versus big business in *A Corner in Wheat* (1909) and labor, management, and the effects of strikes in the modern sequence of *Intolerance*, there was little follow-up through the following decade. *The New Disciple* (1921) dealt directly with the exploitation of factory workers, strike, mediation, and cooperative ownership using passages from Woodrow Wilson's "The New Freedom." Labor strife was otherwise the by-product of melodrama in which labor agitators were hired to induce workers to strike and otherwise cause trouble for the company bosses.

As for slave labor, it was limited to the slave traders of Africa, China, and the high seas. Sixty years after the war that split the nation over the issue of slavery, there was hardly a film touching the subject. Various screen versions of *Uncle Tom's Cabin* and the United Artists' burlesque of the Stowe characters in *Topsy and Eva* (1927) were exceptions, as was the 1927 *The Love Mart*, directed by George Fitzmaurice. But these hardly constitute exploration of the issue. In the latter, a Southern belle who is accused of having Negro blood is sold as a slave to a young adventurer (Gilbert Roland), who frees and ultimately marries her when her true white lineage is known. Here again the perfect example of social issue in the service of melodrama.

The characterization of the social reformer seems also to get its direction from Griffith's *Intolerance*. As in the modern sequence of that film, social reformers were usually characterized as "do-gooders" of the leisure class who undertook social work as a diversion and were likely to end up doing more harm than good. Their work, however, brought them in contact with long lost friends who had gone astray, or with their own conscience. Related to the "do-gooders" in screen melodrama were the scandalmongers, who were featured prominently in social dramas in which a family skeleton needed exposing.

One film which single-handedly took on the topics of insanity, quack physicians, and venereal disease was the 1924 *TNT– The Naked Truth*. It is a full-length sociological drama about a youth who gets infected with V.D., marries, goes insane, and kills his wife. The film might have been a milestone in social consciousness had it been the product of a commercial studio rather than a public welfare organization.

Private Issues and Taboos

Marital complications and extramarital intrigues were so much a part of silent screen drama that any meaningful arrangement or grouping of these to suggest trends and stereotypical patterns is difficult. What is clear is that even in the prewar and prefeature decades (1895–1915) sex was a popular and very saleable commodity, despite the hanging on of Victorian morals. The bathroom film, for example, which one usually associates with DeMille, probably had its beginning with Méliès' *Après Le Bal—Le Tub* (1897), in which a woman disrobes and steps into her bath assisted by her maid. As she steps out she is wrapped in a towel and then exits from the scene. In *The Bride's First Night* (1898) a bride is shown entering a bedroom, undressing and getting into bed, then being joined by her husband, who begins kissing her. Méliès even recorded the antics of a peeping tom in a hotel corridor in a 1903 clip. Edison's contribution to the risqué if not exotic early films included the famous *Irwin-Rice Kiss* and the censored dance of *Fatima*. With narrative development, designing and sometimes fallen women, and worldly and sometimes depraved men became very much a part of screen melodrama. Their function was to provide the evil influence and keep the innocent, like Mary Pickford, Robert Harron, Mae Marsh, Richard Barthelmess, and the Gish sisters, in moral danger and generally keep the plot brewing; their presence was usually non-erotic, however.

The Twenties brought with them a more liberal and sophisticated treatment of sex-related topics and with the appearance of Theda Bara and Rudolph Valentino, the term exotic could certainly now apply.

In spite of liberation and sophistication, particularly in the works of DeMille, sex issues did not come under serious examination during the decade, and under the influence of the Hays Office many subjects remained distinctly taboo. Infidelity was second to none in dramatic complications of films of the late Teens and Twenties and with the arrival of the vamp (*A Fool There Was*, 1915), even healthy marriages were in jeopardy. But despite all of the extramarital hijinks that were constantly being paraded, common-law marriages were rarely shown and mixed marriages, with the exception of the ever popular *Abie's Irish Rose*, were few. Miscegenation, when it was treated, was almost always in the past tense, in terms of the sins of the father. It was a taboo subject which could serve as a plot device or reinforce characterization—in *The Wise Virgin* (1924), the villain, it is revealed, had a Burmese mother—but it could never come under very careful examination as a social issue.

Divorce was a constantly reappearing theme or *Popular Sin* as it was called in a 1926 Paramount film which starred Florence Vidor. Pressures from the Hays Office, however, restrained major companies from frivolous treatment without retribution, or the more common resolution, reconciliation. Mate swapping, though suggested by some titles, turned out to be the innocent fun of romantic comedies. Prostitution was a frequent and accepted plot ingredient as long as it was properly condemned.

Sex-related topics which were even further buried among the array of plot devices, if not completely skirted, included abortion, incest, rape, and sexual perversion. Abortion was rarely suggested and when it was, only as a thought, a bad dream, or the act of a completely depraved woman. In *The Road to Ruin* (1928), Sally begins with liquor and cigarettes, graduates to a love affair with an older man, and after becoming pregnant, has an abortion, and finally dies of shock when she finds she is paired off in a whorehouse with her own father. Incest, as this synopsis might suggest, was a good plot device; the last-minute discovery of the true relationship of a pair of lovers would either avert the union or make it legal, and viewers could be appropriately repelled and titillated by the anticipation. But incest was much too delicate a topic to be used often, even when properly condemned. Rape also occurs in a surprisingly small number of films. When it is treated, it is in the past tense or like incest is anticipatory and averted by the last-minute rescue. Sexual perversion or any deviant sexual behavior simply did not exist either in act or thought in films produced for general release.

Other "clinical" topics, such as childbirth, pregnancy, frigidity, venereal disease, or sex instruction, generally were recognized but usually shrouded in mystery. Even nudity, which became fashionable and was permissible when discreetly concealed, was reserved for the *femme fatale;* there was seldom a suggestion otherwise that a character ever undressed.

Other social evils, such as alcohol and narcotics, which were nonsexual, had wider representation, but fared no better than most other issues in terms of realistic appraisal. The evil of drink was more of a plot requirement or embellishment than meaning-ful focus and though sermonizing was frequent, the film was void of any substantive inquiry. Alcoholism served the necessities of plot in Griffith's *A Drunkard's Reformation* (1909) and *What Drink Did* (1908); it also made a hit of *A Fool There Was* in 1915 and boosted Theda Bara to stardom and vamp status. Reference to narcotics tended to become stereotyped with the smashing of the dope ring responsible for a loved-one's death, a favorite theme. *The Spirit of the Poppy* (1914) was an early attempt to dramatize the effects of drug addiction. In 1923, a flurry of films which approached a more direct and "straight" treatment of the topic were released. *The Drug Traffic* was an independent release which featured the doctor whose despondency leads to drug addiction and death. In *The Great Menace* a district attor-ney's son becomes implicated in drug traffic and murder while investigating the evils of addiction, and in *Human Wreckage*, which was produced by Thomas Ince with the cooperation of the Los Angeles Anti-Narcotics League, a family is driven to ruin through addiction to morphine.

Refinements in style and at least a partial liberation of the libido in the early Twenties was met by public pressures reflect-ing more conservative and traditional mores, which came to bear on film treatment through the Hays Office. These counterforces produced the most bizarre results in films which tended toward the taboo, and yet the very distortions and sidesteps were them-selves reflecting social and psychological stresses of audiences, causing an unrealistic appraisal of social issues within the con-text of screen drama.

Racial Issues

In many respects the most interesting example of how social attitudes and accepted images were used in the service of effi-cient dreambuilding was in the matter of race. Racial stereotypes served the formula film because they provided the necessary trimmings or helped trigger conflict without the need of complex explanation as to motivation—no one need ask why an Indian craved whiskey. Accepted mores regarding relations among the races were also useful plotting material in that they could be used to quickly explain a sudden twist of the story. In *The Red Rider*, made by Universal in 1925, both requirements were met. The Indian chief discovers he is white and gets the girl when the

Indian princess to whom he was originally betrothed offers herself as a sacrifice by taking the white girl's place in a canoe set adrift above a waterfall by the tribe. The taboo of miscegenation and the myth of the Indian princess sacrificing herself for love both help to bind together the tortured narrative, while satisfying the romantic and moral notions of the audience.

The Redman's Way

It goes without saying that the preponderance of silent screenplays that dealt in any way with race were of the incidental or gratuitous variety. In the case of the American Indian, the building and reinforcing of the stereotyped image is particularly significant in that the relative isolation of the Redman from other societies and his constant appearance on the screen gave film a corner in image building.

Stereotyping does not necessarily mean a single image, and the reappearance of Indians in film after film which needed to offer some variation on a theme resulted in some variety of "Redskin" types and situations. The image that most quickly comes to mind is, of course, the whooping savage who threatens the pioneer settlement or wagon train. As early as 1904 the American Mutoscope and Biograph Company had produced a short narrative clip entitled *The Pioneers,* in which a pioneer family is surprised by Indians, the parents slain, and the children captured. The heroes of the drama are a group of trappers who rescue the children and kill the Indians. Biograph and other companies continued through the decade to exploit the Indian massacre theme, resulting in protests from various Indian tribes to the Bureau of Indian Affairs in the period 1908–1912. Whether this had any effect on American filmmakers is questionable, but gradually films appeared which gave some justification for Indians' savage behavior. *A Mohawk's Way,* directed by D. W. Griffith in 1910, showed a white woman treating an Indian child when her doctor husband refuses aid. The settlers' cruelty to Indians later brings on an attack in which the wife is spared while many of the settlers, including the husband, are massacred. In another Biograph film made in 1910, *The Indian Runner's Romance,* the daughter of an Indian chief is abducted by three white men shortly after her marriage to a brave. One of the three, who has won her at gambling, is pursued by her husband, who kills the white man and walks off into the sunset with his squaw. Although many other films of the period showed a more understanding attitude toward the Redman, even to giving him hero status, the massacre continued a favorite theme. Even Griffith, who in 1908 dramatized a chief's rescue of a wounded son from white kidnappers whom he has slain *(The Redman and the Child)*, reverted to the murderous attack on a wagon train in his 1912 *The Massacre*. Half-breed gun smugglers and renegade guides continued popular plot ingredients and Bison's 1913 *Early Days in the West* becomes almost a caricature of the genre. It is the typical story of a Sioux attack on the wagon train and a cavalry rescue, complete with a treacherous Indian guide who kidnaps the daughter of one of the settlers. The Selig one-reel *How Lone Wolf Died* (1914) tells of the renegade whose savagery against the white man leads to a miserable death in the desert. That savage ways could be changed was illustrated in a number of films of the period. In *The Heron Converts* (1916), it is a group of Jesuit Fathers who tame the treacherous Heron tribe and give them religion as well.

The most popular of the stereotypes was not limited to the melodrama potboilers. When feature films of more epic proportions made their appearance, the image of the Indian attack on the defenseless wagon train *(The Covered Wagon,* 1923) and the railroad construction train *(The Iron Horse,* 1924) were further reinforced. Even comedy occasionally made use of the menacing Redskin. A Kalem 1915 short entitled *Ham and the Redskins* featured a comedy team, Ham and Bud, who become Indian fighters. Disguised in war paint, each mistakes the other for an Indian and a fight ensues. As early as 1901 Cecil Hepworth, the British producer, had produced *The Indian Chief and Seidlitz Powder,* in which an Indian Chief swallows a concoction he has prepared in a chemist shop, swells like a balloon, and bursts in a cloud of smoke.

An image of the American Indian which was almost as popular as the scalphunter, and began to flourish early in the development of screen narrative, was that of the noble savage. Favorite themes here included sympathetic accounts of the sacrifices made by chiefs, young braves, and maidens for their own honor and the survival of the tribe. *The Redman's View* (1909) showed the separation of Indian lovers and the death of the girl's father in the advance of the ever-encroaching white man. In *Seminole's Sacrifice* (Selig, 1911), a Seminole tribe is incited to battle with an American garrison by a trader. After their defeat, they are offered amnesty if they will surrender their chief, Red

The Vanishing American (1925). Richard Dix as
Nophaie leaves tribal customs and dress to join his
nation at war.
MUSEUM OF MODERN ART/FILM STILLS ARCHIVE

Jacket. Their refusal leads to the chief's voluntary surrender to
save the tribe. And in Thomas Ince's *Last of the Line* (1914)
Sessue Hayakawa plays the son of Gray Otter, the last of the great
Sioux warriors.

Other sympathetic types that sometimes attained hero status
were grateful Indians eager to return a favor (relationships with
the Northwest Mounted Police were especially amicable), the
faithful Indian companion (which reached stardom with the
Lone Ranger's Tonto), and the selfless sacrifice of the Indian
maiden (often played by Mona Darkfeather, born in Los Angeles
of a Spanish family). Here the trials of the halfbreed *Ramona*
(1928), the heroines of *The Red Rider* (1925), and *The Heart of
Night Wind* (1915) serve as lovely examples. Paramount's *The
Vanishing American* (1924) gives the honor of sacrifice to
Richard Dix, who stars as a Navajo brave who falls in love with
a white schoolteacher, beats an evil Indian agent, warns the
whites of an Indian attack, and dies in the arms of the schoolteacher. But first place should probably go to the heroine of *An
Apache Father's Vengeance* made by Bison in 1912. Here an

Indian girl is dressed up and taken to a dance by some officers' wives. Indians attack the uprotected garrison and when the girl rides to warn the cavalry, she is shot by her own father. The film ends with cavalry soldiers covering her body with the American flag.

By the 1920's another popular image was that of the Indian college graduate whose exposure to white man's ways and women often led to integrated romance. Sensitivity to miscegenation, even with the native Americans, usually resulted in a last-minute change of heart or revelation of true parentage. In *Blazing Arrow* (1922), it is a Columbia student who loses the girl when his Indian identity is revealed and wins her back when it is discovered that he was only adopted by an Indian chief. *The Great Alone* (1922) has as its star a Stanford University football star who is scorned by fellow students because he is a half-breed. He repays the kindness of a white girl by rescuing her, but falls in love with a half-breed girl. First National Pictures made its variation on the theme in 1925 with *The Scarlet West*, in which the son of a chief is rebuked by his people after his Eastern education and joins the cavalry. He falls in love with the commandant's daughter, but eventually gives her up, along with his army commission, to rejoin his people. The most elaborate of the group was doubtless Cecil B. DeMille's offering, *Braveheart*, also made in 1925, in which Rod La Rocque stars as the young brave who goes to an Eastern college to study law and help protect the tribe's fishing rights. He makes All-American playing football and becomes a scholar, but is expelled from college and disgraced by his tribe when he confesses to selling football signals to an opposing team in order to save a friend's reputation. He finally wins back his tribe's respect (and their fishing rights), but denies his love for a white girl and marries an Indian instead.

The popularity of the denouement in these films notwithstanding, interracial relationships and marriage made for effective plot intrigues and were a part of a number of films. DeMille's own first film, *The Squaw Man* (1913), depicted the marriage between an English nobleman and an Indian girl. But such relationships usually resulted in strife for the couple or their half-breed offspring. In Kalem's *The Blackfoot Halfbreed* (1911), a girl returns to her Indian mother when fighting breaks out between Indians and her father's regiment. She is finally rescued by her white fiancée when faced with a forced marriage to the tribe's chief. In *The Flaming Arrow*, produced by Bison in 1913, it is the son of a white man and an Indian woman who returns to Indian life but, caught in the struggle between the races, finally saves the colonel's daughter and defeats the Indians, who have been provided with whiskey by troublemakers. In *Scarlet and Gold* (1925), the tragedy of a mixed union is combined with the theme of the Indian maiden's sacrifice. An Indian girl who is thought near death gives birth to the child of a Canadian Mountie. A friend marries the girl to give the infant a name and the girl recovers but commits suicide later to free her white husband to marry his white sweetheart.

The image of the American Indian in American silent films then was clearly influenced strongly by plot requirements and stereotypes that had already become well established. Collectively they provided the threat to pioneer expansion; individually they triggered personal conflict and interracial intrigues, which were simplistic and exploitative though occasionally reflecting something of the struggle for both races that the coming of the white man produced. Few were the films that attempted an exploration of the internal affairs of the Redman or serious inquiry into the effects of westward expansion. Those that dramatized aspects of Indian life without depending on conflicts with the white man, like Griffith's *The Squaw's Love* (1911), were mainly romantic idylls. Militant racism on an individual and personal level was rare, though given some attention as early as 1912 in *The Vanishing Tribe* and again more elaborately in Universal's *Red Clay,* made in 1927.

In the case of the documentary approach to Indian civilization, motives became suspect, with heroes of the piece ranging from a U. S. Agency to the motion picture industry itself. In 1905, the American Mutoscope and Biograph Company made a series on American Indians under the auspices of the U. S. Department of the Interior, especially for showing at the St. Louis Exposition. An important function was to show work being done by the Bureau of Indian Affairs in educating the Indian. It included a clip described in the Biograph bulletin as "a graceful and interesting drill with American flags by a group of young squaws of the Moqui tribe." And in 1930, with the advantages of sound, Paramount produced *The Silent Enemy,* a "fictional documentary" on the life of the Ojibwa Indian. It featured a prologue by Chief Yellow Robe crediting the white man's civilization with, of all things, preserving Indian traditions via the motion picture.

Uncle Tom and Others

Blacks, like Indians, were very much a part of the film scene from the beginning. Unlike the Redman, however, a popular early role for the black was in a kind of surreal buffoonery of the most exploitative kind. Using white actors in blackface and the trick potential of the camera, a variety of shorts were produced which involved bizarre transformations of blacks to whites and vice-versa. Méliès' *Off to Bloomingdale Asylum* (1902) is the vintage and oft-cited example, but it was only the beginning of an extended series which continued into the Twenties. Another early variation was the British made *The Negro's Revenge* (1906), in which a Negro who has been insulted by a white woman employs two boys to blacken her face while she sleeps so that she is jeered at by people passing by. A soaking by a gardener finally turns her white again. *His Darker Self*, made nearly two decades later, repeats the basic gag:

> Unlucky in love, the despondent Claude tries to enter a cafe for colored people. Turned away, he goes home and blackens his face. Returning, he is admitted and offered a job as target in a knife-throwing act. Forced to flee when he starts to throw the knives back, he hides in a religious meeting on the beach. Thrown into the water to be baptized, he emerges white, to the horror of the rest of the congregation, who flee in terror.

In 1925 Universal produced a series based on "The Gumps" comic strip. One episode involved a pair of black servants turning white in terror when an escaped lion approaches them. Less fantastic, but hardly less demeaning, was the image of the black, not dependent on color change, in comedies. Characterized as shiftless, thieving, or terror-stricken darkies, they reappeared in countless films whose titles alone give insult. *A Nigger in the Woodpile* (1904) ends with two blacks being blown up with their cabin when dynamite is hidden in firewood they have stolen. *The Wooing and Wedding of a Coon* (1905) is described by its producers as "a genuine Ethiopian Comedy," and *Coon Town Suffragettes*, produced by Sigmund Lubin in 1911, shows black "mammies" organizing a movement to keep shiftless husbands out of saloons. *The Chicken Thief*, made by Biograph in 1904, is described by its producers in a film bulletin as follows:

> From the opening of the picture, where the coon with the grinning face is seen devouring fried chicken, to the end where he hangs head down from the ceiling, caught by a bear trap on his leg, the film is one continuous shout of laughter.

It was at the same time that Lubin was producing his *Rastus* and *Sambo* series, slapstick shorts which characterized blacks as complete fools. And even when not characterized as clowns, they were the cause for consternation and chagrin on the part of white men. In *The Masher* (1907), a lady-killer who flirts with a veiled lady runs away in embarrassed shock when he discovers she is black. *A Fool and His Money,* produced by Aolax Film in 1914, is described in a contemporary film guide as "a brilliant comedy featuring James Russell, the American cakewalk king. Acted entirely by niggers."

Such blatant racist humor, though still present, became less evident by the Twenties. The image tended to be that of the good-natured, superstitious servant—Snowball, Excema, Diploma—dedicated to pleasing the mistress or master and perhaps yearning to be just a little bit white. In *Topsy and Eva* (1927), based on the characters from the Stowe novel, Topsy, who has been bought by Little Eva for a nickel, prays, "I won't ask you to make me white as Eva—just a nice light tan will do."

Segregation, like slavery, was virtually ignored by the silent film except for an occasional comedy like *Spyin' the Sky* (1917), a racist romp with action involving a Klan-type group, or Paramount's *The Palm Beach Girl* (1926), in which a farm girl who has been covered with soot is hustled onto a black bus in Palm Beach by a bellhop. What serious treatment of the subject existed was in the form of the trials and tribulations of the girl or boy thought to be a mulatto. In 1926, Paramount produced *Volcano,* with Bebe Daniels as the French girl who is led to believe she is the product of a mixed marriage but wins her lover when she discovers her real white birthright. A more realistic treatment was provided in *Symbol of the Unconquered* (1921), in which a black woman is thrown out of a hotel in a Western town; but it's doubtful that any white audiences saw the film, as it was produced by a black company without general distribution.

In serious films, blacks were generally the faithful darkies of the ante-bellum plantation. When not part of the scenery, they were part of intrigues that involved miscegenation and the woes of mulattos and octoroons. Griffith, who had become central to the issue of the screen's portrayal of blacks with *The Birth of a Nation,* made many other shorts both before and after which were less controversial but which contained stereotype roles of servants and occasionally villains. In what has been suggested as atonement for his earlier racist portrayals, he produced *The Greatest Thing in Life* in 1918, in which a dying Negro is seen crying for his mother. After his death, a white comrade bends over and kisses him. But four years later, in *One Exciting Night,* the Negro was again portrayed by Griffith as the frightened, superstitious, weak-kneed dolt.

By the time the 1914 version of *Uncle Tom's Cabin* went into production, blackface was beginning to give way to black actors and the role of Tom in that film was played by a Negro. Films made by black companies began in 1916 with Lincoln Motion Picture Company, founded by George P. Johnson, and Colored Players Film Corporation in Philadelphia. The films were intended for black audiences, however, and never had general distribution. In 1929, Fox released *Hearts of Dixie*, the first all-Negro production by a major studio. It helped usher in the era of the screen musical and a new role for blacks—that of the song and dance man.

The Cohens and the Kellys

The portrayal of Jews in silent film is virtually one long Jewish-Irish joke. The pattern was set as early as 1903, when Biograph made a short entitled *Levi and Cohen, "The Irish Comedians."* It continued for a quarter of a century, suggesting that just as the Negro's fondest dream was to be white, the aspiration of the Jew was to either marry into a good Irish Catholic family or to have an Irishman as a business partner, or both. In IMP's *Levi and McGinnes Running for Office* (1914), it is a contest for local alderman that brings Patrick, Moshey, and families into conflict.

The cause of Jewish-Irish relations continued to be served by films through the silent era, but was given a special boost in 1924 with the phenomenal success of the Anne Nichols play *Abie's Irish Rose*, which opened in New York that year. Although the screen version was not produced until 1929, with the coming of sound, the success of the play spawned several silent comedies which centered on business and filial relations between Jew and Irishman. Most notable among these was Universal Picture's series which began in 1926 with *The Cohens and the Kellys* and continued into the sound era with the families' escapades in Africa, Paris, Scotland, and Atlantic City. Once the children had been happily married off in the original, the several sequels found the two fathers, now business partners, off to distant lands in search of ivory, plaids, and bathing suits.

First National Pictures, in an attempt to cash in on the success of the series, produced *Sweet Daddies* (1926) and *Flying Romeos* (1928) with Charlie Murray and George Sidney, who had starred in the original series. They play importers in one

The Cohens and the Kellys in Scotland (1930). The Universal Pictures series featured George Sidney and Charlie Murray as business partners, here on a search for Scottish plaids.
MUSEUM OF MODERN ART/FILM STILLS ARCHIVE

film and barbers in love with their manicurist in the other. When other companies saw how successful the First National series had been, they quickly imitated them. Warner Brothers starred George Jessel as *Private Izzy Murphy* (1926). R-C Pictures (under the production guidance of Joseph P. Kennedy) once again focused on the now familiar setting—the apartment over the Jewish delicatessen in New York's lower East side—in *Kosher Kitty Kelly* (1926). And the "Ice Cream Cohens" and the Kellys engaged in both a business feud and the struggle to keep their children apart in *The Shamrock and the Rose* (1927). MGM joined the fun in 1927 with *Frisco Sally Levy*, about the trials of Sally Colleen Lapidowitz, the daughter of Jewish-Irish parents.

After marriage and business partnerships, the next most popular device used to bring the Irishman and Jew together was adoption. It is interesting how many Irish orphans found their way into Jewish homes, while the adoption of Jewish children by Irish families simply did not exist. The cycle also illustrates how a basic theme could be established and then modified just slightly to give it a fresh look. In *Second Hand Rose* (1922), Universal starts the cycle with the adopted Irish daughter of a Jewish family; in First National Pictures' *For the Love of Mike* (1927), the orphan is being reared by two Jewish and one Irish foster fathers; in *A Harp in Hock* (1927), DeMille's entry, an Irish immigrant boy is brought up by a Jewish pawnbroker; in Columbia's *Sweet Rosie O'Grady* (1927), the godfathers are a Jewish pawnbroker and an Irish policeman. And then Columbia tops it off with *Sally in Our Alley* (1927), with the godfathers now being

191

a Scotsman, an Italian, and a Jew. The Jewish-Irish link became so strongly established in comedy and light drama that it affected other genres as well. *His People* (1925), which is otherwise a thoroughly Jewish melodrama, has the Irish ending as Sammy's Irish sweetheart is given the father's blessing. And even in *The Rawhide Kid,* a 1928 Universal Western starring Hoot Gibson, the story centers around the romance between Dennis O'Hara and Jessica Silverberg. The Jewish western, however, goes back at least as far as *The Yiddisher Cowboy,* made in 1915.

Serious screenplays centering on Jews are not numerous from the silent period, even though melodrama was the predominant form. When they do occur, they are not locked into the single-theme syndrome of the comedies, but still perpetuate the myths and stereotypes and virtually ignore anti-Semitism. As with the comedies, Jews were usually stereotyped as regards occupation—they were pawnbrokers, tailors, moneylenders, or proprietors of delicatessens. Conflicts usually involved business crises or family estrangement. Griffith's early entry was *Romance of a Jewess* (1908), in which the daughter of a pawnbroker falls in love with a Gentile bookstore owner. Their marriage brings estrangement between father and daughter and finally reconciliation at the tragic death of the husband. Griffith authored the script for *Old Isaacs the Pawnbroker* the same year, about the kindly Jewish pawnbroker who comes to the aid of a destitute mother and child.

A sympathetic attitude toward Jews continued through the Teens with the plight of Russian Jews becoming a prominent theme by the early Twenties. Discrimination on home ground, however, was not to be given an airing until well into the sound era. Two notable exceptions were *The Woman He Loved* (1922), in which a California rancher shows dislike for a Jewish immigrant who has established a small ranch nearby. With conflicts resolved he finally consents to his daughter's marriage to the Jew's son. In *Welcome Stranger* (1924), a shopkeeper is driven from a small New England town by the mayor, but is later honored by the town when he helps to bring a power plant to the community. Even with serious drama it was still a world of dreams.

From the Orient

The Chinese, like blacks and Indians, were both prominent and multipurpose in the silent screenplay. Biograph's *The Chi-*

nese Rubbernecks (1903), featuring a chase with a Chinese laundryman in pigtails, was joined by *The Yellow Peril* (1908), in which a Chinese servant disrupts a household, is thrown from a window, beaten by a policeman, and set on fire. Griffith's sympathetic treatment of the Chinese laundryman who apprehends the villain and gives the reward money to the hero and his bride (*That Chink at Golden Gulch,* 1910) led in the Teens to a reinforcing of key Oriental types and themes—narcotics pushers and white slaves of the sinister Chinatown setting; Charlie, the good-natured Chinatown tour guide; the exotic world of Mandarin princesses, and assorted house boys and laundry men. *The Mission of Mr. Foo* (1914) was an elaborate Edison production in which Mr. Foo, a lustful and cunning Chinese, plots the overthrow of the Chinese Republic. The portrayal of Chinese as villains and in otherwise demeaning roles was extensive enough to bring formal protests from the Chinese government. At the same time it provided Japanese actor Sessue Hayakawa with the start of a film career in *The Cheat* (1915), *Forbidden Paths* (1917) and *The Tong Man* (1919).

The image was enhanced immeasurably in Griffith's *Broken Blossoms* and then in the Twenties with the star system giving hero status or top billing to Chinese characters played by American actors. Warner Oland turned from his role of sinister Fu Manchu to inscrutable but kindly detective Charlie Chan. Lon Chaney, as *Mr. Wu* (1927), marries the daughter of a Mandarin and takes the life of his own daughter—as custom dictates— when she falls in love with an Englishman. And Constance Talmadge as Ming Toy (*East is West,* 1922) is saved from the auction block by a young American and becomes marriagable when it is discovered that she is white after all, having been kidnapped from American parents as a baby. The favorite Redman theme was perfectly serviceable with a simple change of color.

With the prominent and supporting roles that Chinese played in so many films, it is interesting that there is virtually no use of Japanese types in silent films save the resurrection of the Madame Butterfly theme in *Heart of O Yama* (1916), Famous Players' production with Mary Pickford. *Shadows of the West* (1921), which deals with the attempt of a Japanese immigrant to colonize the U. S. for his homeland, is an oddity and hardly a trend setter. Japanese villainy here was perhaps too strong to contemplate as the "yellow peril" theme and was finally played down in the shorter release print of this film.

Other national, religious, and racial types, though frequently represented, added color, intrigue, or comic relief without much close attention. The Mexican bandit was a particularly durable type, joined eventually by the wealthy Mexican rancher with a beautiful daughter (*The Rose of the Rancho*, Jesse Lasky, 1915) and assorted dancers and sombrero-laden old men. Also popular were Irish policemen and bartenders, Swedish masseurs, English butlers, German tutors, and French maids.

Feast and Famine—Religion and Politics

The popular aphorism suggests that it is useless to argue about religion and politics. Hollywood, as already suggested, was not doing much arguing about any social issue, and in the case of these two it ignored the one and used the other repeatedly for setting, plot intrigue, and general moral tone.

The earliest and most enduring of religious theme films were the historical pageants and passion plays which brought to the screen personalities and events of early Christendom. These prenarrative tableaux ranged from pseudo-documentary clips of well-known Biblical settings to more fanciful visions of religious pursuits, tribulation, and persecution. In 1898, Méliès, in *The Temptation of St. Anthony*, depicted the trials of the Saint at the hands of a group of seductive naked women, one of whom comes down from a cross. An angel then appears to save him from his torment. Pathé's *The Persecution of the Christians* (1905) shows two less fortunate Christians being brought into an arena, tied to a stake, and left to the lions. With narrative form established, Pathé was able to present the original version of the journey to the promised land and the receiving of the Ten Commandments in *Moses and the Exodus from Egypt* (1907).

American studios, like those in France and England, had begun with the tableau, and with the coming of storytelling turned to the parable and allegory, which permitted dramatization of both historical and contemporary themes. In 1907, the Biograph Company undertook *The Life of Christ*, which its bulletin describes as a passion play in twenty-five scenes from Bethlehem to the Resurrection. By the end of the decade, with melodrama well established, films like *The Lesson* were a popular form of film sermon. In this Biograph short, the wayward son who has rejected the faith of his minister father is apprehended by police at his father's deathbed for inadvertently causing the death of another man. At the same time Griffith was using the

Puritan witchcraft purges as a basis for his *Rose O'Salem-Town* (1910), in which the hero saves the Puritan maid from burning at the stake after she has been proclaimed a witch by a church elder whose advances she has thwarted.

The reconstructions of venerated incidents of the Christian past continued through the Teens and became the prototype for the biblical spectacle, which, thanks to DeMille in particular, became an important part of the prestige picture of the coming decades. *The Last Supper,* produced by the American Film Manufacturing Co. in 1914, depicted the last days of Christ, including his walking on water. Along with such dramatizations came religious subjects in the form of documentaries and pseudo-documentaries which sometimes helped to soften the otherwise stern attitude of Christian churches toward motion pictures. In 1900, the Biograph Company had called attention to "religious views" which were part of its offering, including several scenes of Pope Leo XIII. When William Selig made *The Coming of Columbus* in 1912—photographed near Chicago using replicas of the Spanish ships built for the World's Columbian Exposition—Pope Pius X, who had previously looked with disfavor on motion pictures, awarded the producer a medal for elevating the moral standards of motion pictures.

By the Twenties, however, it was the Biblical spectacle and the melodrama which revealed the consequences of Godlessness that best represented Hollywood's contributions to religious inspiration and education. *My Friend the Devil* (1922), *A Woman's Faith* (1925), and *The Road to Glory* (1926) were typical of the many films in which faith is restored after the renunciation of God at some moment of personal tragedy. Although DeMille himself is better known for the historical spectacle, he also made contributions to the little moral drama. His *The Godless Girl* (1929) shows the daughter of an atheist actually from a high school club called the Godless Society. The modern segment of *The Ten Commandments* (1923) also represented his contribution to the modern religious screenplay. But for all the preaching that film undertook during the silent period by way of both historical spectacle and intimate parable, there was little being said of the pressures and anxieties of individuals and groups in their every day contact with prejudice, persecution, and self-doubt.

The kind of grass root and nonideological politics of the hometown mayoralty race or perhaps the city political machine came to be a modestly represented subject for silent screen drama. It was the kind of political intrigue that could be safely handled without fear of getting into the sensitive issues of party affiliation or doctrine. Following the familiar patterns of heroic and villainous enterprises with justice being awarded, these silent dramas fit comfortably within the formula without disturbing the more troublesome questions of ideology.

The Conquest of Canaan (1921) was a Paramount film that rose above the stock melodrama and became a forerunner of the idealist films of the Thirties by Capra and others. It is based on the Booth Tarkington tale of a young political rebel outcast who makes good and becomes mayor of his hometown.

Prenarrative tableaux and moving cartoons provide an interesting early sampling of films dealing with national and international political thought. In addition to the mock-newsreel editorials on the Spanish-American and Russo-Japanese wars, there were both reverent and irreverent clips devoted to national figures and international relations. In Martyred Presidents, made by Edwin S. Porter in 1901, just after the McKinley assassination, a young woman is shown kneeling before a monument as the portraits of the three American presidents assassinated to date—Lincoln, Garfield, and McKinley—appear in succession on the center of the monument. In Terrible Teddy, the Grizzly King, another Porter film of the same year, Teddy Roosevelt, then Vice President, is shown firing a rifle into a tree to bring down a housecat while "press agent" and "photographer" look on. This spoof of the great outdoorsman is one of the earliest examples of political satire on the screen. In another use of the moving tableaux, the Edison Company turned to American political posture with a foreign nation in German and American Tableau, made on the occasion of Prince Henry of Prussia's visit to the U.S. in 1902. It depicts leaders of the two nations and an American and German soldier shaking hands as a curtain consisting of German and American flags is drawn. Franco-American relations are spoofed in the French-made American in Paris (1900), which depicts an American becoming engaged in a scuffle in a Paris café and being escorted out by a gendarme.

The requirements of the narrative precluded the simplistic and stylized treatment of such tableaux and cartoons, and handling of sensitive political issues in the more realistic dramatic mold were few. In 1917, Jesse Lasky decided to focus on Latin American relations in The American Consul, which involved a small-town lawyer sent as consul to a Latin American country to recognize the rebel government. (Rescue comes with the landing of U. S. Marines.) This kind of subject, however, remained scarce despite its benign attitude. National feeling and patriotic fervor on the other hand, were positive enough values, particularly during wartime, to provide popular themes. From Biograph's *American Soldier in Love and War* (1903), through Griffith's *The Honor of His Family* (1910), to the comic heroics of Langdon's *Heart Trouble* (1928), came a host of films in which love of country proved the ultimate virtue. In the latter film, Langdon portrays a German immigrant who is rejected for service during the war when he fails his physical. He becomes a hometown hero, however, when he unwittingly blows up a German base and rounds up the spies. It was Keaton's *The General* given a new war.

Anti-war sentiment, another politically sensitive area, was given sporadic attention through the silent period. Works like Griffith's *Intolerance* and Ince's *Civilization*, and the later *All Quiet on the Western Front* and *The Big Parade*, were among the more prominent works on the subject. But these were compromised in their mission by being either fanciful period pieces in the case of the Griffith and Ince films, or were neutralized by some heroics in the case of the latter. The lesser-known films of the genre tended to be similarly afflicted.

Direct war propaganda became particularly fashionable during the First World War. *The Battle Cry of Peace* (1915) was a star vehicle for Norma Talmadge and one of the earliest features dealing with war propaganda. But the inevitable star of subsequent films of the genre was the Kaiser himself, the arch villain of the war. *The Kaiser, the Beast of Berlin, To Hell with the Kaiser*, and *The Kaiser's Shadow*, which Ince produced for Paramount, are among the studies of the most hated of the Huns. Even Chaplin's *Shoulder Arms* had in its original version a concluding scene showing Charlie capturing the Kaiser. In 1918, when all these films were released, the motion picture industry was recognized by the war office as the major medium for propaganda. In "Wid's Yearbook" for that year, Cecil B. DeMille suggests that "had pictures accomplished nothing throughout their short history but to bring the great war home to the people of the United States, they would have vindicated, eternally, their right to live."

With the conclusion of World War I, events and political strains resulting from the Russian Revolution came to be a popular political subject, if not a preoccupation, of the Hollywood industry. The end of Czarist rule provided romantic potential, and the use of Bolshevism a new type of screen heavy. Numerous films featured the Russian countess who sought refuge from the Bolsheviks with the aid of Russian peasants. In *The Face in the Fog* (1922), a revolutionary terrorist is in search of the Romanov jewels. Lionel Barrymore plays the reformed crook, Boston Blackie, who exposes the Bolshevist and returns the jewels to the grand duchess. The following year Barrymore starred as the Bolshevist himself in *The Eternal City,* which centered on a Communist-Fascist conflict. Here an Italian orphan and the daughter of his foster father become estranged when he joins the Fascists and suspects her of becoming the mistress of a secret leader of the Communist party. He becomes Mussolini's right-hand man and leads the Fascists against the Bolshevists. This First National film, directed by George Fitzmaurice, has key scenes depicting Mussolini reviewing his troops with the king at the royal palace. Though politics remained in the service of melodrama, the film was a rare example of American attention to a Fascist theme.

Other potboilers of the genre involved Bolshevik agitators leading innocents astray, arrest of Red Agents by the secret service, or some unsuspecting soul being suddenly accused of being a nihilist and exiled to Siberia. In United Artists' *Tempest* (1928), John Barrymore follows his brother in the role of the Bolshevik, here a former Russian Army officer who joins the cause after the revolution, saves the princess from execution, and kills his own Red leader to escape with her. Hollywood's Red scare, as depicted in silent films, remained essentially benign, however. Revolutionary extremists simply provided a new dimension in screen villainy.

The Image Abroad

The lack of propaganda motive on the part of Hollywood notwithstanding, it was becoming incontrovertibly clear, even before film found its voice, that American films had become a key source for the building and reinforcement of images on a wide array of social issues. With efficient dreambuilding still the prime concern of most filmmakers, the propaganda that found its way into photoplay was mostly incidental, but the vast and ever-expanding world market made the American film image pervasive. Concern, both at home and abroad, was growing by the late Twenties over the potential of the medium, and particularly the American product, to influence not only social images but even *trade*, and to produce an Americanization of the world. A British report by the Commission on Educational and Cultural Films* observes that national propaganda is often not deliberate but incidental and goes on to say, "The films which a country produces reflect its national life, and every full-length film which a country exports is a gain or loss to national prestige." Iris Barry, writing in London six years earlier had been even more specific when, in *Let's Go to the Pictures*†, she stated,

> I cannot help feeling that the prestige of America is lower, because of the cinema, than it would have been without it. It is hard to retain one's respect for a nation so constantly put before our eyes, as it is almost always on the screen in an unenviable whirl of surreptitious cocktail-drinking, graft, bad taste, hideous domestic architecture, and vile manners.

Concern for the national image via film came from American leaders as well. Herbert Hoover, Secretary of Commerce at the time, took the opportunity of a Latin American banquet in 1927 to speak of the obligation of the film industry to produce pictures which "carry those ideals which build for that respect and confidence which is the real guarantee of peace and progress." Four years earlier Charles Evans Hughes expressed concern over the image of American life in foreign films when he said,

> I wish indeed that the important educational instrument, the moving picture, was not so frequently used in foreign countries to give false impressions of American life. It is most discouraging to reflect upon the extent to which the best efforts of educators and the men of public affairs are thwarted by the subtle influences of a pernicious distortion among other people with respect to the way in which our people live and the prevalence here of vice and crime.‡

Concern in some quarters went beyond the image of American life and ideals being reflected by native or foreign filmmakers and sounded the alarm against the Americanization of the world through Hollywood pictures. The *London Morning Post* in 1925 ran an editorial entitled "Trade Follows the Film" which warned:

**The Film in National Life.* London: George Allen and Unwin Ltd., 1932, p. 109.
 †London: Chatto and Windus, 1926, p. 15.
 ‡*Film Daily,* October 15, 1923.

If the United States abolished its diplomatic and consular services, kept its ships in its harbours and its tourists at home, and returned from the world's markets, its citizens, its problems, its towns and countrysides, its roads, motor cars, counting houses, and saloons would still be familiar in the utmost corners of the world. . . . The film is to America what the flag was once to Britain. By its means, Uncle Sam may hope some day, if he be not checked in time, to Americanize the world.*

The threat of world conquest may have been an exaggeration, and the countless charges on the other hand against "mawkish and maudlin bilge" on the screen must finally be tempered by the knowledge that without a voice, film storytelling was caught between its requirements and its potential. Visual narrative called for simplification and stereotyping if films were to be understood, while the nature of the photographic image, camera, and editing techniques invited realistic dramatization. The Hollywood formula film though a product of American industry was also a prescription for meeting these conflicting requirements. The multiplicity of film's function through the silent years was the result of machination and inspiration, both by accident and design. It was also tied to the technology of the medium; and the coming of sound was to bring further changes.

*Josef Stalin was also quoted once as saying, "If I could control the medium of the American motion picture I would need nothing else in order to convert the entire world to Communism."

7

Sound and Color: A New Beginning

The Impact of Technology

The contribution of a Porter, Ince, or Griffith followed as much from the availability of portable cameras and improved emulsions as it did from their individual vision and talent.

Although this statement may be a little hard for most tradi-tional film scholars to swallow, it is clear from our analysis in Chapter One that the technology of motion pictures was, and is, of essential importance to the total development of the form—historically, economically, and artistically. It seems necessary at this point, on the eve of film's most dramatic and vital technologi-cal revolution, to reassess the contribution of technology to motion pictures. All students of film—historians, critics, and filmmakers—must begin with an understanding of technology and its role in defining the essential nature of the medium. Artists work within the parameters of their mediums, and no artists, including film artists, can transcend the nature of the medium they have chosen to work in.

In films, however, unlike most traditional art forms, the raw materials of reality must be shaped in terms of mechanical apparatus which records, arranges, and projects a filmed image. Control is the essence of any art—indeed, of almost any experi-ence—and control in films is no exception. Even in the more improvisational films of Fellini or Cassavetes, or in the so-called "cinema vérité" films of Wiseman, the medium is controlled to arrange and shape specific realities. In order to exercise this control the filmmaker must conceive of his idea in a total sense from writing the script to projecting the image, and as a result must take into account the basic mechanical nature of the medium. Machines are a reality for any filmmaker and a failure to understand this concept and the machines themselves can result in great frustration and failure, especially for the beginning filmmaker.

Motion pictures was the child of a scientific age. Cinematography was a culmination of events, discoveries, and inventions, most of them mechanical and technological in nature. This historical reality is continually reflected in the parade of film history. Although many historians might not equate the contributions of D. W. Griffith with Norman Dawn, pioneer special-effects creator, it is important to realize that both individuals made important contributions in motion picture history. By recognizing this fact we also recognize the importance and impact of technology in motion pictures.

This impact takes several forms. First, and perhaps most important, technology sets the motion picture as an art apart. "Live" television and still photography are the only mediums to approximate a dependency on technology similar to film. In no other medium, for example, can the selection of a face or performer depend strictly on the quality of the medium's technology. D. W. Griffith used young actresses, such as Lillian Gish and Mae Marsh, primarily because the film stock used at this time revealed every line and fissure in the human face. As Thorold Dickinson notes:

> By the time their (the actresses) figures were fully developed, their faces . . . were already assuming the look of the *femme fatale;* by twenty-five they were regarded as character actresses, by forty as grandmothers.

A second major impact of technology is its expense. Although much of a film's expense comes from nontechnical items, such as story costs and salaries, approximately 20–30% of any film's cost arises directly from the technology required to create it. Motion pictures are fundamentally a mass medium striving to reach as many people as possible. This mass orientation has as one of its primary conditions the costs imposed by films' technological base.

Yet another effect of technology on motion pictures is the great complexity involved in their construction. The efforts involved in creating such spectaculars as *Intolerance* (1916), *Robin Hood* (1924), *Gone with the Wind* (1939), *Spartacus* (1959), and *Tora! Tora! Tora!* (1970) resulted in tremendous expenses, much of them related to the technology required to film massive crowd scenes and various battles.

As a result of the great number of people involved, the making of a film becomes a team rather than individual effort. This fact has important and crucial implications for the state of film art, as will become evident in our discussion of the studio system in Chapter Eight.

Technology has also contributed greatly to film's industrial domination. Both patent rights on inventions and the huge amounts of capital necessary to construct the organization required to produce films on a mass basis have led to industries rather than individuals assuming control over the medium. Individuals such as Adolph Zukor, Irving G. Thalberg, or Louis B. Mayer may represent or symbolize a company, but few men, even at the height of their power, controlled the medium.

A less obvious, but nevertheless important, effect of technology is on the historical patterns that form such an important part of motion picture history. Whenever the industry was threatened and felt its dominance as a mass entertainer slipping, it turned to technology as a means of restoring motion pictures to their rightful place at the top of the heap. This pattern is especially clear with respect to the two major breaking points in film history so far, the coming of sound and the appearance of television. Both developments brought about major technological changes which in turn significantly affected the state of the medium.

Early Attempts at Sound

In the year 1887, the idea occurred to me that it would be possible to devise an instrument which should do for the eye what the phonograph does for the ear and *that by a combination of the two all motion and sound could be recorded and reproduced simultaneously.*

Thomas A. Edison

Motion pictures and sound were conceived as working together in principle from the very beginning. Films were not silent because people wanted them to be; they were always a compromise necessitated by a lack of technological skill and knowledge and by the industry's desire to avoid "rocking the boat," bringing about a new form which would involve great expense.

Throughout the first thirty years of motion picture history few attempts were made to actually exploit silence and make it an integral part of the form. With the exception of the best work of Chaplin, Keaton, and a few other artists working primarily in the field of comedy, most silent films attempted to create sound either by frequent use of titles and/or live and often elaborate musical accompaniment.

Of course, as has been repeated countless times, silent films were never silent. Directors, producers, and exhibitors were constantly seeking ways to add an aural dimension to their films. One of the most popular early methods was to place actors behind the screen and have them speak or sing in synchronization with the projected image. Even D. W. Griffith employed this method in some road-show presentations of *The Birth of a Nation.* James Limbacher, in his book *Four Aspects of Film,* quotes one of the sound men who worked in this manner:

> ... I was given instructions to slap two boards together when a certain red light flashed on. We could see the film through the back of the screen to be sure we got our synchronization correctly. But I was glued to that red light. When it came on, I slammed the two boards together. When I looked at the screen, I discovered I had just shot Abraham Lincoln!

The most common method of adding sound to motion pictures was by piano, organ, or orchestral accompaniment. Pianos were a fixture of the earliest store theaters and nickelodeons, and by 1912 elaborate organs with various sound effect equipment were being installed in many new theaters.

The golden age of movie palaces brought about an equally golden age in motion picture music. Complete orchestras were standard in many theaters and, as Kevin Brownlow points out in *The Parade's Gone By,* people sometimes claimed they went to the movies just for the music.

Most musicians operated from a standard repertoire, which meant that they played certain selections for various moods and tempos. They were aided in this by cue sheets, which indicated standard pieces for particular moments in a film. In addition, certain major films had original musical scores composed especially for them. Most of Griffith's major works, including *The*

Huge organs like this one installed in the Roxy theater provided a wide variety of music and sound effects for silent motion pictures. The Roxy's owner, S. L. Rothapfel, is pictured admiring the new addition.

Birth of a Nation, Intolerance, and *Broken Blossoms,* had original scores. In fact, each of the characters in *Way Down East* had a musical line intended to be typical of him or her.

Amplification and Synchronization

The basic inventions necessary for a perfected sound motion picture began to emerge early in the 20th century. Most of them were designed to solve the two major obstacles to sound motion pictures—amplification and synchronization. As in the development of cinematography itself, the early contributions to sound motion pictures were made by a variety of people in many countries. However, as with cinematography, it was also an American who made the first and perhaps most significant contribution. The inventor was Dr. Lee DeForest and his invention, the audion, initially had nothing to do with motion pictures. DeForest is best known as "The Father of Radio," because his audion tube made possible the amplification of electromagnetic signals, which in turn provided the stimulus for radio broadcast-

205

ing. With this basic discovery in 1907, the age of electronics was born. The audion was simply an amplifier, but performed the task of "unlocking the door to progress and improvement in almost every phase of sound transmission, recording, and reproduction." DeForest later developed an interest in motion pictures and in 1922 offered the industry a sound system called Phonofilm. However, it met with little success, due partly to technical problems, but more significantly because of the cool response received from an industry which had no use for sound at this time.

Despite this response to DeForest's work, research on sound systems began in earnest following World War I, stimulated in part by the war and the place electronic communications had in it.

Synchronization was the next problem which required solution and research centered on two different types of systems—photographic/electronic sound on film and mechanical/disk. There were advantages to each system and as a result both were developed to commercial status almost simultaneously. The sound-on-film system, which ultimately became the industry standard, was expensive and complicated. The disk method, while less expensive and complicated, was decidedly less reliable and more cumbersome.

The earliest successful work in sound on film took place in Germany in 1918, where three men, Josef Engle, Joseph Massole, and Hans Vogt, developed the Tri-Ergon ("work of three") process. Theodore Case and E. I. Sponable, working at Western Electric, developed a system which involved reproducing sound photographically on the same strip of film on which the visual images were photographed. A light in the projector then picked up the various striations and these electronic signals were pushed through an amplifier (based on DeForest's audion) to emerge as sound. Initially cooperating with DeForest, Case and Sponable developed a number of experimental machines between 1922 and 1925 and by 1926, now separated from DeForest, they produced a commercially viable system. The method was demonstrated to representatives of the Fox Film Corporation, was subsequently purchased, and given the name Movietone.

The first use of the system was a throwback to the principle of the earliest motion pictures—the simple recording of reality. In this case it meant sound newsreels, with such subjects as Charles Lindbergh taking off for Paris and in a later edition

Lindbergh accepting a medal from President Coolidge. In both films the camera was virtually locked into place, simply recording the scene in front of it. There were no attempts at composition and editing existed only when the camera had to be stopped to change reels. Everything was dictated by the microphone. Despite the absence of traditional filmic values, these newsreels were very popular and remain valuable today as historical records.

The disk system of sound motion pictures was directly linked to the development of the phonograph, as it produced sound by synchronizing a record with the film. The first disk system was, of course, Edison's. He discarded this initial attempt, but picked up the idea again in 1913 when his company made several films using round cylinder records connected to the projector by pulley. However, the project was soon dropped and there was little further development of the system until the introduction of the Vitaphone system in 1926. Vitaphone utilized seventeen-inch disks played at 33⅓ rpm on a turntable synchronized to the projector. The primary advantage of the disk system was that it was cheaper than sound on film and produced better sound quality.

Warner Brothers and Vitaphone

As noted previously, one of the obstacles holding back sound film development was the film industry's reluctance to encourage and become involved in costly experimentation when business was stable. Despite this general aura of indifference, one company found itself in a position where it very quickly became interested. Barely two years old in 1926, Warner Brothers was on the verge of bankruptcy and desperately needed some kind of competitive edge if it was to survive. It had none of the extensive theater holdings of the other major companies and thus found it difficult to find a first-run market for its films. In 1925, Sam Warner saw a demonstration of Western Electric's sound disk system, became enthusiastic, and quickly convinced his three brothers that sound was the edge they needed to stay alive. In April, 1926, The Vitaphone Corporation was formed with Sam Warner as president.

Don Juan (1926), starring John Barrymore, was the first major film to utilize the Vitaphone process. When exhibited, it was preceded by a twenty-minute short featuring a talk by MPPA "czar" Will Hays and several selected features, such as the New York Philharmonic Orchestra, demonstrating the potential and attractiveness of sound. The sound heard in the feature was limited to music provided by the New York Philharmonic. This use reflects much of the early thinking regarding the potential of Vitaphone.

> ... Vitaphone will revolutionize the presentation of motion pictures. It will bring famous singers and orchestras to the smallest theaters. Exhibitors will be able to get an accompaniment to their feature pictures played by the most famous orchestras. . . . Perhaps, back in their minds, these experts believe that the Vitaphone eventually will make possible a genuine talking picture. However, no definite plans have been made along this line.

Musical accompaniment was nothing new to silent film audiences, however, and the "miracle" of sound would have to do more than this if it was going to revolutionize the industry and keep Warner Brothers from bankruptcy.

Following *Don Juan,* Warners began producing a series of short films encompassing a variety of subjects designed to demonstrate the possibilities of sound in film. These short subjects could be compared to the "demonstration" records which came out with the introduction of stereophonic music in the late 50's. These records contained trains whistling, bells ringing, and all types of sounds designed to demonstrate the two-channel capacity of this new medium. They had little value other than their ability to demonstrate how the system worked and as a result were usually given away by dealers rather than sold. The early Vitaphone shorts were also "demonstrations" which performed much the the same function. Most of the shorts ran less than one hour and presented seven to ten numbers made up primarily of orchestras, singing groups, soloists, and various variety skits. They were simply recordings of vaudeville acts, demonstrating little camera movement, composition or editing. The emphasis was on "showing" people what sound "looked" like.

The Industry Reacts

Warners continued to produce these shorts along with silent features, constantly trying to gauge audience response. In the

The sound projection sytem developed by
Western Electric and used by Warner Bros. under the
name Vitaphone.

meantime, Fox Films began producing their Movietone newsreels with increasing regularity. Consequently, by mid–1927,
sound in its several forms was beginning to make tentative but
definite strides. However, if sound was going to develop beyond
the experimental stage, the industry as a whole would have to
accept and use it for feature presentations. Fortunately, the
industry, *sans* Warners and Fox, was reaching a point where it
would be forced to consider sound.

By 1926, the boom of the early Twenties was coming to a
close. Business was spotty and if one was reading *Variety* of
December 15, 1926, the following headlines would have indicated that something was wrong.

NEW ORLEANS CAN'T ENTHUSE OVER ITSELF

MINNEAPOLIS IN BAD SHAPE WITH HIGH GROSS LAST
WEEK $12,000

BUFFALO SUFFERS BAD DROP

15% AND 20% DISCOUNT COUPONS BY RIVAL MILWAUKEE
HOUSES

There were several definite reasons for the decline. First was radio. Although less than six years old as a broadcast medium, it had grown to include 732 stations and three national networks (NBC Red, NBC Blue, and CBS). Radio was especially strong in large cities. New York had more than 40 stations and Chicago 58. This meant competition for the first-run theaters, the keystones of the studio empires. *Variety* headlined this competition in 1927 with "RADIO ACES HURT THEATERS." The city was Minneapolis, Minnesota, with 25,000 sets and several strong stations offering a wide variety of programs, including symphonies, musical variety programs, and talk shows. The same atmosphere existed in every large city in the country and for the first time in its young history motion pictures felt the direct force of competition from another mass medium. In 1926 alone, more than $500,000,000 was spent on radio sets and parts.

A second reason for declining attendance was the high cost of admission to most theaters. The nickel had been buried a long time ago and the dime was standing with one foot in the grave. These rising admission prices were a direct consequence of the production costs brought on by Hollywood's spectacle binge of the early 20's. Most audiences gladly paid their quarters, half dollars and dollars for such super productions as *Ben Hur, The Ten Commandments, The Trail of '98,* and *Wings.* However, they were reluctant to pay the same prices for ordinary studio potboilers. The studios had grown accustomed to an automatic response to everything they produced. Attendance figures climbed rapidly through the early and mid-Twenties and the studios had become fat and complacent about both their product and their audience. All of this hit especially hard at second-line studios, such as Warners, who were struggling to gain a foothold in the industry. They had come in during the boom days and were now finding it difficult to keep their heads above water.

Despite their success with short films, Warners needed more than the New York Philharmonic and Will Hays to lure audiences away from Buster Keaton, John Gilbert, and Mary Pickford. Warners continued to struggle. They desperately needed something unique to break into the first-run theaters. Sound by itself was obviously not enough. That "something" was *The Jazz Singer.* Al Jolson in combination with heartrending drama was precisely the magic Warners required. *The Jazz Singer* opened in New York on October 24, 1927, and motion pictures were never again the same.

Only portions of *The Jazz Singer* were in sound, but what

Al Jolson displays some of the vitality which made his personality an important part of the appeal of *The Jazz Singer.*
MUSEUM OF MODERN ART/FILM STILLS ARCHIVE

was important was that for the first time sound was being used as an integral dramatic part of a film, not simply as accompaniment or window dressing. The minute Al Jolson uttered the phrase, "Come on, Ma! Listen to this . . ." audiences cheered wildly.

Still, the other studios held back. In addition to sound, other technological wonders such as color and wide screen were being introduced and the studios were reluctant to jump into anything as expensive as sound with the possibility that it might be just a passing fancy. The winter of 1927–28 saw the studios perched on a very uncomfortable fence.

However, by the spring of 1928 public response to *The Jazz Singer* and subsequent films was sufficiently large to convince the major studios to sign contracts for recording equipment. With the new production season beginning in September, the "sum-

211

mer of '28" in Hollywood was one of incredible activity. The
movement toward sound had quickened in pace from a rush to
a stampede. Studios hired construction crews to build sound
stages on a 24-hour schedule. Typical was Carl Laemmle of
Universal spending $1.2 million for four sound stages in Ft. Lee,
New Jersey. In addition to sound stages there was a mad rush
to obtain engineers, voice coaches, dialogue writers, musicians,
and singers. Anyone who had any possible skill related to sound
was immediately put to work by the studios. MGM immediately
made plans for a school where its foreign players could learn
English.

Meanwhile, silent film production was disappearing with
incredible speed. In less than three years more than 95% of what
was once the base of a huge industry attracting millions of people
each week had vanished. Few tears were shed, however, especially by the studios. Sound was indeed the magic needed to
restore financial vigor. Profits were up for all the major studios,
but none more dramatically than Warner Brothers, whose $17.2
million dollar profit in 1929 represented a 745% increase over
1928. Weekly attendance figures climbed close to 100,000,000
per week.

By early 1929, MGM had only five silent films in production.
That same year Fox discontinued silent production completely.
The activity at the studios was closely paralleled by that in
exhibition. When it finally became apparent that sound was here
to stay and that the studios were going to produce nothing but
sound films, theaters began a frantic renovation process. In 1927,
only 157 theaters were equipped for sound. At the end of 1928
there were more than 1,000 and by 1929 more than 4,000 theaters
could handle sound films. By the end of 1930 more than 13,000
theaters were equipped for sound, most of them capable of
handling sound both on film and on disk. Approximately 8,000
theaters were still silent, but these were located in rural areas
where most theaters could not afford to convert to sound. They
continued to play silent films well into the Thirties and then
went out of business. By 1930, only 5% of the films produced in
Hollywood were silent and these few were made by the small
companies which could not afford to convert to sound and were
simply running out their string by supplying the remaining silent
theaters with some new product.

Clear reasons for the immediate and almost universal public
acceptance of sound are difficult to pinpoint. Nicholas Vardac, in
his book *From Stage to Screen,* noted that 19th century theater

produced a "climate of acceptance" for motion pictures by its emphasis on realism and in most cases its ultimate inability to produce complete realism. Much the same could be said concerning the sound film, as both radio and the phonograph had stimulated audience interest in sound entertainment and had created various dramatic forms which audiences readily accepted. By 1926–27 the phonograph and radio had become established household media: 45% of American homes had a phonograph and 40% a radio set. Sound as entertainment was an accepted reality for a majority of American homes and the extension of sound in motion pictures was natural and welcome. Perhaps, once again a "climate of acceptance" had been prepared which made the sound film welcome.

Another reason for the rapid and total acceptance of sound film was that even with elaborate musical scores and varied sound effects, silent motion pictures were considered incomplete and artificial. Spoken dialogue was missing and sub-titles, even when intelligently and sparingly used, were intrusive and usually broke the rhythm of a film. A study in 1914 demonstrated that one-fourth of the audience could read a printed title in one-third the time required by the rest of the audience. As a result most titles were designed for the slower three-fourths. As literacy increased audiences found that titles were on screen for an intolerably long time. The mass audience was also not used to mime as a standard way of communicating. Most actors and actresses were relatively unskilled in its use, with only Chaplin, Keaton, and several other silent comedians capable of effective communication in a natural way through mime. Silent film was basically an incomplete medium. Sound films were accepted by most people as natural and complete.

Problems

Following the tremendous expansion in sound equipment, the industry was still not able to decide which system to adopt. Most studios and theaters hedged their bets and used sound on both film and disk. However, the advantages of the sound-on-film system soon became obvious and once the problems associated with editing were solved, it became the industry standard.

Beyond the basic system issue there were a tremendous number of problems confronting the industry. Most of them were technical, although these technical difficulties caused equally severe artistic problems.

One of the first problems filmmakers faced was the immobility of the camera. The restriction was caused by camera noise, which was picked up along with the intended sound and amplified so that when directors saw rushes they thought an airplane had flown right through the sound stage. The short-term solution was to encase the camera in a sound-proof box, or "blimp" as it was called. This eliminated the noise, but it also eliminated most camera movement. The inability of the microphone to move further compounded the problem and as a result most films were static stage pieces. Edward Everett Horton recalled those days in a recent interview:

> In those days there was no boom that followed you all around. The microphones hung down, all wrapped around with material to make them look like part of the backdrop. We had three or four cameras. In a great big ensemble scene these cameras were sort of coffins covered with tarpaulins so that you couldn't hear the buzz of the camera. They were on turnstiles. . . . We were instructed not to talk until we felt ourselves in the center of the camera. So the scene would go around: "You see this man?" . . . Camera turns . . . "Yes" . . . Camera turns . . . "You know what happened?" . . . Camera . . . "No" . . . Camera . . . "Killed" . . . Camera . . . "What?" . . . Camera . . . "who did it?" . . . Camera.

In desperate attempts to achieve some mobility cameramen resorted to a variety of measures, including using four cameras for a single take. At times this required ten or more changes on the close-up camera for one ten-minute scene.

There were also problems with microphones. Most of the early ones were very crude and had little directional control. They picked up any and every sound on the set. They were also immobile, as the boom had not yet been developed. The result was a new art based on the ability to hide a microphone in everything from flowers, to vases, clocks, tables, costumes—anywhere large enough to accommodate the bulky demon. Actors and actresses suddenly became aware of new patterns in stage direction which stressed walking over to a bush or a table simply in order to be heard when they spoke. An authentic and amusing account of this period of microphone follies was presented in MGM's 1952 musical *Singin' in the Rain.*

Although the problems caused by the microphone's lack of mobility were irritating, they were small compared to those created by the overall sensitivity of the microphone to normal, everyday sounds. Knock-kneed extras, directors' comments, silk bloomers, and virtually everything that created a sound was a potential problem. Rubber suddenly became the latest in fashion as conventional items such as jewelry and shoes created too much noise in their natural states. A new style of manicuring was developed to eliminate the clicking of long nails. Sugar cubes and matchsticks had to be handled with great care. People had to learn to eat and kiss all over again and chewing gum was instantly abolished. Voice dynamics became a feared term. Clara Bow was a victim of this in her first sound film, *The Wild Party*. She entered a room, hollered WHOOPEE!! and all the sound tubes died. Even noise outside the studio had to be controlled. Garbage trucks on the studio lot were equipped with balloon tires and men were stationed on rooftops to wave flags warning airplanes to stay away. When King Vidor was filming his first sound film, *Hallelujah*, he had lookouts stationed all over the lot, but was still restricted to about ten minutes of shooting a day. Even the lights made noise and as a result incandescent lighting replaced arc lights.

Most of these technical problems were solved within a year or

A gospel meeting provided an excellent showcase for sound in King Vidor's all-black film *Hallelujah*.
MUSEUM OF MODERN ART/FILM STILLS ARCHIVE

two. However, the artistic problems took longer. Part of the reason for this disparity lies in the mental attitude of the various groups involved with the medium on a technical and artistic level. The technicians were enthusiastic over sound, eager to solve any problems and develop new and better methods of recording and reproducing sound. However, many artists were somewhat reluctant to embrace the new medium. They had developed a unique art form out of nothing and had created memorable and compelling drama. In addition, many critics were certain that sound was the death of everything artistic in cinema. Typical is the remark by Paul Rotha:

> It may be concluded that a film in which the speech and sound effects are perfectly synchronized and coincide with their visual images on the screen is absolutely contrary to the aim of the cinema. It is a degenerate and misguided attempt to destroy the real use of the film and cannot be accepted as coming within the true boundaries of the cinema. Not only are dialogue films wasting the time of intelligent directors, but they are harmful and detrimental to the culture of the public.

Chaplin was among those most violently opposed to sound and resisted throughout the thirties with such silent films as *City Lights* (1931) and *Modern Times* (1936). They were only silent, however, in that they lacked dialogue. Chaplin made rich use of music and sound effects in much the same way as Clair. In his autobiography, Chaplin states:

> Occasionally I mused over the possibility of making a sound film, but the thought sickened me, for I realized I could never achieve the excellence of my silent pictures. It would mean giving up my tramp character entirely. Some people suggested that the tramp might talk. This was unthinkable, for the first word he ever uttered would transform him into another person.

Ultimately Chaplin did turn to sound with *The Great Dictator* in 1940. However, the tramp was gone, forever silent.

Despite this reluctance from some quarters and outright hostility from others, many directors saw great possibilities in sound and welcomed it. The accomplished Russian silent film director Pudovkin said:

> . . . the sound film is a new medium, which can be used in entirely new ways; sounds and human speech should be used by the director not as a literal accompaniment, but to amplify and enrich

the visual image on the screen. Under such conditions, could the sound film become a new form of art whose future development had no predictable limits?

Pudovkin was, of course, pointing to a basic problem that plagued almost all sound films—the literal reproduction of every sound shown on the screen. This literalness greatly hampered another of silent film's most expressive qualities, editing. At first, the changes in editing caused by sound were beneficial. It was no longer necessary to cut to an object making a sound in order for the audience to "hear" it. The sound of a telephone ringing, for instance, no longer required a cut to a close-up of the phone. Even more significant was *Rain* (1932), where the camera focused on Joan Crawford's face as Walter Huston recited the Lord's prayer. Despite these benefits, however, early sound technique and capability greatly restricted editing, because of the necessity to synchronize sound and image. This, coupled with the camera's immobility, produced single-perspective shooting. The only way to create multi-perspective shooting and introduce some editing was to shoot all scenes with several cameras—a camera for long shots, one for medium shots, and one for close-ups. The development of the Movieola in 1932 helped restore editing to its proper place and function. However, even with improved editing capacity, the simple fact that people in a scene could now talk made establishing relationships much easier and simpler. Editing became less of an artistic tool and more of a functional device. The "invisible" editing style of most Hollywood pictures in the Thirties, where individual shots and entire scenes flowed together in a smooth uninterrupted pattern, was clear evidence that meaning could now be carried by sound with less emphasis placed on the visual elements of the motion picture process.

Impact of Sound

Sound's influence on content was immediate and dramatic. Because audiences wanted to hear any and every sound and because music was cheaper and easier to produce than dialogue, the musical film was quickly established as a new genre. If words were going to dominate, they might as well be put into the most pleasing and dynamic form possible. At first, the genre

consisted simply of Broadway musicals and operettas trans-
ported intact from New York to Hollywood. *Rio Rita* (1929),
starring Bebe Daniels, was a big success and was quickly followed by dozens of others, including *The Desert Song* (1929),
Sunny (1929), *Sally* (1929), *Showboat* (1929), and *Golddiggers
of Broadway* (1929).

With the appearance of MGM's *Broadway Melody* in 1929,
a faint trace of originality began to creep into the form. This
originality was given the label "backstage musical." *Broadway
Melody* was a huge success, with a gross of over $4,000,000 in
addition to an Oscar as Best Film (the first sound film to do so).
The natural reaction was to follow this with more of the same
thing. *Hollywood Revue* came along the same year featuring a
new twist, the "all-star" lineup, which would go on to become
an industry staple. Paramount's *On Parade,* Warner's *Show of
Shows,* and Universal's *King of Jazz* imitated the pattern and the
first wave of what would become a recurring cycle broke from
the gate. A sidelight to this development in film was a rapid
increase in the sale of songs in films as records and/or sheet
music. As *Photoplay* noted as early as 1929, within a month of
a film's release the average motion picture song was selling
almost 100,000 sheet copies and records. For example, *Fox
Follies* opened in late 1929 and within three weeks "Breakaway,"
"That's You Baby," and "Walking With Susie" had each sold
100,000 sheet copies and records. The first motion picture song
to sell one million copies was "Charmaine" from *What Price
Glory* (1926). This tremendous economic potential was not lost
on the studios as Warner Brothers quickly bought Witmark,
Inc., one of the oldest music publishing firms in the country for
$5,000,000. Virtually every major studio followed suit.

Two other forms of content were affected by sound; one
permanently, one only temporarily. The most dramatic and lasting impact of sound on film content was in the genre of comedy.
Silent comedy, especially the work of Chaplin, Keaton, and
Lloyd, had achieved a uniqueness and universality that enabled
it to survive sound, as is easily demonstrated today by the
survival of the form on television and in film societies in most
colleges and universities. However, today's audiences are being
amused by a style and form which disappeared more than forty
years ago. Sound brought an end to the genre and helped create
new comedic forms based on verbal humor. The Marx Brothers
and W. C. Fields became prototypes for the new sound comedy
and although some of their humor depended on physical action

The Marx Brothers,
comedy based on verbal humor.

or gesture, it was Fields' "grumbling" and misanthropic asides and the Marx Brothers' dadaistic, stream of consciousness dialogue that provided the true comic dimension to their characters.

Other, more subtle, forms of comedy emerged throughout the Thirties as writers and directors felt their way through the new medium. A shift took place which saw the verbal assault replaced by light banter. *The Thin Man* series, starring William Powell and Myrna Loy, featured a dry, urbane wit and the technique of overlapping dialogue. Frank Capra's "screwball" comedies, such as *It Happened One Night* (1934), *Mr. Deeds Goes to Town* (1936), and *Mr. Smith Goes to Washington* (1937) featured a solid *Saturday Evening Post* middle-class ethic clearly revealed in Robert Riskin's writing.

The other genre affected by sound was the Western. Although the ultimate effect was only temporary, the immediate impact was catastrophic. Limitations on camera movement and editing imposed by sound hit the Western especially hard. The Western was visual by nature and the public wanted films that talked, so as a result, for the first two years of sound no important Western films were made. However, *In Old Arizona* (1929) proved to be popular and set the tone for future Westerns by demonstrating that while *speech* would add little to the Western form, *sound* could add a great deal. The sound of bacon frying, cattle stampeding, and campfires crackling was dramatic to an audience that had not heard such sounds before in film, and these sounds provided audiences with much the same pleasure they received from talk and song.

New forms and changes in content required new people and soon performers who could sing and talk were being brought West from New York. Just as in any industry, when the supply is low, the price is high, and so too with performers who could provide the new medium with quality speech and song. The singers were among the first to arrive. John McCormack, the well-known Irish tenor, was paid $50,000 for ten weeks work. Marilyn Miller was paid $1,000 *an hour* for her singing. Dozens of other performers with various degrees of talent were pushed in front of the cameras to delight audiences in recreations of their original roles on Broadway, including Fanny Brice in *My Man* (1928), Texas Guinan in *Queen of the Night Clubs* (1929), and Sophie Tucker in *Honky Tonk* (1929). This influx of stage players making their individual attempts at screen immortality was vaguely reminiscent of the original Film d'Art movement and many of them ultimately met with the same fate. After the novelty wore off, only those performers who had some screen presence remained. The rest went back to Broadway.

People who could talk came next. Although it would seem that there were plenty of talented performers who could already talk, the studios found to their dismay that their huge investment in faces and figures did not guarantee voices as well. The following list of "New Faces," as it appeared in a 1929 issue of *Photoplay,* indicates the new orientation.

> Carlotta King—graduate of stage operettas
> Charles King—Broadway musical comedy
> Joan Bennet—sister to Constance and Barbara
> Morton Downey—tenor soloist with Paul Whiteman
> Lee Tracy—Broadway actor
> Jeanette MacDonald—musical comedy
> O. P. Heggie—English stage actor
> Marilyn Miller—Ziegfield's leading musical star

There have been many legends surrounding those silent film performers whose careers were ruined by inadequate voices. It is true that some individuals had "bad" voices that simply did not sound right. Most foreign performers were dismissed immediately, although a few, such as Greta Garbo and Marlene Dietrich, did succeed. However, neither Miss Garbo's nor Miss Dietrich's face and figure hurt their appeal. Some American players faded very quickly as well. The story of John Gilbert is well known and typical of what happened to many silent performers. Gilbert, one of the Twenties' biggest stars, was unsuccessful in sound films, not because his voice was *bad;* it was simply *inappropriate.* Had Gilbert's image as a performer been light and comedic rather than heavy and romantic, his relatively high-pitched voice might easily have been accepted by the public.

Another reason why many silent performers dropped from sight was that sound films required a new sense of realism and naturalism in acting. A softer, more subtle style was required and the broad, sweeping, sometimes deliberately exaggerated styles of such performers as Douglas Fairbanks, Lon Chaney, John Gilbert, and others now appeared foolish and overly dramatic. Historian Leslie Halliwell estimated that 90% of all silent stars faded with the appearance of sound. Such major stars as Milton Sills, Mary Philbin, Aileen Pringle, Blanche Sweet, Renee Adoree, Joblyna Ralston, among hundreds of others were dropped from studio rosters and the public mind with astonishing speed.

Not every star could be retired, however, and with musicals and plays being put into production at a frenetic pace many performers were forced into speaking and singing roles they were ill-suited for. Until new talent could be developed and/or imported, various techniques were implemented to allow actors and actresses with poor or inappropriate voices to continue performing. The most common technique and one still used today was voice dubbing or doubling, in which an off-screen voice was substituted for that of an on-screen performer. The most common form of this practice today is in foreign films, where, rather than subject an audience to subtitles, the dialogue is spoken in English by off-screen voices and dubbed in over the voices of the foreign performers. In addition, some musicals feature a well-known performer who cannot sing and rather than lose the built-in star appeal by replacing the individual, a singer's voice is dubbed in over the star's singing roles. In the early years of sound this practice was much more common than it is today. Richard Barthelmess, who would make several excellent sound films in the 30's, was initially forced into a singing role in the film *Weary River* (1930). The critical reaction to his dubbed and obviously artificial singing was not kind. Paul Lukas' heavy German accent required a double for all his speaking parts, and Lawford Davidson was paid $500.00 a week for his duties as Lukas' voice. Suddenly men and women were being evaluated in terms of beautiful voices rather than beautiful faces. Studio casting offices added new classifications to their card indexes on players, listing type of voice, accent, and such notes as "cultured," "lisper," etc. Fan magazines began writing articles on "The Sex Appeal Voice of Ann Harding," "Baby Talk of Helen Kane," and "Vamping With Sound." Many performers, such as Conrad Nagel, Will Rogers, Claudette Colbert, who possessed the all important "phonetic value" received tremendous boosts to their careers. Quite clearly, the effect of sound on the screen performer was great.

Off-screen performers and artists, however, were affected just as drastically. Certain types of occupations, such as subtitle writers and pit orchestra musicians, simply ceased to exist. More important than these eliminations, however, were the additions. Perhaps the two most important were technicians and writers. The technicians, or "knob twiddlers" as they were affectionately referred to, were not really welcomed with open arms, as they placed new and difficult demands on all creative personnel. Thorold Dickinson reveals this attitude quite clearly in his book *A Discovery of Cinema:*

> And all the time, those interlopers, sound engineers aiming at scientific accuracy, interfered with the temperamental atmosphere of film-making, vetoing voices of unusual character, insisting on flat clarity of speech and precise levels of volume of sound, unable to record a real shout or a real whisper, demanding compromises to meet the narrow limits of tolerance of their yet primitive equipment. It was a hell of mediocrity until the non-conformists began to find a way.

However, because of the crudeness of early equipment, the technicians were absolutely necessary if some reasonable sound quality was to be achieved. Much of their early work consisted of adjusting voices of various performers to acceptable levels. At times, however, they became over-zealous in their efforts.

> Tallulah Bankhead, the late actress, had a low voice and the early attempts by sound engineers to "tinker" with it met with disaster. As Miss Bankhead herself said: "They made me sound as if I'd been castrated! I told the studio that if they tampered with my voice I'd walk off the set. After that they never twiddled any more knobs to change my voice again.

Although this new breed was looked upon by many as a necessary evil, talented engineers, such as Douglas Shearer at MGM, made many significant and lasting contributions to the art and science of motion pictures. Among the many areas which required and received solution were sound editing equipment, combination printers (so the sound and picture could be placed on the same rather than separate print), camera sound insulation, theater acoustical treatment, microphone booms and dollies, improved voice monitoring and level control, and sound transmitting screens.

Writers of both dialogue and song were another vital group. Both types were imported from Broadway and Tin Pan Alley and they ruled early sound films almost as much as the engineers.

Dialogue writers were the first priority. John Howard Lawson was one of the pioneers and in his book *Film: The Creative Process,* his major point and a central thesis for understanding the nature of early sound film was that "Hollywood had not so much mastered dialogue as it had been mastered by it." Lawson goes on to note that this dependence on speech was magnified by the type of people brought in to work in sound films. "Directors, writers, performers did not change their methods of work when they crossed the continent from New York to Hollywood. They were hired because of their stage experience and they had no incentive to abandon it or risk experimentation."

Words in the form of songs were equally important as the "all talking, all singing, all dancing" film dominated the nation's screens. Songwriters, such as Irving Berlin, Jerome Kern, MGM's Harry Warren, Mack Gordon and others, contributed as much to this new rhetoric of film as anyone. Suddenly films became known on the basis of songs as well as stars.

Solutions to Problems

The magic of sound had carried the industry through the first years of the Depression in great shape. There was even talk in industrial and banking circles of a "depression proof" industry. However, as the Depression moved along its grinding, unrelenting path, audiences began to stay home. Attendance figures dropped from 100,000,000 per week in 1930 to less than 70,000,000 per week in 1931. The industry began getting restless and started to search for new formulas and solutions.

At this same time an artistic restlessness was occurring among many directors. Although sound had wiped out silent film as an art form, it could not eliminate the feelings and talents of the many creative artists who had worked in it those first thirty years. Such individuals as Rouben Mamoulian and King Vidor realized that although sound had destroyed something unique and placed severe technical limitations on the state of the art, there was a positive side which needed to be developed. What was missing in these early years was a creative use of what sound could uniquely contribute to film, coupled with a restoration of the artistic visual potential of camera movement and editing.

One of the first problems solved was the restoration of camera mobility. Much of the credit here belongs to Rouben Mamoulian. He recognized, perhaps more than any other director of this time, that there was a basic distinction between the stage and screen and he attempted to reinforce this difference. Mamoulian began his career directing plays in London, but soon came to the United States, where he worked in both opera and legitimate theater. He became well known through his work in the Experimental Theater Guild and for his staging of the first production of *Porgy and Bess*. His "symphony of noise" sequence in *Porgy* perfectly illustrated his stylistic blend of sound and movement and greatly impressed the critics. This was 1929; Hollywood was importing anyone who had anything to do with sound and so Mamoulian was brought in with the other trainloads from the East. Paramount initially wanted to sign him to a long-term contract in which he would spend several years learning the trade. Mamoulian insisted on a one-film contract and went off to study and absorb what he could about the process of filmmaking. He was not satisfied with what he saw. As he stated some years later:

> The camera technique then was to shoot a film as a stage play, with ready-made dialogue. They would put two cameras on the set, and shoot two closeups and a long-shot, then cut them together: all you *could* call these films was talkies!

Although Mamoulian's best work was in the musical genre— *Love Me Tonight* (1932), *Summer Holiday* (1947), *Silk Stockings* (1957)—his first sound film, *Applause* (1929), was a harshly realistic story about an aging burlesque queen. In this film, he liberated the camera by shooting several scenes silent and adding sound later. One particular scene involving a huge crowd was shot in Penn Station in New York and ended with a remarkable crane shot which would have been impossible if shot in the normal manner. Mamoulian also conceived of recording the sound in certain scenes on two channels instead of one. Necessity is often the mother of invention and in this case the cliché proved true. In one particular scene from *Applause,* the burlesque queen is singing a "lullaby" to her daughter at the same time the daughter is saying her evening prayers. Standard practice was to place the microphone somewhere in the middle and try to catch a little of both sounds. However, a whispered prayer and a song were of unequal sound value and so Mamoulian suggested using two microphones and recording each sound on a separate channel. In later films, such as *City Streets* (1931) and *Dr. Jekyll and Mr. Hyde* (1931), he experimented with overlapping dialogue, sound flashbacks, and synthetic sound. However, his most important contribution to the developing art of sound film was restoring a sense of movement to the medium.

King Vidor was another pioneer in using sound artistically. Whereas Mamoulian had been a novice and approached film with little background or orientation, Vidor was an accomplished director with several silent "classics" to his credit. Vidor's background in film was eclectic to say the least. He began producing two-reel comedies in Houston, Texas, made several documentaries; came to Hollywood, where he directed religious films *(The Turn of the Road,* 1918), jazz-age films *(Wine of Youth,* 1924), classic literary films *(La Boheme,* 1925); and climaxed his silent film career with two realistic dramas, *The Big Parade* (1925) and *The Crowd* (1928). In both these films, but especially in *The Crowd,* he displayed a highly mobile camera, which he acknowledged was greatly influenced by the Germans. Thus, unlike Mamoulian, who had no previous film style to discard or "hang ups" to get rid of, Vidor brought to sound film a broad background rich in silent film technique. This was reflected in his first sound film, the all-black *Hallelujah!,* made in 1929. The theme was taken from his youth in Texas, where he witnessed black religious meetings, revivals, and baptisms by the workers at his father's sawmill. Much of the film was shot on location in Tennessee and Arkansas. Vidor's basic method, like Mamoulian's, was to shoot silent and dub sound in later. However, Vidor was primarily concerned with the quality of sound and as such he attempted to achieve a balance between a "free" camera and a wide variety of sounds. This balance is nowhere more brilliantly developed than in the remarkable chase sequence through an Arkansas swamp which provides a gripping climax to *Hallelujah!* The camera relentlessly tracks a pursued man as he flees in terror through the swamp. However, it is the "sound" of the swamp which creates the real atmosphere of the scene. Vidor shot the scene silent and then working back in the studio added sounds, such as a branch breaking, a bird screaming, and a foot pulling out of quicksand. These sounds became integrated with the tracking movement of the camera to produce an atmosphere of impending doom and terror. The bird call becomes a hiss, the broken branch a broken bone, and the sound of quicksand becomes the sound of a man being sucked down into the depths of hell.

Two other important pioneers in establishing an expanded perspective for sound films were Lewis Milestone and Ernst Lubitsch. Both concentrated on freeing the camera from the constraints of the microphone by shooting silent and dubbing sound in later. Milestone worked with realistic themes in the anti-war *All Quiet on the Western Front* (1930) and the behind-the-scenes newspaper story *Front Page* (1931). The battle scenes in *All Quiet* . . . are remarkable, with the camera following the action as huge waves of men move across open battlefields. At the same time the sounds of war shells "crumping" into the ground and "whining" overhead, rifles "cracking," and tanks "rumbling" add realism and set a tone of chaos and destruction. In *Front Page*, Milestone worked primarily with dialogue, creating tempo and pace through rapid speech and quick cutting. Milestone's ability to integrate sound and movement made his films unique in a time of stationary themes and settings.

Ernst Lubitsch worked in a lighter metier, utilizing music and song in romantic fantasies, such as *The Love Parade* (1929) and *Monte Carlo* (1930). In both films, he used a silent camera in order to create movement and establish a distinct visual rhythm. He was especially concerned with integrating sound effects, music, and dialogue as one particularly memorable sequence from *Monte Carlo* illustrates. The scene involves a train, The Blue Express, moving away from a station, and Lubitsch integrates the sound and tempo of the train wheels into the song "Beyond the Blue Horizon" sung by the passengers accompanied by peasants in the surrounding countryside. Critics used the phrase "sound montage" in describing the scene, as sounds and music performed the same function for the ear that an assembly of shots perform for the eye, that of uniting and creating a whole from several distinct parts.

One other artist of this early period deserves mention for his use of sound. Some historians and critics have maintained that René Clair represents the ultimate in the artistic and creative use of sound. However, others disagree. They maintain that Clair fought against sound and used it to mock and satirize current sound conventions. As he stated in an interview some years later: "I am still against the big use of words; not sound, WORDS! We have already got the theatre for words. . . . Even now, every time I have to make an important scene in dialogue, I am ashamed, because it is a proof of weakness." Clair's use of sound was essentially restricted to the use of music and a few sound effects which he employed asynchronously—sound working against the image. In such films as *Le Million* (1931) and *À Nous La Liberté* (1932), Clair created his own magical world of sight and sound. Flowers sing and ornamental cupids trumpet loud blasts. He used sound to comment and create new patterns of meaning, and by working in a nondramatic fantasy genre he made this style easier for audiences to accept. One instance in *Le Million* sums up much of Clair's philosophy of sound. A large crowd is shown fighting over a coat containing a winning lottery ticket and in the background are the cheers and roars of a rugby match crowd. Here, Clair uses the sound of one event to comment humorously on the action of another. While the work of Mamoulian, Vidor, Milestone, and Lubitsch inspired and influenced other directors, Clair's influence was limited. His films reflected a uniquely personal vision which was most likely matched only by Chaplin.

Developments and improvements in sound continued through a combination of technological and artistic invention. Editing of sound film became greatly simplified with the development of the sound Movieola. Improvements in microphones and booms, printers and sound mixers greatly extended the artistic possibilities of sound in film. Individual artists such as Alfred Hitchcock, Walt Disney, Jean Renoir, and Orson Welles used the new technology to make many artistic advances and produce memorable films. However, despite these improvements, it took years for sound to be taken for granted and used and abused unselfconsciously. This, however, becomes another story and another chapter.

The Improvement of Lighting

It has been obvious from the previous discussion that sound brought dramatic and significant changes to motion pictures—economically, technically, artistically, personally, and industrially. One other major effect of sound, which is often overlooked, was its influence on other areas of motion picture technology and craftsmanship. Such areas as scene and costume design, special effects and lighting required almost total rethinking.

Of all these areas, lighting was affected most, as the noise from the old arc lamps necessitated a complete change to incandescent lighting. In addition, new strategies in lighting were required by the presence of the microphone and the various booms and dollies used to transport it.

Since motion pictures are formed as a result of the proper and accurate control of light, the concern for proper light in motion pictures is as basic as film itself. As long as films were records of reality, simple sunlight was all that was required of motion picture lighting. However, as soon as Méliès and Porter began to create drama, lighting, like all other filmic elements, had to be modified and brought under greater control. By 1905, artificial lighting in the form of mercury vapor and carbon arc lamps was being used in East coast studios. However, even these lamps were being used to provide a flat diffused light. A few tentative steps toward truly dramatic lighting were taken by D. W. Griffith, but the inadequacies of both lights and film stock prevented any real advances from being made. By 1916, studio lighting as an artistic adjunct to dramatic effects was being given serious consideration. Cecil B. DeMille began to use lighting for dramatic purpose and coined the phrase "Rembrandt lighting" to indicate his orientation.

The carbon arc and mercury vapor lamp continued to be the staple of the industry throughout the Twenties, even though alternate systems were available. However, with the advent of sound and the development of panchromatic film stock, with its increased sensitivity, a change of lighting standards was in order. Incandescent lighting was the result. This lighting gave a softer, more diffused light, but most importantly it eliminated the sizzling and sputtering noise of the carbon arc. However, the artistic demands of directors for a hard, streaky light and the technical demands of a three-color process for more light soon brought about a change to the carbon arc again. This seesaw tipped once again in favor of the incandescent lamp with improvements in the speed of color film.

From the late '30s on improvements continued to be made primarily in the areas of increased light output and portability. The commercial development of the quartz-iodine lamp, more commonly known by amateur filmmakers as the "sun-gun," gave professionals a light, portable, high-power source of illumination which made possible much of the advances in on-location shooting during the Sixties and Seventies.

The Development of Color

Color, like sound, had existed in motion pictures from the very beginning. As early as 1894, C. Frances Jenkins projected hand-tinted color films. Tinting and toning became the standard method of producing color in film for the first 25 years. The actual tinting was accomplished either by hand, by coloring the positive print, or by having the tint already in the film stock. Porter's *The Great Train Robbery* (1903) was released in a hand-tinted version with various scenes in color, including a red-tinted gunshot blast at the end of the film. Hand-tinting, of course, involved great cost and as films grew in length and increased in sophistication, this process became obsolete, although Robert Paul in England did produce a colored version of *The Miracle* (1910) by hand-tinting 112,000 individual frames.

None of the early work in color involved "natural" tones, however, on which the color either exists in the film stock or is added through optical or mechanical means after the film has been exposed. The first practical natural color process, Kinema-color, was developed in 1906 by two British inventors, Edward R. Turner and G. Albert Smith. Kinemacolor represented a form of color created by the additive process, in which the film itself had no actual color, but color values were revealed through appropriate filters in filming and projection. Encouraged by financier Charles Urban, public demonstrations were given in 1908, and in 1909 Urban showed the process to the MPPC. They considered buying the American rights to the process, but ultimately decided against it. This decision was not surprising, of course, since millions were being made with black and white film and there was no need to upset the status quo.

About the same time that the MPPC was turning a deaf ear toward color film, several American inventors were developing a new color system which they labeled "Prizma." It was a subtractive process, in which the color was in the film and the picture became a complete self-contained color record, requiring no special projection equipment. Several films, including J. Stuart Blackton's feature-length *The Glorious Adventure* (1921), were filmed in the Prizma process.

However, all of this early development was superseded by the introduction of Technicolor in 1916–17. Essentially the brain-child of two MIT graduates, Herbert T. Kalmus and Robert Comstock, Technicolor was a two-color (red and green) subtractive process. It had its commercial birth in a railway car somewhere between Boston and Jacksonville, Florida, where the company had gone to shoot a film called *The Gulf Between* (1917).

The quality and clarity of this process soon established it as the leader in the field. However, its high cost of 27¢ a foot was a major obstacle standing in the way of widespread commercial development. The industry wanted a cost under 10¢ a foot and also needed faster service, which Technicolor simply could not provide. Work continued through the Twenties with various degrees of success. *Cythera* became the first color film shot under artificial light in 1924. Dougas Fairbanks' film, *The Black Pirate* (1926), was the most elaborate vehicle for this early process and the following critical comment is an indication of its success.

> So that while the spectator fails to find any carnival hues shooting across the canvas where this cinema is shown, still the deep rich brown of his pirate ships is there, the faded, gray and brown clothing of the players are there; the weak, green waters of the sea are there.

Extensive work in short subjects continued as the process was constantly being improved and costs lowered. By 1927–28 a commercially feasible system was available. The concern over whether sound film would survive on its own merits in the first years led to a boom in color film production during 1929–30. Even though shooting in color increased film cost, many studios felt the gamble was necessary in order to attract audiences to sound. In 1929, Technicolor contracted for seventeen features and by 1930 this had increased to thirty-six. Lab crews were working three eight-hour shifts and since the Technicolor process required special cameras operated by trained men, the pressure on Technicolor was great. *On With the Show* (1929) was the first all-talking Technicolor film and was quickly followed by many others, most of them from Warners.

There was one major flaw in all this, however, and that was that Technicolor was still a two-color process. Although red and green produced passable color registration, a completely natural color required the addition of a third primary color—blue. In addition, when it became obvious that sound film could succeed on its own merits the demand for color films disappeared. By 1932 the "boom" in color was gone.

Despite this, work on a three-color process continued and a perfected system was finished by 1932. Despite its improved nature, however, Technicolor was finding it difficult to get the industry, now safe and secure with sound, to try it out. However, a situation developed, not dissimilar to that of Warner Brothers and sound, when a struggling Walt Disney, desperately needing something to save his studio, turned to Technicolor for his film *Flowers and Trees* in 1932. The result was a success for both Disney and Technicolor. The film demonstrated the beauty and appeal of the three-color process and Disney's fortunes soared. The first feature to be produced in the three-color process was Mamoulian's *Becky Sharp* in 1935. However, the film that really provided a showcase for Technicolor was *Gone With the Wind* in 1939. Public and industrial acceptance of color films was now certain and Technicolor became the established standard for the industry.

The development of color negative film stock by Eastman Kodak in 1949 revolutionized color filming. Color features could now be filmed with any 35mm camera rather than Technicolor's specialized equipment. The savings made possible the first low-cost feature color films. At this same time the threat of television created panic in the industry and it once again turned to technology as a source of magic. Wide screens, 3-D (three dimensional), and color were the magic this time. Although screen size has stabilized and 3-D films are rare, color has continued to grow to the present. With this increase in color has come some attempts to use it more intelligently and artistically. Color, like sound, had first been used as a gimmick, a novelty which audiences soon tired of. It was often used in musicals and other light genres and there was little attempt to develop any true dramatic value. As such the association of color with nondramatic films would carry on into the Sixties. Only then through the work of Antonioni, Bergman, Fellini, and others did color become integrated as a natural element in film. Natural in this sense does not mean "real" color. Rather, it means that color is now accepted as a natural part of the symbolic language of film and is used to make statements and create meaning rather than simply dress up a film so it will be more attractive.

Summary

Sound brought with it tremendous and fundamental changes in motion picture history. Technology, as one of the pivotal arms of the medium, reigned supreme. Sound and concurrent changes and advances in other aspects of motion picture technology, such as lighting and color, heralded a new beginning for the motion picture. Soon technical innovation began to be used to create and communicate rather than act simply as window dressing or a gimmick placed on display for its own sake. The Thirties, although dominated by an industry that was often responsible for limiting the potential of film, saw this technology brought under control and used to great advantage.

Because the motion picture in the United States was a

product of a business, the impact of sound on the business of film was profound and represented a clear turning point in film history. In a way, history was repeating itself. Like the MPPC's fight against the independents, an old established order once again gave way to a new one. The one unique aspect of this revolution was that no major established company—with the possible exception of First National, which was absorbed by Warners—was hurt. Several new corporate "stars" emerged either through sound-stimulated growth, such as Columbia; consolidation and merger, such as 20th Century-Fox; or outright creation, such as RKO. Conversely, most small independent studios died a quick and unceremonious death. The huge amounts of capital necessary to retool for sound required outside funding by even the biggest studios and as a result Wall Street became even more firmly entrenched. With millions of borrowed dollars riding on the flimsy wings of motion pictures the tolerance for and acceptance of personal grandeur was gone. The organization replaced the individual and that organization extended all the way from New York to Hollywood. It is interesting to note the geographical shift in direction, which again symbolized a broader, deeper change in the industry. The direction was back East again and this meant less flexibility, more financial responsibility, and an obligation that stretched beyond the studio walls.

The introduction of sound brought a profound psychological effect to the industry. As it grew bigger and bigger it grew more self-important. It became standardized, complex, technical. A whole new way of making films emerged. Creatively, because films cost more money, content became more conservative; a new, safe, corporate rhetoric emerged. Artistically, the medium exhibited less freedom. It became more complex as whole new aesthetic dimensions required exploration.

As *Variety* commented on the impact of sound:

> It didn't do any more to the industry than turn it upside down, shake the entire bag of tricks from its pocket and advance Warner Brothers from last place to first in the league.

8

Studio Styles and Forms

Sound in motion pictures brought many changes. One of the most significant was its effect on the structure of the film industry. The money required to convert to sound production eliminated all but the strongest studios and brought most independent production to a swift and final halt.

The changes in industrial structure brought equally significant changes in the types of films produced. A new rhetoric began to emerge; a corporate rhetoric based primarily on a mixture of formula and personal style; a rhetoric influenced by big business, big money, big stars, and big audiences.

This "golden" period of sound and color begins around 1930 and ends in 1946. The dates and adjective are arbitrary to be sure. For some, only the silent era was golden: sound brought with it a tarnish, a lowering of aesthetic standards. For others, the "golden" years are now, a time in which experimentation and independence have become symbols of a break with an old, outdated Hollywood tradition. However, from 1930 to the end of World War II, Hollywood and motion pictures were more firmly established and deeply rooted in the American consciousness than at any other time in history. In a time of economic depression and international conflict, motion pictures, as Hortense Powdermaker observed in her sociological analysis, *Hollywood: The Dream Factory,* helped people escape their anxieties, ease their loneliness, provided them with vicarious experiences, portrayed solutions to problems, created models for human relationships, and developed new value systems and new folk heroes.

235

Studios and Stars

As John Baxter stated in *Hollywood and the Thirties:* "Without the studios, Hollywood could never have existed." It could also be said that without stars—personalities—studios would never have existed. The two were welded together inexorably. As an anonymous critic wrote in a 1933 issue of *Screenland:* "Hollywood was founded on Personality, builded on Personality, exists on Personality. The movies live from one Personality discovery to the next."

The system was built on the already well established studio foundations of the silent period. However, the introduction of sound created even more specialization and division of labor. A large and highly structured system was required for sound films as music and the writing and speaking of dialogue became important factors which called for entire new departments and hundreds of additional people.

The studios were, therefore, an economic necessity. Like television today, Hollywood in the Thirties and Forties faced the weekly pressure of entertaining a mass audience. Consequently, the studio system grew up as a necessary industrial response to the huge public demand for more of its product. Harry Cohn, president of Columbia, in talking to a young film editor stated:

> Listen, kid, . . . I make fifty-two pictures a year here. Every Friday the front door opens on Gower Street and I spit a picture out. A truck picks it up and takes it away to the theatres, and that's the ball game. Now, if that door opens and I spit and nothing comes out, you and everybody else around here is out of work. So let's cut out the crap about only good pictures. How many of those pictures I spit out do you think that I think are any good? . . . I run this place on the basis of making one good picture a year. . . . The rest of them I just have to keep spitting out.

The 500 films a year produced in this period were products of a sophisticated industrial system and as such reflected the general mood and attitude not only of the system itself, but the era and the audience. Films were reflective of the time precisely because they were products of an industrial system. Few aspects of our society are more attuned to the pulse of society than industry. Individuals and small groups often listen internally. D. W. Griffith and William S. Hart, for example, did not really produce films that were in tune with society. Rather, their films were the outcome of an intense personal vision. This vision

Feature Length Production
in Hollywood's Heyday

	All Cos	Para-mount	Loew's	Fox	Warner	RKO	Colum-bia	Uni-versal	UA	Other
1930–31	510	58	43	48	69	32	27	22	13	198
1931–32	490	56	40	46	56	48	31	32	14	167
1932–33	510	51	37	41	53	45	36	28	16	203
1933–34	480	55	44	46	63	40	44	38	20	130
1934–35	520	44	42	40	51	40	39	39	19	206
1935–36	517	50	43	52	58	43	36	27	17	191
1936–37	535	41	40	52	58	39	38	40	19	208
1937–38	450	40	41	49	52	41	39	45	16	127
1938–39	526	58	51	56	54	49	54	45	18	141

Source: *United States v. Paramount Pictures Inc., et al.,* Civil Action no. 87–273 in the District Court of the United States for the Southern District of New York, amended and supplemental complaint, 14 November 1940.

contributed both to their greatness and ultimately their failure to maintain top status in the industry. The studio system as it had developed was completely in tune with what the paying public wanted and as a result the films of this period have more meaning as social documents than as personal works of art.

Individual Studio Profiles

When one speaks of Hollywood studios, the names which immediately come to mind are MGM, Paramount, Universal, RKO, Columbia, Warner Brothers and 20th Century-Fox. These "majors" dominated production without question. Together with United Artists they accounted for more than 60% of all feature production. However, there was that other 40%, and indeed, there were other active production studios. In 1935, according to *The Film Daily Yearbook*, there were 46 production companies, 26 active studios, 174 enclosed stages, and 19,000 permanent employees in Hollywood. Some companies, such as Burrough-Tarzan Enterprises, Superior, and Supreme Pictures, produced only one feature a year. However, others such as Chesterfield Invincible, Alliance, and Tiffany produced from 10 to 25 feature films a year. More importantly, studios such as Monogram and Republic were responsible for entire genres of film, most significantly serials and the "B" Western.

Despite this activity, the seven major studios dominated the scene and set the tone and style of the era. Some historians place United Artists among the majors. However, UA was never a studio as such. It was simply a distribution arm for various independent producers. The only independent producers able to maintain some degree of production parity with the majors were Samuel Goldwyn and David O. Selznick.

Goldwyn's most important work was in association with William Wyler and included such films as *Dodsworth* (1936), *Wuthering Heights* (1939), and *The Best Years of Our Lives* (1946). Goldwyn's great value was the example and precedent he set for other independents. He was not well educated or greatly talented. However, he was able to recognize talent in others and knew the audience as well as any studio head. He brought both cinematographer Gregg Toland and choreographer Busby Berkeley to Hollywood, gave them a start, and provided an economic and artistic climate which allowed both to develop their unique and highly personal styles.

David O. Selznick was like Goldwyn in some ways, but his artistic temperament was vastly different. Selznick came up through the studio system and was one of MGM's top producers in the early 30's, with such films as *Dinner at Eight* (1933), *Anna Karenina* (1935), and *A Tale of Two Cities* (1935). Increasingly annoyed at studio restrictions and spurred on by the example of his late father, Lewis, an early motion picture producer, Selznick went independent in 1935. Taking as his studio motto "In a Tradition of Quality," he produced some of the most memorable films of the period, including *A Star is Born* (1937), *Nothing Sacred* (1937), *Rebecca* (1940), and *Duel in the Sun* (1946). His most memorable and significant film was, of course, the monumental *Gone with the Wind* (1939) and in a sense he spent the rest of his life (he died in 1965) trying to live up to and equal this success. Unlike Goldwyn, who usually left his talent alone, Selznick constantly interfered with his films, making suggestions about everything from editing to music. As a result, most of his films have a curiously uneven quality with form and content seemingly pieced together by Selznick from what others had originally created.

MGM

MGM was the dominant studio of the period. Actually, its corporate name was Loew's Inc., with MGM simply used as a trademark. Louis B. Mayer, as head of the studio, was a power not only at MGM but throughout the entire industry. He was a public figure in every sense of the word, delighting in escorting distinguished visitors around the set, dabbling in politics, and fine racing horses. Mayer ran the studio primarily on an emotional level, alternately weeping and laughing as he "discussed" star's contracts or future productions. Had Mayer had total control over the studio, it is likely that MGM would not have achieved its dominant position in the industry.

Fortunately, Mayer was balanced by Irving G. Thalberg. Beginning as secretary to Carl Laemmle at Universal, Thalberg came to MGM in 1924 at the age of 25 and quickly established a reputation as a boy wonder. Thalberg had the official title of Vice-President in Charge of Production. Unlike Mayer, he preferred to work in the background. However, it is generally accepted that Thalberg was the one individual responsible for MGM's consistently high quality level of production. Thalberg supervised every aspect of studio production. Bob Thomas, in his book *Thalberg,* describes this supervision very well:

> He made the selection of story material. He assigned his associates to supervise the myriad of details necessary to put a movie before the cameras. He retained the responsibility for selecting the writers and directors. He thrashed out the scripts with the writers, repeatedly offering his own original solutions to narrative problems. He cast the films and approved the costumes and sets. He made himself available for problems that arose during shooting. After the picture was assembled, he often made important changes in the cutting. He previewed the film and ordered extensive retakes if the public's reception was not favorable. He even oversaw the publicity and advertising campaign.
>
> He was neither a director, writer, actor, editor, designer, composer nor any other craftsman ordinarily associated with film making. He came closest to being a producer, yet he was not like today's producer, who follows a single film from beginning to end, then commences another one. Thalberg fulfilled the functions of a dozen producers.

Thalberg died in 1936 at the age of 37, after having established himself as the model of the creative Hollywood producer.

MGM's pseudonym as "the home of the stars" was well deserved. They employed the greatest array of production talent of any studio in history. The MGM system was a well constructed, smoothly operating machine. At the top was Thalberg. However, he employed many associate producers who were attuned to his method of operation. Thalberg would assess the particular talents of these men and then place them in positons he felt suited to their interests and skills. Hunt Stromberg, for example, specialized in "sexy" subjects, such as *Our Dancing Daughters* (1929) or *Red Dust* (1932), starring Jean Harlow and Clark Gable. Albert Lewin assumed control over many of MGM's literary works, such as *Private Lives* (1936), starring Noël Coward. Harry Rapf specialized in melodrama, such as *The Champ* (1934) and oversaw all "B" picture production.

These men reported directly to Thalberg and formed an "inner council" by which the vast production empire was controlled. It was a highly efficient system, as Thalberg did not have to waste time and effort with MGM's huge number of directors and stars. Only when Stromberg, Lewin, and the others had problems they couldn't handle did Thalberg step in. This allowed him time to analyze almost all of MGM's output and exercise direct control over the films themselves.

Next in command were the contract directors and here MGM was fortunate to have people who had both talent and long-term contracts. These men included Clarence Brown, who directed both the highly styled Greta Garbo films, *Anna Christie* (1930), *Anna Karenina* (1935), *Conquest* (1937) as well as such typically "American" films as Eugene O'Neill's *Ah Wilderness* (1935) and *Of Human Hearts* (1936). William S. Van Dyke was a versatile director responsible for "The Thin Man" series starring William Powell and Myrna Loy as well as the Jeannette MacDonald-Nelson Eddy musicals. Sam Wood directed most of the Marx Brothers comedies. Sidney Franklin directed MGM's literary films, such as *The Guardsman* (1931), *Private Lives* (1931), *The Barretts of Wimpole Street* (1934), and *The Good Earth* (1937). Victor Fleming was in charge of (rather than personally directed) some of MGM's biggest productions, including *Captain's Courageous* (1937) and *The Wizard of Oz* (1939).

All of these men and many more were highly talented individuals. However, the overall sense of directorial presence at MGM was one of diversity, variety, and executive management. There were simply too many other powerful and talented artists to allow one individual such as a director to stand out. The MGM directors were in effect supervisors and coordinators of talent. They imprinted their films with a certain style, but it was one of only several "prints."

MGM's overall pool of technical and artistic personnel was tremendous. All contributed significantly to the MGM style. The costumer was Adrian, whose influence was seen in everything from elaborate costume spectacles such as *Mutiny on the Bounty* (1935) and *The Barretts of Wimpole Street* (1934) to the flowing satiny gowns worn by such stars as Jean Harlow, Norma Shearer, and Greta Garbo. This modern style set a standard for both the motion picture and the fashion industry and would become symbolic of the era.

The set designer was Cedric Gibbons, whose work again ranged from the huge, elaborate sets for *Mutiny on the Bounty* (1935) to the smaller, yet intricate and detailed backdrops for *Dinner at Eight* (1933). Gibbon's sets were difficult to characterize except for the general comment usually made that they imparted a "glow" and "polish" to the films he worked on. Bosley Crowther remarked that for the 1936 production of *Marie Antoinette* Gibbons was instructed to produce the most exquisite and impressive sets that could be conceived. According to Crowther, "Versailles itself was slightly tarnished alongside the palace Gibbons whipped up."

All of this visual detail, whether through costume or set design, was indicative of the very system itself. Films were reconstructed and totally controlled events—usually made en-

This ballroom scene from MGM's *Marie Antoinette* illustrates the high style of the studio as well as the individual efforts of costumer Adrian and set designer Cedric Gibbons.

tirely within sound stage environments. Even when a film was shot on location, the reality was controlled as much as possible. Little of the "real" world was allowed to intrude as the "reality" of motion pictures was *created* by Gibbons, Adrian, and others.

Sound was supervised by Douglas Shearer, brother of leading MGM actress Norma Shearer, who also happened to be Thalberg's wife. Shearer, however, didn't need connections to assure his place at MGM or in the industry as he was acknowledged as one of the leading innovators in sound technology.

Despite MGM's great array of production talent, however, it was the stable of talented actors and actresses that, more than anyone else, provided MGM with its reputation. To say that MGM had a corner on acting talent is an understatement. Among the better known and more talented stars under contract to MGM in the Thirties and Forties were Ethel and John Barrymore, Wallace Beery, Jackie Cooper, Joan Crawford, Marion Davies, Clark Gable, Spencer Tracy, Robert Montgomery, Mickey Rooney, Jean Harlow, Helen Hayes, Walter Huston, Myrna Loy, Conrad Nagel, Johnny Weismuller, Robert Young, Robert Taylor, William Powell, Nelson Eddy, Greta Garbo, Norma Shearer, Jeannette MacDonald, Rosalind Russell, and Louise Rainer, among many others. As a number of critics have noted, MGM had a distinctly feminine emphasis, as illustrated by the dominance of top female names on the list. Only Gable, Tracy, and Taylor were superstar male leads. Eddy, Powell, Weismuller, Nagel, Rooney, and others were primarily character type stars who played a relatively limited range of parts. The point behind all this talent was simply that MGM had a corner on the market and simply by placing a certain type and number of stars in a film could virtually ensure its success.

However, lest one forget that despite all this individual brilliance it was still "the system" which dominated production, listen to film director Joseph Mankiewicz:

> I'd be willing to bet that in all the years I worked at Metro it would be hard to name a film done by one of the Metro stable of directors, say Woody Van Dyke, Victor Fleming, Bob Leonard, Clarence Brown, Jack Conway, and so on, which some *other* director didn't complete. People forget. Production in those days was such an assembly line, with so many films being turned out that by the time a film was previewed the guy who'd originally directed it would have already gone on to another. After the preview, there'd always be changes and retakes, and the front office would assign another director to handle them. Nobody ever thought anything of Sam Wood, who was a fine director, coming in to do the retakes on a Victor Fleming picture.

Paramount

Paramount was second in power and prestige only to MGM. Due largely to its vast theater holdings, it was the dominant studio of the silent era. Paramount was a studio distinctly opposite in style to MGM. Its films included the comedy of manners of Ernst Lubitsch, the lavish spectacle of Cecil B. DeMille, and the continental intrigue of Josef von Sternberg.

At first, primarily through the pioneering work of Lubitsch and Rouben Mamoulian, Paramount was the acknowledged leader in sound experimentation and development. This was at least partially caused by its dominant position in the Twenties as it easily made the financially hazardous transition to sound. Mamoulian's and Lubitsch's contributions to the development of sound have already been discussed. However, note must be taken of their careers as a whole while at Paramount. Mamoulian departed radically from his early realistic efforts and began to

An aerial view of MGM's back lot reveals a conglomerate environment of cities, castles, villages and lakes.
MUSEUM OF MODERN ART/FILM STILLS ARCHIVE

specialize in fantasy and musical films with such efforts as *Dr. Jekyll and Mr. Hyde* (1932), *Love Me Tonight* (1932) and *Song of Songs* (1933). Lubitsch, on the other hand, maintained a consistent profile with his sophisticated, fast-paced comedies and musicals. Utilizing two of Paramount's major stars, Maurice Chevalier and Jeannette MacDonald, he produced some of the period's wittiest, most charming musicals in *The Love Parade* (1929), *Design for Living* (1933), and *The Merry Widow* (1934). His nonmusical efforts were characterized by the same sophisticated charm and continental gaiety. His humor was distinctly European, emphasizing the sly glance, sharp repartee, and closed door. Some of his most successful films in this genre were *Trouble in Paradise* (1932), *Ninotchka* (1939), and *Heaven Can Wait* (1943).

Two more directors who represented the Paramount style were Mitchell Leisen and Cecil B. DeMille. Leisen is not particularly well known today, but his films of the Thirties and early Forties were well done and well received. Leisen was one of the few directors to come up the studio ladder from costume design. This greatly influenced his work, especially his light comedies, such as *Death Takes a Holiday* (1934), *Murder at the Vanities* (1934) and *Midnight* (1939). DeMille, of course, has achieved a lasting reputation as the great showman, the master of the spectacle film. His work for Paramount beautifully illustrated the coordination and combination of individual and studio. With heavy emphasis on set design, costumes, and casts of thousands, DeMille produced a remarkable number of "big" films, including *The Sign of the Cross* (1932), *Cleopatra* (1934), *The Crusades* (1935), *The Plainsman* (1937), *The Buccaneer* (1938) and *Union Pacific* (1939). DeMille's style is difficult to define. He was primarily concerned with three major elements in all his films: SEX, SIN, SCENERY. He managed to integrate and manipulate all three regardless if the content was the Bible, ancient Egypt, the Middle Ages, or the American West.

However, of all the directors who worked for Paramount in these years the one who represented the studio's style best was Josef von Sternberg. He set a tone of high style and continental romance which came to be known as *the* Paramount style. Most of his best work was done with Marlene Dietrich, beginning in 1931 with *Dishonored* and followed by *Shanghai Express* (1932), *Blonde Venus* (1932), *The Scarlet Empress* (1934) and *The Devil is a Woman* (1935). In all of these efforts, von Sternberg displayed a visual style that can only be described as exotic, emphasizing primarily lighting and decor. Few of his films are distinguished by plot, since content was really not important to him. As John Baxter quotes von Sternberg in *Hollywood in the Thirties:* "The best source for a film is an anecdote." Andrew Sarris has described him as a "lyricist of light and shadow." Von Sternberg is a classic example of a talented director who required a studio to create his best work. He required total control over his environment and utilized all the technical and artistic resources of Paramount to achieve his results. He was also a good example of the dominating power of the star system, as Paramount was willing to put up with some of his eccentricities as long as Marlene Dietrich appeared in his films, virtually guaranteeing their financial success.

As with MGM, technical personnel contributed greatly to Paramount's effectiveness. Perhaps the key individual here was set designer Hans Dreier. His work is especially evident in most of DeMille's and von Sternberg's films. In a recent interview, Garson Kanin described this set style as "rococo" and related the story of Ernst Lubitsch remarking that he had been to Paris, France and Paris, Paramount and preferred the latter.

Although not blessed with a large number of contract stars, Paramount employed some of the most striking and individual personalities of the period. Marlene Dietrich was perhaps the most glamorous. However, of equal if not more important value to the studio was another glamorous woman, Mae West. Beginning with *Night After Night* (1932), she starred in eight films over the next six years, all of which were very successful at a time when Paramount desperately needed income. Gary Cooper was the studio's top male lead and was used constantly in everything from foreign intrigue to high society to light comedy. Another male star was Bing Crosby, whose solo musicals in the Thirties helped Paramount tremendously. However, it was not until he teamed with comedian Bob Hope in *Road to Rio* (1940) that Paramount began to push him as a major star. As a result of his "road film" success and Paramount publicity, Crosby became the top box-office attraction through most of World War II.

In summary, it is difficult to get a solid grip on Paramount. Its profile was a mixture of light comedy, continental intrigue, and lavish spectacle. Perhaps this split personality resulted from a shaky financial base and front office politics. Perhaps it was simply because the studio had a collection of highly talented individuals. Whatever the reasons, Paramount's profile was one of the most fascinating and diverse of any studio.

Warner Brothers

Unlike Paramount's split personality, Warner Brothers had a distinct and unswerving profile. It quickly became known as the studio with a hard, fast, big city style. Warners was a "depression studio," as its films and overall style clearly reflected the mood and atmosphere of the depression more than any other company.

Key films establishing Warner's style were *Little Caesar* (1930), starring Edward G. Robinson, *The Public Enemy* (1931), starring James Cagney, *I Am a Fugitive from a Chain Gang* (1932), starring Paul Muni, *Fury* (1936), directed by Fritz Lang, and *The Maltese Falcon* (1941), starring Humphrey Bogart. In addition, there were scores of lesser-known films, such as *Heroes For Sale* (1935) and *Wild Boys of the Road* (1934), all of which resulted in one of the most prominent social realism cycles in film history. The content was seemingly torn from newspaper headlines and in several cases *(I Am a Fugitive From a Chain Gang)* was based on fact. Just as important to this sense of realism was the basic style of these films, characterized most clearly by the hard, flat, black and white photography pioneered and perfected by Warner cinematographer Sol Polito. Editing also played a key role, as Warner's films were cut to a maximum of 90 minutes, with most running just over an hour.

Another type of "depression film" developed at Warners was the backstage musical. The form took the depression as a basic theme, but spent little time in detailing the reality of it. Society simply served as a springboard from which to launch elaborate musical numbers. Key films in this form included *42nd Street* (1933), *Gold Diggers of 1933* (1933), and *Footlight Parade* (1935). These and several others were known primarily for the work of choreographer Busby Berkeley. Famous for his stylized nonrealistic productions, Berkeley became better known than most of the directors he worked under. Berkeley used squadrons of people, usually scantily clad girls, in intricate and complex designs which often resulted in a surrealistic atmosphere. The depression was still present; however, in contrast to the more graphic social realism presented in *Little Caesar, I Am a Fugitive* . . ., this was a "fun" depression. The plots generally revolved around attempts to produce a musical without adequate money and the air of imminent disaster hung over the entire company. However, the endings were always happy, as the musical went on, the boy got the girl, and some light was seen at the end of the tunnel.

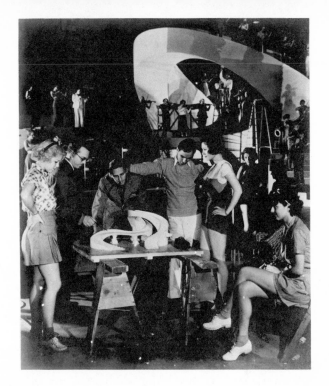

e and after scene showing Busby Berkely at work designing one of his
d production numbers and the end result as it appeared in *Gold*
 of 1933.
OF MODERN ART/FILM STILLS ARCHIVE

These two types of films best represented the basic Warner's style. However, like any studio, it had a large pool of talent and therefore, diversity was almost a built-in quality. Warner's diversity centered primarily around three talented and totally unique stars: George Arliss, Errol Flynn, and Paul Muni.

Arliss was a veteran of many years on the legitimate stage and was used by the studio in such prestige vehicles as *Disraeli* (1929), *Old English* (1930), and *Voltaire* (1933). Arliss won the Academy Award for Best Actor for his performance in *Disraeli*, but in retrospect most of his films date badly and his individual performances are heavy and obviously stage dominated.

At the opposite end of the continuum was Errol Flynn, Warner's answer to Douglas Fairbanks. Less talented than Fairbanks, especially in handling light comedy, Flynn was the epitome of the virile, handsome individualist, battling all types of enemies from pirates to Indians. Flynn moved through his films with a steely-eyed stare and unswerving demeanor. He was always present, but rarely dominated in the manner of Fairbanks. Most of his films, such as *Captain Blood* (1935), *The Charge of the Light Brigade* (1936), *The Adventures of Robin Hood* (1938), *The Dawn Patrol* (1938), and *The Sea Hawk* (1940) stressed action. It was this large, impersonal action, rather than intense personal drama that dominated his films. Nevertheless, he was one of Warner's most productive and popular stars, appearing in more than thirty films between 1935 and 1946.

Besides Spencer Tracy, Paul Muni was one of the most talented and versatile actors in Hollywood. He was used initially in typical Warner films such as *I Am a Fugitive . . ., Bordertown* (1935) and *Black Fury* (1936). However, he soon began to branch out with a series of biographical studies, which included an Academy Award-winning performance in *The Story of Louis Pasteur* (1935) and the major roles in *The Life of Emile Zola* (1937) and *Juarez* (1939). Muni supplied Warner's with most of their "prestige" during this time and became one of the industry's most respected craftsmen.

The two leading stars of the studio were Edward G. Robinson and James Cagney. Both of them had similar careers and suffered from similar career problems. Each was a versatile actor and yet became typed very quickly in their careers as "tough guys." Although they both tried, neither was ever able to completely escape this role definition. Cagney was slightly more successful than Robinson, because of his dancing ability, which he parlayed into an Academy Award-winning performance in

Yankee Doodle Dandy (1942). Both of these men represent how the system was built on and depended on personalities, but at the same time manipulated and controlled these personalities for the studio's benefit.

As should be noted by now, Warner's was a "male" studio. Its female stars were few and all seemed to be cast from the same mold: tough, wise-cracking "dames" who played hard women. The most prominent female personalities of the period were Joan Blondell, Glenda Farrell, Barbara Stanwyck, and Bette Davis. Only Davis achieved some measure of creative independence and versatility as she consistently fought for better roles. The studio soon regarded her as their "female Muni" and she amply rewarded them with an Academy Award-winning performance in *Jezebel* (1938) and nominations for the next four years running.

Warner's directors have received little attention so far and it is with good reason. The Warner system of production placed less emphasis on directing than it did on acting, editing, and photography. To be sure, there were several good contract directors working for Warners, including Lloyd Bacon, who was responsible for several of the Berkeley musicals, and William Dieterle, who directed most of Muni's prestige vehicles. Michael Curtiz was the most prolific of Warner's directors. Curtiz directed most of the Errol Flynn pictures and achieved a light, almost winsome style despite being responsible for action pictures which involved logistic coordination of people and equipment more than artistic direction.

Garson Kanin, again in a recent interview, provided some insight into the Warner's system and how it functioned in relation to its directors.

> ... there were Warner directors, for instance, who never got near a script. It's no secret that Michael Curtiz sometimes started shooting a script without reading it. He would make about four pictures a year, which at those studios wasn't unusual. They would be prepared almost entirely by the front office, they'd be cast and the sets would be designed. And then they would say, "Well Mike Curtiz, he's finishing Thursday ... Do you want him to start on Monday? No, make it Tuesday." They'd call him in and say, "You're going to start this on Tuesday." He'd say, "What is it?" And they'd say, "Well, it's *The Charge of the Light Brigade*." "What's that?" "Well, you'll see ...." He would then maybe read it, maybe not. The director would do his part of the job and the film went to the cutter and he put it together. Frequently a director at Warners wouldn't even see his assembled stuff. It was all organized, assem-

bly line stuff, and I think that's one reason why the general run of pictures was so bland . . . in all my years in Hollywood, and later, I never knew a director who had final say on his work. Not one . . . And if you talked to producers and heads of the studios, they would say, "Why should they? It's our money. . . ." For the most part, they (directors) were employees who got paid so much per week. Not even by the year; they were paid by the week on Fridays, like employees. That's what made the world go round . . .

20th Century-Fox

Although organized in 1935, Fox had a history dating back to 1915; its founder was William Fox. Fox continued to operate the studio until 1932, but was eased out following a series of court actions and stock mergers. He was replaced by Sidney Kent and in 1935 the organization was merged with 20th Century Pictures.

20th Century-Fox achieved its reputation primarily through the efforts of Darryl F. Zanuck, who in 1935, became Vice President in Charge of Production at the age of 33. Zanuck, like Thalberg, supervised virtually every aspect of production. Mel Gussow's biography of Zanuck, *Don't Say Yes Until I Finish Talking*, illustrates this well.

> He announced assignments, assigned credits, including his own (whether a picture should be "produced by DFZ" or "DFZ's production of"), suggested old movies to be rerun as guides for new movies, rewrote dialogue, canceled projects, moaned about the state of Hollywood and the state of the world, welcomed new employees (to Charles Brackett: "the steam room downstairs is at your disposal, and also Sam, the barber"), distributed praise as well as scorn, changed titles, and changed his mind (depending on the grosses, a picture could go from great to terrible in a swirl of memos). Except to his top personnel and specific producers, directors and writers he was working with, he was accessible largely through memos.

20th Century-Fox, had relatively few stars. In 1935, Zanuck inherited Will Rogers, Shirley Temple and Charlie Chan. Rogers died less than a year later, and so Zanuck came up with the motto "Stars don't make pictures, pictures make stars." However badly Zanuck wished this were true, it was equally true that the Fox output in the Thirties and Forties did not make many stars. Had it not been for Shirley Temple and Charlie Chan and later Betty Grable, Fox might not have survived.

Lionel Barrymore and Shirly Temple
in Fox's 1935 production *The Little Colonel.*
MUSEUM OF MODERN ART/FILM STILLS ARCHIVE

The Chan series began in 1931 with Warner Oland in the title role. More than a dozen films were produced in six years, most of them similar in plot and style. The only changes seemed to be in the title, which had Charlie in different parts of the world: *Charlie Chan in London, Paris, Egypt, Shanghai* or in different locations: *Charlie Chan at the Circus, at the Race Track, at the Opera, at the Olympics, on Broadway,* and *at Monte Carlo.* Following Pearl Harbor, Orientals were out as sympathetic characters, and Charlie quickly disappeared.

Almost as prolific and incredibly popular, Shirley Temple was one of the most remarkable phenomenons of the entire period. She took the American public by storm, starting in 1934 with *Carolina,* and for the next six years reigned supreme as one of the industry's top box office attractions. During this time she starred in twenty-three films for Fox, all of them highly successful. For all practical purposes her career was through by the time she was 10. Fox placed her in a number of films as a teenager, but she never regained her success as a child. She made her last film, *A Kiss for Corliss,* in 1949 at the tender age of 21. Fortunately for Fox, Betty Grable arrived on the scene to pick up the

251

slack left by Chan and Temple's decline. Grable headed up the so-called "Fox girls," who were basically nameless, but looked alike. They were placed in films primarily to reveal their physical attributes, which was very successful among a male population separated by war from normal female companionship. Grable, of course, became the prototype of all pin-up girls during the war and was one of the most popular stars of the war period.

Columbia

Harry and Jack Cohn began Columbia in 1924, starting out on what was known as "poverty row." However, through the bulldog tenacity and instinctive "feel" of Harry Cohn, the administrative ability of Jack Cohn and Joseph Brandt, and the films of Frank Capra, Columbia emerged in the Thirties as an important studio. Like most of the other studios besides MGM, Paramount, and Warners, Columbia had a definite lack of star names and relatively few assets to indulge on lavish productions. It was not until Rita Hayworth emerged in the early Forties that Columbia had a star of international magnitude. Rather, Columbia's films were populated by such people as Ralph Bellamy, who starred in thirteen films in one year, Jean Arthur, Grace Moore, and Lee Tracy. Most of Capra's films, for example, had leads "borrowed" from other studios; Clark Gable and Jimmy Stewart from MGM, Gary Cooper and Claudette Colbert from Paramount.

Rather than stars, Columbia relied heavily on creative personnel, especially writers and directors borrowed or briefly lured from other studios. Important directors employed by Columbia included Lewis Milestone, Howard Hawks, George Cukor, George Stevens, and Leo McCarey. Writers of reputation included Dorothy Parker, Robert Riskin, Herman Mankiewicz, and Jo Swerling. Few of these people stayed long, however. This policy of quick departure was due mainly to Harry Cohn. Legends have grown up around the tactics of Harry "King" Cohn. As the only person to be both president of the company and chief of production, he exerted total, domineering control over the studio and its personnel. However, Cohn had an instinct for recognizing talent and a healthy respect for it. This was evidenced by his offering directors the unheard-of opportunity of sharing in a picture's profits. Although almost 70% of Columbia's product was "B" quality, such "A" features as Capra's *Lost Horizon* (1937) and *You Can't Take it With You* (1938), Leo

McCarey's *The Awful Truth* (1937), and Charles Vidor's *A Song to Remember* (1945) provided Columbia with prosperity, reputation, and up to 60% of its profits. Columbia's films were mostly contemporary in content, due both to the lack of money required for expensive period pictures and the tastes of Cohn. Although Capra did his best work as a contract director for Columbia, he

Jimmy Stewart as Mr. Smith makes an impassioned plea
for justice on the floor of Congress in Frank Capra's
1939 production *Mr. Smith Goes to Washington.*
MUSEUM OF MODERN ART/FILM STILLS ARCHIVE

deserves special recognition here beyond his economic value to Columbia. Most of his films bear the stamp of an individual creator, although screen writer Robert Riskin and cameraman Joe Walker must share some of the praise given to such films as *It Happened One Night* (1934), *Mr. Deeds Goes to Town* (1936), and *Mr. Smith Goes to Washington* (1937). Most of Capra's films display a boisterous sense of humor and a knack for improvisation. However, the most striking characteristic of all his work in this period is what one reviewer called "the fantasy of good will." This was a philosophy inherent in Capra's films which said that the little man could triumph over his odds, whatever they might be. This philosophy was especially popular in the depression and Capra himself states in his autobiography, *The Name Above the Title,* that he felt that he had to be the spokesman for the little man; that his films had to contain a message and not simply entertain. This philosophy worked to the extent that Capra won three Academy Awards as best director and his films won the award for best picture twice.

Radio-Keith-Orpheum (RKO)

Radio-Keith-Orpheum (RKO) was actually the top holding company which integrated various production-distribution and exhibition organizations, among them RKO Radio Pictures, Inc. Organized in 1931, RKO was originally conceived by RCA, which was seeking its place in the development of sound pictures. However, the depression soon made its effects known and RKO went into receivership from 1933–1940. However, the studio prospered, due mainly to the efforts and talents of Fred Astaire and Ginger Rogers who starred in a nine film series of smart, fashionable musicals beginning with *Flying Down to Rio* in 1934. The most popular films of the nine-film series and some of the most engaging musicals ever made were *Top Hat* (1935), *Swing Time* (1936), *Shall We Dance* (1937), and *Carefree* (1938). Plot was never particularly important or even relevant to most of these films. Rather, narrative served simply as the thread which strung the individual Astaire-Rogers numbers together. Although some attempts were made to "integrate" the individual productions with the rest of the film, once a production was started it took on a life of its own. Unlike Busby Berkeley's tightly edited and totally constructed fantasies, Astaire performed in a totally "real" situation, with the camera usually recording him alone or with Miss Rogers in full figure in one

The monster plays tenderly with the little girl in
James Whale's 1931 production of *Frankenstein*.
MUSEUM OF MODERN ART/FILM STILLS ARCHIVE

take. Astaire was an original and unduplicated creator; not so
much through his choreography (Hermes Pan did much of this
work for RKO), but through his completely natural and almost
"eerie" physical grace. He used these natural abilities to interpret in both dance and song (Astaire did not possess a "great"
voice, but Irving Berlin called him the best interpreter of his
music of any singer) to capture the very essence and spirit of all
that was light, gay, and fancy.

Universal

Universal was one of Hollywood's oldest studios, dating back
to 1912. The studio established itself as one of the top silent
companies, primarily because it created in areas where it had
little competition. Universal was known as the home of the "B"
film. In 1927–28, for example, the studio produced 26 Westerns,
four serials, 52 comedies, and several feature novelties. They
continued this pattern into sound and in the Thirties became
primarily known for their horror films and "B" musicals. A
teenager named Deanna Durbin was the key to their musical

success as she made a number of very popular films, beginning
with *Three Smart Girls* in 1936 and including among the more
successful, *100 Men and a Girl* (1937), *Mad About Music* (1938),
and *That Certain Age* (1938). The slapstick comedy of Abbott
and Costello also helped to fill Universal's coffers, but its major
creative efforts were in the horror genre. Beginning in 1931 with
Frankenstein, Universal produced some of the classic horror
films of all time, including *Dracula* (1932), *Freaks* (1932), *The
Mummy* (1932), and *The Invisible Man* (1933). Most of these
films were not great commercial hits, perhaps because they did
not simply exploit the grotesque visual nature of the genre, but
presented a moral/philosophical point of view. *Dracula,* as
played by Bela Lugosi, was not simply some bizarre caricature,
but embodied the very essence of evil. Frankenstein's monster,
as played by Boris Karloff, was not some insane creature, but a
driven animal who evoked feelings of compassion as well as
terror.

A Minor Case: Republic

There were, as noted previously, a great number of minor
studios whose story will most likely never be told. However, one
studio formed from the merger of several smaller ones was the
"king" of the "B" film, especially the "B" Western. The studio
was Republic, founded in 1935 by a number of small-time independent producers and located in the old Mack Sennett studios.
Under the leadership of Nat Levine, Republic specialized in the
rapid-fire production of Gene Autry and Roy Rogers' Westerns,
twelve-chapter serials, detective stories, and country-style musicals starring Judy Canova.

Speed and cost-cutting were Republic's and especially Levine's specialty. Republic pictures were the ones which played
every Saturday afternoon in thousands of neighborhood theatres.
The pace of production at Republic was so fast that writers would
often find themselves hard at work on a sound stage, typing
dialogue for scenes which were being shot twenty feet away.

The key to Republic's success, like most of the other studios,
depended on its stars. In this case it meant Autry and Rogers.
This illustrates once again the major dividing line between
success and failure in Hollywood. Hundreds of minor studios
had the same characteristics as Republic, except for attracting
popular personalities.

The Directors

This review of the major studios obviously leads to a crucial question: What difference did it make that the films were produced by an industry and not by a man with a chisel or palette?

In some ways this is an unfair question, since a motion picture by its very nature is a collaborative enterprise. Even D. W. Griffith, one of the most single-minded and highly personal directors, relied upon others for advice and help, especially his talented cameraman G. W. "Billy" Bitzer. Indeed, Lillian Gish, in referring to Griffith in his declining years, said:

> There was no one left among his staff to say "no" once in awhile. He needed the gently abrasive minds and personalities of those who had once been close to him. He had thrived on the tactful suggestion, the quiet hint that some other director had done as well, that a better effect could be found.

This comment can be made about almost every artist who had worked in films. This does not deny the talents and insight of highly talented craftsmen; it only illustrates the very nature of the film medium, especially in the feature film. Collaboration is more than a necessary evil; it is a vital factor contributing to the overall excellence of most motion pictures.

More than 7,500 feature films were produced between 1930 and 1946. Most of them were characterized by the traits of the studios that produced them. However, some of them stand out because a creative, talented director was allowed to place his personal signature on the film. Indeed, as John Baxter has pointed out in *Hollywood in the Thirties:*

> Although the high average standard of Hollywood films during the thirties is directly attributable to the studio system with its pools of talent and techniques, most of the period's major advances in cinema art can be traced to a group of independent producers whose unwillingness to work within the studio system gave them a greater degree of freedom than would have been possible otherwise.

Although this point is highly debatable, it is certainly true that a few key directors deserve special attention. Several, including von Sternberg, Capra, and Lubitsch, have already been discussed in relation to the studios they worked for. However, some important directors of the period did not have any distinct studio affiliation and require separate and individual analysis.

One of the most creative craftsmen in Hollywood was Howard Hawks, who directed several of the outstanding films of the period, including *The Dawn Patrol* (1930), *Scarface* (1932), *Twentieth Century* (1934), *The Road to Glory* (1936), *Only Angels Have Wings* (1938), and *Sergeant York* (1940). Until recently, Hawks was little appreciated by most critics and historians. However, he has come to be recognized as one of the few individuals creating films within and for the studio system that still maintained a personal identity. Hawks' cinema is clean, direct, and functional. He was rarely among the avant garde in technology or content. Rather, as he stated himself: "All I'm trying to do is tell a story." One of Hawks' major strengths was an ability to work in a variety of genres, ranging from the gangster film to screwball comedy to Westerns to science fiction. His films contained few profound themes. Instead, they concentrated on tight continuous narrative action. Although he made films for many studios and under many producers, his work always retained a unique directness and force which made his efforts commercially successful and artistically distinct.

John Ford also stands out in this period as a strong, successful commercial director and artist with a personal vision. Best known for his Western films, such as *The Iron Horse* (1924), *Stagecoach* (1939), and *My Darling Clementine* (1946) among many others, he was also a versatile director comfortable in a number of genres, as evidenced by his success with *The Informer* (1935), *The Grapes of Wrath* (1940) and *How Green Was My Valley* (1941). Like Hawks, Ford was known for his strength and directness. However, Ford was interested in atmosphere and mood and as a result most of his films have a lyric quality which is at the same time very formal and structured. Ford worked in and needed the studio system. Some critics have questioned Ford's status as an auteur at times because of the incongruities in a career that saw him produce not only such critically acclaimed works as *The Informer* but such studio potboilers as *Wee Willie Winkie* (1937) with Shirley Temple. One of the keys to Ford's ability to stamp his personal signature on his films was that he rarely shot any excess footage. He gave a film editor only enough footage to put the film together as Ford essentially shot it.

Ford did most of his best work in this period for 20th Century-Fox. Prior to 1939, his reputation was limited, but with

Some of the power and appeal of John Ford's 1939
classic western *Stagecoach* are revealed in this vista of
the stage moving through Monument Valley.
MUSEUM OF MODERN ART/FILM STILLS ARCHIVE

his production of *The Grapes of Wrath* (1940), *The Long Voyage Home* (1940), and *How Green Was My Valley* (1941), his critical reputation soared. If Ford had any consistent problems in his films, it was his sentimentality. Ford was at his weakest when he attempted the abstract; he was strongest when he was creating visual tableau of simple and poetic action.

Both Ford and Hawks continued as dominant directors in Hollywood through the Fifties and into the Sixties, achieving the one quality above all else which classifies them as directorial auteurs: consistency of vision and the ability to stamp this on every film they made.

A third director came to the era late, producing his first film in 1941. At the age of twenty-five Orson Welles produced one of the most significant films of the period and indeed, of almost all film history, *Citizen Kane* (1941). He soon followed it with an equally creative film, *The Magnificent Ambersons* (1942). So much has been written about *Citizen Kane* that it is difficult to discuss it in a few sentences. Voted by an international panel of film critics in 1972 as the best film of all time, it is regarded by most critics as the American film having the greatest influence on subsequent film development since *The Birth of a Nation* (1915). *Citizen Kane* is famous both for its theme and its artistry. Its story is the ill-disguised and unsympathetic biography of newspaper mogul William Randolph Hearst. This fact alone created tremendous problems both during and after filming. None of the Hearst newspapers carried ads for it and the Hearst critics panned it unmercifully. Welles' technical artistry domi-

The remarkable deep focus composition in Orson
Welles' *Citizen Kane* is beautifully illustrated in this shot
of Kane and his wife Susan.

nated the film and he created scenes of tremendous power. This
artistry lay primarily in Welles' "eccentric" camera angles,
sweeping camera movement, single take, deep-focus scenes, and
the use of audio montage, a technique employing overlapping
sound which he first utilized in radio.

Welles composed and created relationship within shots
through camera composition and movement. The opening scene
of *Citizen Kane* begins with a close-up of a "No Trespassing"
sign and then builds as the camera slowly moves along the iron
grating of the fence which surrounds Kane's estate, revealing
iron flowers, a huge "K" and finally in the distance the towering
and forbidding castle. In all his films, Welles' characters usually
interact with their environment through position within a scene.
He uses his camera to reveal these relationships in a completely
fluid and highly dramatic manner. Gregg Toland was his cameraman for *Kane* and was responsible for many of the deep-focus
effects achieved by creating specially ground lenses which eliminated normal depth of field characteristics.

Welles' second film, *The Magnificent Ambersons*, although
not filmed on as grand a scale as *Kane,* was almost as effective

in its portrayal of the disintegration of a way of life at the turn of the century. Welles utilizes camera movement more in this film and his "last ball" sequence is one of the most dramatic and effective examples of camera movement ever used. The camera starts outside the Amberson mansion and then moves through the front door, past maids and butlers, through archways, into great rooms filled with people, all in one sweeping motion.

With this and other "tour de force" examples, both *Kane* and *Ambersons* tend to overwhelm the audience with technique. However, both of these efforts have come to be appreciated in later years as much for their vision, social comment, and intent as their technical virtuosity. As several critics have correctly pointed out, these films are really the forerunners of the "serious" European films of the late Fifties and early Sixties, as much for their content and personal point of view as their individualistic style.

Both are studio films. Welles required the studio, the accomplished technicans, the company of actors. Above all he required the controlled atmosphere which only a studio could provide. The winter scenes in *Ambersons* were shot inside a cold storage locker because Welles wanted both the realism of frosty breath and real snow and controlled lighting and exact camera placement.

Welles has made only ten films since 1941 and while all of them display his unique style, none of them carries the thematic strength of *Kane* or *Ambersons*. As a result, such efforts as *The Stranger* (1946), *The Lady From Shanghai* (1948) and *Touch of Evil* (1955), while containing brilliant individual sequences, ultimately fall under the weight of Welles' style.

Short Subjects

It is clear from our previous analysis that this period was dominated by a system of production which subordinated the individual creator to the demands of producing for a mass audience. This system resulted in the creation of certain patterns and formulas. Feature-length films were the most conspicuous products of the studios. However, perhaps even more indicative of the way the system worked was the tremendous amount of non-feature material produced. This category, commonly called "shorts," included shorts, serials, newsreels, and cartoons. Only a system anticipating, and subsequently geared toward meeting a huge public appetite for film could afford to produce so much non-feature material.

Shorts were the most important non-feature materials. All of the major studios made them part of their regular production schedule. They were created by separate, autonomous units staffed by people who did nothing but make a particular kind of short. For example, the Three Stooges shorts were made by Columbia under the short subject unit headed by Jules White and Del Lord. Most of these films were shot in three to five days and relied heavily on stock footage and footage from previous films in the series. Between 1934 and 1958 Columbia turned out 190 Three Stooges shorts, a record for both longevity and productivity. At MGM Jack Chertok was head of short subjects and produced, among many others, the famous "Pete Smith Specialties." Chertok's comment that "We had access to most facilities so long as we didn't get in the way" is representative of the studios' attitude toward shorts. They relied on them heavily for overall studio profit and yet only reluctantly recognized their legitimacy in the total studio structure. The longevity of the shorts proved their moneymaking ability and it was only when the total audience for film had declined and the costs for all film, including shorts, had risen that the studios dropped them from their schedules in the mid-Fifties.

Serials were another aspect of production during this era; however, only four studios produced them—Universal, Columbia, Republic, and Mascot. The other five major studios did not find it necessary or feasible to devote time, money, and personnel to serials because of their predominantly "A" feature schedule.

Serials covered almost every conceivable area of content, including outer space (Flash Gordon, Buck Rogers), the West (The Lone Ranger, Red Rider), the jungle (Tarzan, Jungle Jim), and detectives (Flying G-Men, Dick Tracy). They were usually issued in ten-to fifteen-chapter installments and were enthusiastically received almost every Saturday afternoon by millions of cheering children. In 1946, it was estimated by *Film Daily Yearbook* that the weekly audience for serials was 12,000,000.

Like everything else the studios did, serials had a strong economic basis for existence. One of their key functions was to provide a testing ground for new talent and a burying ground for old talent under long-term contract. John Wayne, for example, starred in a number of serials for Mascot in the early Thirties.

Walter Brennan, Mickey Rooney, and Lloyd Bridges all had serial experience before achieving stardom. On the other end, several major silent stars, such as Henry B. Walthall (the "Little Colonel" in *The Birth of a Nation)* and Francis X. Bushman, were working in serials in the late Thirties.

The series film, although feature length, bore strong resemblance to the shorts and serials because of its repetitive nature. Just as the series program is a staple of the television industry today, necessary because of the need to continually program to a mass audience, the series film was a staple of the studio system of the Thirties and Forties. Perhaps no other content characteristic is more indicative of the place Hollywood occupied in American life than the series film. Producing a number of films with the same characters in similar plots signified a confidence, a sureness that what was produced would be accepted. It also reflected the system's dependency on formula and its willingness to repeat a proven concept. Some of the most popular series included "Hopalong Cassidy" (66 films), Columbia's budget series, including "Ellery Queen," "Boston Blackie," and "Blon-

Mickey Rooney gives a typical Andy Hardy kiss to his best girl in *Andy Hardy Meets a Debutante.*
MUSEUM OF MODERN ART/FILM STILLS ARCHIVE

die," MGM's "The Thin Man," starring William Powell and Myrna Loy (four films), and Paramount's "Road" series, starring Bing Crosby and Bob Hope (six films). Perhaps the most famous and successful series was "Andy Hardy." Beginning in 1937 with *A Family Affair*, MGM produced 17 films in the series, ending with *Andy Hardy Comes Home* in 1958. Produced by George Seitz's economy unit and starring Mickey Rooney and a host of stock characters, the series made more than $25 million for MGM.

Animation in the form of the short cartoon was yet another feature of the studio production system. Animation had existed in a number of countries almost from the beginning of motion pictures. In fact, the motion toys of the 19th century were animations. The strip cartoons used in the Zoetrope and Phenakistoscope were drawn by the thousands, but with the development of photography, phase pictures replaced these drawings and animation declined.

Animation by definition is a film that is created frame by frame. It normally takes three forms; the cartoon, puppet animation, and pixillation (animation of the human form). Its simple but arduous technique consists of drawing 24 different phase pictures for every second of screen time. A ten-minute cartoon would require 14,400 different drawings.

Animation did not develop rapidly at first, since most filmmakers were fascinated with their new found power to record reality in motion. Emile Cohl of France was the first animation "mogul" as he produced over 200 cartoons between 1908 and 1918. The first American cartoon units began around 1900 and continued with a moderate level of production throughout the silent period. However, the lack of sound and color greatly hampered cartoon development. Audiences could accept a silent Douglas Fairbanks or Charlie Chaplin, because they were dynamic human characters. Cartoons containing stick figures and crude backgrounds had great difficulty in competing against this.

Into this tentative and relatively undeveloped field came a man from Kansas City who revolutionized the form. Walt Disney began his career making one minute black and white animated commercials. With his partner and chief artist, Ub Iwerks, Disney soon gravitated to Hollywood, where he experimented with a mouse character. This met with little success. It was not until Mickey, as he was later called, was able to talk and sing in *Steamboat Willie* (1928) that Disney's cartoons caught on.

Following this initial success, Disney began to expand his operation. He succeeded primarily because of his willingness to

The most famous mouse in the world makes his debut by playing
a tune in Walt Disney's 1928 production *Steamboat Willie*.
© Walt Disney Productions

gamble and experiment with new technical innovations. This,
plus his perfectionist nature, produced a great many films which
were barely profitable. He expanded into color with *Flowers and
Trees* in 1932 and soon was filming in color exclusively. He
managed to come up with several big films, such as *The Three
Little Pigs* (1933), *Snow White* (1937), and *Cinderella* (1938),
which kept his studio solvent.

The keys to Disney's success were stories and characters. All
of his films had carefully constructed plots, most of them preaching a moral or delivering some sort of message. His characters
were humans in animal disguise. Each one, whether it was
Mickey Mouse, Donald Duck, Pluto, or Goofy, had clearly identifiable personalities. Mickey was the eternal optimist—a personi-
fication of Disney himself. Donald Duck was an angry protagon-
ist, quickly taking offense and ready to fight at a moment's
notice.

In 1940, Disney made his one attempt at serious art in
cartoon form—*Fantasia*. It is a complex and serious film with
many brilliant and visually stunning sequences. However, it is
badly flawed in that its attempt to raise animation to a higher,
more philosophical level worked against audience expectations
and predispositions. Reissued in the late Sixties, it met with

265

great success as a more visually literate and filmically sophisticated audience saw the film as some sort of inner reality—a mind-expanding trip.

After a successful war effort in which Donald Duck taught American soldiers how to handle an M-1 rifle and informed other Americans about South America, Disney turned to live-action nature films, such as *Seal Island* (1948) and *Beaver Valley* (1950).

Although Disney dominated the cartoon field during the Thirties and Forties, almost all of the major studios had cartoon divisions. Columbia produced "Scrappy" cartoons, using a staff of 200 people. Universal's 100-person cartoon unit was headed by Woody Woodpecker creator Walter Lantz. Warner Brothers had its "Merry Melody" series and introduced the two most famous non-Disney characters, Bugs Bunny and Porky Pig. 20th Century-Fox distributed Terry Toons, created by independent Paul Terry, and Paramount distributed Max Fleischer's "Popeye the Sailor."

Besides Disney, however, the industry viewed cartoons as simply program fillers, a little extra frosting on the cake. However, for the audience, children and adults alike, cartoons became an expected and special attraction all by themselves. The characters became "stars" in their own right. Following the war, television began to saturate the audience with hundreds of "new" characters and old stories, and the theatrical cartoon, already weakened by the general industry collapse, died a slow but final death.

In summary, the non-feature film was perhaps the most typical and representative form of film produced by the studio system. Shorts came about as a result of the double feature practices of exhibitors during the depression and the studios' efforts to satisfy their quota agreements. The studio system was the perfect place for these types of films. Contract players were in abundance and newly signed actors and actresses had a safe, obscure testing ground, as most series and shorts were virtually ignored by the critics. The studios employed staff producers, directors, and writers by the year rather than by individual pictures, thus making the shorts inexpensive to produce.

Summary

The amount and type of production along with other factors, such as huge stables of contract directors, writers, and actors has always led to the accusation that the studio was simply a factory spewing out chunks of entertainment and did nothing to further the art of the motion picture. The studio system obviously produced a tension between film as art and film as product. Irving G. Thalberg, production head of MGM, clarified this tension when he stated:

> It is a business, in the sense that it must bring in money at the box office, but it is an art in that it involves on its devotees, the inexorable demands of creative expression. In short, it is a creative business, dependent as almost no other business is, on the emotional reaction of its customers. It should be conducted with budgets and cost sheets, but it cannot be conducted with blueprints and graphs.

This point is further reinforced by Kenneth Macgowan in his book *Behind the Screen*. Macgowan, a long-time producer, maintains that studios were not the same as factories. In a factory, the same men do the same job to produce the same item. In a motion picture studio, there were innumerable combinations of people and material which produced consistently different items. Certainly, because of close supervision and overall management philosophy, there was a distinct studio style, but the films produced by the studios certainly cannot be likened to a car or an electric toaster. In fact, the huge number of films produced had some advantages as *New York Times* film critic Vincent Canby suggested in reference to a contemporary filmmaker:

> Mr. Fassbinder obviously works fast. He doesn't fool around getting things perfect. He tries something difficult and if it works, fine. If not, he'll do it better the next time around. Shakespeare worked this way. So, I'm sure, did a lot of the people in Hollywood in what are called the good old days. Experience doesn't accumulate like dust. You simply can't sit around waiting for it to settle on you. You have to work to get it.

What was the mystique, the power this era had and continues to have on the American mind? The answer is not simple. One element, of course, was visual monopoly. Radio provided the only strong entertainment competition. However, it was both a non-visual and "home" medium. Motion pictures had a home, but it was the Palace rather than the parlor. Often the magic surrounding the films was the environment in which they were seen as well as the films themselves.

At first, theaters were seemingly not affected by the depression. The tremendous appeal and acceptance of sound resulted in a meteoric rise in attendance. By 1930 attendance was at

A theater marquee advertises what for many depression
audiences was more important than the film itself.
MUSEUM OF MODERN ART/FILM STILLS ARCHIVE

100,000,000 a week. However, the prosperity was short-lived
and the depression soon caught up with the motion picture
industry. In 1932 attendance was down to 60,000,000 per week.
By 1935, weekly attendance rose to 80,000,000 and reached
90,000,000 the next year.

A majority of the nation's 14,000 theatres were on a double
feature policy and more than one-third used gimmicks, such as
"Bank Night," "Dish Night," "Screeno," and other giveaways to
attract customers. "Dish Night," for example, involved the purchase of dishes by the theatre owners for about 10¢ each and one
piece was given away to each paying customer as he entered the
theatre. Exhibitors would sign contracts with dish distributors
for fifty-two weeks, indicating the hold this custom had on the
industry.

Another factor, and perhaps the most important, was the star
system and the whole appeal of stars to the American public.
Unlike today, stars did not really function as "normal" people.
Involvement in politics, for example, was severely frowned upon
by the studios, whereas today stars are sometimes known more
for their political activity than their films. However, at the zenith
of the star system, the public saw the stars only as the studios
wanted them to be seen. They were gods and goddesses. The
image of the star is what made the whole system work. They, and
therefore their films, were larger than life. With fan magazines
and studio publicity leading the way, they became the roles they

created. Clark Gable was Rhett Butler, Greta Garbo was Ninotchka, Henry Fonda was "young Abe Lincoln."

As Andrew Sarris noted:

> The idea of casting Humphrey Bogart, Ingrid Bergman, Paul Henreid, Claude Rains, Conrad Veidt, Sidney Greenstreet, Peter Lorre, and Marcel Dalio in a routine studio project such as *Casablanca* suggests the incredible human resources of the period.

It was an intensely personal system ruled by men whose taste, while not as refined as some would have liked, nevertheless was usually accurate. The people working in the system were conscious of the limitations and restrictions, but they were also conscious that their work had more meaning than cranking out cars on an assembly line. Ed Woeher of MGM expresses this feeling well:

> As a unit manager, what we would do is shoot a picture and prepare one at the same time. You'd always be working on a couple of pictures. It didn't give me too much time for myself, but we were dedicated, I mean we just gave our own good life to the studio and we didn't resent it. In fact, we accomplished something and we were pleased with what we did.

This is perhaps one of the best summaries of the time; men and women who performed assigned tasks with professional skill, resulting in a product which more than anything else met the needs of society.

9
International
Style and Form

Sound in a Chaotic Period

The invention of the motion picture camera occurred simultaneously in various countries. So did the perfection of sound technology in the form adopted by Warner Brothers. The sound film was acclaimed by international audiences immediately and by 1930 the medium had been fitted for sound almost everywhere.

The system which was implemented in the United States was not invented here, however. America's Western Electric was licensed to manufacture a sound system invented in 1919, the patents to which were owned by Tri-Ergon of Germany. Tobis-Klangfilm had further perfected the system, which was reshaping the structures and forms of international film.

Eight sound pictures had been made in Germany before *The Blue Angel* in 1930, and in 1931, the year of Lang's *M*, 146 sound pictures were released. Within the same period René Clair was spinning his delightful fantasies, which preserved the visual integrity of the medium and wove the element of sound into his fabrics, both affirming the German applications and demonstrating further uses of the new element. The Frenchman's work was done on equipment owned by Tobis of Germany.

European contributions to the development of film were in no way to parallel the previous decade, however. Beyond certain creative demonstrations of sound applications and singular refinements of style and personal statements from a handful of directors no surge of breakthroughs were to mark the Thirties.

271

It was a decade of world economic depression and threatening intimations of the second world conflict of the century.

In America, the Great Depression and clouds of grit arising from the dust bowls hardly touched the Hollywood industry. For the American studios it was business—big business—both at home and abroad. But it was not so for many European studios. Warner Brothers had gambled and won. In Europe, there was precious little with which to gamble, as Hollywood dominated world production with a product which found near universal approval. Many European companies did not possess the capital required to make the change-over themselves. Others were able to raise funds from daring speculators, but with the infusions of funds came a loss of control. Suddenly the atmosphere which had embraced the talents of serious artists and craftsmen from allied fields had changed. There was little sympathy for experimentation. Functions of the product were reshaped: no longer was the film to serve as an image-builder for a national state and no longer was the medium to serve as illumination of human experience. It was to return whatever profits it could. The economic and political states of affairs saw to that, as did the pre-eminence of the American industry. Equivalents of the Hollywood "B" quickies were not to ask any basic questions about the nature of the medium, nor were they to demonstrate challenging themes or manipulations.

As European studios collapsed or passed into the control of investors or fascist governments, and as Hollywood solidified its control and expanded its international empire, more European talent left for America. By the middle of the decade, when liberal movements were crushed and the hydra-headed spectre of dictatorship slithered into position, even more went into exile. For new movements and styles the world audience would have to endure the coming holocaust and the birth of the atomic age.

Film in Britain

Even in the Twenties, the British film industry was so destitute and so overwhelmed by Hollywood that a quota system was instituted, part of the Cinematographic Act of 1927. British companies would be allowed to distribute American films only if they produced a certain number of British-made films. The "quota quickies" were produced for a fast profit and not with the intention of revitalizing a national industry. In desperation, E. A. Dupont was brought in from Germany to add his lustre to the moribund industry. Neither his *Piccadilly* nor *Atlantic* (1929) brought on the hoped-for miracle and Dupont returned to the Fatherland.

The Act of 1927 also required that for American studios to release their product in Britain they would have to make some movies in Britain. To satisfy the demand, however, Hollywood merely sent to Britain a number of personnel who had already fallen from the firmament or who could not make the transition from silent to sound production. The infusion of has-beens hardly served to energize the British film. By the end of the decade, the British industry having fallen into another severe slump, MGM was using British studios and technicians to produce such films as *A Yank at Oxford* (1938) and *Goodbye Mr. Chips* (1939). These films featured American talent and directors and were released as American productions—which did little to stimulate national recovery.

Paramount had dispatched one of its European-imported directors, Alexander Korda, back across the Atlantic, this time to England. Within a year he had cut his ties with Paramount and had formed his own company. He had learned the Hollywood style and was convinced that the matrimonial exploits of Henry VIII offered good material. With Charles Laughton as Henry, *The Private Life of Henry VIII* (1933) launched what appeared to be a successful model. Soon other talent from America joined Laughton in making frequent trips between the two countries and British production picked up.

But Korda and his investors knew they could not depend upon necessary gate receipts from the United Kingdom alone. As his budgets increased the box office from America did not. American companies did not conduct exciting promotional campaigns and the British product was booked into a few large cities, where limited audiences were not impressed with the titles, since they did not bear the image of middle-America.

There was one viable British director, however, whose unique handling of the who-done-it had captivated audiences with *The Lodger* (1926). *The Thirty-nine Steps* (1935) and *The Lady Vanishes* (1938) realized excellent box office in both Britain and the United States. But Hollywood offered him a contract and Alfred Hitchcock left for America.

Except for the dedicated band of documentary filmmakers, only the work of Carol Reed stands apart from the confused and disjointed production of the period. *The Stars Look Down* (1939) was a simple and straightforward story set in a Welsh mining town. As if affected by the documentary movement, its uncompromising realism and reflection of issues and attitudes offer an approach which was to be developed by the neorealists in Italy after the war. Twenty years later the Angry Young Men movement in Britain would hark back to Reed's maverick piece. The film was withheld in America until 1942, until after John Ford's *How Green Was My Valley* (1941) had run its course. And, because the miners were antagonistic toward their own union, *The Stars Look Down* was not received kindly by American unionists fresh from a decade of intense and bloody labor-management conflict.

What the British were unable to accomplish during the Thirties was swiftly rectified by Hitler, because the Nazi threat quickly established a British cinema reflecting uniquely British values and concerns. Once again the film industry was harnessed to the task of unifying the country and supporting the national will—first toward survival and then victory.

Film in Italy

The situation in Italy paralleled the British crisis on several issues. An industry which had produced as many as 450 features a year and enjoyed vast world markets had fallen on bad times. By 1920 only half as many titles were released compared to prewar years, and fewer than a dozen features were issued in 1927. Unable to discern the temper of the times, the Italian studios continued to grind out the old spectaculars in which the acting talent performed in a style similar to grand opera. The Germans were invited to perform for the Italian industry the magic which had brought the German cinema to world attention. But a remake of the 1912 *Quo Vadis?* (1924) did nothing to help the situation. MGM was invited to Italy for a remake of *Ben Hur* (1926), but the studio scrapped the project and returned to Hollywood, where the horrendously expensive (and profitable) production was shot.

The fascist government under Mussolini centralized all production in 1925 and tried to breathe new life into the industry by drawing from American, German, and Soviet theories and practice. That organization, known as LUCE, was functioning by

1927. In 1935, Centro Sperimentale was trying to develop an Italian "school," but nothing was to come of the organizations except a remarkable complex of equipment and studios. It must be clear that these and other attempts were stimulated because of national needs for recognition and esteem in the world community. The film medium had become, perhaps unintentionally, a yardstick by which national images were being measured. Creativity and experimentation, however, do not appear as qualities to be summoned at will by industrialists or politicians.

But there was in Italy a faint voice being raised, a voice beyond the pale of fascist structures, which contained the seeds of revolutionary change. Writers and critics during the Thirties began to plead for a rejection of studio fakery and a return to the naturally occurring surfaces of the real world; to reject the pompous veneer and the sumptuous settings and the inflated characters of passive entertainment. Only the final collapse of fascism and the Second World War could set free the uninhibited, creative forces and generate the necessity, the impulse, and the will to develop an authentic vitality in the form of neorealism.

Film in the U.S.S.R.

Perhaps inventiveness had run its course in the Soviet Union, but the Stalinist period of the Thirties made sure of it with a few fortuitous exceptions. Eisenstein and his like were thrown into disrepute. He was allowed to teach, but not to make films. "Barren intellectualism" was the charge, and demands were made for mass audience films with themes reinforcing changing party doctrine and interpretations of history.

Pudovkin's *Deserter* (1933), Vertov's *Three Songs of Lenin* (1934), and Dovzhenko's *Frontier* (1935) represent contiguous works within earlier traditions, but slowly and carefully integrating the new element of sound—predictably in ways other than mere synchronous recording.

In 1938, Eisenstein finally found his ground again with *Alexander Nevsky*. Although powerful, his former approach of depicting the masses as hero supported by theoretical expositions was modified by the historical material of the epic. Separated from the event by centuries, the mist of ages made the plot's facts relatively safe in the political sense. In this remarkable film, in no way natural, but artificial in the sense of other

European experimental works, he offers the figure of Prince Alexander Nevsky, a good and kindly aristocrat, for those ruthless times, more at ease with peasants than scheming politicians. Yet he does not permit this individual to dominate the struggle as the Forces of Good wage successful battle against the German Forces of Incarnate Evil.

Symbolism was carried to its near ultimate limits. The Germans are encased in iron masks, devoid of humanity. Nevsky acts as a force of pure good and wisdom, demonstrating leadership capacities made possible only by the wisdom of the masses. Sergei Prokofiev created the musical score, and sound and visual combinations gave new force and energy to the visual techniques he had worked out more than a decade before. In *Ivan the Terrible* (1946), a project he never finished because of government interference and his subsequent death, Eisenstin carried this work toward his formalist climax, the end of one of the most intense, productive, and enriching human chapters in the history of the film.

Film in Germany

As the internal problems worsened in Germany and as the attempt at democratic government proved inept at coping with unemployment, inflation, and political bickering, President von Hindenburg found himself naming Adolph Hitler as chancellor in 1933. Paul Goebbels was placed in charge of directing the state-owned radio system, the press, and the German film industry. Production remained with the various companies, but the function of their production was dictated by the Propaganda Ministry. No longer was the cinema to generate world respect for the German nation, but "to lift the film industry out of the sphere of liberal economic thoughts . . . and thus enable it to receive those tasks which it has to fulfill in the National Socialist State."

With the exception of Leni Riefenstahl's documentary projects and a few other documentaries produced during the war to "document" German military victories, little of any interesting work was to appear under the obscene dictatorship. Indeed, even the German audiences abhorred the blatant, propaganda-ridden features and silly attempts to glorify the former Imperial epoch through empty spectaculars. Audience response was of great concern to the Propaganda Ministry, but no one could suggest a plan to cope with massive audience hissing to be heard throughout the land. The people flocked to the few Hollywood "B" pictures which Goebbels permitted to be shown. Gradually, the Ministry gave up their plans to use the cinema for hard propaganda, concentrating on radio and the press and permitting the cinema to produce trite and vacuous stories.

But the Germans had demonstrated an early intuition for the integration of sound. *The Blue Angel* (1930) preserved the power of composition and lighting control, evoking an atmosphere which in retrospect offers comparisons between the cruel school boys and the rising tide of cruelty within Germany; between the released passions of Marlene Dietrich's Lola Lola and the repressed passions—and hope—of the German people; between the increasing incompetency of Professor Unrat (played by Emil Jannings) and the disintegration of order. Although directed by von Sternberg, imported from Hollywood by Pommer for Ufa's first major sound film, the film draws its power directly from the style perfected by the German system. And the sound factor demonstrated what Vidor was showing in America (*Hallelujah!* 1929), that recording techniques were possible in such a way that the sound film could be something other than "all talking, all singing, all dancing" trivia. When the professor walks into his classroom, it is filled with undisciplined and chaotic noise; when he leaves, it is deadly silent, hate for the old man flowing out of the room on the screen and into the theater. Contrasts are drawn between sounds, such as Lola's torch song and the chimes for the village clock. Moments of silence, of an absence of sound, serve to strengthen the impact of a facial expression or gesture.

Fritz Lang's *M* (1931) further demonstrated a masterful utilization of sound. The strength and power of visual elements draws from the best of the German tradition, as a sequence composed of shots within the little girl's apartment reveals the mother's routine of preparing lunch, the steaming bowl of soup, the table set; the only sound that of the ticking clock as apprehension builds in the mother's face; the clock strikes noon; no little girl appears; the mother calls for the little girl as the camera reveals an empty staircase; and later the child's balloon drifts up and away, caught in telephone lines.

As the psychopathic killer, played by Peter Lorre, steals through the streets, his sickness and compulsion drive him to murder, and as the pressure builds he whistles a Grieg tune. Even when we cannot see him on the screen, hidden in the shadows, the sound of his whistling signals the terror of his presence.

None of the camera techniques were sacrificed to the integra-

tion of the sound element. Just because lips moved it did not
require that we hear the words. Another sound might better
reveal the intended meaning of the shot. Just because sound
technology was available did not mean that every screen moment had to be filled with sound. Silence within the sound film
offered a deeper dimension to the potential of the contrast
between sound and silence.

There is an attitude of futility in *M*, similar to that in *The
Blue Angel*. Even as the order represented by the professor was
rejected by his students and his rational powers subverted by
Lola Lola, ending in his death, so were the capacities of the
police shown in *M* to be powerless to locate the child murderer.
Even their most sophisticated methods could not arrest the social
cancer. Only the underworld had the power to identify the
psychopath, and that only when their own activities were threatened by the police. Dragging the miserable Lorre to their head-
quarters in an abandoned factory, Lang directed the trial in a
fashion approximating the style of the Nazi hordes already loose
in the streets. As the interrogation proceeds, led by a black-
gloved and leather-coated leader, the metaphor was prophetic as
the Horst Wessel song filled the streets outside the movie theaters.

Fritz Lang's *M* gives Peter Lorre an opportunity to
develop his sinister characterization.

Both *M* and G. W. Pabst's *Kameradschaft* (1931) were shown in America. Pabst's work appears as a plea for international brotherhood and understanding, a hope which was bitterly crushed by the Nazi stranglehold. While the German audience did not particularly care for his story, others were impressed by the urgent struggle made by German miners in behalf of their French counterparts. Despite reluctance on the part of the companies and officials, the Germans break through a barrier in a long-unused tunnel and on into French territory in order to liberate the trapped Frenchmen. Pabst implies that the solidarity of the working class is strong enough to surmount political and national differences. Despite the dangers of gas and flooding and the joy which Pabst reveals in the people's success, the barrier is once again erected, cutting off the light which once penetrated through the underground chaos, a parallel to the political chaos above ground.

As the political future became clearer and as the uniformed troops took control the end was obvious for these brave last calls for brotherhood and humanitarian values. Thirty years after the collapse of the thousand year Reich there would be no intimation of a cinematic revival although the scars from the war had disappeared. But the silent film and early sound film heritage left enduring effects upon the medium. Although many of the directors and acting talent who came to Hollywood did not remain, others did and the American film profited from their work.

Film in France

In France, where the studios were perhaps the hardest hit by the depression, the experimentalists turned from their adopted medium to resume former pursuits. The desire to shock and outrage, to stage radical attacks upon the feature story film (which is to say, society), seemed to have run its course. Jean Epstein turned his impressionistic camera upon real life, studying the lives of the simple and primitive kelp gatherers off the French coast, giving understanding and dramatic import to their simple dignity within a harsh environment. Jean Vigo had juxtaposed the economic disparity between rich and poor in his *A Propos de Nice* (1930). Vigo was to incorporate sound, however, in his *Zéro de Conduite* (1933), which was banned in France for twelve years. It was a poetic reflection of his own private school days, preserving both the delightful playfulness of school boys detailed in a slow-motion sequence of a pillow fight in a dormitory room filled with flying feathers as well as the loneliness and incipient cruelty and alienation.

Ideas about uses for sound were generated by the score in the fantasy films created by René Clair. *Le Million* (1931) and *A Nous la Liberté* (1931) preserved the humor and dalliance so evident in his earlier *Paris Qui Dort* (1923), *Entr'acte* (1924), and *The Italian Straw Hat* (1927). Like Lang in Germany and Vidor in America, Clair demonstrated that silence could be tolerated in the sound film. Like Lang and Vidor, his primary emphasis was on vision, shots and editing. To that he *added* sound with restraint in giving synchronous sound to talking heads—but also asynchronous, contrapuntal sound. His camera was free to roam and probe, his action motivated by energy and sudden cuts in time and space. Sound was incorporated as another element which could be used in a sense similar to montage. The Soviets had shown what one shot in relation to another could trigger in the mind; Clair was adept at bouncing a shot against a sound which could do the same thing. So when we see a mantel clock with cupid figures blowing trumpets, we do not hear the chiming of a clock but the sound of blowing trumpets; it is not the fight scene we can barely see in the shadows which suggests the ferocity of the battle, but the sound of chugging locomotives and the screams of passing trains which make the comment; the girl we and the hero think is singing a beautiful song is revealed to be a phonograph record. In a release of fantasy, birds and flowers sing in chorus and, in the tradition of the movies, anything can happen.

A Nous la Liberté presents two convicts who escape from prison, one to become a wealthy tycoon and the other a bum and a free spirit. The assembly line is little different from prison routine, and by the end both tycoon and bum take to the open road, hopefully to leave formal prisons and the prisons of society's conventions and factories behind. Its theme and spirit are similar to Lewis Milestone's *Hallelujah, I'm a Bum* (1933) and Chaplin's *Modern Times* (1936). Clair's insistence on leaving his film totally in the realm of fantasy makes it work better than Chaplin's, and Milestone's film appears to be telling Americans caught in the grip of the Great Depression that money and wealth are not desirable anyway, thus permitting the audience to leave the theater singing a song, their situation redeemed.

Clair remained true to his avant-garde traditions, renouncing conventions entirely but with a light and easy heart.

Having left France as internal problems mounted and the Nazi mutterings were taking the form of sabre-rattling, Clair worked for Hollywood production based in England. True to his style, *The Ghost Goes West* (1936) traced the story of a *nouveau riche* American who buys a Scottish castle and moves it block by block to Florida.

Until the middle Thirties the French cinema reflected the ideals of the Popular Front, a coalition of left-of-center groups who were united in such struggles as the war in Spain and in the hopes for a more humane world order. Feyder's *Carnival in Flanders* (1935), Allegret's *Les Beaux Jours* (1935), and Duvivier's *La Belle Equipe* (1936) exemplified the surge of hope. But as the struggle in Spain turned against revolution and change, and as Hitler was given his first new territory in the interest of "peace in our time," a sense of doom permeated French production. Under German occupation a host of French filmmakers went into exile. But unlike Germany the end of the war would witness the rise of a new and trend-setting cinematic style, the French New Wave.

There was in France another film director, however, who approached his work with an attitude suggesting Reed's *The Stars Look Down* but represented a body of work—unlike Reed —the sum total of which demonstrated a unique approach. Jean Renoir began his career in film as a part of the avant-garde movement, but his seriousness of purpose demanded an independent and personal departure. He was not much interested in fantasy and humor or delightful techniques. His films were saturated with mood and atmosphere, the element of light as carefully controlled as in his father's paintings. His *Little Match Girl* (1928) did not dance happily into the future but disappeared beneath the snow in a deserted street. He made a film for the French Communist Party, thought lost until the discovery of a print in 1969, and went on to direct his own version of Maxim Gorky's *The Lower Depths* (1936).

The Grand Illusion, made in 1937, caused a sensation. Here was a style which renounced romantic fantasies and the artifice of cutting to accommodate talking faces. Without the lenses and film stock which permitted Orson Welles to make his deep-focus opus, *Citizen Kane* (1941), Renoir improvised with what he had to avoid editing on the full face of one speaker to take the response from the other. Here was naturalism transformed by an impressionistic approach. It was a style which was complimentary to his theme.

His subject of analysis was the First World War, the conflict between German and French soldiers, the end of an era, and suggestions about the future. Erich von Stroheim played the German commander, von Rauffenstein, who in Prussian style plays by the fading chivalric rules of war. His head is supported by a metal brace; his chin, having been shot away, is covered by a metal plate; and metal pins hold his limbs together. But Renoir shows him not as a caricature but as a deeply complex, thoughtful person who appreciates beauty, form, and discipline. His French counterpart, DeBoeldieu, his prisoner, shares his values. And they are caught in the Catch-22 of their world, a rule which demands the attempt at escape, and the demand of death for such attempts. So that his men can achieve escape, their captain draws the German's fire. His heart say no, but his training demands no alternative. As the old Prussian sits by the deathbed of his French equal, Renoir has directed one of the most deeply affective moments of its kind in film.

The two Frenchmen who escape from the German fortress represent another level for analysis under Renoir's careful scrutiny. For the pair Renoir casts a gentile mechanic, Marechal, and a cultured Jew, Rosenthal. As the two men make their escape both religious and class differences are explored, differences which erupt in conflict, but conflict which is sublimated in the interest of crossing the border.

For the modern era, survival is paramount. The new soldier, the rich man who might have been a von Rauffenstein under the old rules, cares not a shred more about decorum than the lower class soldier. And as they successfully escape across the border it is to an uncertain freedom and future. Renoir is not the armchair revolutionary who revels in the passage of an era and its seeming hypocrisy, nor is he a sentimentalist who mourns the passing of an age, an age of grand illusion. Rather, he is the humanist who understands the fullness of the time, who sees with sympathy the passing of the old and cautions restraint and care about the future.

The Rules of the Game (1939) extended his analysis of human nature by offering a study of the master and servant classes, both hopelessly bound by traditional behaviors and values. Both classes resist the meaning of the signals which point to the emptiness of their games. So did the French audiences, and the censor banned the film as the war began. The exposure of artifice was too much. This was a time for national unity, not division; *The Grand Illusion* was then banned because of its pacifism. Escaping France as the Germans invaded, Renoir settled in America, where he found work at 20th Century-Fox. Conflict with Darryl Zanuck caused his removal from his first American project, *Swamp Water* (1941).

Renoir was to have an impact far larger than his probing and thoroughly modern films from his French period. There was an Italian whom Renoir hired for *The Lower Depths* in 1936. His name was Luchino Visconti, a name which was to be associated with Italian neorealism, an approach to filmmaking which broke through in Italy even before the Allies had cleared out the fascists. Before he left France for the U.S., Renoir had visited Visconti and friends—Vittorio de Sica, Roberto Rossellini, Cesare Zavattini, and others—at the Centro Sperimentale in Rome, the only place in Italy where foreign pictures were tolerated, and that for purposes of study and analysis. That tolerance of ideas was enough to provide the devotion of time and thought to the nature of film so that in its time a new idea could take wing.

Jean Renoir has said, "No, I don't believe there are such

The Grand Illusion
depicts the passing of an era.
MUSEUM OF MODERN ART/FILM STILLS ARCHIVE

things as absolute truths; but I do believe in absolute human qualities—generosity, for instance, which is one of the basic ones." Integrity might be another, for in his relentless cinema it is ideas which guide his quest and the function of his characters. Under his hard gaze universals of human experience were allowed to shine forth, marvelous and true. He is responsible for paving the way for the modern film, the film expressions which were to emerge from most countries with film industries after the bloodbath of the Second World War.

Summary

Uncertainty marked the decade of the Thirties. Basic premises of Western thought were to be shaken to their roots. The chaos threw institutions and traditions, even established film industries, into a vortex of disarray. But that is to be expected of a medium which reflects the raw pulse of its time, both in terms of mass diversion and serious analysis. Individual free spirits rose above that chaos to point new directions for a medium in existence for barely forty years. Approaches were explored, sound integrated, and American film further influenced by talent from elsewhere in the film world.

Non-narrative Development

Beginnings

Histories of the film often narrow their chronicles to the feature fiction film. The movie often conjures a social event spent watching an entertaining and diverting studio release.

On that first program at Koster and Bial's music hall, however, were "factual" clips including *Seaways, Venice* (showing gondolas), and *Kaiser Wilhelm* (reviewing his troops). The Lumière brothers went trooping about with their hand-cranked cameras "recording" even the most mundane everyday events. Even Méliès had begun in 1896 by making more than 75 short "actualities" of surface movement before turning to the theatrical fantasies with which we have come to associate his name. In America, as in Europe, the first film function was the recording of reality, from the famous stage kiss to the censored version of the hoochie-koochie dance.

Two French cameramen endured the Russian peasant stampede to film imperial gifts at the coronation of Nicholas II in 1896, only to have the police seize their film. America's 1896 presidential campaign and the 1897 and 1901 McKinley inaugurations were events covered in this country, as were the devastating Baltimore and Galveston floods. Funerals, battle surrenders, ship launchings—actualities of every kind—were documented. Charles Urban's British Kinemacolor releases of the 1911 investiture of the Prince of Wales drew large audiences in Europe as

285

well as in America. The early color process was hailed as especially suited to the pageantry of royal happenings and was accepted by audiences as lifelike color reproduction.

Between 1896 and 1906, news events, travelogues, scientific films, and commercials grew in popularity and hence in number. By 1907 in Europe and 1909 in America the newsreel idea was firmly established. In 1910, Pathé Frères scheduled regular production. So popular were these snips of scenes and events from around the world that "compilations" of such footage drew audiences to single-bill programs.* Khanzhonkov had put together such a package of films in Russia (1909), featuring clips shot at various times of the Romanov family. The compilation documentary was to play an increasingly important role as the documentary genre developed in following decades.

Dickson had pioneered in microphotography for Edison's *Unseen World* series (1903). *Problems of Circulation, Laboratory Techniques,* and *Microscopic Magnification* were instructional films developed for use at St. Thomas Hospital in London. Resisting a particularly virulent pressure group of the time, it was believed that "the education of the public mind in this way should do much to destroy the effect of the fabulous tales of vivisection horrors and to make understood to the people the realities and enormous value of laboratory work."

Before long a business began to develop around the purely nonfictional use of film. By 1911 one English company was distributing only factual films to schools, universities, clinics, and institutions. By 1926 there were at least 75 such companies in the United States. Reflecting the mass culture and populist American bias, a trade writer crystallized the goal as early as 1911: "By educational films we do not particularly mean travel and such subjects . . . but of a nature that brings science from its high pedestal right into the ranks of the layman." And because it was seen that film could "explain points difficult to render clearly in the verbal," Massachusetts's Fitchburg State Normal School installed a projector in a college lecture hall. The Mothers' Club of Alameda, California, presented their local school authorities with equipment to show materials suitable for geography and history classes. By 1920 the presidents of Stanford University, the University of South Carolina, Washington and

---

*"Compilation" film as defined by Jan Leyda (*Films Beget Films,* 1964) involves the manipulation of actuality by editing, using pre-existing material taken for other purposes, and creating scenes to serve a particular idea or ideological purpose.

Lee University, and Bowdoin College were advocating the use of educational films.

There had always been severe and harsh criticism of fiction film from religious groups, but in little more than a decade after the first public showing, the Moody Bible Institute was using film to illustrate songs in outdoor evangelistic meetings, and other groups were using and making their own films as a perceived aid to religious conversion. Even D. W. Griffith was later to serve as a consultant to a religious film production company.

Industrial promotional films were abundant. The Western State Illustrating Company of Seattle made a film about the Yakima Valley and it was shown to the Commercial Club of New York to promote agricultural sales. J. J. Hill of the Great Northern Railway produced a film including scenes from Ellis Island to Portland, Oregon, specifically for showing "in those European countries where are to be found the most desirable settlers."

In 1897, Rector had filmed the Corbett-Fitzsimmons fight in thousands of feet, years before the feature-length fiction film appeared. Sports events were at the very beginning a lucrative mass media event, American Mutoscope and Biograph squabbling with Vitagraph over exclusive rights to the 1899 Jeffries-Sharkey fight. In 1916, the Willard-Johnson fight had been staged in Cuba. Unable to be shown in this country because of a federal law prohibiting the import of foreign-made boxing pictures, it was projected inches beyond the border on Canadian soil, the images being rephotographed from the American side. It was shown—legally—in New York City a few days later.

The indomitable Margaret I. MacDonald had championed the instructional film for years in the pages of *Moving Picture World*. In 1911, advocating a film explaining the Eskimo culture she had just been fortunate enough to observe first hand, she said, "All of this would prove very interesting and instructive placed before the public on the moving picture film, and would be productive of an interest in our brothers of the Far North who are so anxious to know and do the best that the white man has to teach him."

MacDonald's dismal ethnocentrism aside, Paul Rainey's *African Hunt* (1912) in eight reels, feature length, was more in keeping with popular entertainment. A year before Flaherty's *Nanook of the North* (1922), in which the Eskimo experience was masterfully put on film, *Wild Men of Africa* (1921) was the rage in New York. A Dr. Leonard Vandenbergh "put the motion picture camera to one of its most productive uses by going into

Africa with it and bringing back in film what his lens found there." And what did his lens find? "[We see] how the tribesmen of the dark continent live, what they look like, what their social and religious practices are, and the nature of the country they inhabit." Those were the facts. But what did the information *mean?* In the words of a *New York Times* critic, the tribesmen of Darkest Africa "are not an attractive people. They have no physical charm, and their customs are revolting to anyone famil-iar wih social refinements. They could hardly be called romantic, these crude, cruel, animalistic savages, whose chief recommenda-tion to sympathy is their simplicity and helplessness."

African safaris, often led by "professors" who later accompa-nied exhibitions to lecture while the film was run, were common bill of fare. *Wonders of the Wild* (1925) trooped to the Mexican interior to film wild Yaqui Indians and then went on to the "wild" Far East. *Red Majesty* (1929) tripped up the Amazon River in search of exotic encounters and Indian life. Under the auspices of the American Museum of Natural History, several serious *documentaries* were made, *Hunting Tigers in India* (1929) and *The Silent Enemy* (1930). Although the latter was a document dramatizing the constant threat of starvation, it was seen as a story "of the redskin of old," and was not perceived as a document of the contemporary struggle for survival.

The Uses of Nonfiction Film

At the very beginning nonfictional uses of film were firmly established, from the single shots of moving reality to news events, scientific, instructional, religious, industrial, promotional films, sports events, and travelogues. Terms such as "factual," "recording," "actuality," "document," and "compilation" have been used to describe these nontheatrical film forms. There was a market, because there was a need and an audience willing to pay. And companies quickly appeared both to service that need and to make those profits.

There are at least two important problems connected with the nonfiction film. In 1898, a film was released purported to be a film of the Oberammergau Passion Play. It was in truth shot on a New York rooftop. In the same year, Francis Doublier was running around Europe projecting his bits and pieces of reality, and when the Dreyfus case broke he took (1) a shot of the French

Army on parade, (2) a Paris street scene with an imposing building, (3) a Finnish tugboat going out into a harbor, and (4) a scene
of the Nile River delta. With his narration those disparate shots
became Dreyfus being arrested, the Palace of Justice where he
was tried, a battleship carrying him off to exile, and Devil's
Island, where he was imprisoned. Another film advertised as
footage from a Russian-Japanese battle was actually fought in the
forests of New Jersey. The nonfiction film has frequently been
revealed to be fake, fiction presented in the guise of the "actual."

It is an ethical problem which has continued into the
present. The *March of Time* series for April, 1935 (issue no. 3)
entitled *Huey Long*, incorporated factual and reenacted scenes
which contributed to the politician's demise, a blend which
worried filmmakers, critics, and politicians. German communists, who in the late Twenties were barred from making their
own persuasive films, simply gathered together available footage
and edited them to make their own political statements. By this
method materials can be made to relate (shots of poverty juxtaposed against wealth) regardless of their contexts. While the
method is legitimate, there is always the danger of forcing meanings from such juxtapositions that are not inherently present in
the primary material. Other styles present similar concerns, for
instance, the "fiction documentary" and the politically explosive
features released in the late Sixties and early Seventies.

17 Flashes of Spring, a Soviet television serial of the early
Seventies, is a "fictionalized documentary" about a Soviet spy
who infiltrates the Nazi heirarchy in order to neutralize a Nazi-
American agreement which would have given Hitler a free hand
on the Eastern Front. While non-Soviet "facts" do not support
the plot, the Soviet people believed that it "must be true
otherwise they wouldn't have shown real film of Stalin and
Roosevelt." The mixing of reality and fantasy continued in
contemporary fiction narratives such as *Medium Cool* (1969),
Z (1969), *State of Seige* (1970), *Serpico* (1973), *The Confession*
(1974). The danger of such mixing, begun by Doublier, is one
which critic Robert Hatch has posed: "[Recent] events of
some importance are being tinted and reshaped by fiction
and passed off to very large audiences as history." The television commercial further dims our perceptions when it passes
off as reality, a testimonial written by an advertising copy-
writer.

Second, beyond the issues of definition and form—integrity
of purpose aside—even when the intention may have been to

offer "true" images of the "real" thing, it is impossible to offer truly objective manipulation of actuality, and there can be no control over the perceptive processes employed by audiences in response to offered images. The Playboy organization learned that painful lesson after a documentary had been made about Hugh Hefner. It was shown to him and was given his blessings. When shown to the public, the images were perceived as satirical and comical, and attempts were made to suppress the film.

Mere recording functions are not simple matters with which to cope. Truth and fiction are not always easy to distinguish. Fact, after all, is a matter of perspective. The predisposition by which we judge the world can play havoc upon creative intentions. The fiction narrative leaves one free to work one's will; the nonfiction use of film poses problems because its material is set amid surfaces of reality and is perceived as a level of reality similar to daily encounter. Yet it may be no closer to the *essence* of truth than the fiction film.

It would be interesting to compare the footage which has passed through cameras for purposes of narrative fiction and for other intentions. One might guess that more film has been shot for nonnarrative purposes. Nevertheless, when considering the history and development of the motion picture, it is possible that actualities, travelogues, newsreels, factual and poetic documentaries; educational, religious, and pornographic films; commercials, and promotional films have perhaps as significantly affected the lives of humankind as narrative fiction forms. Each of the two classifications has learned from the other and each has borrowed techniques from the other. Indeed, most nonfiction film forms are feted by awards which, if not followed by the public as avidly as the Academy Awards and other national and international film festivals, play a significant role in giving attention to new techniques, methods, styles, and creative talent.

Documentary

"Documentary" has come to mean different things to different people. To categorize a particular nonfiction film as a documentary can be a difficult problem. Hans Richter describes the genre this way:

> With the documentary approach, the film gets back to its fundamentals. Here, it has a solid aesthetic basis: in the free use of nature,

including man, as raw material. By selection, elimination, and co-ordination of natural elements, a film form evolves that is original and not bound by theatrical or literary tradition. . . . These elements might contain a social, economic, political, or general human meaning, according to their selection and co-ordination. But this meaning does not exist *a priori* in the facts, nor is it a reproduction. It is created in the camera and the cutting room. The documentary is an original art form. It has come to grips with facts—on its own original level. It covers the *rational* side of our lives.

A survey of documentary film titles reveals a major characteristic: the documentary most often has been used as a tool to persuade, to change or reinforce people's attitudes, to generate social change, to make us see, in the words of John Grierson, "the world under our nose."

Robert Flaherty

It was an American by the name of Robert Flaherty who began to lay the groundwork for the documentary idea. It was his film *Nanook of the North* (1922) which began to set off a chain of events.

Flaherty did not simply set off for the Arctic with a visionary goal to make a film about the Eskimo. He was born and raised in northern Michigan, Minnesota, and Ontario forests, where at the age of ten a pair of genuine Indian moccasins was a gift of unparalleled treasure. Grade school and later academia proved no substitute for the wilderness, so for a living he turned to exploration and prospecting for the Hudson Bay Company. In 1913, his employer, Sir Alexander Mackenzie, urged upon him "one of these newfangled things called a motion picture camera" before setting out on an Arctic prospecting venture. With three weeks of instruction at Rochester—his only formal training—he was on his way. An affinity for adventure he had, but also another quality known to any woodsman or explorer, a humility in the face of an unknown environment. As Calder-Marshall has observed, "He knew that in their country, Eskimo knew best." He had a knack for building authentic perceptions, not so much from his own predispositions, but from the perspective of people who knew the land.

It is that sensitivity which enabled him to put on film the images of Nanook in simultaneously specific and ambiguous form. He seems to have forced few predispositions on the Eskimo experience, but came rather with the purpose of document-

Nanook of the North. "Here was drama rendered far more vital than any trumped-up drama could ever be by the fact that it was all *real.*"
—Robert Sherwood

ing the Eskimo way of life, the demands made by the environment which caused the values and behaviors unique to the Eskimo people. That incidental motion picture camera was to become his prime motive for subsequent trips to the Arctic's mystery.

While surveying the Belcher Islands for the Hudson Bay Company, he filmed some 70,000 feet of Eskimo scenes. Losing the negative in a fire caused by his own cigarette, he was left with a dupe he could not duplicate because of the technological limits of the time. He showed the print to his friends and was depressed to observe that they put up with his film more because it offered them a chance to see where *he* had been and what *he* had done. Said Flaherty, "That wasn't what I wanted to show them, not from the civilized point of view, but as they [the Eskimo] saw themselves, as 'we the people.' I realized then that I must go to work in an entirely different way."

As he and his wife discussed the problem a new approach evolved—follow one man and his family in order to compose a "biography" of an Eskimo, whom the world came to know as Nanook.

But where to get the financial backing? Europe was in the

292

To what degree does the very presence of the camera
alter the reality of the event? It does, and so did
Flaherty's approach.
MUSEUM OF MODERN ART/FILM STILLS ARCHIVE

throes of carnage, of war, revolution, and epidemic. Hollywood
studios had no interest. Banks could see no promise of return.
It was the rival of his former employer (the Hudson Bay Company), Révillon Frères which made his project possible. The
agreement was made in 1920, an industrial sponsor found for a
project promoted by an amateur, but an amateur knowledgeable
about cameras suitable for Arctic temperatures and in the posses-
sion of a new tripod with a gyro head to facilitate smooth pans
and tilts. He took lighting, developing, printing, and projection
equipment along. But it was no *cinéma vérité* documentary film
that Flaherty had in mind.

When he arrived on location, he found that "the people"
were no longer wearing the typical Eskimo clothing and so he
ordered in appropriate but real garb. Many events appearing in
the film were restaged from events he had seen in previous
Arctic trips. An igloo twice the normal size was built so he could
film inside, but even at that there was not enough light, so the
top part of the dome was removed. There is no question that his
very presence and requirements altered the raw life he had come
to film. This was not the method of *cinéma vérité*, but a studied,
formal style imposed upon the vagaries of Arctic life.

He returned a year later to edit his material. That done, he
faced a problem as acute today as it was then: to secure a
distributor for his new film. There was no television market, of
course. Mass distribution was possible only by release through

293

the studios. Paramount and First National were not interested. But his French contacts paid off: Pathé interested the Roxy chain and *Nanook* opened in New York City, billed second to Harold Lloyd's *Grandma's Boy* (1922).

Only in Europe was *Nanook of the North* perceived as something of exceptional value. Despite the sweeping changes in technology (color and sound to cite but two examples), it appears even now a masterpiece. Its quietness, its subjugation of the all-too-typical objective to the subjective is its inherent strength, and above all its integrity, an integrity which is caused by the filmmaker's capacity to understand and share in a universal human truth of experience given specific form in the case of Eskimo experience. The viewer shares in the joys and the heartbreak of a people who stand in sharp juxtaposition to industrial "civilized" life. (Not long after, Nanook died of starvation while on a hunt for food. Mrs. Flaherty remarked on the irony of buying ice cream in a wrapper from which Nanook's smiling face appeared.)

Unfortunately, an established pattern was repeated once again. Jesse M. Lasky, with an ear always to the film ground (he was later to convince Eisenstein to come to America), heard of the European success of *Nanook*. And so Lasky cabled Flaherty, I WANT YOU TO GO OFF SOMEWHERE AND MAKE ME ANOTHER NANOOK GO WHERE YOU WILL DO WHAT YOU LIKE I'LL FOOT THE BILL THE WORLD'S YOUR OYSTER.

As a result, in 1926, Paramount released *Moana*. Flaherty's second film was hailed by some critics as even a greater work of art than *Nanook*. His use of the close-up broke through to an inner sense of presence only hinted at in *Nanook*. But he was working for Hollywood now and this gentle, poetic probe into the life of South Seas islanders was advertised as THE LOVE-LIFE OF A SOUTH SEA SIREN and earned a mere $150,000, a pittance compared to a studio-star million dollar entertainment.

When *Moana* opened in New York, a glowing review appeared in the *New York Sun* by someone (later identified as John Grierson) who ascribed "documentary value" to the film. Grierson's use of the word "documentary" was drawn from the French *documentaire*, a term used to describe serious anthropological/expeditionary/academic films.

Flaherty's ties with Hollywood proved disastrous, similar to that of so many other artists and craftsmen enticed into Hollywood's web. "Let's fill the screen with tits," said a studio mogul concerning a subsequent studio project to be set in the South Seas.

In anger and frustration, Flaherty sailed off to Tahiti with the former German-gone-Hollywood director, F. W. Murnau. And yet what they had in common could not bridge the gap between Flaherty's inquiry for facts and meaning and Murnau's sense of theatricality. The resulting film, *Tabu* (1931), showed little of Flaherty's attitude.

Unable to find backing for further work, Flaherty went to Europe, where he met some of Europe's exceptional film artists, such as Pudovkin, Eisenstein, Joris Ivens, and others. Several co-productions were discussed, but he found Soviet-imposed political limitations as monolithic as the studio mentality. Summoned to England in 1931, he finally met the former reviewer, Grierson, and was hired to work on a project with Grierson's group. The result was *Industrial Britain* (1933).

Flaherty did some of the shooting, but the film was completed under Grierson's direction. Flaherty's initial work had deeply affected Grierson, but Flaherty was unable (or unwilling) to work within such a small budget. Flaherty was a loner, requiring time to sense the locales and the people, and money to film test shots until he found the right approach to begin the particular project.

If one has seen *Nanook*, one may find it difficult to understand how it fits the previously noted persuasive dimension of the documentary genre. It was Grierson, the "father of the documentary film," who understood Flaherty's attitude and to that attitude added the persuasive dimension. Calder-Marshall has analyzed the differences between the two men:

> One sees at this single point at which their work crossed the fundamental division between the two men, Flaherty's individual quest for the long truth and Grierson's with the brief progressive one. Grierson had an articulate social philosophy. Flaherty had an inarticulate human love. The two met in the potter's hand and face [a sequence from *Industrial Britain*], but began to diverge in what was made of them.

That is why Flaherty has earned the title of visual poet, the facility to manipulate his material in camera and to edit that material in the projection room by watching over and over again until an organic truth began to emerge free from didactic intentions, free to celebrate human experience.

Flaherty's capacity for empathy—although it did not offer critical judgments or demand change—laid the fundamental aesthetic and humanist groundwork. It was Grierson and Lorentz who applied that empathy to more direct appeals for pragmatic understanding and action.

Walter Lippmann, in 1922, had warned that the mass media were creating a "pseudo-environment." At the University of Chicago he stated his concern for the modern citizen even then sinking under the load of media information drawn from complex issues and problems generated by the modern industrial society. How could democratic rule function in ignorance, Lippmann queried.

John Grierson

John Grierson had come from Britain to the University of Chicago under a Rockefeller Foundation grant in 1924. Along with others at the University of Chicago Grierson became interested in the processes by which the media were shaping public opinion and assuming educational roles formerly ascribed to home, church, and school.

It was Lippmann who suggested to those political science students that they "follow the dramatic patterns of the film through the changing character of our time." Grierson dropped his studies of print journalism and went to Hollywood, where he gained access to Paramount's box office records. There he analyzed the public response to changing star personalities and thematic trends.

Returning to New York, he joined Robert Flaherty in seeking an American release of Eisenstein's *Potemkin*. Said Grierson, "What I know of cinema I have learned partly from the Russians, partly from the American westerns, and partly from Flaherty, of *Nanook*. The westerns give you some notion of the energies. The Russians give you the energies and the intimacies both. And Flaherty is a poet."

Back in England, Grierson organized a film collective similar to Soviet models, but under the sponsorship of Britain's Empire Marketing Board (EMB).

> The extraordinary thing about the whole atmosphere was that there was no discipline in the Unit, although Grierson was this god. Everybody wandered in and out and there were no hours. We worked every God's hour there was, and wandered out to the pub and had a sandwich and a drink and came back and worked again and very often, if there was a rushed job, slept on the cutting room floor, all for a matter of two to three pounds a week.
> —Harry Watt, EMB Unit

It was a closely knit group that talked and discussed countless hours in such pubs, joined on occasion by the likes of D. W. Griffith, Josef von Sternberg, and of course, Flaherty. As Flaherty had applied a poetic approach to the "primitive" *Nanook* and *Moana,* Grierson revealed the simplicity, beauty, and terror connected with the lives of North Sea herring fishermen. The result was *Drifters* (1929).

As he worked with his group of young educators, newspapermen, and sociologists who had been drawn to his film producing group, he taught them basic film elements by showing them James Cruze's *The Covered Wagon* (1923) and Eisenstein's *Potemkin* (1925). These two films were chosen as models for the evolving documentary creators because in the first Cruze had imposed an authentic quality upon fiction. W. S. Hart bitterly complained that what most viewers and critics accepted as authentic reconstruction of a wagon train's journey actually contained many discrepancies, half-truths, and outright distortions. Nevertheless, Cruze had seen the power of reenacted reality transformed to an artistic level through composition, camera angle, and attention to detail. For most viewers he had successfully recreated a chapter of America's past in terms which allowed the mass audience to share in a variously perceived epic.

That *Potemkin* should have been chosen is hardly a surprise. Although the masterpiece is an example of reconstruction, even as was Cruze's work, the revolutionary approach to emotional and intellectual participation in the filmic reality through the application of montage seemed to suggest a technique valuable to "the observation of the ordinary or the actual" which could aid in "civic education" (Grierson). It was with *Potemkin,* finally freed from a conservative British censor's clutches, that *Drifters* was premiered.

When the EMB was dissolved by the financial pressures of the depression, Grierson's group was placed under the sponsorship of the General Post Office, from which *Weather Forecast* (1934), *Song of Ceylon* (1934), *Coal Face* (1935), *Night Mail* (1936), and *North Sea* (1938) were to follow. These titles may sound pedantic, but in no way do they serve as examples of hack educational, industrial, or travel films. Whether the subjects were maritime short wave, the laying of international cable, mail delivery, or the wonder of a storm at sea, they were revealed in intimate, dynamic, and always human poetic and visual terms. If they were persuasive, it was in subtle terms, for Grierson was pleading for the respect of the working class and for modern phenomena that because of their commonness were often not perceived as worthy of remark.

I was very interested in this question of putting the working class on the screen, bringing the working class thing alive in another form than we were getting on the [political] soapboxes of Glasgow Green. That wasn't good enough for me, the soapbox. You see, I worked in a factory down the Clyde and I didn't think we could live off platforms, platform relationships. And I think I saw early the possibility of other forms. . . . But then, of course, Flaherty was a turning point—*Nanook* hit Glasgow around about 1922, I think. I was on to it by 1924, that film could be turned into an instrument of the working class.

—Grierson

And yet how much social change could be initiated or tolerated by a government bureaucracy? The British documentary movement was political, although certainly not dedicated to advocating radical change. Charged one critic, "Mr. Grierson is not paid to tell the truth but to make more people use the parcel post."

But if these documentaries do not appear to make strong social criticism by current standards, the fact remains that Grierson was able to extend Flaherty's poetic vision from the largely unknown and mysterious human face to those of one's neighbors. The model had been established with earlier photo essayists, and now the motion picture turned not to curiosity and headline material of newsreels, but to the common man who had first endorsed the medium.

The main thing to remember is not that all the films were gems. They were, many of them, amateur and second-rate, but they were revolutionary because they were putting on the screen for the first time in British films and very nearly in world films . . . a working man's face and working man's hands and the way the worker lived and worked. It's very hard with television nowadays and everything to realize how revolutionary this was . . . We started to try to give the working man, the real man who contributes to the country, a dignity . . . away from the Edwardian, Victorian, capitalist attitudes. In this the Establishment didn't like us . . . We were on the razor's edge. We were always financed by the Establishment and the Establishment basically regretted that they'd started this thing.

—Harry Watt

Not long after, Grierson left the Post Office to form The Film Centre, which was not concerned with actual production, but was more interested in stimulating new ideas, approaches, and subjects. It was while with the Film Centre that the paths of British and American documentary crossed once again, when Pare Lorentz visited Britain with a print of his film *The River* (1938).

Subsequently, Grierson left for a trip throughout the Commonwealth and the father of the documentary was to leave in Australia, New Zealand, and Canada film organizations somewhat similar to his EMB Film Unit. In 1939, he became the first Canadian Film Commissioner of the newly created National Film Board. As Commissioner he was committed "to wake the heart and will." The series *Canada Carries On* detailed national concerns. *The World in Action* (1940–46, 48 units) was more global in scope. Soon projectors and generators were being hauled throughout the vast and often isolated reaches of Canada. The visual medium was being used to develop a sense of community and national will, a characteristic which continued to flourish after he left in 1945. To relate "high intentions" with "political realities" had been his objective in Britain, Canada, and elsewhere. But after World War II Grierson admitted that because the "high road" usually led to controversy it was necessary to seek other sources than governments, sources "who are less hamstrung."

In 1946, Grierson returned to America, where he organized International Film Associates, patterned after his earlier Film Centre, designed to serve as a documentary film clearing house and distributing agency. But when United Artists gave up on the short subject film, theatrical distribution for the documentary film

299

effectively came to an end. Without support or funds he returned to England, where he tried to breathe new life into the Central Office of Information. Conditions had changed, however, and people were more interested in a return to normalcy after the chaos of war. The earlier period of excitement and ferment which gave birth to the movement could not be restaged. The feisty old man continued to travel, lecture, and occasionally put his hand to a film or television program. He had personally created but one film, *Drifters* (1929), and photographed one other, *Granton Trawler* (1934). But the pioneer had articulated the noble intention of the genre, which was to focus upon real conditions in the real world faced by real people. Like Flaherty, Grierson demonstrated that artistic manipulation of actuality could help people to perceive the incipient power and even glory not only in kings but in ordinary people and in the common affairs of daily life.

He saw the necessity for organization, and because he was more concerned with illuminating the power structures and institutions which affect the quality of human life in all social and economic strata, he waded into the world at large to provoke and stimulate the kind of commitment and action from other individuals, nations, and the United Nations. In his case, there is ample proof in behalf of the great man theory of history. A man of the people, he had little time for film aesthetics in the sense of art for art's sake, but an aesthetic which would serve the cause of humanity. And it was an attitude that was large enough to ask *first* that the issues be addressed and second to encourage the growth and application of various artistic approaches. His purpose was not to make a work of art on the subject of herring fishermen, but to make many films about fishermen; to inject various points of view and to appeal to mankind's best instincts. For Grierson that was a fundamental cause far more important than secondary political philosophies, a cause which is consistent in both word, and most important, in his deeds. His death in 1972 was noted throughout the world.

Pare Lorentz

Like Grierson, Pare Lorentz believed that the film medium should be turned upon societal problems to illuminate the complex problems which had worried Lippmann in 1922. For the depression-scarred Americans to rely entirely upon government economic infusions was not the kind of problem-solving that would stand in the best interests of an enlightened democratic society. Lorentz was convinced that the government had an obligation to produce film material that was focused upon real and urgent contemporary problems, problems which required more than the studio fiction films' largely disguised allusions to pressing national issues.

Film production under government auspices has always been controversial in America, even though few objections have been made to similar efforts in the print medium. It had been Department of Agriculture photographers who had shot films of the Wright brothers' flying machine, a film unit having been established (1908) in the Department and kept a secret from Secretary James Wilson (who described motion pictures as "the work of the devil, a disreputable medium of expression").

Government films made by the Departments of Agriculture, Interior, Labor, War, Commerce, and such particular agencies as the WPA had become commonplace by the time Lorentz released his first film for the U. S. Resettlement Administration, *The Plow that Broke the Plains* (1936). Previous government films had been created more to teach and to describe. Lorentz wanted his country to open its eyes and ears and to get on with desperately needed problem-solving.

His first idea for a documentary film took the form of a book, *The Roosevelt Year: 1933,* when he found it impossible to locate production funds. But because of the book Lorentz was to make his connection with the New Dealers, and like Grierson his projects were never to be tied to the production attitudes or economies of Hollywood.

The Resettlement Administration had already put various media to work explaining New Deal programs to the citizens affected by the Roosevelt administration. Another objective had been drawn from an ethical consideration framed by such people as Grierson: document the intense physical and spiritual needs suffered by various groups in the depression- and dust-ridden nation and bring those documents to the whole nation so that the will of the country could be brought to bear upon the problems, creating policy to abate human misery and to plan more wisely for the future. Ralph Steiner, Paul Strand, and Leo Hurwitz were hired by Lorentz for the *Plow* project, each with previous documentary film and photo experience. These were socially committed individuals and like Grierson's people, saw a mission to be played by the medium quite different from the entertainment industry's veneer.

Friction developed between the four individual creative

talents, however, and Lorentz fired his crew, leaving him short of the footage he needed for *Plow*. As an alternative he went to Hollywood, where he planned to buy stock footage from studio and archive sources. He had co-authored a book in 1930 highly critical of the industry's censorship policies, and Hollywood in turn tried to prevent access to the material he sought.

Lorentz came to filmmaking an amateur, as had Grierson. His first effort bore the marks of superb visual treatment and critics hailed Virgil Thomson's musical score created for *Plow*. Like Flaherty, Lorentz was unsure of his method at the beginning; his shooting problems made script and sequence weaknesses obvious. Nevertheless, his first work makes clear his insight as to the use of contrapuntal sound: "Settler, plow at your peril," is intoned by the stern narrator as we see the farmer's face surveying the advancing drought without making the connection between plowed fields made vulnerable to the dry winds.

> Thus, with some outstanding photography and music, *The Plow That Broke the Plains* is an unusual motion picture which might have been a really great one had the story and construction been up to the rest of the workmanship. As it is, it tells the story of the Plains and it tells it with some emotional value—an emotion that springs out of the soil itself. Our heroine is the grass, our villain the sun and the wind, our players the actual farmers living in the Plains country. It is a melodrama that only Carl Sandburg or Willa Cather perhaps could tell as it should be told.
>
> —Lorentz, reviewing his own film in *McCall's*, July, 1936

Here again the medium was capturing the life of common men, women, and children, not John Ford's actors in *The Grapes of Wrath* (1939) enacting through their craft the lives of real people filtered through John Steinbeck's literary art and adapted once again by the scriptwriter. The craft of the film medium—visuals, editing, narration, and music—transforms the raw material by manipulating that primary material through film art processes.

Manipulated pictures of reality, pictures ordered through artistic grids, can indeed tap humanitarian wellsprings by ordering the facts in such a way as to pierce through accumulated layers of indifference to, as Archibald MacLeish said in his play *J.B.*, "blow on the coals of the heart." Having moved the viewer to pity and fear, having exchanged glances, as it were, with fellow human beings caught in circumstances beyond their immediate control, the documentary filmmaker, having done what he or she could, waits in hopeful expectation that his or her message will culminate in action. Action, however, must not be construed simply in physical terms. It can also refer to realms of thought, values, and spirit.

Lorentz learned the editing process for himself, cutting first for purely visual sequence; then working with the musical composer so that the attitude and intended meaning could be reflected in the score; and then reediting to effect the greatest possible organic impact from the two elements. Finally, the narrative threat was refined. Lorentz's style is authentic cinema and stands in sharp relief against the common educational documentary which amounts to little more than an illustrated lecture, visual and hack musical elements serving merely as secondary support for language.

Unsure of the quality of his first film, Lorentz sought a response from a liberal friend in Hollywood, King Vidor (who employed a mobile camera and creatively applied sound in his unusual and controversial all-black film *Hallelujah!*, 1929). Rouben Mamoulian and Lewis Milestone supported Vidor's assurance that *Plow* was unusually fine work. Once again world documentary paths crossed, for at the first public showing arranged by the Museum of Modern Art, *Plow* was featured along with British, Soviet, French, and German works.

But what good is a film unless people see it? The historically perennial problem of distribution surfaced once again. Hollywood was largely opposed to Roosevelt's reelection, some studios threatening to fire employees who voted Democratic. No industrial distributor would touch *Plow*. So Lorentz hand-carried his film from city to city, repeating Vidor's method for *Hallelujah!*, arranging for showings to the local press, urging reporters and critics to include the fact that "this picture cannot be shown in your town." In his wake he left glowing press reviews, and the occasional theaters that booked *Plow* employed the old advertising cliché, "The picture they dared us to show!" Throughout, Congress debated, the studios complained, the Hays Office threatened, and various courts ruled. The controversy unleashed by Lorentz's little film was harsh and stormy.

His first Government film had been completed and limited distribution secured only by his drawing from his small personal resources. With enough hassles to discourage most people, Lorentz could not shake a concern for another environmental problem: human misery caused by poor land management and consequent flooding within the Mississippi River system, within

The River. Because of unwise land use, people suffer. The
message: change the policy so that the cause of human suffering
is eliminated.

an eco-system which embraced more than half of the United
States' total population in 1937. *The River* was to be his second
project.

This time he defined his topic precisely and developed a
careful plan. Research was exhaustive and locales were chosen
before filming began. For *The River* Lorentz knew what he was
looking for, a study of the ecological relationship between the

land, the river system, and the people. Subsequent shooting proceeded with dispatch and economy, but just as filming had been completed news arrived of an Ohio River flood of major proportions. This unplanned footage is awesome, giving direct and raw substance to the studied compositions of his artistic argument, but secured only because of his extraordinary perseverance.

It is always difficult for one to view a film from the past and to "see" in it significance beyond those continuities of the present, difficult to perceive the significance attached to the work in its time. From current perspectives these films made by Lorentz may appear in some measures too heavy, ponderous, the music too obvious a parallel or contrast to visual components, the alliterative narration too pretentious. But it is clear that the ecology film did not originate in the Sixties.

The essential truth, however, remains intact. Without wise land use policies people suffer unnecessary consequences. To prove that, Lorentz reached far back into history in order to expose the flaws in westward expansion and reactionary policies. The despair, the pain, the loss, the hunger, the misery offer incontrovertible evidence—faces looking into our faces set amid raging rivers, eroded landscapes.

Its visual, musical, and verbal elements were so combined that its aesthetic, emotional, and persuasive impact stormed the 1938 Venice Film Festival, where it was awarded Best Documentary. Integration of sight and sound elements were compared to Walt Disney's craft with animation. Ironically, Disney spoke against *The River*'s nomination for the Academy Awards, because the American industry had not yet created a documentary category, and Disney felt that it was unfair to have the government compete with industry. And yet Disney encouraged exhibition of *The River* in the same program as his first full-length animation, *Snow White and the Seven Dwarfs* (1938).

The impact of *The River*, however, did set many precedents. The United States Film Service was established after the film; Paramount found that there was a mass audience for such films (*The River* was so popular that it often outlasted the main entertainment feature on local bills); the Academy Awards were broadened to include the documentary genre; it was the first documentary to be shown on television—the BBC; and its success at Venice helped to create a more favorable environment for documentary production. Less desirable, perhaps, film became a recognized tool for political campaign persuasion; *The River* and sequences from it were used as argument for several congressional campaigns.

And yet, as Tom Brandom has observed about the Thirties, neither the newsreels nor the features were exploring the realities of the Great Depression. Hollywood newsreels found the facts inappropriate since ugliness was not the business of studio newsreels. *Gold Diggers of 1933, Hallelujah I'm a Bum* (1933) and *Mr. Deeds Goes to Town* (1936) made it possible for the audiences to leave the theaters humming catchy tunes and gently persuaded that money brought only problems, socialists were comic, bumbling fools, the life of the hobo was to be preferred, and unlike life, justice always prevailed in the courts. It was a period, however, of massive unemployment, hunger strikes and civil disobedience.

The Workers' Film and Photo League

The unemployed and some individuals seeking real political alternatives formed The Workers' Film and Photo League. Between 1931 and 1935 this rag-tag and haphazard group produced their own rough newsreels and documentaries. One spin-off group, The Frontier Film Group, successfully experimented with an improvisational style similar to Cassavetes' *Husbands* (1972), in the 1936 production, *Pie in the Sky. People of Cumberland Gap* (1938), *Heart of Spain* (1937), *China Strikes Back* (1937), *Return to Life* (1937), and *Native Land* (1942) were all titles growing from this group.

Consider the differences between *Native Land* and any of the safer cinematically interesting documentaries. In this film we find a compilation and reenacted episodes including such ugly actual events as a union farmer murdered by thugs; police tracking down sharecroppers, black and white; corporate spies stealing union membership files which led to selective firing and blacklisting of the workers; the massacre of striking workers by Republic Steel. Here were other "facts," facts which were potentially explosive if a mass audience could be reached. Even the safer documentary film makers had problems with distribution and exhibition. But for these films there was no endorsement by the establishment, few doors open, and little encouragement was to be found. Much like underground and "public access" video tapes of the 1970's, these often rough and simple newsreels and documentaries made their way across the country where they reinforced attitudes and helped to focus policy among small, scattered, but politically articulate groups of the working class.

Factual Film in Europe

In Europe even the avant-garde movement was attracted to the documentary approach. Working from visual impressionistic styles these experimentalists turned the camera upon city environments with the purpose of revealing unacceptable conditions arising from industrial capitalism. Their work differed from the conventional styles represented by Flaherty and Grierson primarily in technique. Super-impositions, fast and slow motion, poetic and impressionistic images were woven into visual patterns in a fashion that required an active role from the viewer.

Although the style differed from the conventional narrative forms, they worked from clearly articulated intentions. They referred to their work as "social documentaries."

> In this film, the description of a whole town begging from sheer laziness, we are spectators at the trial of a particular world. After indicating this life and atmosphere of Nice—and, alas, elsewhere—the film proceeds to a generalized impression of gross pleasures, to different signs of a grotesque existence, of flesh and of death. These are the last twitchings of a society that neglects its own responsibilities to the point of giving you nausea and making you an accomplice in a revolutionary solution.
> —Jean Vigo, about *A Propos de Nice* (1930)

Gamla Stan (1931) presented an impressionistic and depressing study of alienation in Stockholm. Joris Ivens' *Borinage* (1933) concentrated on conditions in Dutch slums. His *New Earth* (1934) bitterly detailed the negative effects upon the people caused by a sea reclamation project, and *The Spanish Earth* (1937) espoused the Loyalist cause in the Spanish Civil War in haunting visual terms. Henri Storck filmed the misery of a Belgian slum in *Les Maisons de la Misère* (1937).

The heritage and inspiration for these expressions had been established before the sound film. Cavalcanti's *Rien que les Heures* (1926) had presented a montage of scenes from a day in the life of a city—Paris. Ruttmann's *Berlin: The Symphony of a Great City* (1927) and Ivens' more gentle *Rain* (1929), a beautiful impressionistic vision of wet streets and sidewalks filled with gently moving streams of umbrellas, further explored the form.

Ruttman's *Berlin: The Symphony of a Great City* (1927).
MUSEUM OF MODERN ART/FILM STILLS ARCHIVE

But by the Thirties the intention of these films had changed from poetic or exploratory impressions to hard-hitting investigative studies, reflecting the influence of the socially committed but traditional documentary film makers as well as the economic and political tensions of the period.

These were irritating films to many of the more direct and didactic documentary purists. Grierson complained about *Berlin* (1927), citing a revealing criticism. If *Berlin* created anything beyond the images of factories, workers and the dizzy "swirl and swing" of a modern city, Grierson could not see it. What stood out for him was "that shower of rain in the afternoon. The people of the city got up splendidly, they tumbled through their five million hoops impressively, they turned in; and no other issue of God or man emerged than that sudden besmattering spilling of wet on people and pavements." It has been charged that Grierson's approach merely aestheticised the reality of work and ordinary people. The impressionists, said the realists, took unacceptable liberties in imposing their own meanings upon "Life Caught Unawares."

These films may not challenge the film aesthete, but craftsmanship and art may not necessarily determine the impact or human value represented by some of those locally produced, simple and direct communicative tools. British documentary production was organized, funded and guaranteed. It was humane but it was also a tool of the establishment. In America the movement produced a handful of richly crafted pieces but it was unorganized, often without funds, haphazard, and establishmentarian. In terms of film history it may well be the unorganized and haphazard efforts that contain the seeds of productive change and use. For it was from the ranks of loosely organized groups such as the Workers' Film and Photo League that the purpose of film making was passed into the hands of the people.

The documentary genre, as a film form that made common people, common environments, and societal problems worthy of artistic treatment—making everyday life potentially dramatic—was given impetus in Europe.

Ivens' *Rain* (1929).
MUSEUM OF MODERN ART/FILM STILLS ARCHIVE

Factual Film in the Soviet Union

Lenin had ordered that at least three-quarters of all Soviet film production be allocated to the factual film. *Potemkin* may have been the vehicle which stimulated experimentation throughout the world, but Einstein's work had been seeded and harvested long before 1925 in the forms pioneered by Dziga Vertov, his wife, Elizabeta Svilova, Kuleshov, and others. Vertov was responsible for a series of forty-three newsreels and compilations made between 1918 and 1919 (*Kinonedelia*) and a series of twenty-three releases between 1922–25 (*Kinopravda*). His purpose was to introduce heroes of the revolution, as well as enemies, and events intentioned to promote the penetration and acceptance of the government's ideals and programs. Between his newsreel projects, Vertov edited a number of compilation documentaries and throughout this period montage principles were continuously refined. It was from that epoch that *Potemkin* was to emerge.

Motivating his persuasive hybrid documentary forms was perhaps the first theoretically expressed notion of direct cinema (*cinema vérité*): "Life Caught Unawares." In the very first Lumière, Méliès and Porter clips, interest was to be found simply in the fact that the subject matter moved. Later shorts such as *Buffalo Bill's Wild West Parade* (1902) focused on an event of some sociological importance similar to the political interest associated with McKinley's inaugurations. Newsreels began to present popular headlines as early as 1910 (*Pathé*). But by 1918, following Lenin's edict, the Soviets were making the proletariat newsworthy and even dramatic.

Distribution within the Soviet Union was given a high priority. By 1919 all film making had been nationalized, all production directed toward solving government-to-people persuasion. Special trains and even boats were turned into portable theatres and the government line was reflected from screens throughout the land.

An historic concept in audience feedback was activated during this period. Arriving in a town, Vertov would show the films and while in the same town shoot additional footage of the local people and environment, working this new material into the films he had already shown. By this method Marxist dialectics helped to create a film form which was truly organic, never permanent or static, but rather in a continual state of bio-spheric evolution.

Factual Film in Nazi Germany

It was from Nazi aegis that one of the most controversial documentaries was to emerge: Leni Riefenstahl's *Triumph of the Will* (1936), the film "document" of the Nazi rally organized at Nuremberg in 1934—one of the most impressive pseudo-events ever staged in media history.

No one disputes the compelling power created by the shots and editing style or even the effectiveness of the concept motivating the event. And yet it was only after the passage of some thirty years that critics were able to describe Riefenstahl as a creative force edging toward the rank of honorable artist. For those who suffered and perished in opposition to the Nazi nightmare, it is difficult to label their films as "art." However, aesthetic qualities, art for its own sake, appears to be able to exist in a political vacuum quite apart from moral or ethical considerations. If it is possible to separate artistic achievement from its political context, perhaps Riefenstahl shares with Eisenstein the difficult adjustment between political demands and artistic discovery.

> [My] film is only a documentary. I showed what everyone was witness to or had heard about. And everyone was impressed by it. I am the one who registered it on film. And that is doubtless why people are angry with me: for having seized it, put it in a box. . . . What did I do that was political? I was not a Party member. . . . I should have been able to foresee that one day things would change? At that time, one believed in something beautiful. In construction. In peace. . . . It is history. A pure historical film. . . . It reflects the truth that was then, in 1934, history. It is therefore a documentary. Not a propaganda film. . . . I found myself, me, at the heart of an event which was the reality of a certain time and a certain place. . . . I had sought to make a striking and moving film. A poetic and dynamic film.
>
> —Leni Riefenstahl

> In this monstrous, primeval rite, the mass—anonymous and hypnotized—never acts, but only responds to the Fuerher's initiatives, delivered in an authoritarian, hysterical, obsessive fashion. The film's caressing, sensual pans of Hitler's face are world famous. Everything is designed for seduction (Hitler's term for propaganda): the sensory overload of high-pitched oratory, the massed bands and banners, the dynamism of goosestep and drums, the incantatory rhythms of montage, sound and visuals.

Precisely because of its powerful appeal to such factors and its perfect orchestration of filmic and psychological components, "Triumph of the Will" must be classified as a profoundly subversive work and its creator as Nazism's most effective propagandist. . . . only a fanatic Nazi could have created such a work.

—Amos Vogel

Riefenstahl was proud of her "architecture" and of the rhythm she imposed by editing—proud of the control that she imposed on her material. Politically committed she may not have been, for in her *Olympia* (1937), Hitler does not dominate the event and even the American black hero, Jesse Owens, is not selectively edited out of existence. Her use of slow motion to highlight the beauty and grace of the human body in athletic motion is but one innovative trait which has caused her monumental work to remain an enduring masterpiece, a model for most subsequent efforts.

Compilation Documentaries

There are vaults throughout the world bulging with millions of feet of film containing countless records of past human events, footage which has appeared and reappeared in various contexts serving various purposes. Where Riefenstahl had the Nazi hordes marching, endlessly marching in hypnotic time to the beat of synchronous military band music, Capra, in *Why We Fight* (1945), used the same footage to urge American soldiers on to victory over Hitler's demonic legions (Nazi knife rips into another country), and Resnais in *Night and Fog* (1955) was to use Riefenstahl's black-and-white footage juxtaposed with his own sombre color footage of rusting and rotting concentration camps. The devastating effect is further heightened by a low-keyed narration, and rather than synchronized martial music, dissonant sounds are juxtaposed against Riefenstahl's familiar troops. The compilation documentary film remains commonplace as we seek to coax continuities from past experience.

Ingmar Bergman and Francis Ford Coppola both claim their first work with film began as children, when in their parents absence they re-edited home movies, sometimes shaping stories about themselves from the informal clips. Porter had started it with *Life of an American Fireman* (1902), compiled from various shots of fire fighting material, and in the following years count-less new contexts were found for countless other shots.

Joris Ivens took to borrowing newsreels, recutting them to make pointed social statements, projecting them for his pur-poses, and no one watching the movie newsreels ever guessed that they had served quite different purposes. By the mid-Twen-ties millions of newsreel clips were advertised for rent or copy.

Behind the German Lines (1927), a three-part compilation series, was put together by the German Ufa studios to justify Germany's cause in World War I. Interest groups of all sorts were turning to compilation in order to develop arguments for a myriad of causes.

In the Soviet Union, Esther Schub was assigned to locate and gather whatever pre-revolutionary factual film she could find. Material was found, some of it in personal libraries and collections, some of them Romanov "home movies" which had been buried for safe keeping, and other footage secured from foreign newsreel companies who had been licensed to work in Tsarist Russia. Her first major compilation, *The Fall of the Romanov Dynasty* (1927), composed of found footage together with shots of locale and objects which she shot herself, remains a model of montage as well as the potential for giving new meaning by altering the context of shots taken for disparate purposes.

Today and *Cannons or Tractors* (1930) followed under Schub's direction and were shown in this country. *This is Amer-ica* (1933) presented a social, economic, and political history of life in the United States between 1917 and 1933, and bears great similarity to Schub's technique. Meanwhile, the Germans and British were locked in compilation battle (1933), the Germans releasing *Bilddocumente,* a Nazi interpretation of German his-tory from World War I, and the British, *Whither Germany?,* offering a critical analysis of the Nazi clique's plan for world reorganization.

By 1912 Talbot was talking about taking various bits and pieces of reality and joining them together to "form a continu-ous miscellaneous moving mirror of the world's happenings." Grierson had attacked the studio newsreels as "just a speedy snip-snap of some utterly unimportant ceremonies." And the American compilation filmmaker, Louis de Rochemont was com-plaining that newsreels "never get behind the news. . . . What has led to a given event? What does it portend? . . .Some day I'm going to revolutionize the newsreel."

The March of Time

De Rochemont did not revolutionize the newsreel but for Henry Luce and the Time-Life company he produced *The March of Time* series beginning in 1935 which was to the film medium what *Time* was to print: an attempt to provide an analysis of current events and to suggest causes leading to complex problems in need of solution.

Persuasion was often merely suggested, a fact noted by one critic who said, "I wish that these editors of *March of Time*, since they have at their disposal these fictions which excite and enrage people, would use them for some purpose—I wish they would say—outright beyond question—that somebody was right or wrong."

De Rochemont felt free to include re-enactments of events that were not available, and so we entered a dangerous period in mass communications—the free mixing of truth and fiction. The *March of Time* series reduced the number of covered headline events and developed thoughtful background material to topical issues. A good number of political figures were incensed by various episodes in the series, but as long as the Time-Life foray into controversy was saleable, de Rochemont continued with his work. The series influenced film magazine styles throughout the film world.

As World War II approached the shores of the United States, the attentions of both feature and documentary filmmakers turned toward mobilizing public opinion. RKO-Pathé's *The Last Stronghold*, Paramount's *The World in Flames*, and *The Ramparts We Watch* were all compilations designed to motivate the American public's commitment to her European allies. The war further encouraged an international cross-fertilization of film ideas.

Before the war was over, the Soviets gathered to study Capra's *Why we Fight* series, impressed with his editing of compiled film materials. A tilt up a huge tree trunk dissolves into a tilt up the column of a New England church; the sequence in celebration of America's vast technological power (including blast furnaces, huge hydro-electric dams, mountains caving under explosives and earth machines). Functions of music and narration (Humphrey Bogart reciting a litany of sentimental American characteristics) indicated to the Soviets new uses for sound elements. The *Why We Fight* series was translated into Russian and Chinese while the Soviet's *Moscow Strikes Back* and *Stalingrad* were given English tracks for Commonwealth and American release, a Spanish track for Latin-American audiences.

The possibilities were endless: *The World at War* (1943) and *Why We Fight* used captured Nazi film of German planes attacking British ships and then intercut British clips of the same German attack planes. Walter Houston turned, as had Capra, from fiction to documentary with *The Battle of San Pietro* (1944), and in Britain Carol Reed joined in a British-American coproduction, *The True Glory* (1945), detailing the collapse of the Nazi's Western Front. Editor Helen van Dongen joined her Dutch compatriot, Joris Ivens, in the American effort, releasing her own compilation, *Russians at War* (1943). Even before the war was over, anticipated problems were defined and persuasive documentary scripts were produced such as Capra's *Two Down, One to Go* (1944), which was designed to marshall the resolve of American fighting men in the Pacific, with European victory on the horizon.

Hortense Powdermaker noted that "Movies have a surface realism which tends to disguise fantasy and make it seem true. . . . There is, of course, no necessary correlation between surface reality and inner truth of meaning." Whether the shots contain false or actual surfaces, fiction or actualities, the objective truth escapes. Joris Ivens asserted that a documentary filmmaker, whatever the style, must take a stand if any dramatic, emotional, or artistic value can emerge. "I was surprised," he said, "to find that many people automatically assume that any documentary would *inevitably* be objective. Perhaps the term is unsatisfactory, but for me the distinction between the words *document* and *documentary* is quite clear."

Jay Leyda has summarized the non-fiction film, "This manipulation, no matter what its motive—art, propaganda, instruction, advertisement—usually tries to hide itself so that the spectator sees only 'reality'—that is, the especially *arranged* reality that suits the filmmaker's purpose."

Despite the fact that selection and arrangement can direct the viewer to a predetermined end, the non-fiction film (the elements of which were the very first film functions to emerge) finally developed by 1920 and quickly grew in sophistication, harnassing artistic craftsmanship to films of human life, environment, and social issues. Through that craftsmanship, artistic shafts of light penetrated to every level of human experience bringing order out of chaos by artistic manipulation. The face of humankind was elevated by the moral and ethical impulses of the documentarians. It was after the war that documentary methods began to leave their marks on the fiction narrative, just as the craftsmanship of the fiction film had offered aesthetic foundations for the non-fiction film.

The Turning Point

A Critical Boxscore

Along with the arrival of sound came an increasing battle of ideas over how far film had come and where it was going in satisfying aesthetic and social needs. The following comments illustrate the variance of opinion expressed through nearly two decades of sound film by writers whose association with the medium had itself been diverse.

> At last the movie, being a topical medium too, must recognize the "depression" as subject matter. The audience is lured to see a film pretending to tell the truth and they are shown another picture or the glib studio formula, *American Madness*. With a grand flourish this film opened at the Mayfair. There were spotlights on the theatre but not a flashlight on the truth.
> Harry A. Potamkin, "Dog Days in the Movies,"
> *Close Up*, Vol. IX, No. 4, December, 1932

> Hollywood today is more nearly in tune with the normal honesties of life than it has been since the days when Jesse Lasky and Sam Goldwyn made pictures in a barn and ate their lunches from paper bags.
> Clifford Howard, "American Tendencies,"
> *Close Up*, Vol. IX, No. 4, December, 1932

> Putting aside the individual achievements of Griffith and the single masterpiece of Stroheim, the American cinema of the past two decades had made no fundamental progress.
> Seymour Stern, in *The Bankruptcy of Cinema as Art*, 1935

The Motion picture industry has no notion of how bad it is because
it has developed no commanding artist who has power to follow his
intelligent instincts and to develop an intelligent public.
William Allen White, in *Chewing Gum Relaxation,* 1935

The real problem was never whether the artist should take sides
on social issues. The real problem was whether a form of art which
ignored everything comprehended under the term "social issues"
in this time could have vitality, could have the fourth dimension
of life . . . The reason Hollywood's pictures lack the fourth dimension of life is precisely that they do not know their own time, do
not present their own time, do not belong to their own time, and
therefore, quite naturally, have lost interest of their own time.
Archibald MacLeish, in *Stage,* 1939

In the sixteen years of talking pictures in this country, they have
achieved practically nothing positive as a social force.
Gordon Mirams, in *Speaking Candidly,* 1945

It is a medium with a vivid and wide appeal, exercising in contemporary society an influence which is enormous, though still largely
unmeasured.
Sinclair Road, in *The Influence of the Film,* 1946

As reflected in several of the comments above, much of the
criticism of movies during the period was tied to a recognition
of the greater potential of the medium, particularly as a social
instrument. It was not just that film had progressed so little, even
with voice, that brought it under fire, but that it could accomplish
so much. Exceptional works were establishing an aesthetic base
and social function for the medium, thereby raising standards
and expectations.

But most films were not being produced for social philosophers, theorists, and critics, and despite criticism, they continued to satisfy the requirements of the industry itself, and at least
partially, the needs of the public. As Road states in another part
of his essay,

The typical Hollywood film has given people all over the world an
opportunity to slip away from the disappointment and inadequacies of their own lives to move for an hour or more in a world of
half-truths and happy endings.

The seeming contradictions in critical response to the films
themselves can be at least partially resolved by looking at the
conflicting forces that were influencing their production. Film
studios, now representing a multi-million dollar industry with an

enormous investment in sound film production and exhibition, continued to look to the box office for signs of audience approval and to the formulas which had proven in the past to be most serviceable. Audiences, quickly saturated with the novelty of speech, song, and general din, and faced with world political upheaval and economic strains at home, were looking to the movies for temporary release from both the anxieties and drudgeries of the real world. Though studios were still guessing as to what variations of the formulas might come into vogue, it was becoming clear that the most popular screenplays were those that drew from a combination of the fanciful and the real. These ranged from backstage romances and tales of instant stardom linked to the anxieties of the depression *(Gold Diggers of 1933)*, to Rouben Mamoulian's starkly realistic study of an aging burlesque queen with an occasionally romantic tone *(Applause, 1929)*. In spite of the expressed preference of audiences for escapist formula fare in the early Thirties,* a social awareness was on the increase and the so-called problem picture was soon to become a popular staple.

Filmmakers who had the freedom and incentive to rise above the status of hack director were stimulated to explore and refine the new sound medium while exploring filmic statements of real world issues as well as film world dreams. And evolution in the medium itself, particularly the introduction of sound and the rise of the documentary tradition, raised new questions for all concerned as to how and to what extent films would spotlight the truth and the normal honesties of life.

Preoccupations and Requirements of the Industry

The immediate questions for the industry itself concerned economic stability, the acceptability of film fare by the watchdogs of the industry and patrons, and the continued domination of a worldwide market. The issues, of course, were interrelated and Hollywood's nervous control of both production and exhibi-

*A poll taken in 1932 by the Hays organization covered cities and towns throughout the country with samplings from all social and economic brackets. In response to the request for favorite film types—comedy, romance, mystery, adventure, social relevance, etc.—the first choice among viewers was slapstick comedy with "thrillers" coming in second. These were followed by Westerns and other adventure types, with films dealing with problems of a political, social, or personal nature far behind.

tion were influenced by events both within and outside the industry. But philosophic and critical queries into the true nature and social function of the medium were not foremost in the minds of American producers.

The 1929 stock market crash and subsequent crises of the Thirties plus a resurgence of anxieties about screen morality were factors which strongly influenced both production and exhibition procedures of the films themselves. By 1932, the reduction in foreign markets and the general war jitters resulted in something of an austerity program and retrenchment in production. Cost accounting and personnel cutbacks were accompanied by an all-out effort to keep up production quotas in fear of independent producers getting a corner of the market. To expand a faltering home market in the mid-Thirties, the double feature program was adopted, which, under budget and time limitations contributed to production of the "B" picture. To further bolster attendance at an increasing number of mediocre films, various giveaway schemes were instituted at theatres, and dishes and encyclopedias became the exhibitor's supplement to Hollywood's dream.

If economic austerity and sagging attendance were two parts of the threat to Hollywood, a third was the watchful eyes of would-be censors. Pennsylvania censors had banned the Eisenstein epic *Potemkin* on the grounds that "it gave American sailors a blue-print as to how to conduct a mutiny," and a bill pending in Congress provided for the creation of a Federal Motion Picture Commission which would make the motion picture industry a public utility. It would not only censor all films but supervise production and regulate distribution and exhibition. The need to bolster a sagging box office and to ward off censorship and control from outside the industry made Hollywood receptive to guidelines. Cinemorality thus continued to be a key ingredient of the formula films, with a fresh emphasis on affluence and elegance being the rewards for virtue. With a passing reference to "religion," "national feeling," and "repellent subjects," the Hays Office Production Code centered its attention on subjects and situations regarding crime and sex, with particular applications to murder, drug traffic, vulgarity, obscenity, profanity, and the "low forms of sex relationships": adultery, scenes of passion, seduction or rape, sex perversion, white slavery, and miscegenation. In addition to its specific exclusions, the code provided its own formula for screen narrative. The sanctity of the institution of marriage and the home were to be upheld and "correct standards of life shall be presented on the screen, subject only to necessary dramatic contrasts."

With the code and subsequent ratings by the Legion of Decency as guidelines to acceptability, the studios continued to use story and star appeal as basic lures. The strategy in selection of screenplays involved plugging into tried and proven properties. Popular "photoplays" of the past as well as better known literary and stage works became the base or model for entire series of films, thus introducing the era of film cycles. Particularly vigorous was the fantasy and horror genre which borrowed heavily from European themes and talent, but quickly developed its own distinctive, macabre style. With the aid of fan magazines, imaginative press agents, and elaborate publicity campaigns, the stars were brought to a peak of popularity and appeal. The implications of the star system went beyond adulation or star-worship, which initially drew audiences to fantasize about the glamorous and adventurous life of screen gods and goddesses both on and off the screen. Previous film roles helped to establish in the minds of viewers certain expectations concerning characterization and motivation. When these expectations were played upon, they became part of the formula and aided in the economy of exposition. The appearance of Clark Gable or Joan Crawford brought with it ready-made delineation of motivation and personal traits. Even before his appearance in a film, the very knowledge that the long-awaited new marshal of the crime-ridden Western town was John Wayne or William Boyd would signal how the crisis would be handled once he arrived on the scene.

Star status led for some to superstardom. With the superstar it was no longer a question of recreating the familiar role, perhaps with some variation to lend a touch of freshness and surprise. For superstars, the film itself became a showcase and vehicle in which they performed as themselves with little pretense at characterization. What narrative formula remained served the perpetuation of the star's image.

The need for economy, patronage, and the blessings of moral guardians all helped to reinforce studio formula filmmaking under the unit system of production. The star system gave the formula a new focus, and persistence and vision on the part of the auteurs brought attempts to stretch if not break the mold. But of the nearly 600 films being produced by the American industry in the peak years of the Thirties, the majority were modestly budgeted, highly moral variations of tested themes which satisfied the needs of studios and patrons and perpetuated the practice in efficient dreambuilding established during the silent era.

New Complexion and New Direction of Sound

Technological advances of the early Thirties provided Hollywood with both a new threat and challenge. The Fox Company, which had acquired some 1500 theatres throughout the country, was rumored to be equipping them for showing 70mm "Grandeur Stereoptic Pictures." (Two theatres, one in Los Angeles and one in New York, actually showed 70mm films briefly.) Color was moving out of the experimental stage and into feature production as well as animated shorts. "Stereoptimism," in the words of one British writer, was stirring the imagination of some. And an ominous if generally unnoticed development was taking place on the campus of U.C.L.A., where a course was being offered in film broadcasting in anticipation of commercial demands for "men trained in the operation of ikonophones and of all the other intricate apparatus involved in cinema television."

But it was the arrival of sound that presented the immediate challenge for both industry executives and production crews. Hollywood had invested $500,000,000 between 1928 and 1930 in scrapping old equipment and gearing for full sound production and exhibition in some 22,000 theatres throughout the United States. With such an investment, and what quickly became a total commitment to sound, it was natural that the industry should look to the experts to explore and exploit every potential of the sound track.

The immediate effect on production methods was a further reinforcement of the unit system of production which divided talent and labor into various areas of specialization. Music brought the composer, conductor, and musicians onto the scene; sound effects were the province of other specialists, who could create anything from the chirp of a cricket to a tempest; and the vocal coach cultivated the voices of the stars—and sometimes failed. And over all worked the sound engineer, whose wizardry via mixing and dubbing brought it all together.

With the critical function that dialogue now played, writing departments took on an even greater role, requiring new specialists. Though anonymity still followed the screenwriter through the early years of sound, he became a key member of the production team, responsible now for giving the narrative voice. A studio's stable of stars was complemented by its stable of writers, which included men from the literary world who joined the filmmaker in the production of both original screenplays and the adaptation of stage and literary works. The adaptation had always been a significant part of the industry's output, but the talking film opened new horizons for filmic representation, particularly with regard to the stage play. By 1930, Universal Studios had inaugurated a policy of purchasing the screen rights to plays and novels in advance of publication.

An immediate and significant change in narrative design came about with the new status of dialogue in films. Where story had usually given a film its *raison d'être*, narrative development now often served the need to move characters into new sets of circumstances upon which they could verbalize. In George Cukor's *Dinner at Eight* (1933), it is the Ferber/Kaufman dialogue from the stage original that is central. This subservient role of narrative design had marked screen comedy throughout the silent era with the story serving as a framework for visual routines and byplay. Now other genres became similarly affected, with sophisticated or earthy repartee and the verbal duel becoming ends in themselves. The importance of the well-turned phrase and other attributes of clever dialogue tended to keep cinematic style as well as the story in check. Camera angle, lighting, editing, even the design of settings became calculated to serve the speaking actor, with much of what had been learned about visual statement and inference easily forgotten.

The addition of music to the sound track did more than replace the pit piano as a source of background music; it ushered in a new genre of film—the musical—which usually relegated visual storytelling to a flimsy narrative framework upon which musical production numbers could be hung. Less prominent, but equally self-conscious, was the screen's reproduction of natural sound effects, which gave the promise of greater realism, but which usually, in the formative years, resulted in noisy artificiality.

The most exploitative and banal use of sound, however, could not completely obscure the potential of the sound film for creative storytelling with realistic detail, and ultimately for furthering the cause and complexion of social realism on the screen. Even setting aside the singular contributions of such creative

pioneers as Clair, Vidor and Mamoulian, the positive implications of sound became clear. Speech could not only replace the
clumsy intrusion of titles, it could also make exaggerated ges-
tures and movement unnecessary and allow for more naturalistic
acting. Through the combination of voice and subtle shades of
visual response, characterization could be more finely drawn,
with a quality of realism and intimacy seldom displayed in silent
films save the performances of such masters as Chaplin and
Jannings.

In addition to expanding the range for delineation of character, sound also increased the possibilities for basic narrative
exposition and plot detail. Though screenplays did not necessarily display more significant film content, as is sometimes
claimed, it did provide an additional channel by which information could be readily conveyed. The result was increased specifi-
city and detail, which not only supported more intricate plotting,
but also helped to bring the fiction film a step closer to the
documentary tradition. Fritz Lang's *M* (1931) stands as an important and still impressive example of narrative development,
because it succeeded as both a sensitively drawn character study
and an intriguing document on methods in criminal investigation
and apprehension.

Recycling

Gradual discovery of an aesthetics of the sound medium
continued to be accompanied by the demands of a dominant
American industry through the Thirties and Forties. The star
system and formula filmmaking were still central to the Hollywood method, and the nature of film content and style continued
to be affected by both. The perpetuation of the formula film led
to the observation by Lincoln Kirstein in 1940 that "American
films are about boys and girls with love troubles, unless they are
about character actors disguised as famous men." Though suggesting dominance of the formula picture, what the statement
ignores is the diversification that had by this time developed in
the formula system; the era of film cycles had arrived. With a
finer delineation of the old categories or genre labels (comedy,
melodrama, fantasy) and an accommodation for new types, such
as the musical and horror films, formulas were adopted to serve
a wider range of styles, situations, and settings.

Film cycles usually consisted of an initial film or cluster of films within a particular genre which would set the pattern in style and even in narrative design for others to follow. With this as a blueprint, a studio would launch a cycle, often using the same production team and talent. Styles and story became as familiar to audiences as the stars and when a cycle proved particularly popular, such as the song and dance extravaganzas inaugurated by Warner Brothers with its *Gold Diggers* series, other studios would soon be following the lead and helping to perpetuate the cycle. Warner Brothers and MGM musicals were joined by several other popular cycles during the decade, including the Gothic American horror series, which had its beginning in 1931 with the release of both *Frankenstein* and *Dracula,* and the screwball comedies which Columbia had made the mainstay of its lighter offerings.

Film cycles had usually run their course, reached the limits of their staying power within a few years, and were dropped in favor of new cycles. It had been the sensational news accounts of gangland killings that provided both stimulus and narrative base for the gangster series that featured James Cagney, Edward G. Robinson, and George Raft as underworld leaders. By the Forties these had been replaced by the private eye films like *The Big Sleep* (1946), which were usually taken from pulp fiction and characterized by complex plotting and an aura of sophistication and savvy. The plush musical dramas of the Forties—*Meet Me in St. Louis* (1940), *Anchors Aweigh* (1945), *Blue Skies* (1946)— likewise bore little resemblance to the digest of song and symmetry that made up the Busby Berkeley and Astaire-Rogers films of the previous decade.

Film cycles reflected the means by which Hollywood, still dedicated to formula filmmaking, could meet the social, economic, and technological demands of a rapidly changing industry. The transitory nature of cycles was much less in evidence in such well established and venerated genres as the Western. Here, and to a lesser extent with the crime melodrama, the molding and fixing of dramatic conventions gave such works the quality of folk myth. The design or framework which had been plain formula in earlier examples, now became ritual, and the stories, taken from the most cherished aspects of national heritage became legend. Such genres thus resisted the easy accommodation of film cycles and tended to be the least affected by whims and passing fancies.

The Life of Émile Zola (1937). Paul Muni in the title role
plies the trade of a fishmonger in this film biography.
MUSEUM OF MODERN ART/FILM STILLS ARCHIVE

Social Consciousness
and the American Problem Picture

The preoccupation of the American industry during the
Thirties with myth, legend, and the contemporary dream might
suggest that films of the period would have little social relevance, that is, reveal little about the extent of awareness of social
issues and the nature of attitudes expressed or harbored. But
many Hollywood films served as social barometers, even when
engaged in song, dance, or sophisticated bedroom fun. By way
of subtle, even incidental, reference on the one hand to the more
conscious and concerted effort on the other, American films were
reflecting a social and political temperament and revealing a
growing social awareness. Forsyth Hardy in 1933 was suggesting
that "America's films, more than those of any other country,
reflect the activities and problems of its peoples."

Indirect social commentary came by way of a number of
genres and cycles. "Chinup" musicals like *Gold Diggers of 1933*
and *Footlight Parade* (1933) extolled the simple rewards and

silver linings which made the depression easier to endure if not forget. Warner Brothers' cycle of film biographies—*The Story of Louis Pasteur* (1936), *The Life of Émile Zola* (1937), and *Juarez* (1939)—provided individual fortitude and idealism at a time when people's will was dampened if not broken at home and democratic ideals were being challenged in Europe. Screwball comedies, like the musicals and biographies, exuded optimism and idealism while giving reassurance of values. In spite of tacked-on fairy-tale endings, films like Capra's *Mr. Deeds Goes to Town* (1936) were able to come closer to situations of everyday life and eschewed the social glitter so popular in the Twenties.

The popular escapist genres and cycles were satisfying a social function by indirect means: assuaging fears, inspring confidence, and reinforcing values by way of abstract and general reference. Other films, however, were attempting to deal more directly with contemporary issues. They had had their genesis in the works of Porter and Griffith and later in the films of Pabst, Eisenstein, and Clair. Now they came in sufficient numbers to constitute a genre of their own—"the American problem picture" or, when sufficiently dedicated to the cause, the social protest film. If not the age of social realism, these films did usher in the era of social consciousness.

Most prominent among the original problem pictures were those dealing with crime, corruption, and the evils and weaknesses of particular social mores and institutions. This particular group had been spawned by Warner Brothers' original gangster films and it was the same studio that now led the move to explore and sometimes expose society's responsibility for breakdowns in the system and the effect on the individual. *I Am a Fugitive from a Chain Gang* (1932), directed by Mervyn LeRoy, who had made *Little Caesar* just two years before, launched the movement. Based on an autobiographical account of a man who had been framed for a crime and incarcerated in a Georgia prison, the film attempted to expose the inequities of both our judicial and penal systems and the stark horrors awaiting the unsuspecting citizen. The film proved to be an impressive beginning in the era of film exposé. Not only did it enjoy both critical and popular support, it also brought widespread public outcry and eventual reforms in the chain gang system in Georgia.

Warner Brothers continued to reinforce its image as a reformist studio with other exposés, most of which were based on actual incidents. *Wild Boys of the Road* (1933) was a study of the

Black Legion (1937). Humphrey Bogart and leaders of the hooded society—a secret Fascist organization.

effects of economic crises on adolescents directed by William Wellman. *Black Fury* (1935) was adapted by the studio from a journalistic account by a district attorney who had prosecuted the case of a miner who had been killed by police in a strike-breaking scuffle in Pennsylvania in 1929. Paul Muni, who had suffered the chain gang system, here became the victim of a struggle between management and labor. In 1936, the arrest of members of a secret fascist organization in Detroit led to the production of *Black Legion* (1937), an exposé on the black hooded society. With *They Won't Forget* (1937) the studio moved further into racism with Mervyn LeRoy directing this account of an actual lynching. It followed by just a few months the Fritz Lang study of lynch law and mob psychology, *Fury,* which attempted to uncover the reasons decent men become irrational and violently take the law upon themselves.

Other studios joined Warner Brothers with an occasional glimpse at society's ills, but Production Code pressures and audience disposition usually ruled in favor of safer and more popular fare. Sensitive issues, particularly those related to sex, race, and religion, were carefully skirted, making what social consciousness there was a very selective thing. Once settled in the posh comforts of the movie palace, most patrons still preferred to give up real world ties and be lured into the intrigues of favorite screen personalities or be whisked away to high adventure in exotic distant lands. One could join the sophisticated social whirl of people who never worked for a living (if they did it was to star in a Broadway revue), or could be eased into the suburban colonial with white picket fence and join one man's family's crusade to keep the maid from quitting and help out in some nondescript local benefit. Many films of this prewar period had the appearance of realist social drama, but were actually charting a circuitous route to dreamland. By using events and issues of the time as touchstones they could simultaneously satisfy one's need for escape and identification with real-life "problems."

In 1930, Harry Potamkin, in his "New York Notes" byline, stated, "The movie has been a fairy tale and has had its existence as a compensatory mythology. Only a new social mind can stir it to actuality and positive experience." The stir to actuality was clearly under way by the late Thirties, and with the austere studies in human weakness and want like Ford's *The Grapes of Wrath* (1940), Wellman's *The Ox-Bow Incident* (1943), and Billy Wilder's *Lost Weekend* (1945), the movement continued into the

Forties and demonstrated that in the hands of directors with
independence and vision, the social reform film could win both
the heart and mind. Though representing only a fraction of the
films being produced, the move was being recognized as an
important new avenue for film by the middle of the decade. In
1946, Sinclair Road was suggesting that "this new note of seriousness, and the desire to move in a world of actuality are real
things."

The shift to social awareness was slow and cannot be pinpointed by any single cycle or handful of auteur classics. It
involved not only the stirring of filmmakers and audiences to
explore and accept the new social role of the medium, but also
the education of studio executives still keenly sensitive to economic and political pressures. Part of this education was clearly
in progress by the late Thirties and is reflected in the shift in the
official position of Hollywood on social themes. In successive
annual reports as President of the Motion Pictures Producers and

The Ox-Bow Incident (1943). Dana Andrews and Anthony Quinn
are two of the lynch victims and Frank Conroy (right) the leader of
the mob in this study in mob violence.

Distributors of America, Will Hays makes the following observations:

March 28, 1938

In a period in which propaganda has largely reduced the artistic and entertainment validity of the screen in many other countries, it is a pleasure to report that American motion pictures continue to be free of any but the highest possible entertainment purpose. The industry has resisted and must continue to resist the lure of propaganda in that sinister sense persistently urged upon it by extremist groups. The function of the entertainment screen is to entertain— but there is no place in motion pictures for self-serving propaganda.

March 27, 1939

The increasing number of pictures produced by the industry which treat honestly and dramatically many current themes proves that there is nothing incompatible between the best interests of the box-office and the kind of entertainment that raises the level of audience appreciation whatever the subject treated . . . Today competent critics, in and out of the industry, are able to point to a succession of pictures which dramatize present-day social conditions . . .

The compatibility between entertainment and dramatization of social conditions of which Hays speaks is well illustrated in the films produced by the American industry during the Forties, particularly in those dealing with the world at war. The war provided a panoramic backdrop and limitless dramatic possibilities for films of every conceivable genre. Many reflected short-range and rapidly shifting attitudes as the war progressed. Most showed that social consciousness and social realism are not synonymous and that the dream world could flourish in a setting of harsh realities.

The Hollywood film of the Thirties had provided hardly a hint of the events leading up to World War II. In fact, the domination by escapist fare and isolationist posture was reflected in even the newsreels of the period. Isolationist sentiment began to give way by 1940 and in the three years following America's entry into the war, Hollywood produced nearly 400 features which directly related to some aspect of the conflict. This was nearly one third of the industry's total output.

Many early films attempted to set the stage for American involvement by dramatizing democratic ideals and sorting out friend from foe. Red scare tactics made a new image of our Russian allies necessary and the result was films like

Mission to Moscow (1942), *Song of Russia* (1943), and *North Star* (1943). *Mrs. Miniver* (1942) led a cycle of films dealing with battle-scarred and occupied nations, while anti-Fascist sentiment was best served by casting the Gestapo and SS troops as heavies. The ever serviceable spy formula accommodated films dealing with the fifth column activities of spies and saboteurs *(Confessions of a Nazi Spy,* 1939).

Home-front mobilization and participation in the war effort became favorite topics which allowed for the conscription of a variety of traditional genres. These ranged from civil defense comedies and light dramas involving entertainment of G.I.'s *(Stagedoor Canteen,* 1943), to the family film in wartime dress *(Since You Went Away* and *I'll Be Seeing You,* 1944). Films dealing with the military services and war campaigns likewise covered a broad range of styles, with the boot camp and shore leave comedy and musical sharing the spotlight with the documentary-like combat films in which individual heroism was a major ingredient. Even the films of the immediate postwar period which tend to suggest sober reflection of war's rationale and its aftermath range from the sardonic personal statement of Chaplin in *Monsieur Verdoux* (1947) to the studio-crafted *The Best Years of Our Lives* (1946), the homely and sincere American saga which James Agee says represents "a great and simple, limpid kind of fiction."

The preponderance of Hollywood war films serve to illustrate that representation of a great social issue does not assure a great social document. And the films which in the postwar period showed increased dedication to other social and psychological themes did not mark any dramatic shift in the function of the American film from entertainment to social enlightenment. The industry continued to be preoccupied by old methods, was still sensitive to social pressures, and became nearly paranoid over political spectres raised as a result of the House Un-American Activities Committee hearings and resulting purge. More dramatic changes in both film style and function were to come by way of European New Wave and neorealist movements in the years following the end of the war.

The American film by the end of two decades of sound was still the product of a highly organized and efficient industry. It had conquered the "talkies" and other major technological developments; it had satisfied the needs and requirements of the "watchdogs" and mass audience; and at the same time had made room for creative directors and new ideas. By 1946 it had reached the most profitable year in its history and was on the brink of revolutionary changes that were to rival the coming of sound; a renaissance from Europe, a divorcement ruling from the courts, and the age of television.

Seeds of Change—The Roots of New Realism

One change that was more evolutionary than revolutionary and involved an inherent quality of the medium itself was in the nature of screen realism. From the beginning it was being used to describe, or we should say label, the often undefinable quality of a film that lies at the center of both its popular and aesthetic appeal; the notion as to exactly what it was varied widely. Prenarrative concept of screen realism centered on cinematographic recording of actuality. "All very real and singularly exhilarating" reads the *New York Times* review of the original public showing in 1895. Screen storytelling introduced other dimensions: continuity, historical accuracy and, in general, the extent to which a film satisfied the laws of science and human nature.

A collection of observations by viewers in 1915 under the heading "Realism on the Reel"* illustrates the diversity of the term's application. The restoration of eyesight of a fifteen-year-old girl, blind since birth, is challenged by an optometrist who has seen Biograph's *A Bit of Driftwood*. Another viewer took exception to a heroine's repairs on a cut telephone wire without scraping the insulation off the ends of the wires. Motivation of characters is challenged in a number of films, including the girl who goes on the street dressed in modern hat, but wearing her hair in ringlets, the tightrope walker who fails to check his equipment before a performance, and the minister who strikes another minister, "specially in the house of a millionaire and in the presence of a lady."

If scientific principle and character motivation were the concern of some viewers, others found problems in continuity or discrepancy in detail equally bothersome. These ranged from clocks that fail to tell the correct time, gowns of the wrong period, and horses that change color from one scene to the next. Such oversights were joined by what were considered "desperate inconsistencies" of tortured plot lines, like the one in which

*Pictures and the Picturegoer, September 4, 1915, pp. 428–429.

two detectives are thrown in a dungeon from which they summon the police by a carrier pigeon, the presence of which
remains unexplained. Even the fantasies of the unconscious are
challenged in a film in which a girl faints from a shock and has
a vision of angels. What is touted as "realism beyond all criticism" on the other hand is a scene from Vitagraph's *Juggernaut*,
in which an express train crashes through a rotten railway bridge
and plunges into the river below.

Obviously, many of the negative reactions to screen realism
reflected here were the result of hurried production schedules
which did not allow for correction of even the most basic of
discrepancies. Others, however, form the base of what was to
become the major guidelines in analysis and criticism of film as
a maturing art. Continuity, internal consistency, the believability
of characters and situations—all became part of what was to be
judged as authentic; but truth and reality was finally anchored
in the potential of the medium for visual detail and pictorial
realism.

"Kino pravda" or film truth was the foundation upon which
the Soviet filmmakers built their theory of film in the Twenties.

Confessions of a Nazi Spy (1939). An American Nazi
organization is commanded by George Sanders in this
dramatization based on an F.B.I. case.
MUSEUM OF MODERN ART/FILM STILLS ARCHIVE

Griffith, in the previous decade, had taken special pains to give historical authenticity to his epic films, while Ince's work was being credited for its hard-hitting realism, which was tied to both authentic setting and story. German films, with settings built completely within studio confines, extended screen realism to include the social milieu, and strongly influenced the complexion of both story and setting of the Hollywood films of the late silent, early sound era.

With the coming of sound and the rise of the documentary movement came a renewed interest in photojournalism, not simply for documentary films, but for dramatic narratives as well. True stories shot on actual location demonstrated that reenactment of events need not be artificial and could provide the control not possible in filming actual events. *Confessions of a Nazi Spy* (1939), which concerns the Nazi espionage system in the United States, was based on an investigation by the F.B.I. and the court testimony which followed. Documentary authenticity of this and many other similar films came principally through the ruse of dramatized incidents with functional dialogue being combined with the commentary of a narrator. Louis de Rochemont, who had given the voice of authority to the newsreel via his *March of Time,* also used F.B.I. files as the basis for his *The House on 92nd Street* (1945) and *13 rue Madeleine* (1946), both spy thrillers, which blended fact and fiction in a semi-documentary style. Shooting key scenes in the location they actually occurred in life provided the added element of realism. These dramatic films and the feature-length documentaries that had been made by the military services and shown in commercial theatres had an impact on both audiences and the Hollywood industry. Documentary technique, in the hands of experienced directors, became an effective embellishment to screen narrative and set a new pattern in combining dramatic and documentary styles.

An important boost to Hollywood realism came in 1945 with the release of *The Lost Weekend,* the close study of a few days in the life of a New York alcoholic. Charles Brackett and Billy Wilder, the film's producer-director team made use of both authentic Third Avenue locations and a journalistic commentary to give the film its semi-documentary feeling. Elia Kazan went to the actual Connecticut town in which the murder of a priest had occurred for the filming of *Boomerang* in 1947. The following year *The Naked City* was introduced by its producer as "a motion picture unlike any you've ever seen." Filmed entirely on location, it became the prototype of the New York City manhunt film, with its montage sequences of city life and death, its chase through the lower East Side, and a showdown on one of the towers of the Williamsburg Bridge. The genre continued popular not only in film but became the basis for many television series.

New directions in screen realism were not to be limited to authenticity of setting and the journalistic spirit that character-ized these semi-documents of the late Forties. The genre came under attack by critics who found that greater potential of the screen for truth was being ignored in favor of the easy application of surface detail. *The Naked City* becomes a logical target of such criticism, because of its breezy narration and documentary vignettes—kids playing in the spray of a fire hy-drant or jumping rope—which were designed to provide the stamp of "film-truth" but remained essentially an artificial over-lay.

John Gassner, writing for the *Penguin Film Review* in 1947, suggested that the potentialities of expressiveness were being neglected in favor of the most pedestrian aspects of realism: "The average film has reduced reality to a glossy picture-card." Studio dedication to realistic detail when working within the studio also came under fire: "The Hollywood studio spends much money to be certain that the paving stones in the medieval courtyard or the costume of the heroine are historically correct. Surely authenticity with respect to the structure of human person-ality and human motivations is as important as authenticity in setting."

The humanistic dimension of screen realism was to become the hallmark of postwar film both by way of European renais-sance and in the new American cinema of the Fifties and Sixties. But it had found expression early in the works of Griffith, Chaplin, Murnau, Clair, and a few others of the major silent screen directors. It had been nurtured by Vigo, Ford, Renoir, and others of the prewar auteurs. Although the formula system was not conducive to its growth, it had even become an enduring part of otherwise pedestrain screenplays of a mass production indus-try. Otis Ferguson, the American critic, called it a "magnificent realism" which could make a picture which was otherwise "pure hokum" very true."*

Still another dimension of realism in film which had evolved out of the silent cinema and was to find new expression in the

*Otis Ferguson, "Life Goes to the Pictures," *Films*, Volume 1, No. 2., Spring, 1940, pp. 19–29.

postwar years was related to the atmosphere of the work or its *mise-en-scène*. Putting aside the almost mystical connotation of this term, it represented in this period a link between the realism of surface detail and the human drama, providing the contextual environment of the film.

Murnau, Pabst, Sjöstrom, and Vigo had led the way in the use of environment as milieu into which characters were placed. Hitchcock, Welles, and Ophuls had led the way beyond location shooting or set building for atmosphere and made the total design and dressing of the film a part of the new realism.

Realist cinema had been neither an American invention nor monopoly. The direct look, both in spirit and detail, had been a characteristic of the major silent European genres. Strongest among these had been the social realist films to come out of Germany in the mid-Twenties, and the atmospheric pieces by Sjöström and Stiller in Sweden during the same period. Formalism in the architecture of the Soviet films put them in something of a special category, but they nevertheless represented a redemption of reality, both physical and spiritual. Abram Room's *Bed and Sofa* (1927) provided a singular effort in social consciousness free of party ideology.

Limitations, both physical and ideological, and the preoccupations of peoples on the verge of another war, hampered but did not extinguish the tradition in social realism in Europe through the first decade of sound. While Nazi Germany and Fascist Italy turned their attention to the propagandistic values of documentary shorts and newsreels, individual directors like Pabst *(Kameradschaft, 1931)* and Vigo *(L'Atalante, 1934)* kept the spark alive through their studies in the working class milieu. The British strength in realist cinema, on the other hand, was developing through the documentary tradition, which was itself to provide the training ground and inspiration for the postwar British realists.

By the late Forties ideas on what screen realism might be had been extended far beyond the original notions of having clocks in a scene tell the correct time. It was clear the term was not limited to social awareness or photographic faithfulness. Neither was it synonymous with set-building for atmosphere or with naturalistic character study. With release from the traditional story form as pattern for its design, a film could extend realism beyond all of these. When the lights went on again in Europe in 1945, there were a host of directors ready to show the way.

12
International
Renaissance

In the wake of World War I came a European film renaissance led by German social realists and Soviet socialists. It was marked by exploration and refinement in cinematic styles linked to examination of the social realities of the time. It extended into the late Twenties, until it was finally absorbed by a new revolution and turning point in film history—the coming of sound.

The end of World War II similarly brought with it a new period of aesthetic fervor and enlightenment, this time beginning in Italy, spreading through Western Europe over the next decade, and finally, by the late Fifties, bringing the filmmaking artists of Eastern Europe and Asia into the critical arena and commercial markets of the world.

The New Realism From Italy

The spectacles of 1912, which likely inspired Griffith's *Judith of Bethulia,* put Italy in the vanguard during the early silent era. The political support (and control) of the Fascist government through the Thirties and early Forties resulted in sterile romances—the so-called "white telephone films"—and propaganda films. Though both genres are undistinguished, the training of filmmakers at the large and well equipped Cinecittà studios provided refinement in technique if not assurance of artistic freedom.

339

With the liberation of Rome came the release of a creative spirit in cinema. Italian neorealism, a style of filmmaking which characterized a genre of films that is still considered one of the richest and most inspired of any period or country, brought to Italy in the postwar years the attention and respect that neither the silent nor early sound period could provide. The movement has been called by one critic "the most important attempt by liberal man to realize himself on film." With what Cesare Zavattini, the leading screenwriter for the movement, called "a hunger for reality," this approach to filmmaking began in the early Forties as a reaction to the militant propaganda of the Fascist-controlled industry. International recognition came in 1945 with the arrival of Roberto Rossellini's *Open City*. With German troops still in the streets of Rome, Rossellini scraped together camera and film stock and used the city streets as the setting for his tribute to the underground resistance movement during the Nazi occupation. The harbingers of the movement had come earlier in the war years, with Luchino Visconti's *Ossessione* (1942) and Vittorio de Sica's *The Children are Watching* (1942), which showed the dramatic power of direct and unembellished observation. It was the Rossellini work that gave the movement its form and direction, however, and when released in 1945, it heralded in the new age of realist cinema.

Roberto Rossellini

Filming under the most difficult technical and financial conditions, Rossellini recreated the struggle of the city's resistance movement against the German occupation forces. Plagued by inadequate equipment, inferior film stock, and lack of financial backing, production was frequently interrupted. When filming was completed, the impoverished conditions for production of the film were reflected in the results. The austerity became a virtue, however, and the authenticity of the situations themselves became strengthened by the spontaneous and "raw life" look of scenes shot, often in secret, of activities that were frequently a part of the life of the city.

The immediate success of this film encouraged a small group of directors to join in telling the truth about the war and the difficult period of reconstruction. This group, which included Visconti, de Sica, and Federico Fellini, became the inspiration and guiding force for the neorealist movement, and is even

Open City. In this film which ushered in the neorealist
movement, Rossellini recreated the struggle of Rome's
resistance movement against German occupation forces.
MUSEUM OF MODERN ART/FILM STILLS ARCHIVE

today largly responsible for the complexion of contemporary
Italian films.

Rossellini's leadership of the new movement was further
strengthened in 1946 with the release of *Paisan,* a six-part
story covering wartime episodes following the Allied advance up
into Italy from Sicily to the marshes of the Po valley. Each
segment of the film, which is independent of the others, became
an intimate and compassionate tribute to the suffering and anguish of people caught up in war. In addition to revealing
Rossellini's sensitivity to the subject, the film also showed his
command of a cinematic form that took on the appearance of
documentary reportage.

Vittorio de Sica

While the Rossellini works concerned anti-Fascist activities
during the war, de Sica concentrated on the tragic human results
of war and poverty without using the Fascists as heavies. His

341

The Bicycle Thief. A father's despair over a stolen bicycle, necessary for his work as a bill poster.

Shoeshine (1946), which American critic James Agee called "about as beautiful, moving, and heartening a film as you are ever likely to see," is the story of two street boys who, as part of the black market in Rome, become victims of corrupt state officials. With this film de Sica joined Rossellini as a leader of the neorealist movement and further illustrated what were now becoming the hallmarks of the genre: a deep humanism and sense of compassion together with the feeling of the extemporaneous mode. Using real locations, a combination of professional and amateur actors, and the direct cinema journal approach of Rossellini, de Sica revealed a method which seemed to have its roots in the Soviet films of the silent era.

De Sica's next film, *The Bicycle Thief* (1948), revealed the true flowering of the form. It is a penetrating humanistic study, set in postwar Rome, in which a father and son are engaged in a desperate search for a stolen bicycle, which is essential to the man's work as a billposter. Using amateur actors in the key roles of father and son, de Sica shot the film entirely in the streets, churches, tenements, and other location settings in Rome. After working with Zavattini for nearly a year on the screenplay, de Sica finally shot the film without benefit of script. The result has the extemporaneous flavor of earlier works, but added to this is

342

a strong sense of the depth of the relationship between the father and son. The father's fear that Bruno may be a drowning victim, and the son's realization that his father has, in desperation, himself attempted the theft of a bicycle are moments which reveal the human spirit at its most engaging. Though criticized for its sentimentality, *The Bicycle Thief* brought the movement a step closer to the ideal which Zavattini himself had pronounced; here was "the reality buried under the myths."

Umberto D (1952), made by de Sica with Zavattini four years later, was the third and final contribution of the writer-director team to the original movement. It was an intense character study of an old man's struggle to salvage some dignity out of his lonely and impoverished life. *Miracle in Milan* brought the two together in 1950, but this time in the production of a fanciful social satire that showed a distinct departure from the stark realism of earlier collaborations.

Luchino Visconti

A third key director, Luchino Visconti, had pioneered the movement with his *Ossessione* in 1942, and was also responsible for extending its life into the Sixties with his *Rocco and His Brothers* (1960). It is *La Terra Trema* (1948), however, that comes closest to the direct and uncompromising ideal set down by Zavattini. Here the subject was the disintegration of a family of Sicilian fishermen under punishing economic strains. The film develops along more expansive lines than the Rossellini and de Sica films. Like his later works—*Rocco and His Brothers* (1960), *The Damned* (1970), *Death in Venice* (1971)—it becomes almost operatic and shows, in the words of Penelope Houston, "the grandeur as well as the misery of aspiration defeated." Despite the grand design of the film, it still easily meets the basic tenets of the movement. In addition to location shooting and the use of nonprofessional actors, Visconti also encouraged improvisational speech. The resulting Sicilian phraseology and dialect made parts of the film unintelligible even to many Italians.

Cesare Zavattini

It was Cesare Zavattini, scenarist for *Shoeshine* (1946), *The Bicycle Thief* (1948), and *Umberto D* (1952), who served as theoretician and spokesman for the neorealist movement and articulated its function and style. He saw the role of the film creator as "being able to observe reality, not to extract fiction from it." He not only saw the affinity of film for realistic detail, he found also the potential for real drama in the homely details of everyday life, particularly as lived in the streets and tenement homes of working-class families. Central to his notion of form was the recognition that invention of a story was "simply a technique of superimposing dead formulas over living social facts." "Reality is hugely rich" said Zavattini, "to be able to look directly at it is enough." It was through the normal qualities rather than the spectacular that he found material worthy of attention, and at the same time capable of producing adventures in exploration of the "dailiness"—the everyday banal details that usually go unnoticed.

The films which evolved from this theoretical base, and from Zavattini's own screenplays in several instances, were the works of independent and creative directors and they therefore showed individual style. But certain key features characterized most of the films of the movement. These included a narrative taken from a close study of situations as they occur in life, without concern for traditional dramatic elements. Though the films usually told stories, they were not concerned with plot intricacies and neat resolutions. What the modest stories did convey was a sense of the social conditions to which characters were subjected and which served as motivation. The films, through their attention to visual detail, also conveyed a sense of the immediate experience—a cinematic journal of the times.

In a sense, Italian neorealism was a reaction to both the slick and sophisticated stories common during Fascist rule and to the Hollywood films which exhibited technical superiority but produced a reality which was "unnaturally filtered." Lack of stylistic refinement became a virtue in the hands of filmmakers seeking to reveal the truth of the unadorned and unexceptional. But the movement was not only a liberation from the studio, the stars, and externally imposed style; it was a liberation from the past tense. It was an Italian film version of "See it Now" or "You Are There," using the nation's recent past as the common wellspring of ideas.

The French Experience

The French film industry found itself in a state of disarray at the end of the war. The government was unstable, as was the economy. Government financial aid came at the cost of freedom from pressures by officialdom, which was looking for both films supportive of national prestige and potential moneymakers.

Joining established directors like Renoir, Cocteau, Clément, and Carné, who had been favorites of prewar cinema, were Robert Bresson, Henri-Georges Clouzot, and Jacques Tati, whose work suggested individualistic style, even if it did not herald the "New Wave." Bresson's *The Diary of a Country Priest* (1950), like most of his other works, was the product of the scenarist tradition, which required a polished script as a blueprint for a film. Here Bresson examined the life of a young cleric who is dying of cancer, concentrating on his spiritual search for life's meaning. The strength of the film, which has some of the flavor of the Italian neorealist works of the same period, was in both its artistic direction—particularly its exceptional photographic composition which, with choice of setting, provides a strong sense of atmosphere—and the appeal of its simple story of the young priest's struggle to give moral guidance to a country village.

Tati and Clouzot were at the same time demonstrating their special talents in the fields of comedy and suspense, respectively. Tati followed the Chaplin tradition of adversary relationship between modest man and modern world in both *Mr. Hulot's Holiday* (1953) and *Mon Oncle* (1958). Seaside resort characters and life styles are spoofed in the former, suburban conveniences and living standards are the target in the latter. In both, Tati used his gift of mime to create, as both director and star, choice moments of comic art. Clouzot secured his place as a master of suspense with his *The Wages of Fear* (1953) and *Les Diaboliques* (1955). They reaffirm the importance of the carefully crafted screenplay, which leads, anticipates, controls attention and pace, and keeps the viewer continually on edge.

Each of these directors in his own way demonstrated the importance of formative and preparatory stages of filmic representations. Each became a master of his material before it became part of a film. Each employed conventional methods in composition and montage and followed rather traditional patterns of structure. For all the merits of these major postwar directors, it was clear that there were few ripples of the New Wave here.

Through the early Fifties, young directors, unable to find financial backing for films because of studio monopolies, turned to criticism of the postwar scenarist films. Several, like Francois Truffaut, Claude Chabrol, Jean-Luc Godard, Alain Resnais, and

Jacques Rivette, joined *Cahiers du Cinema,* the esoteric film journal that had been founded by André Bazin, noted film theorist. Bemoaning the regression in French cinema since the creative efforts of Renoir, Clair, and Vigo in the Twenties and Thirties, they turned to "camera stylo" and the importance of *mise-en-scène* as essential to creative filmmaking.

The New Wave began as an idea on cinema authorship by film critics and theorists who were dissatisfied with the traditional approaches to cinematic expression and the lack of freedom and individuality on the part of practicing directors. André Bazin was the guiding force behind the new spirit, which became a *cause célèbre* in 1954 when Truffaut, in a *Cahiers du Cinema* article, denounced the "tradition of quality" represented by the works of the established directors. In what came to be known as the "Politique des Auteurs," he attacked the finely crafted studio productions which depended heavily on scenario, which in turn was strongly shaped by dialogue. Truffaut wanted the filmmaker to create his own visual conception of an idea, rather than be limited to the production of an already existing screenplay.

Even before Truffaut's dictum, there was concern expressed for creating a film with a camera rather than the pen. In 1948, Alexandre Astruc wrote an article calling for what came to be called "camera stylo." It was this that became the foundation of New Wave style; and it was the works of such earlier masters as Clair, Vigo, Renoir, and the American based directors—Hitchcock, Hawks, and Preminger—that had provided the inspiration.

By 1959 theory was turning into practice as top awards at the Cannes film festival went to three relatively unknown directors —Marcel Camus for *Black Orpheus,* Truffaut for *The 400 Blows,* and Alain Resnais for *Hiroshima, Mon Amour.* In that year, some two dozen directors were engaged in the production of first features. Between 1959 and 1963 more than 150 directors made feature films for the first time. Many were undistinguished and threatened to submerge the work of the more creative. Those that survived the deluge and became the focus of international attention were those who had been recognized as the pioneers— Godard, Resnais, Truffaut, and Chabrol—all original members of the *Cahiers* staff.

As a reaction to "well-made movies" which had lost contact with the meaning of the modern world, New Wave films attempted to demonstrate a new freedom of deliberate artlessness. It was a rebel cinema, which often, particularly in the hands of

Godard, approached the nihilistic. Of the several major national genres, it came closest to reflecting the contradictions, ironies, hazards, and the otherwise imponderable and unresolved aspects of life. Though style changed from director to director, and in fact from film to film, the films were similar in their modest and spontaneous look. Although they ranged in theme from social realism to surreal spoof, they almost invariably revealed a freedom in style and an extemporaneous quality that frequently made use of location settings, hand-held camera, and improvised dialogue, though they were by no means dependent on these devices.

Unlike the neorealists, the New Wave filmmakers could not be pegged to a common approach or singular style. Their range extended from the naturalistic and humanistic spirit of *The 400 Blows* to the cerebral and formal architecture of *Last Year at Marienbad* (1961). Their common ground was a reaction to past and existing styles in filmmaking, and in the case of the major figures—Truffaut, Godard, Chabrol—a common background in film criticism as founders and regular contributors to *Cahiers du Cinema.* Truffaut expressed a common interest in avoiding the big budget production with large technical crews, foreign actors, too many screenwriters, and pressures from distributors. The solution he suggested was "working freely and making cheap films on simple subjects."

Francois Truffaut

Truffaut not only articulated the theory which gave New Wave cinema its direction and drive, he has also proven himself the most versatile and durable of the cinema auteurs. His *The 400 Blows*, along with Godard's *Breathless* (1959), came to be regarded as the key works to launch the movement. His subsequent films have shown a wide range of moods and styles, proving that Truffaut is an auteur with a good deal to say. His short, *Les Mistons* (1957) and his first feature, *The 400 Blows* are models of grace and humor with something of a social conscience. In the former, he examines with affection a group of boys engaged in games and pranks in a sometimes humorous, sometimes painful passage from childhood to adolescence. In the latter, he suggests the strains of his own childhood as he follows Antoine from schoolroom confrontation (he is punished for cribbing an essay from Balzac, whom he idolizes) to the resentment of parents at home and the forays into petty larceny. Truffaut's disturbed childhood, which involved a period of confinement to a reform school as well as association with a local film club, has entered into much of his work. This first feature and his more recent *Day for Night* (1973), though light years apart in virtually every respect, are clearly both autobiographical.

The 400 Blows, which won him the Best Director award at Cannes in 1959, has little of the self-conscious reaction to previous cinema styles and subjects that is characteristic of much of the New Wave films. It is rather a cinematic idyll, which combines the poetry, compassion, and sense of realism of such other directors as Flaherty and de Sica. The combination of the lyrical and documentary is characteristic of much of the Truffaut work and becomes strong in such recent works as *The Wild Child* (1970) and *Day for Night* (1973). In *The 400 Blows*, Truffaut neither provides pat answers to the causes of Antoine's conflict and delinquency, nor does he sentimentalize over it. The final freeze frame of Antoine's face as he rushes to the sea suggests both kinds of restraint. He is able to romanticize about the innocence of youth without becoming indulgent. He also incorporates a revolutionary theme—much in the spirit of Vigo's *Zéro de Conduite*—while using quite conventional cinematic technique.

The film which comes closest to the spirit of nihilism of new French cinema was *Shoot the Piano Player* (1960), which Truffaut made as a comment on the American gangster film, as Godard had done in *Breathless*. More significantly, however, the film attempted to defy any typing or characterization as to genre, mood or form, and became a reflection on the contradictory, unexplained, and unresolved incidents of life. Charlie, a former concert pianist who has taken a job as piano player in a bar, tries to help his two brothers escape gangsters. The bartender is accidentally killed by Charlie; Lena, the waitress with whom Charlie has become involved, is shot in a showdown gun battle; and brother Fido, who has been kidnapped by the gangsters, is saved. This mimicry of the plots of the American "B" gangster film is Truffaut's way of paying homage to the movies and at the same time provide a framework for his shifting style and humor. Truffaut has himself admitted to the self-indulgence of the film, which was made to please himself and other movie buffs.

In *Jules and Jim* (1961), Truffaut celebrated both the freedom of the human spirit and the freedom of the cinema, but in a quieter, less flamboyant way. It is the story of the friendship between two men—a Frenchman and a German—and their relationship with the impulsive, free-spirited woman whom they both love. The film sustains a delicate lyric quality that surpasses his first feature and is never quite recaptured in subsequent works. Camera zooms, slow motion, and freeze frames are employed to reinforce the idyllic mood. The contradictory and even self-destructive nature of Catherine, however, is responsible for the film's sobering reality of incompatibility with human and physical restraints.

Since his initial efforts at cinema auterism, Truffaut has ventured into such varied styles as melodrama in *The Soft Skin* (1964), the curiously distant and stylized adaptation of the Ray Bradbury story, *Farenheit 451* (1966), and his homage to the Hitchcock thriller, *The Bride Wore Black* (1967). With *Stolen Kisses* (1968) and *Bed and Board* (1970), Truffaut has once again demonstrated his mastery over the light, good-natured but wise love idyll, and with *The Wild Child* (1970), shown his talents as actor/director. Through these works he has continued to show his interest in the complexities of human relationships and a whimsical sense of humor and familiarity or closeness to the characters he portrays. At the same time he has kept his distance from direct social issues and political causes. Many of his films are marked

The Wild Child. Truffaut himself stars as the doctor who brings a young savage to civilized ways and a loving relationship.
MUSEUM OF MODERN ART/FILM STILLS ARCHIVE

by equivocal or unresolved endings: Antoine's indecision caught in freeze frame, Jules' adjustment to the death of Catherine and Jim, and Victor's progress and relationship to Dr. Itard in *The Wild Child*. While exploring new stylistic approaches, Truffaut also refrains from conveniently dramatic resolutions to social observation. Consequently, his work has escaped the convenient labels and stereotyping experienced by other filmmakers.

Jean-Luc Godard

Like Truffaut, Jean-Luc Godard came to directing via film criticism for *Cahiers du Cinema*. His first feature, *Breathless* (1959), which Truffaut helped script, is a testament to Truffaut's aspiration to the cheaply and simply made film. From here, however, the cinematic approaches of the two directors varied widely. Godard's work has clearly dramatized the use of film for stylistic experimentation in which subject matter has little meaning outside the context of film. *Breathless* is less a representation of the anti-hero in the form of small-time gangster as it is a satire of such anti-establishment celebration by the American "B picture." In *A Woman is a Woman* (1961), Godard again pro-

Breathless. Jean Seberg and Jean-Paul Belmondo
portray young rebels in Godard's tribute to the American
"B picture."
MUSEUM OF MODERN ART/FILM STILLS ARCHIVE

duced a tribute to the American film genre—this time the Hollywood musical.

Godard has continually reminded his viewers that they are watching a film. It is something of an attempt to counter the tendency in traditional cinema of total absorption, and to keep the viewer at a distance that will permit a more objective recep-tion to the work. It is a technique that quickly brought Godard under fire, charging him with a self-conscious use of the medium. It is not a device that is peculiar to Godard, however. Truffaut and Alain Resnais have both tried, by varying means, to counter the conditioning that puts a viewer in lock-step with narrative development. Bergman draws the viewer out of the story in both *Persona* and *Passion of Anna* by "it's only a movie" techniques, and Fellini in 8½ and Truffaut in *Day for Night* carry the device to the ultimate. In both films, the central conflict is that of the filmmaker trying to make a film.

Although Godard shared New Wave celebrity with Truffaut as a result of his original contributions to the movement, he has not enjoyed the wider appeal that Truffaut has through his more recent works. *Le Petit Soldat* (1960), *A Woman is a Woman* (1961) and *My Life to Live* (1962) were all original studies of women in which Godard's wife, Anna Karina, performed in leading roles. Though well crafted and insightful, they lacked the cult appeal of *Breathless* and were given little attention by foreign audiences. His *Les Carabiniers* (1963), a parable on war, had less support, even from home audiences, but brought Godard further along the road to cinematizing his own attitudes toward his characters and their environment, and in providing more of an intellectual exercise than emotional trip through conventional narrative. In *Alphaville* (1965), he composed a futuristic Orwellian setting for his study of the dehumanization of civilization and the corruption of its ideals. *Weekend* (1967) rails against the modern consumer-oriented society and the butchery and violence of modern civilization, which Godard represents metaphorically by guerilla warfare that leads to cannibalism. The serious purpose of these films does not prevent Godard from wry commentary on the arts that characterized his early work. In *Alphaville*, Lemmy Caution, the main character, reacquaints us with the Private Eye, and in *Weekend* with the storybook characters first introduced by Truffaut in *Farenheit 451*.

One Plus One (1968) and *Le Gai Savoir* (1968) brought Godard to almost total absorption in Marxist polemics, though,

Weekend. Godard's chilling metaphors for contemporary social values include life (and death) among weekend travelers.

like Truffaut, he usually manages to mask ·his own political position in ambiguity. But his continued willingness to challenge accepted precepts of film form and function remains unchallenged even through what many critics consider static, longwinded diatribes.

Alain Resnais

Alain Resnais, an important creative force of the New Wave period, was not a typical New Wave director. Unlike Truffaut or Godard, he came up through the ranks as an assistant director and producer of short documentaries after attending film school. His early art films, *Van Gogh* (1948) and *Guernica* (1950) and his time study of Nazi concentration camps, *Night and Fog* (1956), established his reputation before he began directing feature films. It was while directing these shorts that he also developed the discipline that characterizes his later work and clearly distinguishes it from that of other New Wave directors. Dedicated to the idea of mastery of material, Resnais has worked in the scenarist tradition from a highly polished script, with editing the key to creative design. *Night and Fog,* with its movement along a dual time track, provided a prelude to the special structuring of film involving the interplay of past and present which is central to the design of his major feature films.

Resnais' highly ordered but unconventional approach to the dramatic unities of time and place have brought his work under the harshest critical assault, in spite of his traditional background and more conventional productions. Responding to *Hiroshima mon Amour* (1959), one critic observed, "He has the skill to say whatever he wants to say on film. Unhappily he has nothing, or almost nothing, to say." Centering on the fusion of present experience and the memory of past events, the film concerns a French actress who falls in love with a Japanese architect while working on a peace film in Hiroshima. A strain in the relationship develops as a result of the girl's memory of her experience at age 18, when she was in love with a German soldier during the occupation. (He is shot and she banished in disgrace.) The cross-cutting between past and present becomes basic to the film's structure, both in the personal story and that of the city itself. As in *Night and Fog,* Resnais uses the interplay of present and past not simply as a means for direct comparison, but to comment upon the fragile quality of memory. The actress is fearful that she will forget her former lover and the horrors of Hiroshima, just as Resnais himself expresses the fear that nobody "is on the lookout . . . to warn us of the coming of new executioners," because memories are so short. The film was the product of close collaboration between Resnais and scenarist Marguerite Duras and illustrates the importance of script to Resnais' approach to filmmaking. It was Resnais as editor, however, who gave the film its final balanced and cohesive form.

Following his Cannes triumph with *Hiroshima* in 1959, Resnais won the Golden Lion award at Venice in 1961 for his second feature, *Last Year at Marienbad.* A new storm of controversy broke over his unorthodox exploration of mental as well as physical time. Here, as in *Hiroshima,* Resnais and scenarist Alain Robbe-Grillet have dealt with the visualization of mental images and given the past qualities of the present. Rather than move into past tense, Resnais showed the past as present remembrance influenced by present stimuli. The film follows a group of people who roam through a baroque chateau in evening dress and centers on the relationship between a man and a woman who are uncertain whether the events we see have occurred in the past, the present, or perhaps never. The importance of mental reality to the film is suggested by scenarist Robbe-Grillet, who says, "When we say that what goes on in our minds is just as real as what goes on in front of our eyes, we are laying the foundation for a cinematic style which can switch to and fro between the things around us and the subject of our conversation." Resnais suggests that the film is about degrees of reality and that the film represents "an attempt, still crude and primitive, to approach the complexity of thought and its mechanisms."

Resnais, like several other directors who gained initial prominence in the European renaissance, has continued making films which have won critical acceptance but only limited distribution abroad.

Claude Chabrol, Claude Lelouch, Jacques Demy, Louis Malle, and Eric Rohmer are the other major directors who, along with the inexhaustible Truffaut and Godard, have helped mold and maintain the image of French cinema through the Sixties and early Seventies. While working within the traditional genres and more conventional forms of dramatic structure, and meeting the production requirements of the industry, they have managed to explore and extend the limits of style and story (or statement) open to film. Chabrol has combined the tension of the murder mystery with the psychological study in motivation in films from *Les Cousins* (1959) to *Le Boucher* (1969). Jacques Demy challenges Hollywood's expertise in the mounting of musical fantasy in *The Umbrellas of Cherborg* (1964). Eric Rohmer's delicate and graceful studies in human passion challenge notions on the supremacy of the visual image in film. Louis Malle's *Murmur of the Heart* (1972) challenges Rohmer's work for its delicacy and grace, and notions about what can be treated tastefully on the screen. His *Lacombe, Lucien* (1974) further extends his firm hand and delicate touch. The French cinema, traditionally nonconformist and in the vanguard in exploration of new ways of using the medium, has continued in the period of European renaissance and beyond to nod respectfully to past masters in film and the other arts, and then go its own way.

Kitchen Sink Realists

Britain's legacy in film from the years prior to World War II had been overwhelmingly in favor of the documentary form. Out of the welter of silent and early sound comedies, spectacles, and intrigues which were made to compete with the products of the German, Soviet, and French "golden ages," and the staggering invasion of American films, only a handful of works received anything like an international reputation. These were mostly the early works of Alfred Hitchcock and Alexander Korda's mounting of *The Private Life of Henry VIII* (1933). While John Grierson and his associates and disciples were combining social purpose and artistic experimentation in the first documentary movement, feature filmmaking was involved in the subversion of the 1927 "quota law"—quickly and cheaply made British films becoming the ransom for the highly prized American features.

In the decade following World War II, the British feature began to distinguish itself in several diverse genres. Droll satirical comedies made for Ealing Studio by directors like Alexander Mackendrick (*Whiskey Galore,* 1948, *The Man in the White Suit,* 1951, *The Ladykillers,* 1955), Robert Hamer (*Kind Hearts and Coronets,* 1947), and Charles Crichton (*The Lavender Hill Mob,* 1951), were favored with both popular appeal and moderate critical acceptance. The films also won plaudits and a boost to star status for such players as Alec Guinness, Peter Sellers, and Terry-Thomas.

Also distinguishing themselves during the period and establishing a strong tradition in dramatic narrative were such directors as David Lean, Anthony Asquith, and Noel Langley. Their films included several adaptations from classic literature, with Lean's *Great Expectations* (1946) and *Oliver Twist* (1947) gaining special prominence. Most prestigious of the dramatic features, however, were the costume spectacles, including the ballet extravanganzas *The Red Shoes* (1948) and *The Tales of Hoffman* (1950). Laurence Olivier's acting/directing triumphs in *Hamlet* (1948) and *Richard III* (1955) were distinguished followups to his *Henry V* (1944) made during the war, which further extended the genre of literary and stage works in translation. Original dramatic narrative was best represented in the works of Carol Reed (*Odd Man Out,* 1946 and *The Third Man,* 1949), whose *The Stars Look Down* (1939) had been a foreshadowing of the social realist cinema to come.

Given virtually no notice, but more significant than any of these in terms of the direction of British cinema in the late Fifties and Sixties, were the products of what came to be called the "Free Cinema" movement. Following the tradition in social realism established by the original documentarists, directors and writers who wanted to "celebrate the significance of the everyday" came together between 1956 and 1958 to examine, via film, the life of the streets, dance halls, clubs, and markets of the British working class. Their purpose was to fulfill what Lindsay Anderson, one of the directors, saw as the prospectus to which the movement was dedicated: "If you're going to get attention, you've got to get together and make a row." The row was a reaction to what Anderson called the "emotionally frozen" British features currently in vogue. *O Dreamland* (1954) by Anderson is a harshly satirical commentary on the seedy and hollow pleasures of the "Fun Fair" or amusement park. Karel Reisz, another key figure in the movement, dealt with the drab routine of work and play in *We Are the Lambeth Boys* (1958), a study of a progressive London youth club. Tony Richardson, another free cinema pioneer, worked with Reisz on another look at London youth in a dance hall setting—*Momma Don't Allow* (1956). Another Anderson work, *Every Day Except Christmas* (1957), was a celebration of the work ethic and like some of the earlier documentaries—Harry Watt's *Night Mail* (1936)—lent a lyric quality to the subject, here the fruit and flower dealers of Covent Garden Market.

While these filmmakers were developing style through these experiments in social observation, young novelists and playwrights, such as John Osborne, Arnold Wesker, Alan Sillitoe, David Storey, and Shelagh Delaney, were producing first works which represented a challenge by East End and North Country working class liberals to the more affluent, conservative, and traditional values of Southern and metropolitan locals. With a fresh stimulus to the social realist tradition coming in the dramatic and literary arts, the free cinema filmmakers moved from documentary shorts to narrative features, with these same novelists and playwrights serving as scenarists for their own works.

Jack Clayton

The director to launch the movement, sometimes referred to as the "British anti-establishment film," was not one of the documentarists, however. Jack Clayton had come up through the ranks in feature film production as production manager and producer. His *Room at the Top* (1959) became the first of the new socially conscious features and set the pattern for several key characteristics of the genre: the drab industrial setting, the class consciousness **and other preoccupations** and drives which motivate the workers, and finally the young hero who gave human form to social protest. The hero in Clayton's film was Joe Lampton (Laurence Harvey), an ex-RAF sergeant who strives for social status. While realizing his goal—by marrying the daughter of a wealthy industrialist—he destroys the woman he really loves and finds his victory in upward mobility a hollow one. The first feature film by Clayton did more than establish a pattern for protest against the drab and restricted life of the working class in the industrial north; it also depicted the dreariness at the top of the social ladder. Laurence Harvey's portrayal of Joe as the scheming and cynical opportunist is not the more prevalent view of young rebellion, but does provide the necessary perspective for viewing the class snobbishness and lack of emotional depth of the industrialist and daughter with whom Joe casts his lot. The strength of the film rests not only in the sense of social realism Clayton captured with his camera, but also in the choice and handling of actors. There are exceptional performances by the cast generally, with a particularly arresting performance by Simone Signoret as Joe's mistress.

Tony Richardson

Tony Richardson came from the London stage to begin his career as filmmaker and made a major contribution to the new British movement. Working with adaptations from works by John Osborne (*Look Back in Anger,* 1959 and *The Entertainer,* 1960), and Shelagh Delaney (*A Taste of Honey,* 1962), Richardson created his own gray world of dingy flats, sleazy seaside midways and music halls, and shabby, smoked-filled pubs. Although Richardson occasionally tried to open up the plays by moving outdoors, the result was something of a forced attempt at naturalism. It was the drab, airless interiors that usually provided the setting for the more powerful dramatic moments. These came to life chiefly through the combined talents of scenarist, director, and the performances of such acting talents as Richard Burton, Rita Tushingham, Laurence Olivier, and Joan Plowright. Olivier's portrayal of Archie Rice, the broken-down song and dance man in *The Entertainer,* is both a tour de force for the actor and an indication of Richardson's ability to adapt theatre to film without becoming self-consciously cinematic.

In his next work, *The Loneliness of the Long Distance Runner* (1962), based on the Alan Sillitoe story, Richardson moved more clearly into the style of the British realist tradition. It is a study of an 18-year-old boy from the slums who is arrested for a bakery robbery and becomes the top track star of a Borstal reformatory. Through flashbacks Richardson establishes the grim realism of Colin's life in the slums, both in action and decor —his witnessing his mother with a lover before his father is buried, the disarray, noise, and general dreariness of his working class neighborhood. It is here that Richardson's earlier training in the free cinema movement, rather than his theatrical background, becomes apparent. It is also here that he comes closest to the anti-establishment mood that characterizes the genre. Colin's chance to rebel against the Borstal system and the society that produced it comes with the eagerly awaited competition with members of a public school for a coveted trophy.

It was with Karel Reisz that Richardson collaborated on *Momma Don't Allow* for the free cinema movement. And it was Reisz who in 1961 worked again with Richardson on the film that seems the most controlled and uncompromising of the social realist films. *Saturday Night and Sunday Morning*, which is based on another Sillitoe story, makes few of the usual demands on viewer indulgence. It neither proclaims its role as social observer nor impresses with its search for naturalistic detail. With a loose, freestyle structure reminiscent of some of the early Italian neorealist films, it follows the little daily doings of its hero, Arthur, with the unbroken and deadly regularity of a metronome—from factory job to row house "tele," to Saturday night drunk at the local pub, to Sunday morning recuperation on the river bank. Rather than the embittered young victim of social injustice, Arthur Seaton, as the lathe operator from the industrial Midlands, accepts his dreary routine, occasionally attempting to break the monotony by inventing pranks or engaging in sexual escapades or, when all else fails, the escape which itself has become part of the routine—the Saturday night binge. "What I'm out for is a good time" Arthur declares, "all the rest is propaganda." It is Reisz's control of both his characters and the milieu of Nottingham's factory and pub that give the film both authenticity and dramatic strength, despite its low-key style.

Lindsay Anderson

Lindsay Anderson had left his work in the free cinema movement to spend several years in the theatre. When he returned to begin a career in feature filmmaking, he joined his old co-workers Reisz and Richardson in forming the core of the new movement. His *This Sporting Life* (1963), which Reisz produced, is a study of the physical and emotional strains on a British rugby player who finds the sport a means of social climbing. His reward, however, is a hopeless relationship with his widowed landlady and exploitation by unscrupulous sports promoters. Like Reisz, Anderson employed many documentary techniques learned in his years with the free cinema movement. The rugby field during a match becomes a brutal challenge not only for the players, but for Anderson's camera, which bobs, weaves, and jostles newsreel fashion into the center of the action. Like the Reisz work and others of the genre, it has an appropriately gray Midlands city setting and equally gloomy prospects for its hero's future. Unlike the simple and direct narrative approach of Reisz, Anderson works the narrative through a series of flashbacks to establish the professional and personal commitments and drives of Frank (Richard Harris). Even Richardson's flashback technique in *The Loneliness of the Long Distance Runner* seems ordered and conventional by comparison with the spontaneous and disassociated flashback sequences here. Though strongly criticized by many, the device does give Anderson the means of exploring the character and makes the work more of a psychological than sociological study.

The anti-establishment films were not the sole province of the free cinema directors, and several others provided variations on the spirit of social protest in the early Sixties. John Schlesinger, whose training had been in television documentary, contributed *A Kind of Loving* (1962), which came as close to a documentary style as anything by Reisz or Richardson. Sidney Furie's *The Leather Boys* (1963) featured naturalistic acting that included improvised dialogue, while an intrigue of the occult, Bryan Forbes' *Seance on a Wet Afternoon* (1964), and Jack Cardiff's adaptation of D. H. Lawrence's *Sons and Lovers* (1960), though hardly at the center of social realist cinema, did command respect for visual detail and their sense of the social as well as physical climate that had become a significant trademark of British cinema.

By the middle of the decade an unmistakable shift in focus had begun. Less angry in tone and less devoted to the "Kitchen sink" school of realism, such films as *Alfie, Morgan, Joanna, Georgy Girl,* and *Darling* showed interest in the social environment in which their characters moved, but they were found in color bedecked London rather than some dreary Midland town. They were vaguely better off than their North Country cousins and more devoted to play than work.

With Richard Lester's *The Knack* (1965) and the Beatles' films *A Hard Day's Night* (1964) and *Help* (1965) the shift went even further, and by the time *Joanna* (1967) arrived in mod London to study art and take a black lover, most vestiges of the social realist cinema were gone. Reisz and Richardson adjusted their style to accommodate box office and big production methods. From *Morgan* (1966), Reisz went on to the even more rarified atmosphere of *Isadora* (1968) and Richardson and Forbes to the richer baroque trappings of such period pieces as *Tom Jones* (1963), *The Charge of the Light Brigade* (1968), and *The Madwoman of Chaillot* (1969). Lindsay Anderson, though a long way from documenting the day-by-day activities of Covent Garden and the fun fair, was still devoted to the survey of British social institutions. His *If* (1968) moves by way of surrealism to examine the possible results of continued extremes in discipline at a boys' boarding school. Anderson has declared that his sympathies are always with the revolutionaries, and *If* comes much closer in spirit to Kubrick's *Clockwork Orange* than to Vigo's *Zéro de Conduite*, with which it has so often been compared.

The kinship of American and British industries and the increased exchange of talent has, in recent years, obscured the distinctive style and singular purpose of British film. This includes not only the angry anti-establishment features of the early Sixties, but the mod, off-beat and elegant successors as well.

Italian Encore

The original neorealist movement had run its course by the time de Sica's *Umberto D* was released in 1952. Though still applauded by critics, worshipped by art house patrons, and studied respectfully by filmmakers around the world, the neorealist films were a flop with home audiences and played down by the Catholic church and the Italian government. Particularly by the early to mid-Fifties, when economic and social stability produced an appetite for romantic sensory delights, the reminders of poverty and social injustices that had been so much a part of the recent past were rejected. By the middle of the decade directors were turning to more fanciful and erotic themes, with such stars as Gina Lollabrigida, Silvano Mangano, and Sophia Loren, as a way of winning the patronage of Italian audiences. Unlike American filmgoers and subsequently those of Europe, who were lured away from the theatres to home screen entertainment, the gregarious Italians continued willing to support the moviegoing tradition, given the right attractions; and sex and spectacle proved to be the appropriate ingredients for the times.

The arrival of the Italian love goddesses and earth mothers (often one and the same) in the mid-Fifties did not really bring the neorealist movement to an end, but rather marked a critical stage of evolution. Ermanno Olmi's *Sound of Trumpets* (1961) extended the spirit and much of the style of the original movement with a blending of compassion and a realistic perspective that marked the original works. In this film, the anxiety and exhilaration of entering the adult world was set against the beginning of a deadly life routine. It was a mild but moving protest against the dehumanizing effects of big business told through the story of a shy boy who lands his first job with a large corporation. Visconti's *Rocco and His Brothers* (1960) was a study of the corrupting influence of city life on a family of five brothers who migrate to Milan from their impoverished farm. Both films, one by a pioneer of the movement and the other by a relatively unknown director, were very much in the spirit of the original movement, while suggesting less of the rough-hewn style.

Federico Fellini

The pivotal director in the evolution of the form, however, was Federico Fellini, whose *La Strada* (1954) was to provide the link between the two major Italian movements. Although Fellini's approach was basically neorealistic—real locations and scripts developing from a single situation—the focus of the film was on the individual rather than the relationship of the individual to his society. Loneliness, the need for love, the tragedy of selfish cruelty, and ignorance of emotional needs, though hardly original themes, were given a controlled and understanding treatment within unadorned, often stark settings which reflected the personal emptiness experienced by the film's characters. Fellini chose the story of a simple-minded waif who becomes the mate and assistant to a brutish migrant who travels through the country on a motorcycle trailer performing a strong-

man act. Rivaling Fellini's own contribution to the film was that
of his wife, Giulietta Masina, in the role of Gelsomina, univer-
sally acclaimed as a masterpiece in characterization. In Fellini's
next film, *The Nights of Cabiria* (1957), Masina's acting and
Fellini's imagery once again combined effectively in telling the
story of the lonely streetwalker whose spirit and hope remained
unshaken through the deceptions and exploitation of several
men.

It was in this same year that Michelangelo Antonioni made
Il Grido, which served as a prelude to his major works of the
Sixties. By 1960, with the release of both Fellini's *La Dolce Vita*
and Antonioni's *L'Avventura*, the two directors were firmly
established as the leaders of a new Italian movement. In spite of
individual styles that were virtually the antithesis of one another,
they led a move toward psychological subtlety, social sophistication, and aesthetic experimentalism that was to distinguish their
own films and influence their contemporaries. Though the tex-
ture of the worlds they composed were strikingly different, the
increased importance of atmosphere to both directors was clear.

In *I Vitelloni* (1953), *La Strada* (1954), and *Nights of Cabiria*
(1957), Fellini explored human emotions and social forces in
comtemporary Italy with fluent, assured mastery of both his
characters and their environment. In subsequent films, he
turned to more expansive and elaborate themes and, in the
rococo tradition of the early Italian spectacles, achieved monumental studies of the mores and lifestyles of a decadent, plea-
sure-loving society. In *La Dolce Vita* (1960), Fellini dropped the
single situation and close psychological study in favor of a grand
fresco of depravity and tragedy within Rome's social set. Using
a young journalist as a focal point, he leads the viewer through
a series of incidents representing societal values, and one by one
reveals the corruption and hypocrisy of each. Though the product of a realist tradition, Fellini turned to the peculiar, the
bizarre, and if in no other way exceptional, than the larger-than-
life in his study of "the sweet life." It was Rome of Fellini's
imagination, more valid as vision than any documentary record.

Fellini has also worked successfully on the psychic front and
given visual form to the tortured mental battlefield. In *8½*
(1963), the study is of a film director who is plagued by social
contacts and by his own childhood memories and self-doubt in
his struggle to come up with a suitable subject for his next film.
Fellini is dealing with both autobiography and personal myth
here and begins to provide the kind of visual extravagances that

became so much a part of his later work and which was just hinted at in *La Dolce Vita*. In *Juliet of the Spirits* (1965), he leads his viewer on an even more subjective tour, but this time less autobiographical and more fanciful, and the result is his most visually lavish and also most Freudian work. Giulietta (Masina) has visions of both past and present happenings which provide transport to some of the most exotic images of the surreal ever composed for film. "I'm interested in man, but on all his various levels, in his miscellaneous conditions and dimensions," Fellini has declared.

It is the broad, elaborately dressed sociological landscape that Fellini is most quickly associated with, and which has earned him the title of "grand showman." In both *Satyricon* (1969) and *Roma* (1972), he returned to his favorite setting—the city of Rome. In the former, it is the pre-Christian Rome of Petronius and other classic literary writers. Fellini's approach

Juliet of the Spirits. Giulietta Masina as Juliet searches for meaning in her marriage; which leads to dreams, fantasies, and childhood memories.
MUSEUM OF MODERN ART/FILM STILLS ARCHIVE

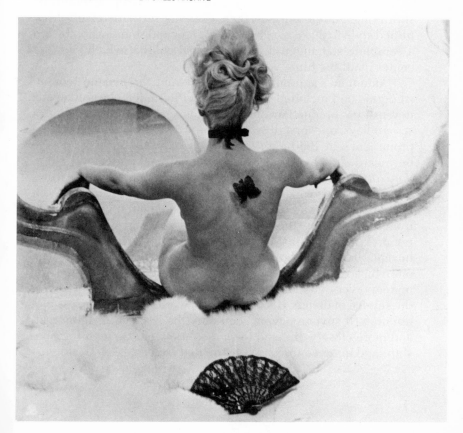

was "authentic reconstruction, as reflected over two thousand light years." Here the view, according to Fellini himself, is of "a cynical society, impassive, corrupt, and frenzied." *Roma* is again a Fellini image of the city, this time seen through the eyes of a boy from the provinces visiting the city for the first time. He further extends the image in *Amarcord* (1974) by relating the adventures of a young man in Rome during the Fascist takeover in the late Thirties.

Michelangelo Antonioni

It is Michelangelo Antonioni, however, who has become master of psychic drama and particularly the cinematic representation of the soulless, emotionally barren, and isolated set in the modern world. His characters have lost the sense of the meaning of life, yet find themselves tied to social conventions and moral precepts they distrust or reject. They wander into and out of relationships, attempting to resolve doubts about their own identity and reason for being and the meaning of such relationships. In the hands of a lesser talent, such an atmosphere would be stultifying. Antonioni, however, uses his restrained, self-disciplined style to make every detail of sight and sound work toward a complete statement of the emotional conflict which is at the center of all his films.

Antonioni's apprenticeship in film came through the neorealist period and included writing film criticism for a local Ravenna newspaper, production of documentary shorts, and writing of screenplays, one for a Rossellini film. He came into international prominence in 1960 with *L'Avventura,* the first of what was to be regarded as his trilogy on emotional bankruptcy and ennui (*La Notte* and *Eclipse* came the following year). In his earlier, less celebrated work, *Le Amiche* (1955) and *Il Grido* (1957), it was already clear that his approach to the medium varied widely from Fellini's; now their styles were approaching direct counterpoint. Where Fellini was increasingly the extroverted, flamboyant showman who leaned toward the extravagant, opulent, often bizarre, Antonioni was self-disciplined, restrained, looking to keep every element of a film under complete control and in the service of theme. His trilogy films were successively less plot oriented (if anyone having seen only the first can imagine that) and more closely directed toward subtlety of character relationships and inner conflicts. With *The Red Desert* (1964) the aliena-

Blow-Up. David Hemmings' obsessive search for reality
via the photographic image is set by Antonioni in a
frenetic and lonely mod London.
MUSEUM OF MODERN ART/FILM STILLS ARCHIVE

tion and disorientation of Giuliana is not only central to the film's
statement, it is expressed in subjective terms. With his mastery
over detail and with the aid now of color, Antonioni could give
a visual representation to the mental state of Ugo's neurotic wife.

The study of emotional conflict is hardly a subject that is
unique with Antonioni. With his characters, however, it becomes
a struggle to adapt to the emotional hazards of modern life. After
the anguish of betrayal and mistrust, Claudia and Sandro of
L'Avventura learn to adapt to a more stable and realistic, if less
idyllic, human relationship. Guiliana in *The Red Desert* articu-
lates the lesson in adaptability she is learning when she stands
with her son on the desolate Ravenna factory site at the end of
the film. The photographer hero of *Blow-Up* (1966), after a

365

unique struggle to come to grips with what is real and controllable in his life, finally seems to make the necessary adjustment which will enable him to live with some sense of belonging.

What becomes evident in all of Antonioni's films is a new and critical role for the concept of *mise-en-scène*. The film's environment goes beyond being simply complementary to the film's meaning and becomes the key to understanding the characters, their motivations and conflicts and ultimate adjustment. The action of the first half of *L'Avventura* takes place on a bleak and forbidding volcanic island. After Claudia and Sandro return to the mainland, the deserted streets, shuttered houses, and cold and impersonal apartments and hotel they frequent continue to provide a gauge to emotional aridity. The Ravenna landscape of *The Red Desert* is likewise more than an accommodating setting. Gray marshes, impenetrable fog, stark white corridors—all become a visualization of Giuliana's world and thereby what Antonioni calls "a reality of the moment." The world of mod London in *Blow-Up* is both the controlled, ordered, and revealing world of the photograph and the unpredictable, capricious real one through which the photographer himself moves. In *Zabriskie Point* (1970), the American desert is sufficiently broad both physically and spiritually to accommodate the youthful rebellion of the theft of an airplane, communal lovemaking, and the spectacular vision of an exploding desert mansion.

Antonioni is not the popular showman that Fellini has become, but is generally recognized as one of the most disciplined and uncompromising of modern directors. The jeers that greeted him when *L'Avventura* was shown at Cannes were followed by a first prize for *The Red Desert* in 1964 at Venice. He has earned his place, along with Fellini, as a major force in the Italian cinema of the Fifties and Sixties and an international star among auteur filmmakers.

In the wake of increased French-Italian co-production and American support, several Italian directors have been able, along with Fellini and Antonioni, to preserve some individuality and secure or retain international visibility among contemporary filmmakers. Pietro Germi, a social satirist whose career in feature film production goes back to the Forties, is less concerned with subtlety of mood and character delineation and more interested in direct social observation through comic narrative. His *Divorce –Italian Style* (1962) and *Seduced and Abandoned* (1964) dramatize outmoded and pretentious codes, particularly those concerned with filial relations. Frantic attempts to neutralize a marriage in the former and legalize one in the latter, are equally pointed in their reflection of how tortured a sense of honor and propriety can become, and also how hilarious it can be.

It is dramatic narrative as represented in the works of a number of directors that makes the stronger showing, however. Rossellini and de Sica, who pioneered the original neorealist movement have moved into richer, less austere historical impressions *(The Rise of Louis XIV,* 1966 and *The Garden of the Finzi-Continis,* 1971), which continue to show mastery over visual detail in recreation of the mid-seventeenth century French court and the Ferrara estates of Jews in Fascist Italy of the late Thirties. Some directors have revived something of the spirit and style of the original movement. Ermanno Olmi and Luchino Visconti have been joined by Vittorio de Seta *(The Bandits of Orgosolo,* 1961) and Mario Monicelli *(The Organizer,* 1964) in showing an unvarnished look at working class struggles. Pier Paolo Pasolini, who began his feature film career in the neorealist mode with *Accattone* (1961), has moved steadily away from the direct look at social fact to the relatively austere but formalistic and allegorical style of *The Gospel According to St. Matthew* (1964) and *Teorema* (1968). Visconti himself has also abandoned the direct look and the austerity in *The Damned* (1969) and *Death in Venice* (1972). Both films are heavily hung in visual detail intended to support the films' density of mood.

Also heavily dependent on visual detail in conveying his films' meaning or mood, but more successful than Visconti in total creation of *mise-en-scène* is Bernardo Bertolucci, who represents new vitality among young Italian directors. He was only twenty-two when he made his first feature, *Before the Revolution* in 1964. His *The Conformist* (1970) won him acclaim, both for its stylistic control and the intricate working out of the political/sexual theme. With *Last Tango in Paris* (1973), Bertolucci worked with an American star, and Hollywood backing and production techniques, but managed to retain a sense of control over the atmosphere that best accommodates the action and the feeling of film.

The Bergman Touch

Certain film directors stand alone, not only because of distinctive style and fresh ideas, or old and profound ideas freshly expressed, but also because they emerge at a propitious time for influencing the direction of cinematic art. When prolific enough, and unrivaled in their art among countrymen, they become one-man national genres. Méliès, Porter, and Griffith came close to the distinction in the early days, while the Swedish directors Victor Sjöström and Mauritz Stiller shared the honor. The worldwide expansion in production has made such prominence and singular identification with a nation's film art less likely today. Still, the emergence on the international scene of Japan's Kurosawa, India's Satyajit Ray, and Spain's Buñuel, though not all strong trend setters (and in the case of Kurosawa not unrivaled), does illustrate the phenomenon of the one-man national genre.

The director who has not only become synonymous with his nation's industry, but is also recognized as an important influence in setting the course of cinematic form and function is Sweden's Ingmar Bergman. A number of things help to explain Bergman's success and prominence. First, he has a long tradition of prestigious filmmaking behind him, with a particularly rich heritage in the works of Sjöström and Stiller, from whom he has taken inspiration and instruction. He has also, through his experience as a theatre director, learned the handling of actors and has assembled a distinguished company of players who perform on both stage and screen. From his first screenplay for Alf Sjöberg's *Frenzy* in 1944 through many of his own films, he has also learned the art of the film scenario.

It was in collaboration with Alf Sjöberg, then the leading Swedish director, on the screenplay of Bergman's own short novel, *Torment* (Frenzy), that Bergman had his beginning in film. His career as director began in 1945 with *Crisis* and continued with virtually a-film-a-year output through the Sixties. Bergman's early period as filmmaker was one of exploration of moods and styles. *Sawdust and Tinsel* (The Naked Night—1953) stands out as one of his important early accomplishments. It is a somber study of humiliation reminiscent of the Murnau and Dupont films of the Twenties. Set in a circus world, it involves the relationship between a circus owner and a passionate girl performer for whom he has forsaken his family. The film served as a prelude to Bergman's dark poetry that was to follow, but not before the director turned first to a much lighter vein and produced his two most successful comedies—*A Lesson in Love* and *Smiles of a Summer Night*—both made in 1954. Both are high-spirited commentaries on manners and morals, but the latter in particular provides the wit and elegance that stand in marked contrast to the somber, often anguished films which were to follow. Though *Smiles of a Summer Night* was Bergman's last successful comedy, it marked the beginning of an extraordinary series of accomplished works that received worldwide recognition and extended the European renaissance to the studios of Svenskfilm-industri, one of the oldest motion picture companies in the world.

Bergman's coming-out internationally came with the release of *The Seventh Seal* and *Wild Strawberries* in 1957 and 1958. It was at this time that a cycle of Bergman films was shown in Paris which helped provide the impetus for the New Wave. Truffaut explained the Bergman influence and his stature as auteur:

> He was a man who had done all we had dreamed of doing. He had written films as a novelist writes books. Instead of a pen he had used a camera. He was an author of cinema.

Wild Strawberries. Victor Seastrom, veteran Swedish director, plays the role of the aged professor who becomes haunted by nightmares of his own death, and memories of youthful romance at a family summer home.
MUSEUM OF MODERN ART/FILM STILLS ARCHIVE

Bergman's wide imagination and mastery of technique began to flower in *The Seventh Seal,* a dark allegory on man's
search for God in a world of suffering and evil. The story is about
a 14th century knight who, on his journey home after a decade
of crusading, meets Death, but gains a respite in order to resolve
his doubts concerning God and the meaning of his existence.
Plagued by his inability to either find God or end his belief in
him, the knight journeys homeward with his squire, alternately
experiencing the exquisite beauty and contentment of a family
of wandering players, and the anguish of flagellation and witch
burning inspired by the Church. A distinguishing feature of the
film, in addition to its original scenario, is the performance by
Max von Sydow as the knight, and Bergman's exceptional command of visual composition and use of realistic detail in developing his metaphysical drama.

Bergman again focused on the search for the meaning of life
and death in *Wild Strawberries,* but here used a contemporary
setting and incident as the dramatic base, and reserved the
allegory for dreams and fantasies of the central character. Isak
Borg, who is summoned to receive an honorary degree for his
service to science, is haunted by nightmares and recollections of
his past which make him aware of his failures and the emptiness
of his life. Here once again Bergman had the opportunity to
juxtapose the idyllic scenes of human feeling and aspiration with
darker scenes of emptiness and fear. The summer retreat of
Borg's boyhood and the nightmare in which he witnesses his
own death are among the most memorable in film, both for their
fine detail and for their very containment within the same work.

The hope of finding God and meaningful human relationships continued to dominate Bergman's films—*The Virgin
Spring* (1960), *Through a Glass Darkly* (1961), *Winter Light*
(1962), and *The Silence* (1963); but each became successively
more somber and despairing. The miracle of the spring was
followed by the faintly hopeful observation that "God is love"
in *Through a Glass Darkly,* the first of what is considered
Bergman's trilogy. A stark and desolate country parish provides
the setting for the second trilogy film, *Winter Light,* in which a
pastor finds himself in a spiritual vacuum through his inability
to accept the love of his mistress, to comfort a despairing pa-
rishioner in fear of nuclear disaster, or to regain his own faith.
The search for God is abandoned in *The Silence,* which completes the trilogy. Here Bergman concentrates on the alienation
and isolation of two sisters for whom meaningful human contact

has been replaced by lustful indulgence. The trilogy, while further establishing Bergman's reputation, also marked the director's move toward even more subjective landscapes and set the stage for intense psychological conflicts which were to characterize his later works.

It is difficult to generalize about the characteristics and quality of Bergman's work. One critic has called him "a metaphysical poet whose pictures are chapters in a continuing allegory of the progress of his own soul in its tortured and solitary search for the meaning of life, for the experience of God." Bergman himself has described his function as that of a conjurer and entertainer, but has also indicated that he is "trying to tell the truth about the human condition," and the majority of his films have addressed themselves directly to fundamentals of human existence—the meaning of birth, life, death—and such human values as faith, love, understanding, and fulfillment. Man's solitude in a hostile environment and the loneliness that comes of one's inability to feel or communicate emotions are pervasive Bergman themes. Stylistically his films are characterized by reserve in the use of cinematic technique, but also by technical perfection generally and special compositional quality that reveal Bergman as a master of *mise-en-scène*.

Cries and Whispers. Ingrid Thulin, Harriet Anderson, and Liv Ullmann, three of Bergman's leading performers, are brought together in a penetrating study of the female psyche.
MUSEUM OF MODERN ART/FILM STILLS ARCHIVE

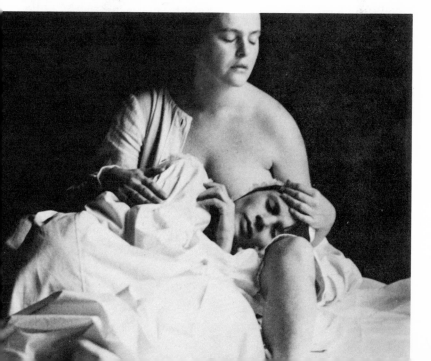

In recent years, Bergman's work has continued to display both profundity of theme and stylistic control, which produce images of extraordinary power and beauty. He has moved beyond the original queries into the metaphysical to examine the impact of war on individuals in *Shame* (1968) and the impact of individual wills and personalities on one another in several of his more recent works. *Persona* (1966), *The Passion of Anna* (1969), *The Touch* (1971), *Cries and Whispers* (1972), and *Scenes from a Marriage* (1973) all provide intensive studies of human contact and psychic relationships which lead in some instances to personality transfer and in others to irreversible imprinting. In all, we find Bergman's relentless probing of the human, particularly the female, psyche.

Among Bergman's many accomplishments in carrying on the Swedish tradition of filmmaking are a demonstration of impeccable craftsmanship in visual representation of theme and in providing intriguing if disquieting intellectual exercises. He has also earned the distinction of being one of the most analyzed and criticized of film directors, and has to some degree fulfilled his announced purpose as filmmaker: ". . . to please, to distress, to mortify, and to injure."

Buñuel and Bourgeois Charms

Luis Buñuel has for nearly fifty years been periodically reaffirming his sardonic and irreverent wit at the expense of the bourgeois class and the Catholic Church. Like Bergman, he stands apart from the film waves and represents not one but two countries (Mexico and Spain) as a one-man national genre. His film career extends from his original avant-garde *causes célèbres* —*Un Chien Andalou* (1928) and *L'Age d'Or* (1930) —to a Hollywood stint as adviser to both MGM and Warner Brothers in the Thirties and Forties, and several years of feature filmmaking in Mexico in the early Fifties. After working for a period in France, he finally returned to his native Spain, where in 1961 he produced *Viridiana*, the film that was to win him renewed infamy and a place among the major world directors.

Although Buñuel's surreal imagery is prevalent and has become something of a trademark, his visual style is less distinctive than that of some of the other major directors and his use of camera technique is generally restrained. It is his sense of irony realized through grotesque, blasphemous, often hilarious juxtapositions that clearly identify all his work. Buñuel's attitude and humor defy easy classification, however. His ridicule, which seems anarchic, is usually softened by an ambivalance toward his targets. This is particularly true in his dealings with human frailties; a tolerance if not compassion is usually detectable. When dealing with social institutions and structures, particularly the Church, less moderation is in evidence.

Los Olvidados (1950), the first of Buñuel's major works, is an essentially realistic, and for Buñuel conservative, approach to studying human weakness and social injustice. The focus is on "the young and the damned" (an alternate title for the film) who live in the slums of Mexico. Buñuel actually used records of Mexico City reformatories in preparing his screenplay and the hard facts of adolescent crime, perversion, and child abandonment, which became part of the film, won for Buñuel a petition for his expulsion from Mexico and the Best Director prize at Cannes.

Viridiana (1961), a study of repressive clericalism which he made after his return to Spain, and *The Exterminating Angel* (1962) constitute the major works of his middle period. They also reveal Buñuel's special talents for fashioning cinematic metaphor. In *Viridiana* a young novice, about to take her final vows, visits the estate of a rich uncle who becomes sexually aroused by the girl and attempts rape. Though he never goes through with the violation of the unconscious girl, he makes her believe that he has. Unable to return to the convent, Viridiana decides to use her uncle's estate as a haven for homeless derelicts. Her good deeds are rewarded by the drunken feasting and brawling of her charges, who break into the house in her absence. Her final disillusionment is revealed as she goes to the bedroom of her cousin to "play cards" with him. Linking of the rape attempt to the playing of Handel's *Messiah*, and the beggars orgiastic feast to the Last Supper make this one of the most demonstratively perverse of Buñuel's films. But despite such ironic outbursts and allegoric references, the film is essentially a realistic one. With *The Exterminating Angel*, however, Buñuel moves further into metaphor and a surrealist style. He follows a group of socialites to an after-the-opera dinner at a patron's home. When they discover that they are mysteriously unable to leave the house, the social veneer begins to crack and slowly peels away until debasing and vicious behavior, which at one point borders on cannibalism, takes over.

Buñuel's assault on human and institutional faults has mellowed over the years, but is still very much in evidence in his more recent films. In *Belle de Jour* (1967), the attack is on contemporary sexual mores, and Buñuel makes marriage synonymous with impotence and the brothel the place for true passion by way of the fantasies and memories, as well as real life relations, of a young wife. His mockery of organized religion continued in *Simon of the Desert* (1965) and *The Milky Way* (1969). Exposure of human frailties and attack on social mores are once again prime motives in *Tristana* (1970), *The Discreet Charms of the Bourgeoisie* (1973), and *The Phantom of Liberté* (1974). The indefatigable Buñuel continues, in his seventies, to follow Bergman's own precept—to entertain, injure, and mortify.

Kurosawa and Ray

In 1951, six years before the Bergman festival in Paris and eight years before the New Wave was signaled at Cannes, a Japanese film was shown at the Venice Festival which caused

Belle de Jour. Catherine Deneuve is the wife whose sensual and psychic needs are met by a part-time foray into prostitution.
MUSEUM OF MODERN ART/FILM STILLS ARCHIVE

Rashomon. Kurosawa's dramatic exercise in search of truth
involves the recounting by each of the principals of the attack by
a bandit on the wife of a samuri.

critics and devotees to sit up and take notice. The film, *Rasho-mon*, was adapted by its director, Akira Kurosawa, from two Japanese short stories. Set in Kyoto in the year 1200, it is made up of four conflicting accounts of an incident involving the attack by a bandit on the wife of a samurai and the death of the husband. Each of those directly involved (the wife, the bandit, and the dead husband who speaks through a medium) and a presumably unbiased witness (a woodcutter) tells a significantly different story. Here was not a single narrative but four, and the function of the film was not storytelling but the fashioning of an intricate parable on the nature of truth—what we believe we experience or what we want others to see.

With the release in Western Europe and the United States of the Kurosawa film, it became apparent that Japan could boast a master director, whose sophistication in handling multiple points of view and whose pictorial sense were equal to that of western filmmakers. This reputation was further supported by other Kurosawa films—*Ikuru* (1952), *The Magnificent Seven* (1954), *Throne of Blood* (1957), *Yojimbo* (1961)—which demonstrated his mastery in dealing with contemporary as well as traditional subjects.

With the discovery of Japanese cinema through the works of Kurosawa came the serious examination of films by other Japanese directors. Such distinguished and varied works as *Ugetsu* (1952) by the veteran Kenji Mizoguchi and *Gate of Hell* (1953), a version of Macbeth by Teinosuke Kinugasa, were receiving respectful attention and even adulation by critics and film art devotees, though not popular support. Later films, such as Kon Ichikawa's *The Burmese Harp* (1955) and *Fires on the Plains* (1959), Yasujiro Ozu's *Tokyo Story* (1953) and *Early Spring* (1956), reflecting contemporary urban life; Kaneto Shindo's *The Island* (1962) and Hiroshi Teshigahara's *Woman in the Dunes* (1964), both about the survival of primitive ways of life, have continued to enrich the international film scene. The nation whose film output had been virtually unknown outside its own borders before 1950 had become by the mid-Sixties one of the most highly respected sources of film in the world.

An additional nonwestern filmmaker to become enshrined in the pantheon of world's great directors and have his works reach an international market is Satyajit Ray of India. With little concession to European and American standards, his work in many respects seems the most distinctive in style. A slow, serene, lyric kind of eloquence marks his films which are dedicated to revealing the everyday life, love, joy, and pain of ordinary Indian people. Despite this distinctiveness in style, a comparison with the spirit of the films of Robert Flaherty and Vittorio de Sica is inevitable. The work which won him an international reputation in the mid-Fifties was his trilogy—*Pather Panchali* (1954), *Aparajito* (1956), and *The World of Apu* (1959)—which follows the lives of three generations of an Indian family who struggle with the conflict between ancient tradition and modern life. Ray, like Kurosawa, has led his nation into the international film arena and given a new dimension to screen narrative.

Eastern Europe

That art thrives on its limitations has many proofs in film. From the ashes of revolution arose the new Soviet cinema; Germany's "golden age" came in the wake of defeat in the First World War; and the Italian and Japanese renaissances, which form a prelude to the new cinemas of East and West, rose from the collapse of the Axis powers after World War II.

The limitations under which filmmakers in parts of Europe have labored in recent years have not been the result of such dramatic dissolution, but rather, of strong ongoing political pressures to which the several nationalized cinemas have found themselves subjected since the war. Under the continuing pressure of the state-controlled industries in Poland, Hungary, and Czechoslovakia for the "socialist realism" doctrine, several filmmakers were able to sidestep the approved socialist themes in favor of personal statements through experimental styles. The result was the emergence on the world scene of an Eastern European cinema in the Fifties and Sixties which involved an opening to Western European and American markets and broad critical acclaim.

First to find recognition in the West was the Polish cinema. With a reorganization of that industry in the mid-Fifties developed a vigorous semiautonomous group whose work, although frequently censured by the state, won popular and critical support. The first wave of directors, who had known the trauma of the occupation, the resistance movement, and the horrors of the Warsaw ghetto, followed heroic themes of occupation and resistance. Aleksander Ford's *That Others May Live* (1943) is one of the more prominent examples. After several years of close con-

trol and benign, often vacuous, themes, a reorganization of the
industry into independent production units brought about a new
era in Polish filmmaking. Leading the movement was Andrzej
Wajda, with his romantic trilogy—*A Generation* (1954), *Kanal*
(1956), and *Ashes and Diamonds* (1958)—dealing with elements
of heroism in the war years. Also establishing himself as a major
figure in the late Fifties was Andrzej Munk, whose focus was also
the war hero, but whose ironic style contrasts with the romantic
approach of Wajda. His promising career was cut short in 1961,
when he died in a car accident.

The Sixties brought a new group of young directors to
prominence, among them Roman Polanski and Jerzy Skolimowski, both of whom had strong ties to Western cinema. Although both men received their formal film training at the National Film Academy at Lodz, their films reveal nonheroic
themes of western, particularly French, cinema. Polanski's first
feature, *Knife in the Water* (1962), which won him international
recognition, centers on the emotional tension arising out of the
relationship of husband, wife, and a young man whom they have
invited to join them on a sailing holiday. The struggle, which
includes a masochistic kind of self-doubt on the part of the
husband, is far removed from the heroic tradition of earlier
Polish cinema.

Knife in the Water. Polanski's first
feature film centers on the
emotional tension arising out of
the relationship of husband, wife,
and young hitchhiker.
MUSEUM OF MODERN ART/FILM STILLS
ARCHIVE

Jerzy Skolimowski, who co-scripted the screenplay for *Knife in the Water* with Polanski, has cultivated a series of nonconformist hero types in his own films. The purpose, however, is criticism of social systems and values, and in the case of *Le Départ* (1967), the values of the hero as well. The film stars Jean-Pierre Leaud (a favorite actor of Truffaut) as a hairdresser whose enthusiasm for sports cars leads to a love affair with a Porsche.

Krzysztof Zanussi, Witold Leszczynski, Andrzej Kondriatuk, and Roman Zaluski are not known to Western film audiences or to many critics. They are among the new generation of Polish filmmakers who were born during or after the war. Free of the trauma of the Warsaw uprising, they are dedicated to articulating the problems and dreams of their own generation. The majority are low-key, and give increased attention to individual experience and less to the social order and the historical hymn to national survival which is predominant in earlier films. Directors of the original New Wave who have continued working in Poland, such as Andrzej Wajda, have also turned to inner worlds and formal problems in cinema. The exhibition of Polish films in Western theatres in recent years has been limited mostly to festivals and national cinema studies.

In spite of early national support for cinema in Hungary, repressive government control left little room for experimentation. Many filmmakers over the years have left their homeland for the freedom of Western film industries: Alexander Korda to England, Bela Balazs, famed theoretician, to Germany, and Michael Curtiz to Hollywood. In 1945, Balazs returned to Hungary to direct the Academy of Dramatic and Film Arts under a new spirit of esteem for cinema, but nationalization once again proved repressive and films were obliged to reflect proper socialist ideology.

By the early Sixties, a liberalization was under way which brought Miklos Janscó, Andras Kovacs, and István Szabó to prominence. The new Hungarian cinema was characterized by a turning away from the literary tradition which had a strong influence on earlier directors. The new filmmakers used the cinema for inquiry into socio-political conditions rather than the mounting of familiar and revered literary narrative. The behavior of individuals in a historical context became central to the works of Janscó. His *Confrontation* (1969) became one of the more controversial films. István Szabó, who had his formal film training at the state-run Budapest Academy of Dramatic and Cinematographic Art, began to distinguish himself as a director with *The Father* (1966), a study of a father-son relationship and of a young man's progress from the world of illusion to the world of reality. This film, together with his *The Age of Illusions* (1966), which follows a similar theme, put Szabó in the forefront of Hungarian directors. New thematic range coupled with vigorous and varied stylistic approaches have characterized the work of these and other Hungarian filmmakers, yet the country remains the least well represented of the major Eastern European nations on the international market.

The film industry of Czechoslovakia was nationalized in 1945 under the control of an Artistic Council. Although a system of autonomous production units was allowed to continue, decisions on films were finally centralized under the council, and the resulting films generally served to further propagandize for the socialist ideology. Meanwhile, FAMU, the Academy of Dramatic Arts, turned out dedicated and free-thinking directors who, by the early Sixties, were challenging the Artistic Council's absolute control and providing the spark for a Czech New Wave. Milós Forman was one of the first of the Czech directors to emerge on the international scene. His finely drawn studies of individual behavior were often akin to those of the Italian neorealists. *Loves of a Blonde* (1965) and *The Firemen's Ball* (1967) both poke gentle fun at conventions of Czech society, particularly the older generation. Forman's intimate portrait of everyday life revealed humor and compassion seldom seen in the works of the directors who were closer to the horrors of the war.

Among these older directors, the best known and most influential on the Czech New Wave was Jan Kadar. His international reputation rests chiefly on *The Shop on Main Street* (1965). With a World War II setting in a Czech town, the story centers on the moral conflict faced by a carpenter in saving an old Jewish shopkeeper from a concentration camp at the risk of his own life. Another anti-Fascist film from Czechoslovakia to find exhibition in the West and critical plaudits for its director, Zbynek Brynych, is *The Fifth Horseman is Fear* (1964). It is the study in Nazi oppression centering on a Jewish doctor who treats and facilitates the escape of a political refugee.

Jan Schmidt, like Brynych, is little known outside Eastern Europe, but has also helped to extend the range and quality of social commentary. His *The End of August at the Hotel Ozone* (1966) is an allegory on the changing of social orders. It follows eight girls, led by an older woman, who search the desolate countryside for other survivors of a nuclear holocaust. It is at the decrepit resort of the title that the party finds an old man living alone and where the old woman dies. The girls ignore the pleas of the old man to stay, and kill him when he refuses to give up the phonograph and single record that he treasures. This new civilization as represented by the girls is frightening in its emotional void, and the killing of a human being of the old order trying to preserve one of its relics is bitterly ironic.

Decidedly more human is the work of Jiri Menzel, who won recognition, including an Academy Award, for his *Closely Watched Trains* (1966). It blends a haunting Fascist theme with humor in the story of a young railroad station attendant's first sexual encounter and, after a suicide attempt, a final brush with death when he is killed trying to sabotage a train. More sobering and surreal than either Forman or Menzel, but less cerebral and distant in his allegorical treatment, is Jan Nemec. His *A Report on the Party and the Guests* (1966) is a study in totalitarian suppression which begins as a pleasant country picnic and ends with a terrifying manhunt and thematically, the linking of conformity with the condoning of persecution and atrocities. The film was suppressed in Czechoslovakia for two years, was cleared for showing by the Dubcek regime in 1968, and banned again after Soviet occupation.

Closely Watched Trains. Fascism and first love provide the subjects for Jeri Menzel's 1966 offering from Czechoslovakia, which won an academy award.
MUSEUM OF MODERN ART/FILM STILLS ARCHIVE

Since 1968, many films, including one by Menzel, have been suppressed and few have made their way to foreign audiences. Many leading directors are now working abroad, and political surveillance at home keeps new talent in check.

As in Czechoslovakia, a state-run industry was set up in Yugoslavia in 1945. Here also, international recognition was not to come until the mid-Sixties. Of the new Yugoslav directors, Dusan Makavejev is best represented (if not well known) in Western film circles for his *Man is Not a Bird* (1966) and *Tragedy of a Switchboard Operator* (1967). Most distinctive of the Yugoslav films in general and the works of Makavejev in particular is an experimental free-form style, including the blending of interviews and other documentary-type material with staged footage that together develop the film's story.

Stylistically, the most distinctive contribution of the Yugoslav cinema has been in the field of animation. Zagreb Studio, with government support, has gained worldwide recognition in the field since its foundation in 1949 by a group of artists and cartoonists for a Zagreb newspaper who decided to experiment with the film medium. Influenced at first by Disney, they soon abandoned the fantasy world and began to animate real world situations. Still using folk stories and fables as a narrative base, the filmmaker/artists focused on contemporary social themes that have a universal quality and appeal. The satirical edge of much of the work is not sharp or coldly calculating. The Zagreb animators equate their art with "giving warmth." The Zagreb style is characterzed by a kind of visual shorthand or reduction of drawings to simplified designs and movements. In addition to the basic visual design, experimentation and refinement in animation style includes work with color collages and contrapuntal use of music and sound. Artists at Zagreb refer to animation as "a protest against the stationary condition."

The establishment of cinema institutes and production facilities to support them have given a new surge to film activities in Rumania and Bulgaria as well, albeit within the parameters of "socialist realism." Although not a part of an international market, the studios near Bucharest and Sofia provide evidence of new creative energies in animation and documentary as well as feature film genres. State control here, as in the other socialist states, results in a combination of benign entertainment and abstract experiments, with any sense of inquiry safely limited to technique. The new cinema from Eastern Europe continues to show new potential, but remains ideologically in tow.

13
Film and the Age of Television

A New Era Begins

World War II saw the Hollywood economy rise beyond all expectations. The American public spent an average of 23% of its total recreation dollar from 1942 to 1945 on motion pictures, compared to 3% in 1969. Much of this resulted from wartime restrictions on travel and other recreational activities which provided motion pictures and radio with a virtual entertainment monopoly.

However, it was not only "take," as Hollywood's war effort also included tremendous contributions of personnel, time, and money. In 1943, more than 4,000 Hollywood personnel were in uniform. By the end of the war film celebrities had made more than 120 overseas tours, the Hollywood Canteen had entertained approximately 3,000,000 servicemen, and troops had watched more than 43,000 16mm feature prints donated by the industry's War Activities Committee. Key Hollywood personnel, such as John Ford, Frank Capra, and William Wyler, were responsible for some of the war's best documentary films, including Ford's *The Battle of Midway* (1942), Capra's "Why We Fight" series (1942–45), and Wyler's *The Memphis Belle* (1944). In addition, Walt Disney produced hundreds of training films using his well-known cartoon characters.

Despite this effort, however, Hollywood conceived of its major function during the war as entertaining the home front. There was, of course, the initial burst of war films in 1942, but this soon decreased to the point where fewer than one-third of

383

the films released by Hollywood between 1943 and 1945 concerned themselves with the war. The top-grossing films of 1944 and 1945, for example, were two Bing Crosby musicals, *Going My Way* and *The Bells of St. Mary's*. On the basis of these and other films, Crosby became the top box-office attraction of the war period.

On August 28, 1946, *Variety* magazine headlined "Film Industry's Fattest Six Months in History." This was the apex, the peak, the industry's all-time high. Box office receipts were $1.7 billion, representing 1.2% of all U.S. consumer expenditures, compared to 0.19% in 1969. For the last time Americans would spend more than 1% of all their money and more than 20% of their recreational money on motion pictures. Weekly attendance peaked at 90,000,000 and the number of theatres (21,500) was the largest since the boom year of 1930.

It was quite natural for most industry executives to look at the end of the war as beginning a new age of prosperity. This thinking received solid support from the first postwar box-office figures. However, the situation simply was not as rosy as it appeared. Problems in a variety of forms quickly appeared. Surprisingly, many of them were not new concerns. The two biggest, anti-trust action and television, had loomed on the horizon long before the war even started. World War II simply delayed their emergence and following the war they wasted little time in rising to the surface.

Basking in the glow of its immensely successful war effort and healthy box-office returns, Hollywood was caught unprepared. The government resumed its anti-trust investigation in 1945. Labor problems appeared, again delayed because few employees wanted to be accused of hurting the war effort, and Hollywood suffered through an eight-month union strike which resulted in a 25% pay increase for many employees in 1946. England announced a 75% tax on foreign film earnings and other countries followed with similar measures. As a result, despite record high earnings in 1946 of almost $2,000,000,000, the industry began to economize.

There were some immediate casualties as a number of small independent studios, which had been hanging on the fringes of the industry such as Rainbow and Liberty, went out of business. Even the major companies felt the impact. RKO was taken over by Howard Hughes in 1948, David O. Selznick ceased production in 1949 and in the same year one of the oldest studios, Universal, merged with International Pictures. Even MGM, the king of them all, felt compelled to gather all of its stars together for a group picture "show of confidence." As Andrew Sarris noted, "Studio identification was still meaningful . . . but usually at the lower levels of production. The fact that Metro (MGM) had the best lab work, Fox the best process shooting, Warners the best night quality is interesting, but hardly crucial." Studio employment fell off 25% as contracts were allowed to lapse and for the first time since the early years of the depression the industry was in a state of decline.

Despite these problems, however, things had not fallen apart completely. The reality of television and anti-trust legislation was still several years away and the industry was still confident of its ability to meet the needs of the American public. As such, the studios continued to produce 300–400 films a year, including the usual complement of "A" and "B" features, shorts, cartoons, and newsreels. In 1950, for example, MGM made 41 features, 16 cartoons, 12 "Traveltalks," 9 "Pete Smith Specialties," 8 "People on Parade," and 104 "News of the Day." Some expansion in theaters occurred, especially in the drive-in category and by 1950 there were more than *22,000* theaters, including 3,000 drive-ins.

Following the war, Hollywood picked up and continued themes and styles which had proven popular in the past. *The Green Years* (1946) described a boy's growth into manhood, while *Road to Utopia* in the same year continued the Bob Hope, Bing Crosby comedy series. Cary Grant played an angel in *The Bishop's Wife* (1947), Loretta Young a farmer's daughter in *The Farmer's Daughter* (1947) and Edmund Gwenn starred as Kris Kringle (Santa Claus) in *The Miracle on 34th Street* (1947). Gregory Peck was characterized as a "warm and gentle father" in *The Yearling* (1947), a far cry from his "heavy" image in *Duel in the Sun* (1946). Even the international tensions surrounding the "cold war" between the United States and Russia received the standard Hollywood treatment, as evidenced in the following review of *A Foreign Affair* by Bosley Crowther in the *New York Times*.

> Maybe you think there's nothing funny about the current situation of American troops in the ticklish area of Berlin. And it's serious enough, heaven knows, what with the Russians pushing and shoving and the natives putting on their own type squeeze. But at least, Charles Brackett and Billy Wilder have been happily disinclined to wax morose about the problems. . . . Rather, these two bright filmmakers have been wryly disposed to smile upon the conflicts in self and national interests which proximities inevitably provoke.

Ray Milland in alcoholic terror
in Billy Wilder's *The Lost Weekend.*
MUSEUM OF MODERN ART/FILM STILLS ARCHIVE

Social Realism

However, Hollywood could not fail to be affected by the tremendous changes taking place in society following, and in many cases, caused by, World War II. The immediate onset of the cold war, along with domestic tensions caused by the problems of returning servicemen, gave the American people little opportunity to relax and enjoy the "fruits of victory." If there was a trend, a dominant theme, or pattern to be observed in the films of this immediate postwar period, it was Hollywood's response to these changes. There was a new sense of realism, focusing on many of society's problems, including race relations, prejudice, politics, alcoholism, even Hollywood itself.

One of the first "new" films was Billy Wilder's stark portrayal of alcoholism, *The Lost Weekend* (1945). Bosley Crowther's use of such adjectives as "shatteringly realistic," "morbidly fascinating," "graphic," and "candid" provides some indication not only of this particular film's style, but sets the critical tone for many which would follow.

Racial intolerance was the most developed theme of the period, with films about anti-Semitism and anti-black prejudices getting about equal treatment. The treatment of anti-Semitism in *Till the End of Time* in 1946 was soon followed by Edward Dmytryk's *Crossfire* (1947) and Elia Kazan's *Gentlemen's Agree-*

ment (1947). All of these films had obvious "messages"; the major characters were supplied with "speeches" which left little doubt about what the films were saying. One of the better examples occurs in *Till the End of Time,* when Robert Ryan says: "My best friend, a Jew, is lying back in a foxhole at Guadalcanal. I am going to spit in your eye for him, because we don't want to have people like you in the U.S.A. There is no place for racial discrimination now."

Discrimination against blacks received heavy treatment in 1949, beginning with Stanley Kramer's *Home of the Brave,* and followed in quick succession by Clarence Brown's portrayal of mob rule in *Intruder in the Dust,* Louis de Rochemont's "reenactment style" treatment of the Negro trying to pass as white in *Lost Boundaries,* Elia Kazan's *Pinky,* and Sidney Meyer's documentary *The Quiet One.* With the exception of *The Quiet One,* all of the films were commercial products, made by major studios or independents and designed to make a profit. As such, they were infused with audience attracting elements, such as

Jeanne Crain stars as a "white" black in Elia Kazan's 1949 production *Pinky.*
MUSEUM OF MODERN ART/FILM STILLS ARCHIVE

major stars and melodramatic themes. Themes were explored through highly dramatic and visually explicit scenes depicting the cruelties and injustices heaped on the unfortunate victims of racial prejudice. The characters were almost always played by major stars who had built-in audience appeal even if they did not "resemble" the people they played. *Crossfire* starred Robert Young, Robert Ryan, and Gloria Grahame. *Gentlemen's Agreement* had Gregory Peck, *Lost Boundaries*, Mel Ferrer, and *Pinky* starred Jeanne Crain and Ethel Waters. It is in reference to *Pinky* that Bosley Crowther wrote what could pass for a sociological analysis of most of these films' function.

> The hopeless discomfort of poor housing, the ignominy of police abuse, the humiliation of Jim Crowism and the sting of epithets are sharply sized. Likewise, the mean antagonisms of certain bigoted elements in the South are vividly caught when the camera—and the story—takes the heroine into court. . . . With all its virtues, however, this scan of a social problem has certain faults and omissions which may be resented and condemned. Its observations of Negroes, as well as whites, is largely limited to types that are nowadays far from average. . . . No genuinely constructive thinking of relations between blacks and whites is offered. A vivid exposure of certain cruelties and injustices is all it gives.

In addition to racial intolerance, the films of this period examined other social ills, such as corruption in the world of boxing, with such films as Robert Rossen's *Body and Soul* (1947), Robert Wise's *The Set-Up* (1949), and Mark Robson's *Champion* (1949). Mental illness and the horrors of mental institutions received graphic illustration in Anatole Litvak's *The Snake Pit* (1948). *All the King's Men* (1949), directed by Robert Rossen, revealed the sordid side of politics in the thinly disguised story of Louisiana Governor Huey Long.

The problems of the returning veteran were portrayed in two films. One was of course, the well-known *The Best Years of Our Lives*, produced on a grand scale by Samuel Goldwyn. The film was over three hours long and featured an all-star cast headed by Fredric March, Dana Andrews, and Myrna Loy. The one conspicuous exception was the casting of Harold Russell, a Navy veteran who had lost both hands in the war, as one of the major characters. The film won many awards, including Best Supporting Actor for Russell, and was hailed as giving off a "warm glow of affection for every-day down-to-earth folks." This description would hardly apply to the other "veteran" film, *The Men* (1950), starring Marlon Brando and produced by Stanley

Kramer. Here producer Kramer and director Fred Zinneman dealt with the "raw human anguish" of the paraplegic veteran. Much of the film was shot on location at the Birmingham Veteran's Hospital near Los Angeles, where Zinneman recruited several minor players for the cast. As a result, the film has a documentary-like quality which is greatly intensified by Brando's performance. This was Brando's first major role and he brought to it a unique combination of power and pity which fully communicated the problems of the crippled veteran.

Billy Wilder and screenwriter Charles Brackett helped initiate this trend of screen realism with *The Lost Weekend* in 1945 and it is perhaps fitting that their 1950 film *Sunset Boulevard* helped cap the period. This is not to say that screen realism stopped. The Fifties were, as we shall see, filled with memorable realistic films. However, the impact and influence of World War II had lessened and as American society began to change films began to change in response. In 1947, for example, 28% of all films released in the United States were classified as "social problem and psychology" oriented. By 1954 this category had dropped to 9%. The reason, then, that *Sunset Boulevard* becomes a significant and almost symbolic film is that in the midst of the turmoil Hollywood found itself in 1950 it is remarkable that the harsh spotlight of realism was focused on the film

Jack Webb talks to a bitter Marlon Brando in the paraplegic ward of a veteran's hospital.
MUSEUM OF MODERN ART/FILM STILLS ARCHIVE

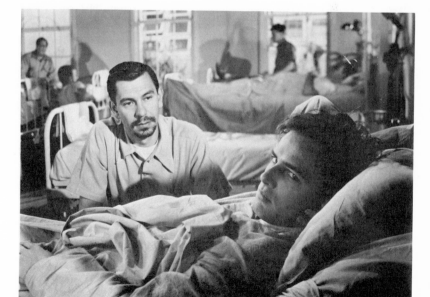

William Holden and Gloria Swanson dance their lonely way
through a ballroom filled with mementoes of Miss Swanson's
silent screen career in Wilder's *Sunset Boulevard.*
MUSEUM OF MODERN ART/FILM STILLS ARCHIVE

institution itself. The story of an aging silent film actress trying
to recapture former glories is not particularly remarkable by
itself. The emotional drama of the plot is greatly intensified,
however, by the players Wilder chose to act out the narrative.
Gloria Swanson was lured out of semi-retirement to play the
aging star, a role she must have found frighteningly familiar.
Erich von Stroheim, the great silent film director, played the role
of her butler, a position he assumed after having discovered her
and become the first of three husbands. Here, too, the "role" was
all too familiar. Perhaps the most pathetically realistic scene
involved a simple card game with three friends, cynically referred to as "the wax works." They were in the film and in reality
three former silent stars now living in obscurity—Anna Q. Nil-
son, H. B. Warner, and Buster Keaton. Indeed, if one looks at the
film's credits, the people listed as playing "themselves" is almost as large as those playing a role.

While most of the films discussed had a common core of

theme and content realism, they were widely varied in actual content and style. One characteristic that was common, however, was the tremendous success of these films. Best Picture Academy Awards were won by *Lost Weekend, The Best Years of Our Lives, Gentlemen's Agreement,* and *All the King's Men.* Social realism was not an underground movement—it was out front in the "A" level of production.

Film Noir

Another group of films were made during this same period which, while fundamentally realistic in treatment, were bound much closer together in style and content; so much so, that they emerged with a common heading/classification—*film noir.*

Literally translated, the term means "black film" and both the films and their creators have received increasing attention in recent years. The films are characterized primarily by their cynical, violent, and brutal themes, accompanied by a psychoanalytic tone which tries to get under the surface of the issues. As Paul Schrader points out, "Film noir is not a genre such as the Western or gangster film. It is defined by the subtle qualities of tone or mood." However, this does not really tell us much, so Schrader clarifies the concept by stating that film noir is really a specific period of film history. " . . . Hollywood films of the Forties and Fifties which portrayed the world of dark, slick city streets, crime and corruption." Indeed, the following list of film titles clearly illustrates this:

> The Dark Mirror (1946)
> So Dark the Night (1946)
> Somewhere in the Night (1946)
> Nightmare Alley (1947)
> Cry of the City (1948)
> The Naked City (1948)
> He Walked by Night (1948)
> They Live by Night (1949)
> Night unto Night (1949)
> Where the Sidewalk Ends (1950)
> Panic in the Streets (1950)
> Night and the City (1950)
> Dark City (1950)

The films dealt with the seamy underbelly of city life, crime in the streets, political corruption, and police action. In a sense, film noir seemed to be a creative release for people in the industry. Previously forbidden themes could now be filmed and highly mannered and sophisticated styles in cinematography and lighting could now be emphasized. Again, these films, like those outside film noir, were basically displays of manner rather than sociological essays. Film noir, despite its uniqueness and individualistic style, was still commercial cinema, and as such utilized well-known actors playing in entertaining dramas.

It was a "black" cinema because of style and content. Films such as Robert Siodmak's *The Spiral Staircase* (1945), Henry

Dorothy MacGuire and George Brent in Robert Siodmak's *The Spiral Staircase.*
MUSEUM OF MODERN ART/FILM STILLS ARCHIVE

Hathaway's *Kiss of Death* (1947), and Raoul Walsh's *White Heat* (1950) all dealt with "black" characters—psychopaths to use a more modern term. The major element separating these characters from their 1930's counterparts in such films as *Little Caesar* and *The Public Enemy* was the sadistic nature of their acts and motives. There were few upward mobility themes present. James Cagney in *White Heat* is not the kid trying to make it to the big time as in *The Public Enemy*. Here, he is driven, not by his own needs or social pressures, but by an obsessive mother love which strangles and suffocates him. *White Heat* provided no poetic, sympathetic end, such as Cagney's death on the church steps in *The Roaring Twenties* (1939). Rather, Cagney, laughing maniacally, blows himself up atop a huge gas tank.

Hollywood had every right to be enthusiastic about this new vitality and infusion of fresh themes and talent. As Andrew Sarris observed, "Hollywood was still close enough to its beginnings and far enough (so it thought) from television to look forward with some confidence, but everything seemed to go wrong at once." The old, latent, long-ignored issues of television and anti-trust legislation suddenly sprang alive. To these were added the two new problems of an anti-communist "witch hunt" which threatened to engulf the industry and competition from foreign countries. It is clear that the industry would have been severely damaged by any one of these, but all four combined dealt a crippling blow from which the industry would not recover.

Hollywood and Communism

Of the four events, perhaps none caught the industry as unprepared as the investigation into alleged Communist activity. Hollywood, like the rest of the country, had been forced to switch its attitude toward Russia several times in the past ten years.

Prior to the war, Russia had originally aligned itself with Germany via the Sino-Soviet Pact. However, with Germany's attack on Russia in 1941, the Soviets became uneasy allies. Hollywood responded with several pro-Russian films, the most notable being *Mission to Moscow* (1943) and *Song of Russia* (1945). However, the cold war soon replaced these tenuous ties as the Iron Curtain became a forbidding and feared symbol. The former "Uncle Joe" Stalin became, for most Americans, a ruthless dictator bent on overthrowing free society. The political machinery in this country began to gear up for a fight and, prompted and promoted by several publicity-seeking congressmen, began the search for and elimination of known Communists.

The entertainment industry, especially motion pictures, was a good place to begin the search, primarily because it was so highly visible. In October, 1947, the House Un-American Activities Committee (HUAC) began a two-week series of hearings to consider the problem of Communism in the motion picture industry. Representative John E. Rankin of Mississippi had set the tone for the hearings with a speech in the House earlier in the year in which he said: "Unless the people in control of the industry are willing to clean house of Communists, Congress will have to do it for them." Under the chairmanship of Representative J. Parnell Thomas, the Committee began to call "friendly" and "unfriendly" witnesses to testify. The industry's initial reaction was anger and defiance. This, however, soon turned to fear. On November 26, 1947, the industry issued the Waldorf Statement, which summarized its attitude at the time.

> Members of the Association of Motion Picture Producers deplore the action of the ten Hollywood men who have been cited for contempt of the House of Representatives. We do not desire to pre-judge their legal rights, but their actions have been a disservice to their employers and have impaired their usefulness to the industry.
>
> We will forthwith discharge or suspend without compensation those in our employ and we will not re-employ any of the ten until such time as he is acquitted or has purged himself of contempt and declares under oath that he is not a Communist.
>
> On the broader issue of alleged subversive and disloyal elements in Hollywood, our members are likewise prepared to take positive action.
>
> We will not knowingly employ a Communist or a member of any party or group which advocates the overthrow of the Government of the United States by force or by any illegal or unconstitutional methods.
>
> In pursuing this policy, we are not going to be swayed by hysteria or intimidation from any source. We are frank to recognize that such a policy involves dangers and risks. There is the danger of hurting innocent people. There is the risk of creating an atmosphere of fear. Creative work at its best cannot be carried on in an atmosphere of fear. We will guard against this danger, this risk, this fear.
>
> To this end we will invite the Hollywood talent guilds to work with us to eliminate any subversives; to protect the innocent; and to safeguard free speech and a free screen wherever threatened.
>
> The absence of a national policy, established by Congress with

respect to the employment of Communists in private industry, makes our task difficult. Ours is a nation of laws. We request Congress to enact legislation to assist American industry to rid itself of subversive, disloyal elements.

Nothing subversive or un-American has appeared on the screen. Nor can any number of Hollywood investigations obscure the patriotic services of the 30,000 Americans employed in Hollywood who have given our Government invaluable aid in war and peace.

What the industry feared most, of course, were not Communists, but government regulation. The Waldorf Statement was really an attempt by the industry to ward off outside regulation. Whereas, in the 1930's, the industry produced a set of rules and regulations called a "code," it now produced a series of names called a "list." The blacklist, while not as visible as the code or even the Waldorf Statement, was far more powerful than either. In the 1920's the victims of industry fear were primarily two talented comedians, Fatty Arbuckle and Mabel Normand. In 1947, the toll was much heavier. The headlines were made by the so-called "Hollywood Ten"—a group of unfriendly, highly vocal witnesses first called before HUAC. However, these people were just the top of the iceberg—the list itself was huge.

> *The Hollywood Ten*
> Alvah Bessie
> Herbert Biberman
> Lester Cole
> Edward Dmytryk
> Ring Lardner, Jr.
> John Howard Lawson
> Albert Maltz
> Samuel Ornitz
> Adrian Scott
> Dalton Trumbo

While the HUAC hearings of 1947 captured more attention, the second set of hearings, conducted in 1951, had a far greater impact for one very simple reason; business was bad. In 1946, domestic film rentals were at $400,000,000 and more than 80,000,000 people attended motion pictures each week. By 1951 the attendance figures had dropped to 64,000,000. The country was involved in another hot war, this time in Korea, and Americans were more security conscious than ever before. The sale of fallout shelters increased rapidly and Herbert Philbrick became a national hero as a spy for the FBI. Hollywood simply could not afford to take a stand. Ninety witnesses were called and asked to reveal names of people they knew or suspected of being Communists. Thirty individuals provided a total of 324 names, all of whom were immediately blacklisted.

The blacklist was particularly insidious because few acknowledged its existence, yet everyone on the list was unable to work. The toll in human terms was tragic. Talented artists— some of whom openly admitted they had once been members of the Party, others who were simply declared guilty without benefit of a trial or even public hearing—were quickly dropped from studio rosters. Many went to Europe; continued to work in the industry using aliases, and accepted low wages. An example of this emerged publicly in 1956 when a "Robert Rich" won the Academy Award for best screenplay for *The Brave One*. When his name was called, no one came up to accept the award, because "Robert Rich" was in reality the blacklisted writer Dalton Trumbo.

Some anti-Communist films were produced as a further response to the climate of fear sweeping the industry and the country—six in 1949 and thirteen in 1952. Most of them were cheap potboilers with such obvious titles as *The Red Menace* (1949), *Guilty of Treason* (1949), *Red Snow* (1952), and *Red Planet Mars* (1952). However, the industry seemed to favor eliminating possible subversive content rather than creating patriotic content. Since this was also a time when the studios needed to cut back on personnel because of poor business anyway, the blacklist became a convenient way of killing two birds with one stone.

The blacklist and its effects lasted more than twenty years and there are those who say it is still in force in some capacity today. Although out of work for a long period, several blacklisted people have made "comebacks" in recent years, including Abraham Polonsky, director of *Tell Them Willie Boy is Here* (1969), Dalton Trumbo, screenwriter for *Hawaii* (1966), *The Fixer* (1969), and *Johnny Got His Gun* (1971) among several films, and Howard Da Silva, who, ironically, portrayed Benjamin Franklin in the musical *1776* (1971).

Television

Another blow to hit Hollywood was one that should have been anticipated. Television had existed in an experimental form since the late 1920's. It was licensed for commercial use in 1941. However, World War II intervened and not until 1948 did the medium begin to assume national significance. By 1949, there were 98 stations on the air in 58 cities. There were 1,600,000 TV homes, but since 40% of the population lived within range of a TV station, the communal pattern of early TV viewing either in a neighbor's home or at the local tavern meant that the actual viewing public was much larger. By 1950, the number of TV homes increased to 6,000,000 and while the number of stations increased only slightly (to 104), these existing stations began to link up with national networks and suddenly the film industry found itself in competition with corporate giants who had large pools of talent carried over from radio, since the three major TV networks were also the three major radio networks (NBC, CBS, ABC).

In 1952, the Federal Communication Commission lifted its "freeze" on station growth and authorized 2,053 channels in 1,291 communities. The holding action was over and television began to take off. By 1955, there were more than 32,000,000 TV homes and 458 stations. Practically every reasonably large community in the country had access to a signal. Motion picture attendance in the meantime was dropping at an accelerating pace from a peak of 80–90 million in 1948 to 46,000,000 in 1954. Production declined from 369 releases in 1950 to 232 in 1954. This drop becomes even more dramatic when compared to the 500-per-year average that existed throughout the 1930's.

Why did people stay home? The question may seem obvious, but consider the following *disadvantages* of television.

1. The home environment was not necessarily more comfortable.

2. The home environment probably was not as glamorous or attractive.

3. The content of television was certainly inferior, especially on the local level.

4. The quality of the TV image was decidely poorer with a black and white image on a 12-inch screen subject to all types of interference.

So, why did people stay home? Two basic reasons stand out. First, television was "free." After the initial $400–500 investment, the only price paid by the audience was having to sit through commercial interruptions. Also, once a family had invested $500 in a set, they made sure they got their money out of it. The second reason, and possibly the more important, was novelty. Television was new, people had the money to spend on it, and everyone got caught up in the surge to buy his own set. TV set ownership increased 696% in the 1950's and with this increase the motion picture lost an audience it would never regain.

Again, all of this occurred at a time when Hollywood could least afford competition and so its initial reaction to television was fear and hostility. Film stars were forbidden to appear on television and the studios clutched their huge backlogs of films to their corporate breasts. However, this simply could not last for long. Television was expanding too rapidly and film attendance and production were declining too rapidly to allow the film industry to stand back and ignore the problem. The first tentative steps in establishing a more cooperative relationship began in 1952 when Columbia Pictures formed a television subsidiary, Screen Gems, to produce commercials and programs. Soon, other relationships were established. ABC and Paramount Theaters merged in 1953. In 1954, Walt Disney and Warner Brothers contracted to produce programs for ABC and soon after Warner Brothers established Seven Arts as its own television subsidiary. The dam really burst in 1956 when Hollywood made more than 2,500 pre-1948 films available to television.

The relationship between television and motion pictures ultimately moved from competition to cooperation. Television did not kill motion pictures any more than it killed radio. What it did was displace a key function of both mediums. The loss of a prime-time evening entertainment function for radio forced it to adjust to a different formula, which it did remarkably well. Motion pictures, however, did not adjust as quickly or efficiently. The industry was slow to react, primarily because it had become too big, unwieldy, and inflexible, and when television replaced the major forms of the "B" film, the short, newsreel, and cartoon, the industry found it had little alternative but to cut back. Radio expanded with FM and the youth music market. Motion pictures had no comparable market. Television became the "B" movie—the national habit, mass produced, "spit it out once a week" medium. The Sixties would see the relationship between television and motion pictures grow closer until the word symbolizing the relationship was merger rather than simply cooperation. In fact, as we shall see, the motion picture industry has survived only to the extent that it has been able to accommodate and serve television.

The Divorce

The industry might have survived the blacklist and television reasonably intact if its internal structure had remained the same. The vertical integration of the industry in which production, distribution, and exhibition were all controlled by the studios allowed them to produce practically anything they wanted, because there was always an outlet for the film. The key to the system was studio ownership of first-run theaters in major cities and lesser control over many other theaters.

The system encouraged and sustained two major selling techniques. The first was block booking, under which, in order to get certain big films, the exhibitor had to take many others. The other technique was blind selling, in which the exhibitor was asked (required) to take films he was not able to preview. Therefore, the studios had an automatic outlet and a guarantee of reasonable success for almost every film they produced. The studio's control even extended to where they, rather than the theaters, often determined admission prices and length of run.

The problem of control was not a new one, of course. It dated from the 1920's and had been looked at closely by the Justice Department since the early 1930's. By 1940, the courts had asked the studios to stop buying theaters. They agreed, but further action was delayed by the war. Following the war, court action began again and after lengthy proceedings lasting almost five years, the U. S. Supreme Court in 1951 in what is known as the "Paramount Decision," (it was against Paramount that the case was being tested) ordered the "Big Five" (MGM, Paramount, Warners, Fox, and Universal) to get rid of their theaters and told the "Little Three" (RKO, Columbia, and United Artists) to stop making binding contracts with theaters. In effect, production was "divorced" from exhibition.

The impact of the decision was enormous. The studios no longer had a guaranteed outlet for their films. This had its primary impact on the "B" film. The "A" film, with its big stars and high production value, was not in immediate trouble. However, as the studios were forced into making more and more "A" films that would attract an audience, the "B" film was all but eliminated from production schedules.

For the theater owners, the decision was a good one, as it allowed them to pick and choose from a variety of films offered by sources other than the studios. As a result, independent and foreign film makers, who for years had beaten on the doors of the industry with little success, suddenly found their product in demand.

The Foreign Affair

Eric Johnston, President of the MPPDA, stated in 1953: "It's a little known fact that nine out of ten United States films cannot pay their way in the domestic market alone. It is only because of revenue from abroad that Hollywood is able to turn out pictures of high artistry and technical excellence." He was, of course, stating a simple fact, that the economic and technological nature of a motion picture forces its manufacturer to try to obtain the largest possible audience for it. This means an international market plan for virtually every film Hollywood produces.

Following World War II, the United States had a tremendous backlog of films which had not been marketed internationally. This was an obvious goldmine. However, foreign industries, especially in Europe, were trying to regain lost ground and feared American competition. As a result, protective measures in the form of restricting imports and levying taxes on income earned within a particular country were instituted.

England was the first to impose a tax. In 1947, they levied a 75% export tax on earnings of foreign companies. This was modified somewhat so that in 1948 an agreement was reached where United States film companies could take out $17,000,000 a year. This was a huge loss, since the "take" over the past two years had been more than $60,000,000. France arrived at a similar policy in 1948. Italy imposed a tax in 1949 and then went to a quota system allowing only 225 American films to be imported in 1951. By 1954 this number had dropped to 209, down from 668 in 1940.

As Eric Johnston adroitly observed, "This rising foreign competition has come at a time when the financial position of the domestic industry has been adversely affected by a combination of factors."

In addition to restricting American films and earnings, many countries, especially France, England, and Italy, began developing plans to get their films distributed in the United States. In 1951, Italian Film Export was founded for the sole purpose of promoting and distributing Italian films in the U. S. With the divorcement ruling in effect, the market for foreign films was greatly increased, so that by 1954 almost 12% of all films released in the U. S. were foreign. If the goal of all this activity was to achieve some sort of parity with the U. S., it succeeded very well, as the following table indicates.

FEATURE FILM PRODUCTION

	1950	1955	1960
U. S.	383	254	154
England	125	110	122
France	117	95	119
Italy	98	114	141

In addition to these four events, other causes of the decline in motion picture attendance included a distinct shift in the population to the suburbs, a tremendous increase in the popularity of spectator sports, more automobiles, and increased travel.

The result of all this change within four years was a type of panic, a loss of confidence. Hollywood started to become self-conscious, no longer sure that what it produced would be accepted. What had given Hollywood superiority was its absolute mastery of so many types of films—comedy, musical, Western, gangster, horror, etc. While some independents and other national industries might produce an exceptional film or series of films, they were limited in the breadth of their output. Hollywood did them all well. The result of this strength and confidence was a seemingly indestructible system of production which seemed destined to continue forever. André Bazin, the late French film critic and theorist, spoke of an "equilibrium profile" in film which can be applied to Hollywood at its peak. Bazin was using a geographical term which referred to the characteristics of a river, which flows effortlessly from its source to its mouth without a further deepening of its bed. Hollywood had achieved an equilibrium profile, but this was quickly disrupted by the events of the postwar years.

Hollywood had been hit over the head with a sledgehammer, not once, but four times. Its instinctive reaction was to fight, to try to win back the declining audience. To do this it chose a variety of methods.

A New Technology

The first and most obvious method, especially since it had worked before with sound, was to introduce some new form of technology. The key was to emphasize the technical differences between film and TV and the immediate thinking went along the lines of "bigger is better." With most television screens measuring at the most, 21 inches, the industry thought a bigger screen would bring the audience back. The idea of enlarging the screen image was not new, of course. Tinkering with size developed almost immediately in film history and it was only because Edison's 35mm film size was the most widely used that a 4:3 screen ratio became the accepted norm.

One of the first commercially successful big screen developments was the Magnascope, developed in 1924 by Lorenzo Del Riccio. This involved projecting a scene through a special lens which blew up the scene to as much as four times its original size. It was used primarily in climactic scenes in such films as *Ironsides* (1926), *The Big Parade* (1926), and *Wings* (1927). Magnascope remained the principle method of increasing image size for almost thirty years. There were other attempts to increase size through a variety of methods, but since there was no real need to provide something different, little commercial development took place. However, in the early Fifties the industry found itself in need of some new miracle to rescue it from financial ruin and so it turned again to screen size.

The first attempt utilized a multiple camera/projector technique. Three cameras recorded various portions of the same scene and then the film was projected through three projectors using standard 35mm film. Three films were projected as one image, rather than blowing up a normal shot, as had been the case with Magnascope. Again, there had been some early experimentation with this method, the most famous being the triptych developed in the early 1920's by Abel Gance and Claude Autant-Lara and used with some success in Gance's *Napoléon* (1924). The technique lay dormant, however, until a process known as Cinerama burst on the scene in 1952. Developed by Fred Waller, the process utilized stereophonic sound as well and the first production, *This is Cinerama,* was a huge success. There was one major problem, however, and that was that the process required a special theater equipped with Cinerama machinery, thereby limiting its potential from the very beginning. However, the initial attractiveness was so great that soon every major city had a Cinerama theater. Now, the problem became one of supplying films. *Cinerama Holiday* followed the initial effort in 1955 along with *Seven Wonders of the World. Search for Paradise* was released in 1957 and the last production, *South Seas Adventure,* came in 1958. By this time the novelty had worn off. The major

These two stills from the 20th-Century Fox production *How to Marry a Millionaire* illustrate the "squeezed" and expanded frame images of the CinemaScope process.

problem was that the concept did not really lend itself to a narrative approach and travelogues soon grew tiresome. Cinerama literally ran out of scenery to present. The technique itself lives on only in a few special presentations, such as Walt Disney's Circlerama and other similar shows.

Despite a limited life span, Cinerama caught the industry's attention and stimulated experimentation in other methods of presenting a bigger image. The second method to appear was the anamorphic lens system, in which an image is squeezed onto the film in the camera and then spread out when projected. The theory was originally developed in 1862, but it was not until almost 100 years later that its first real impact was realized. In 1953, 20th Century-Fox released *The Robe* in a new process it

403

This scene illustrates some of the effective wide screen
composition used in *Bad Day at Black Rock.*
MUSEUM OF MODERN ART/FILM STILLS ARCHIVE

called CinemaScope. Actually, the process was developed in
1927 by Henri Chretren and bought by Fox some time later. The
size of the image was 2½ times as wide as it was high (a ratio
of 2.66:1) and since it required no special equipment other than
the lenses itself, the process was compatible with every theater
in the country. Other studios began to film in CinemaScope and
by 1954, 75 films using the process were in production. In
January, 1954, seven of the top ten films in *Variety's* poll were
"new dimension" films—four CinemaScope, one Cinerama, and
two 3-D.

The studios soon developed their own anamorphic systems.
There was little difference in technique and content as the real
competition seemed to center around coming up with a dramatic,
ear-catching name. RKO brought out Superscope in 1954. Republic used Naturama, Paramount coined Panavision. Other names
included Panascope, Techniscope and VistaRama.

The anamorphic process held the greatest artistic potential
of all the new dimension techniques. It did not rely, as did
Cinerama and 3-D, completely on gimmickry. The key was to get
beyond the scenery and spectacle and begin to use the process
as an integral and dramatic part of the narrative.

Perhaps the best integration of wide screen and narrative
construction occurred in 1955, when John Sturges' *Bad Day at*

Black Rock, Elia Kazan's *East of Eden* and George Stevens' *Giant* appeared. In these films the requirements and demand of the story were considered as well as those of the anamorphic lenses. Both character and scenery were integrated to form compelling and dynamic films. With the exception of these few films, however, and some intelligent work by Hitchcock in VistaVision with *To Catch a Thief* (1955) and *The Man Who Knew too Much* (1956), the process was not really developed. The primary reasons for this were increased costs and the necessity to produce films in a size ratio compatible with television.

The third method of achieving a large screen image was accomplished by using wider film. 35mm film had been the standard since the beginning, but again there was a great deal of experimentation. The most successful early method was RKO's Grandeur process, which used 70mm film in two Westerns in 1929 and 1930. However, sound and the depression stopped further development. It was not until 1955 that motion picture entrepreneur Mike Todd reintroduced wide film with a 65mm process he modestly called Todd-AO. Todd chose the film *Oklahoma* for his premier, and the appeal of a popular stage musical, color, and wide screen proved enormously successful. Even more impressive was his next production, *Around the World in Eighty Days,* released in 1956. Using fifty stars in cameo roles and possessing a theme song which quickly became the best-selling record in the country, *Around . . .* became the year's most popular film and received the Academy Award as "best picture."

Todd himself was killed in an airplane crash in 1958 but his process remained one of the most widely used and visually dynamic of all wide-screen methods. 20th Century-Fox purchased the process and throughout the Sixties shot most of its "blockbusters" with the system, including the disastrous *Cleopatra* (1963) and the successful *The Sound of Music* (1965).

There was one final method used to create a bigger screen and it came about strictly because of economic necessity. When the wide-screen movement started, the studios had a backlog of unreleased films shot in the normal 4:3 ratio. Just as when sound came in, the studios wanted to market these films as profitably as they could, so they dubbed in size, just as they once dubbed in sound. This dubbing was accomplished by masking the top and bottom of the projected image to increase length and reduce height. Using a special gate in the projector, this method achieved ratios ranging from 1.66:1 to 1.85:1. The result was an artistic disaster. Heads and feet were the main casualties, but whole films became stretched and chopped completely out of shape. George Stevens' *Shane* (1953) was one of the more prominent casualties and it is to the credit of the story, direction, and acting that the film survived at all.

In addition to the search for a bigger screen, the panic of the early Fifties also saw the industry turn to an age-old fascination —reproducing reality with a third dimension. Crude 3-D processes were introduced in the early 1900's, using two cameras with two lenses and mirrors. This was replaced in the 1920's by a process in which images were photographed and projected through different colored filters (usually red and green) and when an audience viewed the film through special glasses the images separated, creating the illusion of depth. A great deal of experimentation with 3-D took place in the Twenties, but with the coming of sound the process was put on the shelf.

In 1952, *Bwana Devil* was released in a polarized filter 3-D process and despite offering audiences little else but depth, broke box-office records across the country. Warner Brothers soon followed with *The House of Wax* (1952) and the race was on. Almost all the major studios made several 3-D films in 1953 and 1954. Most of them were Westerns or horror films in which objects or people could be projected at the audience. The

An early 1950's audience equipped
with 3-D glasses.
MUSEUM OF MODERN ART/FILM STILLS ARCHIVE

screens soon became filled with tomahawks, arrows, bodies and bullets—all aimed directly at the audience. A few shorts and cartoons were produced, but the novelty soon wore off and by 1954 3-D was already dying.

There were several reasons for this, including the expense and trouble of projecting the films and the necessity to wear special glasses. More important, however, was the limited potential of the process for telling a story. Despite all the gimmickry, the essential attractiveness of motion pictures was their ability to tell interesting stories. Hollywood, in its mad rush to find a quick and easy formula for winning back the lost audience, simply forgot this basic fact. At their best, films involve an audience; 3-D simply assaulted its audience.

There have been several attempts to revive 3-D in recent years, the most successful involving X-rated sexploitation films, such as *The Stewardesses* (1971) and Andy Warhol's *Franken-stein* (1973). However, here too the appeal is strictly novelty. One has to wonder whether audiences will ever be ready for 3-D. The "flat" experience in film has become an accepted reality and the attempts to *create* feelings of depth and space are far more successful and certainly more artistic than attempts to *demonstrate* the reality itself.

One other technological trend that emerged at this same time was a rush to color. In 1947, 88% of all films made in the U. S. were in black and white. In 1954, this figure had dropped to 42%. Economic need was again the major reason for the rush to color, since a three-color process had been around for almost fifteen years. Color was something TV could not produce at this time.

The trend toward color motion pictures continued from this time and again the reason was TV. However, today the reason for color motion pictures is because TV *can* produce color. Because a film's potential market and potential profit include TV and because 90% of all TV programming is in color, and over 70% of the American public have color sets, a motion picture made in black and white is at a distinct disadvantage when bargaining for TV play time.

Independent Production

Although, not exactly an industry reaction, the rise of independent production outside the major studios was certainly a direct consequence of the events of the early Fifties. As the studios cut back their payrolls, they released a large number of writers, directors, and actors who began to form small production companies of their own. The independents also flourished because they were more assured of an exhibition outlet, since the divorcement ruling allowed theater owners to choose films from any source.

Following the introduction of sound, few independents had the financial stability to maintain any consistent level of production. Only Sam Goldwyn, Walt Disney, and David O. Selznick were able to produce films outside studio control. Even these independents had to go to the studios for help in obtaining talent and in getting films distributed. Selznick, for example, in order to get Clark Gable from MGM for *Gone With the Wind*, had to give the studio distribution rights to the film.

Following World War II, a number of individuals began careers as independent producers. Stanley Kramer started his career in 1948 and produced a number of notable films in the postwar period, including *Home of the Brave* (1947), *Champion* (1949), and *High Noon* (1952).

The most significant development stimulating independent production, however, was the sale of United Artists. Originally formed in 1919 by Mary Pickford, Douglas Fairbanks, and Charles Chaplin, the organization had been long dormant. In 1951, two young men, Arthur Krim and Robert Benjamin, bought the company and immediately sold the studio, making United Artists primarily a financing and distributing organization. Two of their early successes included *The African Queen* (1951) and *Moulin Rouge* (1952). This success prompted several other independents to enter the field as individual producers, including Walter Mirisch and Seven Arts. The independent movement continued to grow throughout the Fifties, as witnessed by the fact that when the screenwriters went on strike in 1960 they blacklisted 56 independent companies.

However, perhaps the greatest single indication of industrial strength, success, and acceptance was that from 1954 to 1962 seven of the "best picture of the year" films were independently produced. Helping this growth was a new financial trend in which actors, directors, and even writers "participated" in a film by taking a smaller salary in exchange for a percentage of the anticipated profits. Quite obviously, this was a gamble, but it paid off so well (William Holden's share of *The Bridge on the River Kwai* [1957] profits will pay him $50,000 a year for more than 50 years) that by the middle Sixties almost 80% of all films made in the U. S. were independent productions.

A New Morality

In terms of film content, the Fifties were a strange decade—a period in which it is difficult to pinpoint trends, a time lacking a distinctive style. This is not unusual, given the circumstances; the winds of change blowing through the industry were not designed to produce content stability. However, the one distinct trend which did emerge was a movement toward greater freedom of expression. The movement actually began with another Supreme Court decision, this time involving a film called *The Miracle* (1951).

The position of motion pictures in American law up until 1951 was governed by a 1915 Supreme Court decision. In Mutual vs Ohio the court said:

> The exhibition of moving pictures is a business, pure and simple, originated and conducted for profit, like other spectacles, not to be regarded, nor intended to be regarded by the Ohio Constitution, we think, as part of the press of the country, or as organs of public opinion.

As a result, censorship of motion pictures was not against the law. By 1950, six states had censorship laws and 150 to 200 communities had a variety of municipal codes and regulations governing exhibition of certain types of content. Despite advances in literary freedom, motion pictures were still under a heavy legal yoke. However, the postwar period brought changes here as well. In 1947, in the Paramount divorcement case, Justice William O. Douglas said in a "dictum," "We have no doubt that moving pictures, like newspapers and radio, are included in the press whose freedom is guaranteed by the First Amendment."

The real breakthrough, however, came in 1952 in the so-called "Miracle Case." The situation involved the Italian film *The Miracle* brought into this country by importer-distributor Joseph Burstyn. It opened in New York in 1951 and subsequently ran into trouble with the New York Board of Regents, which revoked the film's license on the ground that it was "sacrilegious." A struggling independent, Burstyn needed the film badly, so for reasons both of economic survival and civil liberty he decided to fight the decision. The battle continued all the way to the Supreme Court, where in May, 1952, it declared in a unanimous decision that motion pictures fell under the First and Fourteenth Amendements guaranteeing free speech and free press. The specific ruling applied only to the concept of "sacrilege" and did not, in effect, strike down the right of a state or municipality to censor motion pictures. However, the mood of the Court quickly became apparent when in four other cases over the next six years, it overturned bans involving racial themes, crime, and sexual frankness. The impact of these decisions on censorship laws was dramatic. By 1961 only fourteen local censorship boards were in existence.

As the Sixties began, the legal status of motion pictures was distinctly and significantly altered. A way had been paved for the expansion of motion picture themes and content which would make the Sixties one of the most exciting decades in film history.

External legal restrictions were not the only boundaries on motion picture content. The industry itself had its own censorship system dating back to 1922, when the Hays Office was set up in response to the threat of federal action. This threat, along with pressure from outside groups, most notably the Catholic Legion of Decency (formed in 1933), kept the industry self-regulation system strictly in force.

The Code remained fairly intact through the Thirties and early Forties. However, in the postwar period, it was amended to permit films on drugs and drug addiction. A further relaxation occurred in the early Fifties with the influx of independent and foreign films and the decline of the studio system. The studios had always strictly enforced the Code, since as one of the biggest corporate structures in the country they feared government regulation the most. The independents, however, had little to lose and needed something different than the standard studio product to attract an audience. Sexual and social frankness was something different. One man, Otto Preminger, spearheaded the push of the independents in this direction. Preminger brought the issue of Code conflict to a head with two films, *The Moon is Blue* (1953) and *The Man With the Golden Arm* (1955).

Both films were denied a Code "Seal of Approval" because of content indiscretions. However, Preminger released them without Code approval and since theater owners were now free to accept any film, both films succeeded financially. This, of course, was the key. Had the films failed at the box office, the effect of Preminger's effort would have been greatly diminished. The crucial ingredient here, as in *The Miracle* case, was money. Preminger was no social crusader. He was and is a realist, a man who thought his films would sell, and since the time was ripe to defy the system, he pushed the issue.

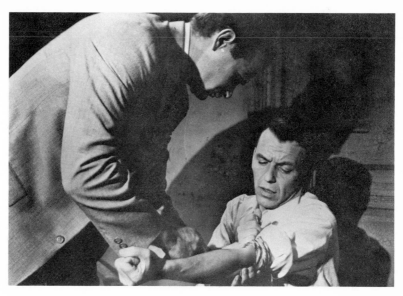

Frank Sinatra prepares to inject himself in Otto
Preminger's code-busting film *The Man with
the Golden Arm*.
MUSEUM OF MODERN ART/FILM STILLS ARCHIVE

The rest of the industry quickly saw the light. If this was the
type of film that would make money, then they would not only
allow such films to be made and released, they would make them
themselves. In 1956, *Baby Doll* became the first film of a major
studio to receive a "C" (condemned) rating by the Legion of
Decency. Prior to this time the Legion, by the threat of economic
boycott, had held enormous power in Hollywood. Legion officials were called in on every film and exerted great influence.
If the Legion wanted something removed or altered, it was done
with little argument. This was all changed, however, by Preminger's example. In a few years, both the Legion and the Code
ceased to function as effective filters through which Hollywood's
films had to pass. Their "do's and don'ts," "goods and bads,"
became so fuzzy and watered down as to be meaningless. Eventually, the Code was replaced by a rating system and the Legion
ceased to exist altogether.

The System Changes

Perhaps the most significant, and yet least noticeable, overall effect of the changes taking place was the gradual yet radical
change in the Hollywood system of producing motion pictures.

411

Forecasts of what was to come could be seen in a number of places, including the forced resignation of Louis B. Mayer in 1951. Formerly the most dominant personality in Hollywood and at one time the highest-salaried individual in the U. S., Mayer found himself squeezed out by a nervous front office.

The old order was beginning to crumble and nowhere was it more apparent than in the profit-and-loss statements. In 1950, 1951, and 1953 Paramount released 70 pictures, of which 51 failed to recoup their negative costs in the U.S. and Canada. Here was the real issue: money and how to keep from losing it. Perhaps the biggest financial concern was the percentage (usually 20%) of any picture's budget allocated to studio overhead. In the old days, this money was a legitimate investment, but now it was simply intolerable. As a result, the studios began to cut back. Feature production declined almost 50% between 1950 and 1960. The number of actors, writers, and directors under contract to studios declined even more drastically until 1960, when there were fewer than 200 of these "creators" under contract, compared to more than 1,400 in 1945. Ultimately, the studios retrenched to the point where they killed off certain types of productions altogether. The "B" film was the chief casualty. It had been the staple of the industry, the assembly line product which had underwritten the occasional excursions into art and spectacle. However, as TV took over more and more of the habit audience, the "B" film quickly became a liability. If color, wide screens, and big budgets were what Hollywood needed in order to compete, the "B" film was doomed. Some statistics on film costs bear this out. While there was some decline in the number of big-budget films made between 1947 and 1954, the real drop occurred in the $150,000–$200,000 category of "B" picture, where production declined over 18% in seven years. Shorts, cartoons, serials, and newsreels also felt the crunch. By 1957, both serials and newsreels were no longer part of studio production schedules.

In an effort to further cut expenses, more and more films were being shot outside the U. S. Instead of constructing castles, streets, or entire villages on a back lot, crews shot the scene or film on location, with substantial savings. Whereas in 1947, over 90% of all films released by Hollywood were made in the U. S., by 1954 over 25% were being made outside the country.

Studios themselves were in trouble. Universal, one of the oldest studios, was absorbed into a huge entertainment conglomerate in 1955, and RKO stopped production in 1956. Republic

Studios, a major producer of "B" westerns, faded and died in 1958.

The overriding philosophical problem was a lack of confidence. Before, the industry had been strong and confident enough to weather anything—depression, war, competing media—but the combined power of TV, loss of theaters, pressure from Congress, and foreign growth and expansion weakened the studio system's faith in its own product, in its ability to produce what people wanted. As a result, the postwar period became a time of searching—for a new audience, new films, and new formulas.

This search is never more evident than when one examines the films of the period and sees the great variety produced. The Fifties have been something of a lost period in film history. It seems that the films followed no patterns, established no trends, and as such the period has usually been dismissed by most historians. However, as Andrew Sarris states, this is "forest" criticism and in order to truly evaluate the time we need to look at a few "trees."

There is little question that the quality of the product as a whole declined. Certain genres, such as comedy, declined more noticeably than others. This was to be expected simply because of the huge decline in the number of films made. In order to analyze what trends or patterns did exist it is necessary to look at some of the major genres, since this enables us to focus more closely on a smaller content area and tradition.

Musicals

Since the coming of sound, the musical has been one of Hollywood's most solid genres. During the Thirties they were characterized primarily by certain individuals who dominated through their particular style, such as Fred Astaire or Busby Berkeley. With the development of color film and the emergence of several talented song and dance teams in the Forties, the musical really took off. Two studios dominated the period—20th Century-Fox, because it had Technicolor and Betty Grable, and MGM, because it had practically everything else. Fox's reign was short-lived, as the other studios perfected their own color process and audiences tired of a steady diet of Grable with occasional relief supplied by Sonja Henie and Alice Faye.

It was MGM which really brought the musical into its "golden age." With former lyricist turned producer Arthur Freed and director Vincente Minnelli spearheading the movement, MGM gathered together the best available talent and then gave them the freedom and material with which to produce their best work. Musicals demanded a large studio operation. As John Kobal notes: "More than any other genre, the successful musical requires the harmonious blending of many talents—design, dance, direction and performance." MGM, with its traditional huge stockpile of talent, was the logical studio to lead the musical to new heights. Some of the key musicals produced by MGM include *Meet Me in St. Louis* (1944), *Easter Parade* (1948), *The Pirate* (1949), *An American in Paris* (1951), and *Singin' in the Rain* (1952). Key performers included Judy Garland, Fred Astaire, and Gene Kelly.

Kelly was perhaps the most important individual of the group, since his talents went beyond performing. He was a highly accomplished choreographer and, teaming with producer Stanley Donen, he produced such musicals as *On the Town* (1949), *Singin' in the Rain* (1952), and *It's Always Fair Weather* (1955). There were many other musicals produced, all similar in style and content. Fred Astaire made several excellent films in the Fifties, including *Funny Face* (1957), produced by Donen. Donen, himself, made one of the most original musicals of the period with his *Seven Brides for Seven Brothers* in 1954.

Based loosely on the legend surrounding the Rape of the Sabines, Donen transformed the "reality" of rape and conquest into a fantasy world of quilting bees and wedding festivals. This type of approach characterized most of the musicals of the period. The films were elaborately constructed "fluff," with little if any connection to the real world. Unlike the Berkeley musicals of the Thirties, these films had no ties to society and its problems. Instead, they were set in Paris, America of the 1800's and Hollywood of the Twenties.

This would soon change, however, as the concept of "integration" became dominant. Integration meant that plot and music were interrelated in a semi-realistic fashion. Content itself moved from the backstage and high society glitter to New York street gangs, Nazi Germany, and Czarist ruled, anti-Semitic Russia.

The keys to this golden age in musicals were an efficient, highly organized studio system and several creative production teams writing *original* screenplays. Following this period as the studio system continued to decline, many of the creative person-nel were forced to work apart from each other and as money for expensive productions got harder to justify, the musical began a long, gradual decline. The form did not die, but much of its creativity and originality were lost as the studios turned to safe, presold themes based on biographies or stage adaptations. The era of the musical as a significant staple of the industry ended, oddly enough, with four of its biggest hits—*West Side Story* (1961), *My Fair Lady* (1964), *The Sound of Music* (1965) and *Mary Poppins* (1967). The key here was that despite record-breaking grosses for most of them, the cost of production, includ-ing buying film rights, simply got too expensive. Jack Warner paid $5,000,000 alone for the film rights to *My Fair Lady* and another $20,000,000 or so to produce it. With a film needing to take in approximately 2½ times its cost in box-office revenue just to break even, this clearly was a risky course to follow. Several disasters, such as *Star* (1966) and *Dr. Doolittle* (1968), finally convinced the studios that the musical could no longer be pro-duced as a genre, but had to be relegated to "special" status.

Western

The Western went through a dramatic metamorphosis during this period, becoming on the one hand more complicated, so-cially conscious, and personal, and on the other, in the case of the "B" western, fading completely from the scene.

George Fenin and William K. Everson point out in their book *The Western* that the postwar Western became dominated by three elements: sex, neuroses, and racial consciousness. Sex was first and both Howard Hughes' *The Outlaw* (1943) and David O. Selznick's *Duel in the Sun* (1946) seemed to signal a new era. However, the trend was short-lived and sporadic as the Western heritage thrived better on violent action and pictorial landscape than on sex. Jane Russell's cleavage in *The Outlaw* may have caused public controversy, but it could not save the film from being a box-office failure.

The maturation process continued as the genre began to explore psychological themes, most importantly the individual against society. This confrontation was symbolized particularly well in Henry King's *The Gunfighter* (1950) and in the Western which on a popular level probably symbolized the new adult

Gary Cooper as the archetype western
hero in *High Noon*.

orientation more than any other single film, Stanley Kramer's *High Noon* (1952). Gary Cooper became the archetype for what Americans believed was good in a man and good in this country's heritage. Cooper's portrayal of a smalltown sheriff—tall, lean, silent, courageously facing a group of killers alone, scorned even by the woman he loved—is, alongside the rebel youth of James Dean, perhaps the best-remembered role of the Fifties.

The Western also picked up on and followed the trend in racial consciousness. *Broken Arrow* (1950), starring Jimmy Stewart and Deborah Paget as interracial lovers, broke new ground in the genre's treatment of Indians. The Indian in film had been characterized at first by a noble savage concept in which the Indian was romantically symbolized by a proud, silent chief or warrior. The "noble" was soon eliminated and for three decades the Indian was a pestilence, a natural hazard which got in the way of white settlers like drought or brush fires. Few individual portraits were painted, as the typical Indian role was a member of a large, screaming horde.

The shift with *Broken Arrow* was, although welcome, not really a realistic one. White actors and actresses were still playing most Indian roles and the content became heavily stereotyped in the opposite direction as the screen became filled with neurotic traders, evil Indian agents, and bloodthirsty Army colonels. It was not until the late Sixties, with such films as *Tell Them Willie Boy is Here* (1969) and *Litte Big Man* (1971) that the Indian issue received even a basic sociological appraisal.

The change in the Western was partially a response to the times and a search by several directors for new meaning in the genre. Increasingly, the genre and its basic formula began to serve as a springboard for personal styles and statements. John Ford was a key figure here, although his Westerns were classical and heavily mythic in their conception. There was little concern for documentary detail or sociological analysis in such films as *My Darling Clementine* (1946), *Fort Apache* (1948), *She Wore a Yellow Ribbon* (1949), *Wagonmaster* (1950), *The Searchers* (1956), *The Horse Soldiers* (1959), or *The Man Who Shot Liberty Valance* (1962). In these films and others, Ford was concerned with a simple message and communicated it in a simple yet vivid style. Ford loved the west and found Western films tremendously enjoyable to work with. His films are filled with beautiful images (his favorite location was Monument Valley), not realistic detail.

Anthony Mann is perhaps the only other director of the

period who established a Western style and tradition as he directed eleven westerns in the Fifties. In contrast to Ford's romanticism, Mann's films were much darker and heavily psychological, concerned with tragic even neurotic men standing alone as the forces of society swirled around them. Beginning with *Winchester '73* in 1950, Mann began an eight-film collabration with Jimmy Stewart in which he probed and explored the moral ambiguities of men caught in a swiftly changing society. An excellent, if somewhat esoteric, analysis of Mann's work can be found in Jim Kitses' book *Horizon's West*.

Many other directors worked in the Western genre during this period. Howard Hawks (*Red River*, 1948, *Rio Bravo*, 1959), Fred Zinneman (*High Noon*, 1952), and George Stevens (*Shane*, 1953) are just a few examples. However, as an entire genre, the Western began a gradual decline. The wide screen, which should have proved beneficial, was surprisingly not used with any real impact. Perhaps the tension between wide open spaces and the psychological forces of society created a similar tension in terms of style. By 1954, the "B" Western series was gone. Even more dramatic was the decline in Western stars. The genre lost most of its standard characters, replacing them with stars who played in Westerns. Gary Cooper, John Wayne, and Jimmy Stewart emerged as the dominant actors, but the real stars were going to or coming from TV. Gene Autrey was the first Western star to make the switch in mediums, followed closely by Roy Rogers and William Boyd. In 1955, *Gunsmoke* and *Wagon Train* appeared and the TV Western was off and running, reaching an all-time peak in 1960 with 27 different prime-time Western programs.

As the era ended, several new directors and styles began to appear, bringing a new, personal, almost idiosyncratic style to the Western. However, the genre's reign as a significant and at times dominant force in American film had passed.

Comedy

Here too was a genre which suffered from an identity crisis. TV and the trend toward social realism were perhaps the two biggest influences creating the problem. The family comedy, especially, declined in the Fifties. Where before some of the most popular studio series, such as MGM's "Andy Hardy," Columbia's "Dagwood and Blondie," and Fox's "Thin Man" had been family oriented, now TV with *Mama, I Love Lucy, Make Room for Daddy,* and *Father Knows Best,* among many others, was usurping this role. Only Walt Disney consistently dealt with family comedies, with such films as *The Parent Trap* (1961) and *The Absent-Minded Professor* (1961). Comedy declined from 19% of Hollywood's output in 1947 to under 10% in 1954.

In response to the many changes taking place, Hollywood began to concentrate on more realistic comedy, replacing, as Raymond Durgnaut notes, the "comedy of manners" with the "comedy of behavior." Instead of the sophisticated high-class comedy of the "Thin Man" series, audiences got *Born Yesterday* (1950) and *The Apartment* (1959). As Milton Berle's zany slapstick continued to lure away the motion picture audience, the studios began to explore more mature comedic themes. Marilyn Monroe became a major star with such "adult" comedies as *Bus Stop* (1954), *The Girl Can't Help It* (1956) and *Some Like It Hot* (1958). Doris Day and Rock Hudson starred in a series of pseudo-sex comedies beginning with *Pillow Talk* in 1959. Raymond Durgnaut characterizes two types of comedy in this period: "rosy" and "black." Rosy comedy embraces themes and characters which have inherent plausibility, but are nevertheless basically non-sociological. Durgnaut points out with reference to George Cukor's comedic style that while Cukor was basically realistic in his interpretation (for *Born Yesterday* he went back to Washington, D.C., to "study the real thing"), he had no "axe to grind," and therefore his comedies are "rosy," smooth and well rounded, avoiding any real clash with social issues or problems. In *Breakfast at Tiffany's* (1960), Audrey Hepburn plays a prostitute, yet her character and the situations she becomes involved in are not presented to us for social analysis; they are comedic ingredients designed to make us laugh.

However, as the era moved to a close, "black" comedy, which uses characters and situations for satiric comment and even biting social analysis, began to replace rosy comedy. Billy Wilder's film *The Apartment* (1959) was one of the first major black comedies as audiences witnessed a callous system in which people were reduced to pawns and manipulated for someone else's pleasure. Even stronger is Stanley Kubrick's *Dr. Strangelove* (1963), with its biting satire of right-wing military/government paranoia. Here, black comedy with its characteristic "implausible central idea" makes a heavy social comment on the cold war and its possible consequences. Likewise, in a film such as *The Americanization of Emily* (1965), we are told that since war is insane, the only sane men are the cowards. This trend would continue in the Sixties and Seventies, with such films as *The Graduate* (1967), *M.A.S.H.* (1971), and Woody Allen's numerous social satires among many others.

Very few comedy stars maintained their appeal and even fewer stars emerged. Perhaps the key comic personality was Jerry Lewis. Lewis has evoked a wide variety of critical opinion. He is generally ignored or maligned in this country, while in France he is almost deified. The American reaction to Lewis may stem from the fact that most American audiences regard slapstick as noncerebral and totally farcical. The attitude toward Lewis is that he is an idiot. He plays a wide variety of idiots, but who in the long run can take an idiot seriously? However, upon closer analysis we see in such films as *The Patsy* (1964), *The Disorderly Orderly* (1964), and *The Nutty Professor* (1963) an increasingly complex character with strong elements of pathos among the chaos. It is this integration of elements that give Lewis' comedies their special appeal. The chaos always has a meaning; it's usually more than a simple pie in the face. In his most subtle roles, Lewis plays a misfit in a world which is unnecessarily cruel. The chaos he creates operates as a necessary antidote to a sick society.

One other minor genre, the science fiction film, deserves mention here. The genre came of age, so to speak, in the atomic age. Prior to this time "sci-fi" films were singular and usually adopted from popular works, such as H. G. Wells' *The Invisible Man* (1937) and the space serial "Buck Rogers." As the atomic age began to pervade society and as an increasingly large body of sci-fi short stories began to appear, the sci-fi film took on increased stature. Beginning with *Destination: Moon* in 1950 and continuing with *Five* (1951), *The Day the Earth Stood Still* (1951), *Invasion of the Body Snatchers* (1956), and *The Incredible Shrinking Man* (1957), among others, a whole body of work began to accumulate. Most of it was low-budget "B" film material, however, and as the reality on TV began to surpass the fiction on the motion picture screen, no Hollywood backlot could hope to substitute for the real thing.

Some General Observations

We have reviewed a few of the dominant Hollywood genres to try to better understand how the events of this period affected the content of film. In a sense, the genres themselves became more complex and the films within them more individualistic. The traditions of a genre, such as the Western or the musical, had relatively little effect on the new films emerging in response to the times and certain directorial philosophies. However, as the decade wore on the genres began to fall back into place or die (the "B" western serial).

To replace and complement the established genres Hollywood came up with a new one based on size. The small film and the big film replaced many of the standard genre productions. The small film—independent, black and white, often adapted from TV—spurted briefly in the mid-Fifties, beginning with *Marty* (1955). Independently produced by the Hecht-Lancaster organization, the film starred Ernest Borgnine as a butcher who falls in love with a school teacher. The film has a distinct neorealist heritage as it looks at two ordinary people living ordinary lives. *Marty,* however, had a freshness and vitality, a genuineness which many had found lacking in most of Hollywood's Fifties products. It won a Grand Prix at the Cannes Film Festival and an Academy Award as best picture of the year. These awards, of course, stirred a beehive of activity. Immediately, producers began a search for small stories to make into small films. As such they looked to TV and the huge number of original 60-minute dramas being presented once a week. Here was a bonanza and soon such TV writers as Rod Serling and Paddy Chayefsky were being wooed by Hollywood. While some of the adaptation succeeded, the old Hollywood game of imitating a popular trend took over as studios tried to create a small-film formula. Unfortunately, despite limited success with Chayefsky's *The Bachelor Party* (1957), Serling's *Patterns* (1955) and *Requiem for a Heavyweight* (1956), the small-film formula did not save Hollywood.

If the word was not small, then perhaps it was big. The spectacle, which had always been part of Hollywood on a limited scale, suddenly erupted in 1956 with *The Ten Commandments* ($13.5 million), *War and Peace* ($6.5 million), *The King and I* ($6.5 million), *Around the World in Eighty Days* ($6 million) and *Moby Dick* ($5 million). The pattern continued through the decade with *Ben Hur* (1959), *El Cid* (1960), *Spartacus* (1960), and the biggest spectacle of them all *Cleopatra* (1963). By the time the smoke had cleared following *Cleopatra's* failure the studios were on such shaky ground that despite the fact that spectacles were still possible and occasionally profitable, costs had increased so enormously that few organizations could afford the gamble.

An Assessment

We are arbitrarily breaking this period at 1963. It is difficult to pinpoint an exact time, since the decades seem to slip into one another. There are no real dramatic events, like sound or television, to mark off the time. If anything serves as an industrial signpost, it might be the film *Cleopatra,* which in many ways was the last of the old Hollywood movies. For society as a whole 1963 became a breaking point as President Kennedy's assassination marked time for all those involved.

In looking back on this postwar period of almost 20 years, it is clear that Hollywood and the whole system of making motion pictures in America underwent a radical adjustment in response to several significant events. Prior to this time Hollywood had thrived on regulated efficiency. There were rules, but more importantly there were *expectations*—those of the system itself and those of the audience. The two were interwoven, since the system imposed its expectations on producers, directors, writers, and stars based on those received from the *mass* Ameri-

A spectacular scene and one of the reasons why the 1963 production of *Cleopatra* lost money.
MUSEUM OF MODERN ART/FILM STILLS ARCHIVE

can audience in the *habit* of attending motion pictures. However, all expectations changed when both "mass" and "habit" were eliminated from "audience."

As a result of this loss, the period became one of trial and error, of new forms emerging and old forms dying. Hollywood developed a split personality, desperately trying to hang onto the old, while trying to adjust to the new. Unlike the Twenties, Thirties, and early Forties, the postwar period cannot be easily characterized. Society was more complex; there were multiple pressures which ultimately caused fundamental changes. Contrary to some thinking, Hollywood and the American film industry (up to this point the two were synonymous) did not die; rather, it was cracked wide open. At times the content of this period gets overshadowed by the emphasis on technology and a few special films or people. However, the most significant content characteristic was the amount of variety which was introduced as the industry was forced to open itself up to new ideas. There were few film categories of overriding importance. Hollywood was beyond the pigeon-holing of the past, where the Thirties could be characterized by the studio system and the Forties by distinct themes and styles. More new voices entered the American film than at any time since the studios had solidified their hold in the early Twenties. In a way the Fifties were a testing ground for many of the ideas and people which would characterize the films of the Sixties and Seventies.

A case in point is the standard cliché that Hollywood in the Fifties was strictly "bubble gum and bobby sox"; a period in which few films of any meaning or consequence were made. Indeed, this might have very well been true, as Hollywood was looking inward most of the time, nursing its wounds and looking for a quick, easy formula to win back the audience. Even when the HUAC/McCarthy atmosphere polluted the air over Hollywood, however, most studios did not simply stop treating certain issues. Rather, they disguised them and dressed them up in the form of Westerns and war films. Westerns dealt with the past and, therefore, could not really be linked to any current social thought. War films were obviously patriotic. Such films as *The Gunfighter, Broken Arrow, Shane,* and *High Noon* in the Western genre and *The Red Badge of Courage* (1951), *The Caine Mutiny* (1954) and *Twelve O'Clock High* (1959) dealt with the individual in society and the problems he faced because of certain beliefs or standards. Of course, a prime motivator in all this was money; and much of the realism was simply the result of a "frenzied search for material that would galvanize the public." Otto Preminger's deviance from the Motion Picture Code is another case in point, as is the appearance of Tennessee Williams as one of the most frequently used playwrights of the time. Although in Williams' case, this was partially due to his cinematic style of writing, his most attractive quality was his themes and the way he treated them. He dealt with subjects such as impotence in *Cat on a Hot Tin Roof* (1958) and cannabalism in *Suddenly Last Summer* (1959), which would have had great problems being filmed previously.

Problems of youth received increased emphasis with James Dean in *East of Eden* (1953) and *Rebel Without a Cause* (1954). Other youth-oriented films of this period were *Blackboard Jungle* (1955), *The Dark at the Top of the Stairs* (1960), and *Splendor in the Grass* (1961). This semirealistic emphasis was soon diffused, however, as rock music began to create a youth culture and Hollywood jumped into the trend with Elvis Presley, Fabian, and other assorted heroes.

The beginning of black consciousness can be seen in two Sidney Poitier films, *Edge of the City* (1957) and *The Defiant Ones* (1958). Although he was a stereotyped larger than life character, the more common ordinary concerns of race relations were stated in films of this period.

Stanley Kubrick's *Paths of Glory* (1958) presented the strongest antiwar statement of the period—perhaps of any period.

One side issue which contributed greatly to the growing trend in realism was a new style in acting known as "the Method." Its origins are found in the Russian theorist Stanislavsky and his book *An Actor Prepares*, in which he stated the central thesis of the movement: "You must live the part every moment you are playing it." The method was popularized in the U. S. by Stella Adler, who taught acting in New York, and by the Actors Studio, organized by Lee Strasberg and Elia Kazan. Marlon Brando was the most famous public communicator of Method acting and through strong performances in *A Streetcar Named Desire* (1951) and *On The Waterfront* (1952) made what was essentially a very small movement one of immense reputation and appeal. The key here was the impact Method acting had on the nature of the star system with its basic conflict between real people vs. stars. This conflict would anticipate the trend of the Sixties and Seventies, where the emphasis on a star playing a role with its almost built-in artificial distance gradually lessened. Although the Method was subscribed to by relatively few players, the versatility and impact of such people as Rod Steiger, Ben Gazzara, Paul Newman, Lee J. Cobb, Eli Wallach, Julie Harris, and Brando would have a major effect on films of the Sixties and Seventies.

Post Script

As the decade ended David O. Selznick said to Ben Hecht:

Hollywood's like Egypt, full of crumbled pyramids. It'll never come back. It'll just keep on crumbling until finally the wind blows the last studio prop across the sands.

Selznick was wrong only in the way the props would go— they did not blow away, someone bought them at an auction. Hollywood as it existed for most people—the golden city, moguls, stars, gods and goddesses—was gone. However, like the phoenix rising from its own ashes, a new Hollywood would quickly grow up in its place.

14
Changing
Form and Function

For most people only two types of films exist: feature-length fiction and "the rest." Primary attention is focused on the feature film, because of its economic importance. However, if one were to consider social influence, education, aesthetic freedom, and experimentation as important as box-office receipts, "the rest" would play an equally important role in most peoples' minds. This second category encompasses a wide variety of film and to attempt to cover them all with any degree of thoroughness would be impossible for any general film history. Rather, we will look at three of the more important and dominant types: the documentary, the animated film, and the avant-garde/experimental film.

Documentary

We are continuing the story begun in Chapter 10 and in doing so find immediate and revolutionary changes. The late Thirties and the period of World War II were truly a "golden age" for the documentary film. More people watched more so-called nonfiction film than at any other time in history. Sources of support were plentiful, as the governments of nations at war spent millions on education and propaganda through the medium of film. The postwar period, however, saw both these sources of support and the size of the audience decrease significantly.

There are obvious reasons for this. Society as a whole and the motion picture industry in particular was in a state of flux, of rapid and at times unforeseen changes. The documentary film as a "fringe" genre was in jeopardy. The black and white issues which it had used to such great advantage during the depression and World War II were gone, as was the equally important fact of government sponsorship. There was some resurgence of commercial sponsorship in England through such organizations as the Cadbury Brothers, the International Tea Bureau, and BOAC. However, American industry had never been kindly disposed toward film sponsorship and there was very little support for the documentary film in the United States.

Although few films were produced, two stand out as classics, even today. Both deal with the unique and private world of a young boy, but there the similarity ends. Robert Flaherty's *Louisiana Story* (1948) is a lyrical mood piece emphasizing the changing yet eternal world of a young Cajun boy in the bayous of Louisiana. Sponsored by the Standard Oil Company, the film superficially dealt with an oil rig drilling in the swamp, and yet the film had very little to do with oil. Rather, it demonstrated in Flaherty's typical humanistic style and vision, the world of youth, of nature, of life as it existed in this "out-of-the-way"

Robert Flaherty and his editor Helen Van
Dongen examine footage from *Louisiana Story.*
MUSEUM OF MODERN ART/FILM STILLS ARCHIVE

Sidney Meyer's *The Quiet One* examines the world of youth in a
radically different environment from that of Flaherty.

environment. Most critics consider the film to be Flaherty's
masterpiece and a fitting climax to a career marked by few films,
but a remarkable consistency of vision.

Sidney Meyers' *The Quiet One* (1949) treats life at almost
the opposite extreme. Instead of an idyllic rural landscape and
the untroubled world of a happy child, Meyers focuses on the
urban jungle of New York and the disturbed world of a young
black as he struggles to survive in a hostile environment. Aided
greatly by James Agee's moving and simple commentary, *The
Quiet One* reflected the struggles and frustrations of the young
boy, Donald, as he tries to find himself through the help of The
Wiltwyck School. Meyers, like Flaherty, communicated with
his audience in a very natural way, allowing the boy and his
worlds (Wiltwyck and "outside") to emerge easily, without a
great deal of obvious structure. This is not to say that either film
was plotless or shot "off the cuff." Indeed, Flaherty and his
editor, Helen van Dongen, spent nearly two years "constructing" *Louisiana Story* from Flaherty's original footage. However,
both filmmakers allowed the natural story to emerge by becoming a part of the world they were filming. Instead of "looking
down" through a microscope, they "looked around" and caught
the "real" world with remarkable fidelity.

429

Television and Documentary

Aside from these two monumental efforts little else of significance was produced in the United States during this period. Most filmmakers, commercial and documentary, were watching with a fearful eye the development of a new medium—television. As it turned out the stronger of the two groups, commercial film, was the real casualty as television revitalized the documentary form and provided it with the showcase it had always lacked. One can argue, of course, that television hurt the theatrical documentary badly. This may be true, but that is a little like arguing that champagne tastes better in crystal goblets than in plastic cups. Some aesthetic appeal is certainly lost, but the ingredients remain the same. Television may not have been as glamorous to some traditionalists, but it provided the documentary film with the sponsorship and organization it so desperately needed in order to survive.

Sponsorship was the crucial element. The documentary film has never been and is perhaps not meant to be self-supporting. If its creators are to be free to explore a wide variety of issues, the concept of audience popularity must be viewed with a different perspective. At least at the beginning, commercial television provided this sponsorship. We hear, especially today, complaints about the lack of, or the type of, commercial sponsorship on television for news and public-affairs programming. This was not always the case, as one has only to compare the brief tenure of the United States Film Service (less than two years) with television's backing for *See It Now* (seven years), *The Twentieth Century* (seven years) and *Project XX* (eight years).

The story of television and the documentary form has been told in superb fashion by William Bluem in his book *Documentary in American Television* and we will not repeat him here. However, a few basic observations are necessary.

The television documentary was formed from the twin heritage of radio and motion pictures. This all came together in the early Fifties, most effectively through the work of Fred Friendly and Edward R. Murrow at CBS, particularly in their program *See It Now*. Beginning in 1951, this program explored a wide variety of individual and social issues, most notably the Communist "witch hunt" conducted by Senator Joseph McCarthy. It was this issue and this man that saw *See It Now* reach the height of its effectiveness and power. In 1954, Murrow went on the air and publicly denounced McCarthy and his tactics. Although the program was not as polished or definitive as Murrow's early treatment of some of McCarthy's victims, such as Annie Lee Moss and Milo Radulovich, its power as an editorial statement was unsurpassed and in the light of passing years unduplicated.

What television provided at this time was not only sponsorship and organization, but individuals who had the courage, integrity, and ability to use the documentary for social investigation and analysis. Edward R. Murrow and Fred Friendly were to the television documentary what John Grierson, Pare Lorentz, and Louis de Rochemont were to the theatrical documentary. This personal vision has always been a vital part of the history of the documentary form and while television's more recent documentary pattern reveals a continued, albeit lessened sponsorship and organization, it clearly lacks the personalities who helped make the early Fifties a "golden age."

The editorial approach of *See It Now* was just one of television's approaches to documentary. Bluem indicates three major approaches: the compilation form, as illustrated by such series as *Victory at Sea* and *Project XX*, the biographical form, as illustrated by *The Twentieth Century* series and hundreds of individual films, and the dramatic form used in *Circle Theater* and Robert Drew's *Living Camera* series.

The initial strength and force of these approaches ebbed gradually through the Fifties, and when Murrow left CBS in 1962 to head the United States Information Agency, the cycle was complete. *See It Now* continued in the form of *CBS Reports* and other series, such as NBC's *White Paper* and ABC's *Project XX*, maintained some of the form's early vigor, but by 1970 there was no regular prime-time documentary series on the air. The emphasis in the Sixties switched to hard news coverage as the network evening news expanded to thirty minutes and television's coverage of big events became almost commonplace. It was television's *live* coverage of assassinations, political conventions, and space shots that established its news reputation and took the place of the formal, structured documentary.

Perhaps the major element which provides the television documentary with both its greatest advantage and its greatest disadvantage is audience size. The advantage is, of course, the huge *potential* inherent in an audience of more than 200,000,000 people. The disadvantage, however, is the *reality* of a much smaller audience and television's dependency on audience size for survival. As long as ratings of 15+ are necessary for program survival and as long as most documentary programs and series receive ratings far below this figure the future of the television documentary is open to question. Its survival will depend upon public noncommercial television and the public-interest policies of the commercial networks and stations.

Other Developments

With television experiencing huge growth and popularity in the Fifties and the motion picture industry declining, theatrical documentary in the U. S. was scarce. There was little commercial or government sponsorship and most documentary production occurred on an independent, partially underground level. This activity would link up with the avant-garde movement of the Sixties, but for the time there was little activity. There were few major styles and most critics find it difficult to describe the period with any real definition. Richard Barsam in his book *Nonfiction Film* says of the time: "American nonfiction film making since World War Two has been characterized by social conviction, sincerity, and high standards of production skill." Perhaps all that can be done is to point to a few individual films.

Benjy (1951) stands out not so much for its subject matter concerning a crippled boy, but for its director, Fred Zinneman, and what he represented. Zinneman was and is a well-known Hollywood director. This fact alone made his association with a documentary film unusual. His effort, while flawed by an overreliance on professional actors and a highly structured script, offered some hope that the documentary form had a future. Unfortunately, with the industry struggling desperately to survive, the luxury of Zinneman's effort was not to be repeated.

If one individual can be said to represent Fifties theatrical documentary, it would be George Stoney. With such films as *All My Babies* (1952) Stoney continued the classical tradition of John Grierson and Pare Lorentz. Stoney's films are marked by a strong sense of dramatic conflict, but at the same time are much "freer" than those of Lorentz or Grierson. He allows the natural flow of events to emerge and as a result his films constitute a "bridge" between the classical tradition and the "direct cinema" of the Sixties.

Besides Stoney's and a few other singular efforts, such as

Alan King's *Skid Row* (1956), Lionel Rogosin's *On the Bowery* (1957), Dennis and Terry Sanders' *A Time Out of War* (1954), and Sidney Meyers' *The Savage Eye* (1959), the quality and quantity of the American documentary effort was lean. As Lewis Jacobs said of the time: "The American documentary revealed itself in a neutralism that offered no challenge to the national temper."

In England, the situation was a little better, helped mainly by The Festival of Britain (1951), which focused attention on the documentary and supported such films as *The Coronation of Queen Elizabeth* and *Mt. Everest*, both produced in 1953. The most important development, however, was the emergence of the Free Cinema Group in 1956. This was a group of filmmakers, headed by Lindsay Anderson, Tony Richardson, and Karel Reisz, who had become dissatisfied with the Grierson tradition. They wanted to create actualities rather than interpret or propagandize. Obviously influenced by neorealism, they revealed in such films as Anderson's *Every Day Except Christmas* (1957) and Reisz and Richardson's *Momma Don't Allow* (1955) a concern for the common man in everyday environments which heralded the beginnings of a "vérité" philosophy. Important here also was the fact of an organization which allowed for the exchange of ideas and mutual stimulation so necessary to any strong documentary movement.

In Sweden, the work of Arne Sucksdorff must be noted. Working with nature films, Sucksdorff achieved a Flaherty-like mood of romanticism about the world of animals and children with such films as *Shadows on the Snow* (1945), and, most notably, *The Great Adventure* (1953).

The most outstanding documentary effort of this period occurred in Canada. John Grierson established the National Film Board of Canada in 1939 and served as Commissioner until 1945. As such, he set forth a philosophy of film committed to public information and education. The Film Board's strongest point was its variety, as films were produced ranging from Norman MacLaren's abstract work to solid "March of Time" efforts. Many films stand out in this effort and selecting any for description and analysis is difficult. However, two personal favorites are the much acclaimed *City of Gold* (1957) and the controversial *Fields of Sacrifice* (1962). *City of Gold* uses a still picture technique which attempts to recreate a sense of the past reality of Dawson City during the Alaskan gold rush of the 1890's. The stills almost seem to come alive, especially as the film moves in on close-ups of long-dead bearded men walking on muddy

streets or working cold streams. *Fields of Sacrifice* also evokes
a sense of the past, but here it becomes fused with the present
by overlapping the sounds of war and pictures of green and
peaceful battlefields. The juxtaposition of sound and image col-
lides with powerful effect and this film, intended as a tribute and
memorial to Canadian war dead, emerges as an anti-war statement of great power.

The Film Board continues its support of the documentary as
it fulfills its original purpose "to produce and distribute films
designed to interpret Canada to Canadians and other nations."

The Past Decade

In significant and dramatic contrast to the relative dearth of
documentary film in the late Forties and Fifties, the past ten to
fifteen years have been ones of enormous growth and development.

One of the major factors stimulating this growth has been
improved technology. The development of lightweight, portable
16mm cameras, direct synchronous sound recording, and 8mm
sound film equipment gave great impetus for new films and new
styles. One of the most important stimuli in this development
was the Vietnam war, as the demands of journalists for quick and
widespread coverage of events under all types of conditions
created a need for new, portable, sturdy equipment.

Perhaps the most significant stimulus was the time itself.
The decade was an explosive one, filled with dramatic events
which provided rich grist for the documentary mill. The documentary film seemed to rise to the occasion these events provided. From the tragedy of President Kennedy's assassination,
for example, came three vital and powerful films: Mel Stuart's
Four Days in November (1964), Emile de Antonio's *Rush to
Judgment* (1967), and Bruce Herschensohn's *Years of Lightning,
Day of Drums* (1967). The Vietnam war, strangely enough, however, did not really stimulate the documentary effort. Perhaps
there was too little unity and consensus and too few black and
white issues. Pierre Schoendorffer's *The Anderson Platoon* (1967)
and Eugene Jones' *A Face of War* (1968) are two of the most
significant efforts. *The Anderson Platoon*, despite the obvious
and "heavy" use of commentary music (shots of combat boots
slogging through swamp water with Nancy Sinatra singing the

pop song "These Boots Are Made for Walking"), is particularly impressive and powerful. Schoendorffer pleaded no particular cause, practiced no demagoguery as he revealed the horror and brutality of war through the tired faces of men as they struggled just to stay alive.

As society broke apart and fractionalized, as issues such as politics, race, war, peace, and youth emerged quickly and explosively, the variety of documentary films increased. More and more emphasis was placed on the exploration of subcultures, probing areas of society not usually examined. *A Time for Burning* (1966) looked at the problem of race relations in a small Lutheran church. *The Queen* (1968) revealed the bizarre world of the transvestite. *Titicut Follies* (1967) looked at the equally bizarre world of a mental institution. The list is endless. Just as important as the particular topic or theme is the style which many of them illustrated.

This development in style and form was the key ingredient in the "new" documentary of the past decade. The last ten years witnessed a dramatic break with the Grierson tradition of documentary as the "dramatization of actuality"; "cinéma vérité" became the prevailing stylistic philosophy. Coined by Jean Rouch, the cinéma vérité approach was based roughly on the Russian director Dziga Vertov's theory of film as a "direct encounter with uncontrolled life."

The key terms in a cinéma vérité philosophy are immediacy, involvement, and participation. Cinéma vérité postulates a concern with purity and clarity in film. To accomplish this, film must move in the direction of the unscripted, unrehearsed revelation of reality. By looking at the surface of life through as few obstacles (filters) as possible, cinéma vérité films attempt to get below the surface of reality; they possess a self-revealing power accomplished by recording and revealing the "true" reality of an event, time, place, or person.

All this philosophy sounds awesome and as a theory, cinéma vérité has great potential. In practice, however, problems appear. First, it must be stated that the attempts by filmmakers using handheld cameras and portable synchronous sound equipment to become a part of the event they are filming have on no occasion succeeded with powerful results. The ability of the camera to reveal through simple recording is powerful. The recording becomes all the more powerful when the filmmaker and his equipment become a part of the situation, with the event itself being only partially "contaminated" by the filmmaker's presence. However, the reality of a truly objective film is impossible. The camera will always contaminate and the filmmaker will always interpret, no matter how physically or psychologically unobstrusive he may try to be.

Despite this difficulty, the ability of filmmakers like Richard Leacock, John Pennebacker, Robert Drew, Al Maysles, and Frederick Wiseman, among others, to penetrate and get behind the facades of various institutions, such as politics, religion, education, etc., has made cinéma vérité something unique.

While vérité filmmakers may not succeed completely in achieving their purist end of an encounter with uncontrolled reality, they have certainly succeeded in revealing new aspects of reality which had previously been hidden.

One of the seminal films of the movement was *Primary* (1960), an "inside" look at the Wisconsin presidential primary campaigns of Senators John Kennedy and Hubert Humphrey. Although it is far from "objective reporting," it does offer revealing insights into the nature of both candidates, their campaign machines, and the voters of Wisconsin.

Although many people are associated with the cinéma vérité movement, two men, Richard Leacock and Frederick Wiseman, are of primary importance. Leacock is in a sense the father of the movement, although Robert Flaherty can lay legitimate claim to being at least a spiritual sire. Leacock worked with Flaherty on *Louisiana Story* and then began to develop a vérité philosophy with work in the television series *Omnibus* in the early Fifties. He continued his work in the Sixties, concentrating more and more on the development of new equipment. The past ten years have been spent primarily at MIT developing a Super 8mm sound system.

His place as an active filmmaker has been taken over to a certain extent by Frederick Wiseman. With the help of public (educational) television, Wiseman has had his films seen by more people than almost any other contemporary documentary director. Beginning with *Titicut Follies* in 1967 he has concentrated his efforts on the exploration of institutions, with such self-explanatory films as *High School, Hospital, Basic Training, Essene* (a religious order), and *Primate,* the study of an animal research laboratory.

Wiseman's films represent cinéma vérité at its very best. At the same time, however, they reveal some of the limitations inherent in the approach. The key to the success of the style seems to lie in the situation or person focused on. If the subject matter is inherently interesting, the method seems to work. The simple and unobstrusive recording of a young boy "coming down" off a drug trip in *Hospital* is frightening and powerful. Wiseman's camera almost brings us in too close to the boy's terror. In situations like this, by allowing the camera to become a participant-observer, vérité achieves a personal perspective unattainable with any other approach. However, when the subject is dull and uninteresting, recording this reality produces a dull and uninteresting film. In these instances the vérité filmmaker falls back on the standard creative elements of composition and editing to make his point. It is this "point making," this use of film as editorial statement which works against the purist vérité philosophy. For example, Wiseman's *High School* has been subjected to intense rhetorical analysis and in doing so researchers have taken great pains to point out the intent of certain scenes, implying in the process certain strategies at work on the part of Wiseman beyond simply recording a scene. Most vérité filmmakers will admit this emphasis. The Maysles brothers have been working in cinéma vérité for almost twenty years and editing has always played an obvious and accepted role in their films, especially such later works as *Salesman* (1969) and *Gimme Shelter* (1972).

What has ultimately emerged in vérité development is the fusion of point of view with an unobstructed camera philosophy. The handheld camera can offer revealing glimpses at life as it pretends to be. Without a structure, however, these glimpses can often be boring and meaningless. The following statement by Wiseman illustrates this fusion perfectly.

I remember one day poring through hours of film I'd shot in nursing homes where I was trying to capture the essence of what it was like to be old and infirm and incarcerated in one of these institutions. There was one interview with an old man whose legs had been amputated because of an advanced case of diabetes. He was dying, and time seemed to stretch out for him as he waited for an exit from the world. For 10 minutes I interrupted the wait, asking him questions about his life, his family, conditions at the nursing home, and how often he had visitors. They were, I thought then, 10 depressing emotionless minutes. The old man seemed to keep a stone face. But the camera saw something I didn't. I had asked the old man how frequently his children came to visit him, and he replied that they never came, but that that didn't bother him, because he had his friends at the nursing home. I had paused . . . and continued on. But my cameraman, Dick Roy, had used his zoom lens at that moment to slowly fill the screen with a shot of

438   *Changing Form and Function*

nothing but the old man's eyes. Weeks later, for the first time, I could see those eyes up close on film brimming with tears. I stopped the film and looked at a single frame: one-twenty-fourth of a second in the old man's life. There was fear in the eyes, and bitterness, and sorrow, and hurt, and a hundred other emotions that well up when a human being is abandoned by his loved ones at his weakest hour. So I used that film in the program and cut out thousands of feet, dozens of minutes of nothingness that didn't quite tell what it means to be endlessly dying in an antiseptic box.

The best documentaries are the ones with lots of such vivid moments left after clock time has been thoroughly cut down. The art of editing is to show in a few minutes the essence of hours or days or even weeks of elapsed-time material. Of course, the editing must be done honestly. Otherwise, time is distorted—and dishonored.

Some of the most powerful examples of vérité documentary to appear in the Seventies have been two television series, *An American Family* (1972) and *Religious America* (1974). In both films the vérité approach combined with a filmmaker's point of view offers intense and at times disturbing insights into two of this country's most sacred institutions. Although subjected to a great deal of criticism, much of it from the "family" (the Louds) itself, *An American Family* opened up a whole new area of thought concerning the role and function of the traditional family institution.

The vérité approach has quite naturally crossed over into feature films. Haskell Wexler's *Medium Cool* (1969) combined a vérité approach with a standard narrative. At times, the film achieved tremendous force, especially during scenes involving the demonstrations at the 1968 Democratic National Convention in Chicago. John Cassavetes is perhaps the best-known Hollywood director to use vérité in feature films. His work in *Faces* (1968), *Husbands* (1970), *Minnie and Moskowitz* (1972), and *A Woman Under the Influence* (1974) demonstrates the great possibilities in the vérité approach. The films also reveal how boring unconstructed reality can be if simply allowed to appear before the camera. Even Wiseman himself is moving into fiction film with his proposed study of a murder trial *Yes, Yes, No, No.*

With the great push toward vérité in recent years, there have been some objections to the report approach and several critics have asked for a return to some form of balance between the report and the statement. One such critic is Arthur Barron, who stated:

As for me, I'd like a little less information and a lot more feeling. I think we know enough facts; what we don't know is how to feel, to identify with others. I think the goal of the filmmaker should be to help make us more feeling, more human. We should try to be novelists and poets of film, rather than such damn good reporters.

In retrospect, the documentary film has not died or even declined. Certainly the golden age of the documentary in the depression and World War II and the magic names of Lorentz and Flaherty are gone. However, the issues examined and the films made today are far more varied in both content and style than anything that took place before. Simply, the amount of activity in the documentary field today is indicative of, if not at least a new golden age, a healthy and vibrant form.

Animation

The story of animation in the postwar period is closely tied in with the fortunes of the industry as a whole. The general decline of the system led to the extinction of most forms of the commercial short—the serial, newsreel, travelogue, "specialties," and the comedy short. The only form to survive with any degree of vigor has been animation in the form of the cartoon.

Following World War II, animation took on new forms and styles. The war itself had a big impact, as the Communist domination of Eastern Europe fostered the establishment of several state film schools which would ultimately result in the development of new styles of animation. A strike at the Walt Disney studio in 1941, however, was the key event. When the strike was finally settled, there were a number of defectors, including Stephen Bosustow, who in 1945 founded a new animation studio, United Productions of America (UPA). Gathering together a number of former Disney animators, UPA began producing cartoons in a wide variety of styles and with a great deal of personal freedom, the very thing Disney forbid. The general UPA style involved a move away from realism, utilizing greater economy in characterization and story. Most of the UPA cartoons used stick figures against sparse backgrounds. The philosophy of the films was decidedly realistic, however, in distinct contrast to Disney's prevailing mood of romanticism.

UPA's most famous character was Mr. Magoo, developed in 1949 and produced with great regularity and popularity for more than twenty years. Other well known characterizations included Gerald McBoing Boing and Madeline, both created by Bob Cannon. Outstanding individual films included Bill Hurtz's *Unicorn in the Garden* (1953), and John Hubley's *The Hole* (1962) and *The Hunt* (1964).

Just as important as UPA perhaps in its overall impact was a more informal school of animation characterized by a strong sense of violence. Beginning with the Tex Avery and Chuck Jones character Bugs Bunny, this new school grew rapidly with such cartoon characters as Tweety Pie and Sylvester, Daffy Duck, Elmer Fudd, and perhaps the best-known figures, Tom and Jerry. This new school dominated the theatrical cartoon in the Fifties and early Sixties. However, the financial crunch finally caught up with the form in the early Sixties and the cartoon was ultimately pushed into television. William Hanna and Joseph Barbera led the way into TV and throughout the Sixties and Seventies dominated the television cartoon market.

Mr. Magoo, the most famous character
from the UPA animation studio.
MUSEUM OF MODERN ART/FILM STILLS ARCHIVE

At its peak in the mid-Sixties the team produced more than 25,000 feet of cartoon material a week and created such popular characters as Ruff and Reddy, Quick Draw McGraw, Yogi Bear, Huckleberry Hound, and The Flintstones.

Television animation took two forms, children's cartoons and advertising. With few exceptions this has remained the pattern. The dominance of animation as standard children's fare drew heavy criticism beginning in the early Seventies and slowly but surely live performances and performers have been creeping back into the Saturday morning scene. However, the television cartoon still remains the dominant form of children's programming and the reasons are quite obvious. The cartoon produces spectacular events and characters at less cost and with greater control than any other film form. Animation began to fade as an advertising vehicle in the early Seventies as market researchers recognized the need of products to "talk straight" and of spokespeople who looked real and communicated directly with the television audience.

Animation was also affected by the avant-garde experimental movement of the Sixties. Several new filmmakers began to work with animation to produce highly abstract and personal films. The Whitney brothers have used computers to create abstract forms and patterns along with synthetic sound in such films as *Celery Stalks at Midnight* (1951–1958) and *Permutations* (1967). Robert Breer, Stan Vanderbeek, and Jordan Belson have all used animation to help create their niche in the new American cinema. Other independent filmmakers working in animation include Ernest Pintoff, who produced the hilarious parody on contemporary film thought in *The Critic* (1963) and John Hubley, long-time animator who, along with his wife Faith, produced in *Moonbird* (1960) one of the most fascinating and touching films of recent years. The film is built around the couple's two young sons' conversations at night, which included the fantasy game of catching a Moonbird. Using stick figures against an abstract background, they achieved unique and revealing insights into the world of children and their fantasies.

In all of this activity, the styles varied greatly. However, there was a general tendency toward simple, clear lines and shapes, as most of the creators were not trying to create enduring mythic characters, but were simply interested in expressing a particular point of view.

Much of this experimental work in the United States was preceded by twenty years in Canada, where Norman MacLaren

One of the most successful feature length animation films of all time, *The Yellow Submarine* starring The Beatles.
MUSEUM OF MODERN ART/FILM STILLS ARCHIVE

was working in animation in the late Forties, producing such classics as *Begone Dull Care* (1949) and *Neighbors* (1952). Mac-Laren developed a number of styles, ranging from the purely abstract in *Vertical Lines* (1960) to his famous pixillation style illustrated so well in *Neighbors*. Here he used live actors and real settings, but created animated movement by stop-action photography and manipulating the speed of the film. MacLaren has continued as a singularly strong force in developing new animation forms and films.

Additional work in animation took place in England chiefly through the work of John Halas and Joy Batchelor, who produced the controversial *Animal Farm* in 1954. However, the most significant and popular work to come from England was George Dunning's *The Yellow Submarine* (1968). This feature-length film about the Beatles literally deluged audiences with images in a variety of styles, including abstract, cartoon, and pixillation. Quickly achieving cult status, it became for many youthful audiences a unique and mind-bending "trip."

Important animation innovations were also taking place in Eastern Europe. Jiří Trnka of Czechoslovakia developed puppet

442

animation to its highest form. He used puppets because they had "more presence" and created complex forms of great charm and genuine involvement. His major work was *A Midsummer Night's Dream* produced in 1959.

Yugoslavia was the other Eastern European country to produce new innovations in animation with the founding of the Zagreb Studio in 1956. Headed by Dusan Vukotic, the school emphasized a clean, functional style obviously influenced by UPA. However, Zagreb's animators went beyond their American counterparts in developing the cartoon form as a rich vehicle for satire, parody, and political comment, with such films as *Concerto for a Sub-Machine Gun* (1959), a parody of the American gangster film, and *Ersatz* (1961), the first non-American cartoon to win an Academy Award.

Current developments in theatrical animation have stressed feature-length animation. Of the 125 such films produced since 1917 almost 100 have come since 1945. *The Yellow Submarine* was probably responsible for some of this activity as Disney studios began to turn to live-action films in the late Sixties. The two most important feature animations to emerge in the Seventies have been Ralph Bakshi's and Robert Crumb's *Fritz the Cat* (1972) and *Heavy Traffic* (1973). In somewhat contradictory

This typically "heavy" scene represents a new use for animation in Ralph Bakshi's *Heavy Traffic*.
MUSEUM OF MODERN ART/FILM STILLS ARCHIVE

fashion, they use animation to portray a real world of drugs, sex, and life in an urban ghetto. In *Fritz the Cat,* all of the characters are animals, but *Heavy Traffic* uses the human form as well. Obviously influenced by both the content and style of the new underground comic books, both films depart strikingly from the child orientation of most American film animation as evidenced by the industry's X rating for both films. They are basically satiric in intent, but strike with an axe rather than carve with a knife. They are both visually and orally blatant and present a view of life "as it is" in the city ghetto. Although many critics considered the films in bad taste, there is little question that they are major works and will greatly influence the future development of the form.

Animation today exists in many forms all over the world. It is used for many purposes, including formal instruction, popular entertainment, social comment, and abstract personal expression. At one time it was threatened with extinction as a commercial short. However, like the documentary film, it has grown far beyond this limited structure and is one of the most contemporary of film forms today.

The Avant-Garde Experimental Film

Of all the recent developments in film none has been more dramatic and at the same time more confusing than the tremendous explosion of experimental film forms in the past fifteen years.

The movement is highly elusive and almost impossible to characterize. Simply finding an acceptable definition is difficult. "It" has been called Underground, Experimental, Avant-Garde, New Wave, New American Cinema, and more. These are all labels and have the built-in limitations of labels. In a sense the movement is all of these things and yet it is more. Further compounding the problem is that the terms themselves are not new, but have been used throughout film history to describe different styles of film. The avant-garde has always been a part of film history. The function of exploring and developing new forms and content in film started when Méliès and Porter stopped recording reality and began to tell stories. Griffith was just as much an avant-garde artist for his time as Andy Warhol was for his. Luis Buñuel, Salvador Dali, Man Ray, René Clair,

Orson Welles, Jean Renoir—the list is endless. All form a part of what film history has always known as the avant-garde. Therefore, trying to pin down the movement by time or definition is difficult, to say the least. As one of the pioneer experimental filmmakers, Gregory Markopolous stated: "The foundation of the New American Cinema is molded out of invisibility and decorated in invisibility. Within such a foundation, films are begun like quick-fire even as others are being completed."

Since the movement escapes complete definition by label, time, or category, perhaps the best way to describe it is through the concept of process—something which is constantly evolving, changing, developing, and becoming. Behind this process are individual filmmakers and if anything offers some hope of definition it is these men and women. The basic and original purpose behind all avant-garde film is the need of filmmakers to express their personal artistic visions in ways appropriate to them. As Jonas Mekas, one of the philosophical fathers of the most recent movement in the Sixties, stated:

> Our movies come from our hearts . . . our movies are like extensions of our own pulse, of our heartbeat, of our eyes, our fingertips; so personal, so unambitious.

Ken Kelman elaborates further:

> The New American Cinema is a spiritual medium; and more physical than Hollywood ever dreamed. In it the conscious and the deep images are reunited, man himself is reunited with passion and no apologies. It seeks to project genuine experience and direct vision. The new cinema attempts to restore subjectivity to its proper realm, and urges the balance of human nature.

Historically, the New American Cinema movement of the Sixties began with Maya Deren, who formed a link between the European avant-garde of the Twenties and the New Wave that appeared after World War II. Although she made only six films in a career beginning in 1943 (she died in 1961), she was the first American to reach a large audience with "personal" films. Her real importance, however, was as a lecturer, writer, and organizer for the fledgling avant-garde movement.

The contemporary avant-garde movement as it emerged in the late Fifties and early Sixties was born out of frustration, frustration with a system of production which stressed uniformity of content and style, frustration at beating on the doors of a closed shop. This lack of aesthetic variety and the absence of opportunity coupled with a new inexpensive 16mm and 8mm technology created a revolution. Jonas Mekas postulated a credo:

> In cinema, this search is manifested through abandoning of all the existing professional, commercial values, rules, subjects techniques, pretensions. We said: We don't know what man is; we don't know what cinema is. Let us, therefore, be completely open. Let us go in any direction. Let us be completely open and listening, ready to move to any direction upon the slightest call, almost like one who is too tired and too weary, whose senses are like a musical string, almost with no power of their own; blown and played by the mystical winds of the incoming age, waiting for a slightest motion or call or sign. *Let's go in any direction to break out of the net that is dragging us down.* (emphasis mine)

"Any direction" was the general road map that was used and yet critics and historians have been able to discern three major types of films: social protest, social anarchy and liberation, and abstract. Regardless of label, essentially all of the films made were protesting something—politics, sexual mores, aesthetic values . . . Regardless if it was Jack Smith's *Flaming Creatures* (1963), Shirley Clarke's *The Connection* (1960), or Andy Warhol's *The Chelsea Girls* (1966), a protest was being made through film.

At first the protest was partially economic. The movement stressed cheaply made films and seemed to find some sort of justification in this alone. John Cassavetes, for example, made his first film, *Shadows* (1960), for $15,000 and this fact seemed to insure the integrity and purity of the movement. Some of this philosophy still exists, but personal vision is not always cheap and some filmmakers have found that an expensive film can still be experimental—witness Stanley Kubrick's *2001* and *Clockwork Orange.*

The geographical dimensions of the movement were scattered, but the primary focus and orientation was located on the two coasts, specifically in New York and San Francisco. What made these two cities important was that they contained several key individuals and organizations which would give the movement power and visibility. The organization came from various film societies and individuals, but the real key was the establishment in 1960 of the magazine *Film Culture* by Jonas Mekas. Although New York based, it quickly became a rallying point and voice for the entire movement.

Other important organizations included Amos Vogel's

"Cinema 16" program in New York and Frank Stauffacher's "Art in Cinema" series, which provided the first real showcase for the movement. Starting in 1947, they provided recognition for new films and new filmmakers. As the movement began to pick up speed in the Sixties many more societies and festivals sprang up and these original two lost most of their power. A key event was the New York Film Festival's official recognition of the New American Cinema in 1966, when they showcased many previously unknown films.

Because of this widespread festival recognition, distributors began to acquire and promote many of the new films. Grove Press, Newsreel, and The Filmmakers Cooperative became vital elements in helping the movement grow and develop.

Andrew Sarris wrote of the movement:

> Finally, the collectivity of Independent cinema is not worth writing about. Only individual films . . . Add it all up and you have an interesting footnote to the history of world cinema. Much ado about nothing? Hardly. Someone has to man the outposts of culture, and the Independent Film is uniquely qualified to express the chaos and confusion of our time.

Individual films? Where do we begin? Where do we end? Where do we settle in between? Obviously, film descriptions say very little, especially to those who have seen a film. Even to those who have seen a film, descriptions do not add much to their experience. We describe these films simply to indicate the types of approaches and styles used.

Any selection is arbitrary, but it is generally acknowledged by many critics of the avant-garde that three of the key filmmakers of the movement have been Kenneth Anger, Gregory Markopolous, and Stan Brakhage. These three represent the diversity which makes up the very fabric of the avant-garde movement.

Kenneth Anger made his first "public" film in 1947. Called *Fireworks*, it was typical of the movement in its total rejection of a Hollywood style. Anger himself, however, did not continue with this style as he began to create "polished" films which explored various areas of the American popular myth. Perhaps his best-known work is *Scorpio Rising*, made in 1963. In it, Anger examines the myth of the motorcyclist and in the process creates a ritual-like film which looks at all aspects of the myth—the dressing of the cyclist, the cultlike worship of the bike, the orgy of power and speed, the relationships between the cyclists and myth heroes such as Marlon Brando and James Dean. Anger's films, with the noted exception of *Fireworks,* all have strong associations with Hollywood, characterized primarily by careful attention to detail and an almost classic approach to the construction of elaborate montage units.

Gregory Markopolous is another pioneer in the movement. Although he studied under the "classic" director Josef von Sternberg at UCLA, his films consciously destroy all the standard Hollywood narrative ingredients. For example, his film *Galaxie* (1966) consists of thirty portraits of various friends, using one roll (100 feet or three minutes) for each individual. The film consists of the rolls attached to each other, with all editing done in the camera. Working in the camera has become a Markopolous trademark. In *Ming Green* (1964), he photographed his flat in New York and by overlapping images and juxtaposing objects created a remarkable portrait of a common environment. Unfortunately, Markopolous' technique of working in the camera has been conceived as an "easy" way of making films by many so-called avant-garde filmmakers. There is nothing "easy" or lazy, however, in Markopolous' work. His effects are carefully designed to present his point of view and to create images of the reality he wants to present.

Stan Brakhage is yet another pioneer who has worked consistently in experimental film for more than twenty years. Brakhage probably represents "underground-experimental filmmaker" to most audiences, because he works in a style which departs most radically from accepted film technique. Brakhage's films have no story, no acting, no narrative editing, no conscious camera composition. Instead, he seems obsessed with the purity of film recording. His films usually "look at" a subject and only when he feels

A baby's mouth is radically transformed in Stan Brakhage's *Dog Star Man.*

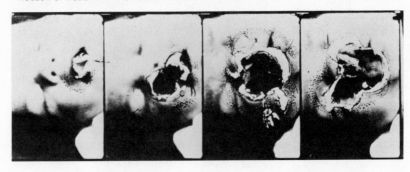

that this revelation has been accomplished does he begin to structure the experience. His most ambitious and well-known work is *Dog Star Man*, which took him more than four years to complete (1961–1965). The basic structure involves a man and a dog climbing a mountain to cut down a tree. As the man climbs his mind becomes flooded with memories of his past. The camera constantly shifts perspective and the reality of the film becomes a constantly changing visual pattern of clouds, sun, dog, internal organs, sky . . . Brakhage is a pivotal figure, as he represents a clear turning point in which experimental film moved away from a literary base to a highly personal vision.

To sum up, we quote Shelden Renan in his comprehensive and detailed book *An Introduction to the American Underground Film:*

> Some underground films are good. Some are bad. A few are great. But whatever they are, underground films are the film artist's unmitigated vision. No banker, no producer, no patron has dictated what they must be or can later change them. Underground films are banned, but they are never cut.
>
> Therefore, the underground is free to look outward with an unblinking eye and inward in complex and mystical ways. It is free to be poetic and to be obscure. It is even free to go mad.
>
> The underground film has a vitality, an arrogant originality and an integrity that today is almost unique in cinema. It has unleashed the artist in the young and still unexplored medium of film. . . .
>
> The underground has many forms, and some are being absorbed into the commercial cinema. Commercial cinema has always used the personal art film as a laboratory culture to be watched for usable material. The real importance of the underground is in its works. Alive, unpredictable, complex, and above all, personal, they are what is happening in cinema now. Their many forms are the true shapes of the vision of the contemporary individual.

15

An American Renaissance

New Styles, Freedom, Audiences, Markets, and Films

Like the Fifties, the last decade of American film is difficult, if not impossible, to characterize. Trying to piece together the many economic, artistic, technological, and social trends making up the fabric of American film is like trying to piece together the parts of a jigsaw puzzle blindfolded.

Part of the problem comes from the simple lack of historical distance as it is difficult to describe an ongoing process by which you are surrounded. There is little opportunity to step out of the so-called "ego-centric predicament"; to look around and look back.

Adding to the problem is the speed with which much of this change has taken place. Instant trends were the norm of this decade. With the exception of James Bond and a planet full of apes, few lengthy cycles were established. In 1964–65, with the huge success of *My Fair Lady, Mary Poppins,* and *The Sound of Music,* musicals were in. Two years later, with such disasters as *Star* and *Dr. Dolittle,* they were out. Following *The Graduate* (1967), *Easy Rider* (1969), and *Alice's Restaurant* (1969), youth films were booming. Two years later, with Elliot Gould and others leading the way in such films as *Getting Straight* (1970), *The Magic Garden of Stanley Sweetheart* (1970), and *The Landlord* (1970), the boom was busted. Old-fashioned love was flowering once again in 1971 with *Love Story,* but less than two years later *The Godfather* exhibited a different form of affection.

All of this serves to illustrate the number of directions

451

American film has been traveling. The search for a lost audience, for a return to some semblance of past success, continued unabated throughout the Sixties and into the Seventies.

Changes in the industry, content, and overall pattern and structure of the American film began, as we have seen, in events of the late Forties and early Fifties. Like the jack pine tree, which spreads its seeds only by the intense heat resulting from a forest fire, so the roots of the "new American cinema" began in the fires of the Fifties. Also like the jack pine, whose seeds explode in all directions, the Sixties witnessed similar explosions in film—explosions which created new styles, new freedom, new audiences, new markets, and new films.

Interest in film on an academic level is a perfect illustration of this explosion. As Arthur Knight noted: "Back in 1960 when I joined the staff of USC's Department of Cinema there were many—teachers as well as students—who suspected that we might be taking money under false pretenses." This all changed quickly, however. By 1969, The American Film Institute (itself a product of this increased interest) was conducting an annual survey of film study in colleges and universities. The latest figures published in 1973 reveal almost 3,000 film courses at more than 600 schools. Approximately 200 schools offer a degree or major in film, with enrollments close to 7,000.

An American renaissance? Yes, but one without clear direction or focus, still in the process of becoming, and more importantly for this chapter and book, still in the process of being understood.

Takeover and Change

One of the most significant areas of change was in the structure of the industry. The studio system in general and the major studios in particular had been floundering in a sea of red ink for some time, looking for the key to success. With production costs soaring to an average $3,000,000 per feature by 1966 and box office figures still plunging, the studios were desperate. Independent production companies were now making over 30% of all films and "runaway" productions (films made outside the U. S.) had reached the 50% level. *Unfortunately*, along came a film called *The Sound of Music* (1965), which Hollywood instantly translated into "The Sound of Money." Grossing more than $135 million, it quickly spurred the studios into a big-

Julie Andrews in the 1965 blockbuster *The Sound of Music.*
MUSEUM OF MODERN ART/FILM STILLS ARCHIVE

budget-spectacle trend which ultimately proved disastrous.
Since spectacles take longer to produce than the average feature,
the industry found itself with some very expensive films in
production when audiences began lining up for blocks to see *The
Graduate* and *Bonnie and Clyde* in 1967. 20th Century-Fox's
Star and *Dr. Dolittle* flopped badly. *Tora! Tora! Tora!*
($25,000,000) did even worse. All of a sudden Fox found itself
with a film inventory of more than $300,000,000 and a 1969 loss
of more than $30,000,000. Paramount was also caught up in the
so-called "Sound of Music syndrome" with *Darling Lili*
($19,000,000), *The Molly McGuires* ($17,000,000), and *Paint Your
Wagon* ($20,000,000).

453

By the late Sixties it was clear that the studios were in deep trouble. Traditionally, the system had thrived on size. Huge sound stages and backlots were symbols of prestige and power; now they were liabilities draining away badly needed resources. The belt had to be tightened and so people were fired, films were shelved, and backlots sold to eager real estate developers. The only extensive backlot to survive was Universal's, which was saved by TV and tourists.

Badly weakened by all this, most of the studios succumbed to the fate of all small fish in a big pond—they were eaten by larger fish. In this case the big fish were huge corporate conglomerates which wanted to diversify and thought a motion picture studio would be a nice acquisition. Paramount was absorbed by Gulf and Western, Warner Brothers by Kinney National Services, United Artists by Transamerica, Inc., and MGM by real estate magnate Kirk Kerkorian.

Soon, a faceless, impersonal, remote corporate power began to dominate a historically individualistic industry. Instead of Harry Cohn looking out his office window trying to catch some writer leaving early or Louis B. Mayer alternately raging and weeping in order to coerce some star into accepting a new contract, the industry had Charles G. Bluhdorn, Board Chairman of Gulf and Western, who stated at one time: ". . . I oversee all our divisions. One of them is called Leisure Time, and Paramount is just a part of it." Individual studio style was destroyed, physical plants demolished, and where previously 20% of any film went into studio overhead, now 95% was allocated to "on-screen" costs.

Conglomerate takeover has had both positive and negative effects. Gulf and Western and Kinney have kept their respective subsidiaries functioning as active production units. This is certainly healthy. However, even when a studio is functioning questions can be raised about the effect of corporate ownership. Certainly, studio moguls such as Harry Cohn, Louis B. Mayer, and Jack Warner controlled their studios with an iron hand. However, what, for instance, might be the effect on Paramount films of Gulf and Western's 1974 $32,000,000 bullet contract with the U. S. Army? Would a *M.A.S.H.* or *Paths of Glory* or *Dr. Strangelove* be possible? Obviously, there are no easy answers. It is quite clear, however, that new ownership patterns bring with them new concerns and there is no easy solution to financial problems.

Another important change involved small independent producers emerging from the fringes of the industry. The unit of film production as it slowly evolved through the last decade is no longer the studio, but the production company, often formed to make a single film. Typical is Cannon Films, which was created to distribute the sex potboiler *Inga* (1968) and then hit the big time with *Joe* (1971). Made for less than $300,000, it grossed more than $20,000,000. Although the rise of companies such as Cannon was a phenomenon of the entire decade, it was not until 1969 and the success of *Easy Rider* that the establishment finally became convinced that movies made for less than $500,000 by relatively unknown people could succeed. *Easy Rider* returned a box office gross of more than $50,000,000 on an investment of $370,000 and the rush was on. Of the total $1.8 billion box office gross of 1969, $1.2 billion came from independent producers.

The result of all this activity was some strange production patterns and combinations. David L. Wolper signed an agreement with the Quaker Oats Company for a series of family movies which included the very successful *Willie Wonka and the Chocolate Factory* (1971). Reader's Digest funded *Tom Sawyer* (1973) and *Huckleberry Finn* (1974). The advertising agency Wells, Rich and Greene backed *Dirty Little Billy* (1973), and Mattel Toys provided funds for *Sounder* (1973). One of the more unusual sources of outside money was for the film *Gunfight* (1971). The Jicarilla Apaches, a tribe of about 1,800 New Mexico Indians, put up $2,000,000 which they had received from income on oil and gas investments. As Chief Charles Vigil stated: "We consider ourselves a corporation like any other."

One of the reasons why independents flourished in the past decade in addition to the general decline of the large studios was the increased flexibility on the part of Hollywood unions. This did not come easily, however. Most producers, independent or otherwise, realized that the studios had built up the finest collection of craftsmen and technicians in the world. However, the unions to which these people belonged were rigid in their rules concerning working conditions and salaries. As one director stated: "Hollywood is great as long as you're working inside a studio. But the minute you go on location, even if it's only ten blocks from the studio gate, the unions will kill you every time." An example from John Sturges' film *The Satan Bug* (1971) clearly illustrates this point. Sturges had as a climactic scene an auto chase through the downtown freeways of Los Angeles. The Screen Extra's Guild wanted to charge him for every car that appeared in the shots, plus a stiff penalty fee, alleging that Sturges was depriving extras of legitimate work.

Consequently, in order to produce their low budget films,

most independents left Hollywood to work abroad, usually in England or Spain. These so-called "runaway" productions were causing up to 90% unemployment in some unions. As a result, the unions agreed to a new contract in 1970 which allowed producers to use a basic nine man crew and members of one union could help members of any other. In the past, of course, when a lighting man needed help, a prop man could not step in to assist him. Thus, a Hollywood film crew was often two or three times larger than it actually needed to be.

With all this independent activity going on around them, the studios found their traditional position as the major film producing organizations usurped. In most cases, they functioned primarily as financing and distributing organizations for independent producers. One of the most ambitious and successful cooperative ventures occurred in 1972 when Paramount put up $31.5 million against 50% of the profits to back three young, highly successful directors, William Freidkin (*The French Connection,* 1971), Francis Ford Coppola (*The Godfather,* 1972), and Peter Bogdanovich (*The Last Picture Show,* 1971) in an organization called The Director's Company.

Thus, the studios were not completely dead. Walt Disney continued to grow, producing family films on realistic budgets. Columbia kept its head above water by avoiding the big film trap, concentrating instead on such reasonably budgeted films as *Cat Ballou* (1965), *Guess Who's Coming to Dinner* (1967), and *In Cold Blood* (1967), among others. Its two excursions into the big time were with very safe projects—*Funny Girl* (1968) and *Oliver* (1968). Paramount was very happy with *Love Story* in 1971 and *The Godfather* in 1972.

The pattern for most studios was either feast or famine. Despite some success, they ceased to exist as major production organizations. They stand alongside the independents as peers in production, holding the upper hand only because they still retain sound stages and technical facilities and a nationwide distribution system. TV, of course, provides the studios with most of their income by renting facilities and personnel.

New Faces and Old

The Sixties and Seventies have witnessed great changes in the people making up the film industry. The star system, which had dominated American films ever since Florence Lawrence received on-screen credit, declined noticeably. Some of this was partly due to old stars dying and very few new stars emerging to replace them. Just when Hollywood needed fresh faces and new images the most, it found that the economy measures of the Fifties resulted in few new contracts signed and many old contracts cancelled.

The whole concept of role definition through leadership patterns has long been recognized by sociologists and studio heads alike. Indeed, this may have been the most powerful effect of the entire studio star system. The consistency of Hollywood in the past depended heavily on these roles and as such the roles themselves became institutionalized in the form of a star system which used certain faces and names in carefully constructed patterns. Clark Gable was the rugged he-man, Gary Cooper the strong silent individualist, Jean Arthur a kooky blonde, and Marlene Dietrich a sultry seductress. Men and women often defined themselves in terms of these screen images and Hollywood became very comfortable (perhaps unconsciously so) in the knowledge that its role as "social reflector" was working so well. Throughout the Sixties the studios struggled with and attempted to perpetuate this system. From 1958 to 1967 only twelve of the fifty top grossing films lacked major stars. However, by 1967 many old faces were gone, new ones were being used badly (Julie Andrews in *Star*, Sidney Poitier in *The Last Man* and *Brother John*), and production schedules were no longer large enough to allow contract players time to develop skills or publicity departments time to develop images.

Society had changed also. It was divided and fractionalized. Youth was a part of this division and as films began to reflect this orientation the Richard Burtons and Elizabeth Taylors playing highly manicured roles were no longer acceptable to this very significant part of the American film audience.

Along came *The Graduate* in 1967. This film went against most Hollywood standard operating procedures. Its director, Mike Nichols, was primarily a stage and television personality. Its major star, Dustin Hoffman, was unknown. The property itself was a minor novel with no built-in audience. However, with the picture's success most of the old formulas went out the window. Here was a film in which the theme was the star and relatively unknown people were acting mainly as attractive vehicles for the theme.

Almost, as if by magic, new faces began to appear. Unknowns were in and studios were willing to gamble on such people as Jack Nicholson, Richard Benjamin, Alan Arkin, Donald

Sutherland, and Jon Voight, among others. As one of these new faces, Gene Wilder, stated: "Ten years ago, they wanted the kind of face that only a few hundred people in the world possess— the Hollywood face. They didn't want people who looked like the people in the audience. Now they realize that they can make money by letting the audience see actors with whom they can identify." Richard Zanuck stated it somewhat more bluntly: "We're hiring the uglies." As a result, from 1968 to 1972, thirteen of the top twenty-five films featured performers who had little box-office value.

These so-called "uglies" did not perform in the traditional star manner. Dustin Hoffman, for example, did not continue to play confused adolescents. Instead, he made a remarkable and thoroughly convincing transformation in *Midnight Cowboy*, playing a Times Square derelict. A pattern was beginning to appear. Star mystique was no longer vital as the film itself became the main attraction. Actor and actress adaptability in the total context of a film became the crucial element. Role emulation, the extension of a film character into a national myth, was no longer a dominant feature of the system. Elliot Gould is a perfect example

Dustin Hoffman stares helplessly at a seduction-minded Anne Bancroft in *The Graduate*.
MUSEUM OF MODERN ART/FILM STILLS ARCHIVE

A radically transformed
Dustin Hoffman and Jon
Voight in *Midnight Cowboy*.
MUSEUM OF MODERN ART/FILM
STILLS ARCHIVE

of the failure to understand this. Following his success in *Bob and Carol and Ted and Alice,* he embarked on a series of youth films, playing essentially the same character. His career bottomed out quickly and only by playing "different" roles (Ingmar Bergman's *The Touch* for example) was he able to emerge from under his screen image. Sean Connery stopped playing James Bond because he did not want to be typed. Of the "old" stars who survived only those like Marlon Brando, Paul Newman, Rod Steiger and Julie Harris, among others, who fought for roles which would not type them, met with any reasonable success.

The Director as "Star"

The star system was not only altered, it was expanded as well. Now the men and women behind the camera became just as well known and important to the audience as the people in front. Although, the "behind the scenes" people include writers, cameramen, set designers, ad infinitum, it was the director who really stepped into the spotlight. Once again, the American film became, at least partially, a director's medium. Once again? Certainly, for film history began with Méliès, Porter, Griffith,

459

von Stroheim. The "discovery" of the director as star was not really a discovery at all, but a reassessment and shift in audience attitudes, industry policy, and, perhaps most importantly, critical evaluation.

Much has been written about the so-called auteur theory in which a film is evaluated primarily on the basis of the director and the film's relationship to the director's total body of work. Emerging from French critical thought in the early Fifties the theory has been both praised and maligned. It is not our purpose here to discuss its individual merits. However, whether one agrees with the theory or not, the movement as such toward recognition of the director as a vital and at times dominating force in the filmmaking process was welcomed. In fact, the movement as it took force in the Sixties not only recognized directors, but encouraged them to take some type of auteur control. Helped by the decline in the studio system, the director *as an individual with ideas he wanted to express in film* became a significant force in the American film of the Sixties and Seventies.

The emphasis in the sentence above suggests an important, but often overlooked, fact. The director is not some sort of god creating a work of art from the pictures inside his head. He still works within a system, with a crew of highly trained professionals. He still functions as a coordinator, an organizer of people and machinery. Directors have always had ideas—some good, some bad. The difference now lies in the *opportunity* to express these ideas and the *recognition* received for them. Equally important is recognition of the fact stated so well by Alan Casty: "For an individual artist's style, whether intuitive or conscious, however distinct or even idiosyncratic, bears significant relationships not only to those of his contemporaries, but to a pervasive style of the times, the intricate fabric of a culture." Each director, then, is tied to his culture, both society at large and the industry in which he works. Each director has certain ideas and approaches them in a distinct style. Trying to pinpoint and extract a common denominator from these many approaches is impossible, and yet this diversity is exactly what had made the 60's and 70's one of the most exciting periods in film history. In comparing the following two statements by two of contemporary cinema's leading directors it becomes obvious that we could spend a great deal of time analyzing individual directorial styles and themes and only scratch the surface of where film has come and is going.

Mike Nichols: "It's not a film-maker's job to explain his technique. His job is to tell the story the best way he can. I wish that people who don't know what the hell they're talking about would leave it alone instead of throwing around half-assed technical terms that have no meaning. For instance, I read that I used hand-held, wide-angle shots (in *Catch 22*). I didn't, whatever they are." (Lillian Hellman, *New York Times*)

Lindsay Anderson: "Probably all my work, even when it has been very realistic, has struggled for a poetic quality—for larger implications than the surface realities may suggest. I think the most important challenge is to get beyond pure naturalism into poetry. Some people call this fantasy, but these terms are dangerous because words always mean different things to different people." (From the book *Lindsay Anderson* by Elizabeth Sussex)

The careers and films of such men as John Frankenheimer, Robert Mulligan, Sidney Lumet, Arthur Penn, Mike Nichols, Sam Peckinpah, Stanley Kubrick, and Robert Altman provide us with various individual glimpses of life and reality as they perceive it. What is unique in their work is obvious. What is common, however, although not as obvious, can provide us with clues to the general direction American film is taking.

The American cinema of the Sixties and Seventies is characterized primarily by the work of individuals rather than studios and as such is filled with all aspects of contemporary life. The "problem" picture has become a catch-all phrase for many of these films, but problems and problem pictures have always been with us. What is significant now is that filmmakers have the freedom to explore *all* problems and present them with straightforward honesty. This is not to say that all problems are treated or that those treated are dealt with honestly; the key is that the opportunity is there.

Many new directors emerged in the Sixties. Of these, several stand out for their consistent contributions to an expanding cinema.

John Frankenheimer

John Frankenheimer became concerned with a variety of social issues, ranging from brainwashing (*The Manchurian Candidate*, 1962) to car racing *(Grand Prix*, 1966). In all of his films, he demonstrates a distinct style influenced primarily by his early

Rod Steiger confronts one of his customers in Sidney
Lumet's *The Pawnbroker.*
MUSEUM OF MODERN ART/FILM STILLS ARCHIVE

work in television. Some have called this style flashy and synthetic, but there is little question that Frankenheimer has expanded the language of film, using shock cuts, slow motion, and
multiple-image photography to add visual excitement and tension to his narrative context.

Sidney Lumet

Sidney Lumet also came out of television and brought to
such films as *Long Day's Journey Into Night* (1962), *Fail Safe*
(1964), *The Pawnbroker* (1965), and *The Group* (1966) a televi-
sion-oriented sense of space and character. Using tight camera
angles and highly expressionistic lighting, Lumet outlined his
characters and their concerns with solid brush strokes. Although,
perhaps a little too self-conscious in his treatment of socially
significant issues (Lumet rarely lets the inherent drama of an
event carry the day as he infuses most of his films with heavy
emotionalism) one finds in American film of the Sixties few

images to match the old man in *The Pawnbroker,* isolated behind his cage, trapped in an environment of his own making. He has continued this work into the Seventies with such films as *Serpico* (1973) and *Murder on the Orient Express* (1974).

Arthur Penn

Arthur Penn became an instant celebrity with *Bonnie and Clyde* in 1967. Coming from a Broadway stage background, Penn demonstrated early his ability to break away from this tradition with such experimental works as *The Left Handed Gun* (1957), one of the most psychological of all the "adult" Westerns. He began to demonstrate his ability to capture a further psychological sense of the American landscape with *Mickey One* (1964). Utilizing a jazz musical score, Penn told of a night club comic's disjointed flight through the urban jungle of Chicago. Utilizing stark black and white photography, Penn seemed to be expressing some of the disjointed, fragmented feelings beginning to emerge in the middle Sixties. It was, however, *Bonnie and Clyde* and to a lesser extent *Alice's Restaurant* (1969) which saw him develop into, as one critic called him, the "American Truffaut." In both of these films he continued to display his concern for the

The three remaining members of the Barrow Gang, Bonnie (Faye Dunaway), Clyde (Warren Beatty) and C.W. (Michael Pollard) are attacked as they try to escape a police ambush in *Bonnie and Clyde.*
MUSEUM OF MODERN ART/FILM STILLS ARCHIVE

character of the American scene, but coupled this with a force and strength which created for the films a unique mythology almost unconnected to any historical reality.

Mike Nichols

Mike Nichols also came from Broadway by way of television (with Elaine May). His first effort, *Who's Afraid of Virginia Woolf* (1966), was closely tied to the stage and was dominated by the acting of Richard Burton and Elizabeth Taylor. Overshadowed by their performances and playwright Albee's language, he emerged finally as a star in his own right with *The Graduate* (1967). His light, satiric approach to the problems faced by Dustin Hoffman as he was about to enter adult society touched a responsive chord in America's youth and the "young adult" market was opened up for the first time. His later efforts in such films as *Catch-22* (1970) have not been particularly successful, as he seemed to stick to literary interpretations and adaptations, forgoing some of the obvious visual dimensions inherent in his earlier work. Nichols remains an intelligent craftsman who has been fortunate enough to select the right themes and present them in a light, socially relevant style for the times.

Robert Altman

Robert Altman burst onto the contemporary film scene with *M.A.S.H.* in 1970, in which he tightroped a thin line between comedy and social comment. The anarchical spirit of the film established Altman as a key "black comedy" auteur. However, instead of continuing in this direction exclusively, he chose to explore a wide range of topics, including comic fantasy in *Brewster McCloud* (1971), the American West in *McCabe and Mrs. Miller* (1971), the 1930's depression South in *Thieves Like Us* (1973) and the contemporary West coast landscape with *California Split* (1974). In all of these films, Altman has focused on the realities of the social setting, most significantly experimenting with audio patterns and characteristics, including overlapping dialogue and "under-heard" conversation.

While all of the directors just noted and many more, including Martin Ritt, the late Robert Rossen, Alfred Hitchcock, Robert Wise, and John Cassavetes influenced and set the tone for Ameri-

William Holden in Sam Peckinpah's *The Wild Bunch*.
MUSEUM OF MODERN ART/FILM STILLS ARCHIVE

can film in the Sixties, two directors stand out above the rest in terms of their influence and effect upon the direction contemporary film is taking. These two are Sam Peckinpah and Stanley Kubrick.

Sam Peckinpah

Opinion is somewhat divided concerning Peckinpah. In 1968, before he made *The Wild Bunch* (1969), Andrew Sarris classified him among the "oddities, one-shots, and newcomers." Indeed, Peckinpah was a little of each, as he had produced only three films up to 1968—*The Deadly Companions* (1962), *Ride the High Country* (1962) and *Major Dundee* (1964). He had an extensive background directing TV Westerns and brought this heritage with him as he began to develop the Western genre in new ways, combining elements of poetry and realism with statements evoking the lost mythology of the West. Working almost exclusively within the Western genre (one notable exception was *Straw Dogs*, 1972) he became, more than any other director, the apostle of new violence. His film *The Wild Bunch* was

465

germinal, as it utilized slow motion to both heighten and diffuse the impact of violent death. In a sense, Peckinpah's vision has perhaps been too large for the Western tradition and heritage. Although labeled as pro-violence, he has been essentially concentrating on men and their conflicts, not simply with each other, but with themselves, and with time itself. In one of his lesser known, but most cohesive films, *Junior Bonner* (1973), he reveals in Steve McQueen a man out of place and time, desperately trying to cope with a modern reality. In this film, Peckinpah continues his traditional concern for and visualization of violence. In this case, however, it takes the form of a bulldozer, smashing the boyhood home of McQueen, almost running over a car, and in general wreaking havoc on an old familiar landscape. Even McQueen's role as an aging rodeo star is symbolized by a desperate and useless conflict with a brahma bull. Thus, even though labeled as a violent director, Peckinpah's images are seldom violent for their own sake. His violence has a meaning—usually the new committing violence against the old.

Stanley Kubrick

Stanley Kubrick's career has extended longer than Peckinpah's and his interests and themes have been much broader. He too is concerned with violence, but his films look at broad social violence and utilize the methodology of satire to create their messages. He is concerned primarily with man's hypocrisy and through a relatively small body of work (ten films in all, five of which are considered germinal) has developed his theme in a

The parts storage area of the spaceship Discovery in Stanley Kubrick's *2001* provides evidence of the intricate design work which, along with special effects, was the real star of the film.
MUSEUM OF MODERN ART/FILM STILLS ARCHIVE

bold and innovative style. Essentially a social satirist, he has looked with a devastating eye at war, both hot (*Paths of Glory,* 1958) and cold (*Dr. Strangelove,* 1964), New England social and sexual norms (*Lolita,* 1962), technological overkill (*2001,* 1968) and futuristic society (*A Clockwork Orange,* 1972). Kubrick works slowly and controls every aspect of his work. What is perhaps most remarkable is the wide range of styles and cinematic forms he has worked with and perfected, ranging from the harshly realistic, semidocumentary style of *Paths of Glory,* to the futuristic special-effects-dominated style of *2001,* to the baroque high design values of *A Clockwork Orange.* In all his films he uses a combination of humor and pathos—laughter leading to thought—as he strives to make his audiences see the foolishness and tragedy of man.

With an increased emphasis on the director as auteur or at least interpreter and with directors concentrating on highly personal themes, the problem of meaning in film has become crucial, although at times overstated. Kubrick's films often fall into the trap of meaning vs. meaningless. Kubrick has perhaps been the least understood American director of the past decade. *2001,* especially, evoked an entire body of literature designed to probe the ultimate meaning of the black slab. In this film, Kubrick attempted a union of mysticism and cynicism and the result was not always too clear.

The problem, of course, does not lie completely with either the director or the audience. Audiences must become more aware and intelligent, while directors must be aware of their own thoughts and the audience they are addressing. Alain Resnais best summarized the obligation of the director when he said: "This is the problem of all communication, whether between two people or ten million. One must know to what extent one can share one's subjective reality with everyone." The director as auteur is certainly a force which is likely to remain in contemporary cinema. In order for a balanced approach to meaning and reality in film to take place, both audiences and directors must understand and implement Resnais' maxim.

Technology

Two major technological developments dominated the Sixties. Both were born out of the need for and desire of filmmakers to shoot films away from the studio. With location shooting and

The Cinemobile Mark IV: a movie set on wheels.

"runaway" productions becoming the norm, there was a need for a portable, compact film unit which could effectively duplicate the studio. The need was met by an Arab immigrant, Fouad Said, who developed the Cinemobile Mark IV in 1967 as a movie studio on wheels. Approximately 35 feet long, the Cinemobile contains dressing rooms, bathrooms, space for a crew of 50 and large amounts of equipment. Its effectiveness was immediately felt. One example is producer Al Ruddy, who used the Cinemobile extensively in the making of *Little Faus and Big Halsy* (1971). He related a typical incident in which he wanted to shoot a motel scene and found it would cost him between $6,000 and $8,000 to use a Paramount sound stage. Instead, he rented rooms at a Los Angeles motel for $100.00 and by using the Cinemobile saved money and created a greater sense of reality. By 1971, Cinemobiles were being used in some 70 pictures, over 50% of Hollywood's total output.

The second technological development, while not as dramatic or conspicuous as the Cinemobile, was probably more important in the long run. The general development of portability and miniaturization of equipment—along with generally decreased costs were welcomed by both professionals and amateurs alike. 16mm filmmaking became a standard subject at many colleges and universities and the home movie market spurted tremendously with the development of Super 8mm film and cassette packaging. Documentary filmmakers received a tremendous boost with the development of low-cost, portable 16mm sound cameras and sound equipment. Hollywood, itself, found new possibilities in on-location shooting with portable 35mm cameras and the cinéma vérité method of shooting from the perspective of the participants in a scene became standard procedure. New developments in Super 8mm synchronous sound equipment are expanding the portability of film to an even greater degree.

Additional developments included experimentation with video tape as a substitute for film, most notably by Frank Zappa for his film *200 Motels* (1971). The flexibility and economy of instant playback and erasure are strong factors in tape's favor and its use as a tool for rehearsal is increasing. However, the image quality which results from transferring tape to film for theatrical release is at present too poor to make it a practical substitute for film.

The anamorphic wide-screen process became the standard in the Sixties for most large productions, resulting in a new screen ratio of 1.85:1 replacing the old 1.33:1. However, little artistic development has occurred, as directors still compose for the squarer ratio.

Expo '67 saw a surge of multiple-image techniques sweep the industry and for awhile, with such films as *Charley* (1969), *The Thomas Crown Affair* (1970), and *The Comic* (1970), audiences were beseiged with multiple images of their favorite stars. However, once the gimmick potential had been mined, directors lost interest and little has been done to integrate the technique into the total context of film narrative.

Films of the Decade: An Overview

Any attempt to describe the films themselves is doomed to almost instant failure. There were too few trends and too many individual successes. However, some patterns are visible and clearly marked.

At first, the early years of the Sixties saw Hollywood still seeking the magic formula which would bring back the habit audience. At the same time, however, the studios were afraid to gamble and so films were pretty well limited to guaranteed box-office hits, especially Broadway musicals and best-selling novels. The blockbuster became a standard product, as big was considered synonymous with better. After the mid-Fifties experimentation there was little further development of the small film. Musicals were very popular in the period 1960–1965, with such major films as *West Side Story* (1961), *My Fair Lady* (1964), *Mary Poppins* (1964), and *The Sound of Music* (1965). Spectacle films with all-star casts and thousands of extras were well represented by *Spartacus* (1960), *El Cid* (1961), *Lawrence of Arabia* (1962), *The Longest Day* (1962), *Cleopatra* (1963), and *The Great Escape* (1963). Even the Westerns and comedy genres were infected as *How the West Was Won* (1962) and *It's a Mad, Mad, Mad, Mad World* (1963) displayed size, but little else.

The prestige film suffered, however, as Hollywood could not really afford to take chances with message films. A few films were produced, such as Stanley Kramer's *Inherit the Wind* (1960), a version of the Scopes Monkey trial starring Fredric March as William Jennings Bryan and Spencer Tracy as Clarence Darrow, *Judgment at Nuremburg* (1961), a highly dramatized version of the war crimes trial starring an all-star cast and *A Man for all Seasons* (1966), the story of Thomas More's conflict with Henry VIII and the establishment of the Church of England.

The one observable trend outside of the emphasis on size was the spy thriller genre begun by the James Bond series, quickly followed by other series featuring "Matt Helm" played by Dean Martin and "Our Man Flint" starring James Coburn. In a sense these were not really spy melodramas at all, but more in the line of Thirties screwball comedies which treaded a thin line between reality and fantasy. The fantasies were primarily involved with some new ways of killing people and old ways of seducing others.

Toward the end of the Sixties, the series film made a brief comeback as a highly successful film, *Planet of the Apes* (1969) spurred three sequels, each of which was progressively worse than the original.

The major reasons why such few cycles emerged in this period are changes in the audience and the creators. The audience for films was becoming increasingly fragmented and splintered. There was no mass audience as such, only smaller separate audiences, which were not economically strong enough to support lengthy cycles. On the other hand, the new independent filmmakers did not want to be typed or tied to a certain genre. They made films on whatever interested them with little interference from a studio structure forcing them into films they did not want. The relationship between these new creators and new audiences was fluid, to say the least. The films of this early period illustrated a constant shift between highly personalized work and safe commercial success. For example, although 1963 was one of the biggest years for the blockbuster film, small films, such as *Hud* and *David and Lisa*, also made an impact. Everyone was searching—the studios for formulas, the independents for fresh ideas, the audience for new films.

Much of this search seemingly came to an end in 1967 with the appearance of *The Graduate* and *Bonnie and Clyde*. Suddenly, the "New American Film" was here. The youth audience was "discovered" and films appeared which would prove to be a barometer of things to come. The new violence was graphically expressed in *Bonnie and Clyde* and *In Cold Blood*. *Cool Hand Luke* continued the exploration of the anti-hero, the amoral, yet highly sympathetic character begun in a sense by *Hud* four years earlier. *In the Heat of the Night* began to reflect racial tension and conflict in a realistic way for the first time since the late Forties.

The "NOW" film was in vogue. NOW was in essence a label for American society in turmoil. It was anti-authority, violent, and sexual. If a film was not NOW, it was doomed. 1968 was a holding year as most NOW films were still in production, but 1969 witnessed an explosion which would alter the face of American film. All of the forces which had been developing through the decade —all the ideas, all of the freedom—seemed to burst forth at once. The old restrictive Motion Picture Code was replaced by a liberal rating system and a new sophistication in content quickly resulted.

Butch Cassidy and the Sundance Kid, while not expressing a particularly new or radically different theme, continued the exploration of the anti-hero and in this case made the criminals into folk heroes much like those in *Bonnie and Clyde*. *Alice's Restaurant* was a continuation of the youth film movement as Arthur Penn looked at American society with a critical, satiric eye and caught the mood of young America perfectly.

However, of all the films released that year, four stand out as marking a significant change in the direction of American film. The first film was the Swedish production *I Am Curious, Yellow*. It was initially banned as obscene in 1967 by U. S. Customs. This ruling was overturned in 1969 and the film was distributed to an eager audience. The explicit sex in the film included male and female frontal nudity and simulated copulation in a variety of positions—all of it usually with great detail. It became one of the all-time top grossing foreign films and indicated a large majority of the American audience wanted to see sex on the screen in more detail and with greater frequency than in the past.

Midnight Cowboy also dealt with sexuality in graphic terms and broke new ground as it became the first X-rated (under 17 not admitted) film to win an Academy Award. It was one of the top-grossing films of 1969 and further opened up the realistic and graphic treatment of sex.

The Wild Bunch did for violence what *Midnight Cowboy* and *I Am Curious, Yellow* did for sex. Peckinpah's film set a new standard for violence with explicit and prolonged blood-letting, much of it in slow motion. This particular technique seemed to divide the critics more than anything else, as some felt it heightened and intensified the violence while others saw it as a diffusing device. The precedent, however, was set.

A precedent of another type altogether was set by the fourth important film of the year, *Easy Rider*. Artistically, the film had a few bright moments, but its real significance lay in its continuation and in a sense peaking of the theme of alienated youth. The fact that this theme earned more than $50 million was the most important feature, however.

Suddenly, studio doors and pocketbooks were opened to young eager filmmakers anxious to make another big profit. In some respects the time was like the French New Wave of the early Sixties, as many came, but few conquered. Even the head guru himself, Dennis Hopper of *Easy Rider*, was unable to duplicate his initial success. Despite this limited success, a resurgence hit Hollywood. A new era was beginning. A new breath of freedom was being felt. In a sense, however, this euphoria was short-sighted. From the vantage of 20-20 hindsight it can now be seen that what really happened is that a lot of gambles, risks, and long-shots paid off all at once. Audiences responded to these new films, especially the youth (18–29) audience. Attendance figures not only leveled off from the steady nose dive they had been taking for the past 20 years, they actually began to rise. However, the new wave quickly broke up on the rocky shore of a fickle audience and a nervous industry.

The next several years saw many attempts to duplicate the "success of '69," but there was little permanent change. The youth film, with its new heroes and new myths, proved to be a cycle like many others before it. Disenchantment soon set in and Arthur Penn, one of the movement's leading apostles, was one of the first to speak:

Dennis Hopper and Peter Fonda
ride the open road in *Easy Rider*.

Some movies are creating the myths of the young. They promote the notion that freedom from all authority is an unqualified good, that mobility as a life style is superior to permanence, that the older generation is totally corrupt, that cool is the only legitimate response.

Much the same could be said for the visual styles which began to accompany this new content. A shift occurred from a literary to a visual base as evidenced in such films as *Reflections in a Golden Eye* (1967), *2001* (1968), *If* (1968), *Slaughterhouse Five* (1970), and *A Clockwork Orange* (1971), among many others, even though most of the films had strong literary origins. The industry, witnessing the success of these films, got on a style bandwagon and began to ignore plot. The emphasis shifted to juggling normal space-time relationships, and mixing black and white with color. At times style was handled well, but it was looked upon as another formula for commercial success. Ordinary films suddenly became infused with stylistic significance. *Newsweek* reported in 1968:

> *Two For the Road*, otherwise an ordinary Audrey Hepburn vehicle, has as much back and forth juggling of chronology as any

473

film made by Alain Resnais—not to mention a comic acidity about marital discord that is as candid as anything the Swedes have said.

How naive this all seems today in the light of the huge commercial success of *Love Story* (1970), *Airport* (1970), *The French Connection* (1971), *The Godfather* (1972), and on and on. The industry was again clutching at straws, tacking on style and pointing to it with pride because it made their films "legitimate." Like the Europeans, we too had "cinema." Richard Lester stated that television's abrupt leaps from news about Vietnam to Gomer Pyle to toothpaste ads had expanded people's vision. "TV is best," according to Lester, at those sudden shifts of reality. "TV, not *Last Year at Marienbad,* made the audience notice them for the first time."

Here was technology with no meaning. The key in Lester's statement is the absurdity of the switches, not the ability to create them or even the ability of the audience to understand them.

However, despite its cyclical nature, something lasting did come from all of this. In the searching and seeking out of new answers to many old questions and values, the new directors began to explore a wide scope of subcultures. As Michael Laughlin, producer of *Two Lane Blacktop* (1971), said: "The movie business used to be dominated by middle Europeans who imposed a fantasy landscape. Now screenwriters . . . are not afraid to write scenes about Americans in bowling alleys or about waitresses." Laughlin overstates his point, of course, since Hollywood was always open to a limited amount of social realism. However, the difference now was that the system was open to many more voices exploring many more areas of society. Robert Altman was able to produce *M.A.S.H.* and *McCabe and Mrs. Miller;* Mike Nichols was able to do *Carnal Knowledge* (1971); John Cassavetes was able to find an audience for *Husbands* (1970) and *Minnie and Moskowitz* (1971). Robert Rafelson produced *Five Easy Pieces* (1970).

Variety was an important result of all this activity. Despite the so-called "vacuum cleaner" syndrome of 1970 and 1972 when *Love Story* and *The Godfather* "sucked up" most of the business, the difference in the types of films which achieved success is remarkable. Reviewing the top-grossing films of 1971 provides a perfect illustration of this. Love led the way *(Love Story),* closely followed by nostalgia *(The Summer of '42),* Walt Disney *(The Aristocats),* sex *(Carnal Knowledge),* rats *(Willard),* science fiction *(The Andromeda Strain)*, the West *(Big Jake)*, and blacks *(Shaft)*.

It was in these films and many others that the new American cinema flourished. Like all movements in film, the outcome was a mixed bag. But overall, the freedom to innovate and explore in both theme and style, formerly confined to underground, experimental or foreign films, had surfaced and the main-line American movies were now capable of demonstrating and revealing new ways of looking at society.

If any one trend has appeared so far in the Seventies besides the continued exploration of sex, violence and race, it has been a replacing of the NOW film with the THEN film. Nostalgia entered the motion picture industry with *The Summer of '42* in 1971 and reached a peak in 1974 with the huge publicity and promotion surrounding *The Great Gatsby*. The period picture has long been a Hollywood staple. The medium is capable of reproducing the visual sense and style of a time and as such nostalgia has provided a perfect theme for filmmakers looking for new areas to explore. Whether it is *The Great Gatsby* trying to duplicate the splendor of Fitzgerald's Twenties or Robert Altman's *Thieves Like Us* (1973) trying to create the atmosphere of the rural South during the depression, or *Badlands* (1974) taking the audience back less than 20 years for a look at two troubled teenagers on a killing spree, the motion picture continues to demonstrate its ability to recreate historical realities and fiction.

Decline of the Genre

With all of this variety and activity, the genre film declined even further. A few types, such as science fiction and the musical, declined primarily because of the costs involved in making them and obvious lack of audience interest, especially among the young. *Fiddler on the Roof* (1970) and *Cabaret* (1972) were two of the few successful musicals of the Seventies and their place is probably due as much to the mixture of social comment and drama concerning prewar Germany and Czarist Russia as to the music itself. The industrial importance of the musical as evidenced by *The Sound of Music* (positive) and *Star* (negative) is gone. Most independents do not have the time, money, or inclination and the studios do not want to gamble the kind of money it takes ($10,000,000 minimum) to create a big musical.

Genres as a whole have become diffused. For example, men such as Peckinpah, Altman, or Penn infused the Western genre with their own personal styles. For a period of time the Western continued in its traditional role. However, with such films as *Tell Them Willie Boy Is Here* (1970), *Little Big Man* (1971), *McCabe and Mrs. Miller* (1971), and *Doc* (1971), among others, the traditional morality of the Western has been severely questioned. The genre has become a vehicle for personal style and themes. As Arthur Penn noted about *Little Big Man:* "It challenges the notion that the heroes of America are the ones you read about in the history books . . . It exposes the rotten values of commercialism."

The comedy genre has gone much the same way. The Sixties saw the decline of Jerry Lewis and the rise of Woody Allen and Peter Sellers. The Seventies saw the rise of Mel Brooks (*Blazing Saddles,* 1973, *Young Frankenstein,* 1974) who along with Allen dominate comedy film. Brooks, with his wild, zany humor and Allen, who satirizes contemporary society, are the huge exceptions to the decline of comedy films. Each has large, devoted followers and their films in the mid-Seventies earned spectacular grosses. Black comedy in the Wilder tradition continues to flourish with such films as *M.A.S.H.* (1970) and *Diary of a Mad Housewife* (1972) among others.

In general, the American film of the past ten years and

Woody Allen escapes from his pursuers in the 1973 production *Sleeper.*
MUSEUM OF MODERN ART/FILM STILLS ARCHIVE

especially in the Seventies has gone through a period of isolated successes. As Paul Mayersberg states: "Among the Hollywood studios, strategy in production is replacing style." Genres as a whole have little appeal for the American audience anymore. They are more attracted to individual films regardless of the genre they operate within.

The Big Three: Sex, Violence, Race

If anything has replaced the genre film of the past it is probably the preoccupation of contemporary film with these three themes. Films have always used sex and violence as staple ingredients. However, the freedom to treat all aspects of them has usually been very restricted—both by legal regulation and social attitudes.

Sex

The Sixties started out with little indication of the revolution to come. Sex was a game played with clothes on and hands off. Doris Day and Rock Hudson were the most representative non-lovers of the period, with such films as *Lover Come Back* (1962) and *That Touch of Mink* (1962). This cute sex philosophy was probably best summed up by Bosley Crowther in his review of *The Facts of Life* (1961), starring Bob Hope and Lucille Ball. Crowther called this romp "grandly good natured, winsome and wise," and closed with "anyone who is worried about the state of the nation and of home life should see it and be refreshed."

Meanwhile, some realism was beginning to creep in, especially with Billy Wilder's films *The Apartment* (1960), *Irma La Douce* (1963), *Kiss Me Stupid* (1964), and *The Fortune Cookie* (1966). However, the real effort was being made at the so-called underground level by such people as Randy Metzger, Russ Meyer, Andy Warhol, and others. In such films as *The Immoral Mr. Teas*, *Not Tonight Henry*, and *Three Nuts in Search of a Bolt*, waist high nudity was common in a burlesquelike atmosphere.

With the introduction of the rating system in 1968 replacing the so-called "Seal of Approval," the emphasis on sex increased. *I Am Curious, Yellow* and *Midnight Cowboy* have already been discussed as trend-setting films; however, the one film which probably did more to legitimize or at least popularize "soft-core" pornography was *Vixen* (1968), directed by the self-proclaimed "king of the nudies" Russ Meyer.

Meyer has been making skin-flicks since 1959 and the crucial distinction between his films and others of the same kind are that his made money. Meyer's films are primarily exercises in voyeuristic fantasy. They have been described as "good-hearted," having a "barracks-room heartiness." His nudity has always had a strange prudishness which reveals itself in his almost exclusive from-the-waist-up composition. Audiences laugh at a Meyer film and the response is a legitimate one which Meyer consciously builds into his work. *The Immoral Mr. Teas*, for example, revolves around a man who has an uncontrollable gift of being able to undress women mentally. Meyer takes the audience through episode after episode in which Teas "sees" nude women in doctor's offices, behind secretary's desks, etc. In addition, Meyer's films differ from most porn productions in that they are professional productions, shot by Meyer himself with great care. *The Immoral Mr. Teas* (1959) returned more than $1,000,000 on a $24,000 investment. *Vixen* (1968) was the real eye-opener, however, as it earned more than $6,000,000 against a $72,000 cost. These kinds of figures (both monetary and physical) caught the eye of 20th Century-Fox President Richard Zanuck, who signed Meyer to direct *Beyond the Valley of the Dolls* (1971). This was the big breakthrough. What had formerly been strictly an underground, stag film movement had suddenly surfaced.

The barriers were broken. Sex was legitimate in every sense of the word and with *Playboy* showing pubic hair, films were not far behind. The mood of the industry and the public changed rapidly. Whereas in 1968, *Midnight Cowboy* was given an "X" rating for "suggesting" certain taboos, such as fellatio, less than three years later Peter Bogdanovich used full frontal female nudity in *The Last Picture Show* and received an "R." Ann-Margret won an Academy Award in the same year for doing little more than allowing herself to be photographed walking in the nude from the bedroom to the bathroom. Two years later Jane Fonda won an Academy Award for playing a prostitute. Glenda Jackson also won an Academy Award for *Women in Love* (1972) in which she appeared nude. Male nudity appeared here for one of the first times as well. However, the male body has not been heavily exposed in films.

While nudity and sexual themes were "open," most actual sexual activity was suggested. Hard core films still played to small art houses in large cities. However, in 1972, a movie entitled *Deep Throat* changed all this and a hard-core trend appeared. Sex in *Deep Throat, The Devil in Miss Jones,* and *Behind the Green Door,* to name probably the three most successful films, was graphic and not simulated. Although most of these played in specialized houses showing nothing but "X" films, the key was that these houses were now located in Des Moines, Iowa, as well as New York. By 1972, it was estimated that more than 700 theaters all over the country were playing nothing but "porn" films, an increase of 60% from 1968. The pendulum had definitely swung. However, like youth films, bike films, etc., etc., etc., the porn film was a cycle. Audiences grew tired of watching copulating bodies and the cycle began to die. Andrew Sarris pinpointed one of the reasons for this when he noted that "the fantasy of superhuman restraint has been replaced by the fantasy of superhuman release." Like all fantasies, this one had a limited life span. One could achieve the same results with home movies, and indeed this is what most porn films have been. The realistic and artistic integration of sex both as theme and visualization is something that is not easily achieved. There is a natural tendency to exploit any new phenomenon. However, the key for today's filmmakers is that at least they have the freedom to use sex in whatever way they see fit. How they choose to treat it and the audience's response to that treatment may be legitimate or non-legitimate, artistic or non-artistic, but at least the opportunity to try exists.

Violence

Many of the things said about sex in films could be applied to violence. Without question, violence has played a large role in film history. Arguments concerning its effects and impact are almost as numerous as those concerned with sex. Again, filmmakers have used violence legitimately and simply for effect. As films began to explore more realistically the various subcultures of American society violence became a natural part of that exploration. As films moved from the boy next door to the gang on the street, the amount and nature of violence changed radically. On the other side of the coin, studios needed a new gimmick to attract audiences and the ability of film to graphically depict violence in all its forms made violence a natural. As one producer stated:

> You can't say it's a bad thing per se—it all depends on how it's integrated into the story. Violence has always been an element in drama, from Shakespeare to Japanese tragedy. Violence doesn't guarantee success in movies, but it reaches the audience on an emotional level, and that's very important.

There were, however, as with sex, rules by which Hollywood played. These rules usually discouraged graphic bloodletting and most killing and violence was "clean." One remembers such films as *Guadalcanal Diary* (1943), where entire platoons of men simply fell over in their foxholes as if they were asleep. However, these rules were graphically broken by *Bonnie and Clyde* in 1967 and destroyed altogether in the next three years in such films as *Bullitt* (1968), *Madigan* (1968), *The Wild Bunch* (1969), *The French Connection* (1971), and *Shaft* (1971). Violence was now "dirty," as audiences saw bullet holes, blood, and torn flesh.

There are many reasons for the change and we can not possibly explore them in any depth here, but one of the dominant reasons was simply that directors such as Peckinpah, Don Seigel, and Roger Corman were expressing personal styles and visions. These men pictured a violent society, filled with conflict. Whether it was the old West or an urban ghetto, man was looked upon as violent with much of his essential nature being expressed in violent ways. Another reason was that society was changing as well. The Vietnam war was a nightly occurrence on television and exposed most people to more graphic violence than they had seen before. As the producer of *Bullitt* and *The French Connection*, Philip D'Antonio, said: "People are used to seeing the war on television. They know what the real thing looks like. So, how can you fake it? Audiences won't buy that anymore."

Whether audiences would "buy it," of course was, and is, the real issue and as long as they are willing to accept violence, filmmakers are going to produce it. Some, such as Samuel Z. Arkoff, board chairman of American International Pictures, may demonstrate a social conscience and set "a limit on the number of blood bags used. . ." but the attitude of most seems best summed up by Joe Wyman, producer of *Kansas City Prime* (1972): "The effect on society? I don't give it a thought. Psychiatrists don't have the answers, why should I?"

Race

Yet another significant development in film content in the Seventies was the emergence of the black film. It was born out of economic necessity involved with exploiting a relatively untouched portion of the American audience and the cultural necessity of blacks striving to find a reasonably reflective screen image.

Recent population demographics revealed that half of the black population lived in fifty cities. As white America moved to the suburbs, the urban area, with its huge downtown theaters, filled with a new population, which required new motion pictures. A few individual efforts appeared in the late Sixties, such as Melvin Van Peebles' *Sweet Sweetback's Baadasssss Song* (1969), but the real boom began in 1970 with Gordon Parks' *Shaft* and *Cotton Comes to Harlem*. There were thirteen black films in 1970, eighteen in 1971, and then the movement really exploded with sixty films in less than two years. The black film integrated virtually every genre, including comedy, horror, the musical, and Western. However, it was the detective gangster genre which held the most potential. Here the urban black

Cicely Tyson helps Kevin Hooks get ready to leave home for a distant school in *Sounder*.
MUSEUM OF MODERN ART/FILM STILLS ARCHIVE

experience could be reflected easily and such 1972 films as *Super Fly, Hit Man, Trouble,* and *Trick Baby* exploited this orientation with tremendous success.

With this exploitation, primarily by white producers using black actors, came strong concerns over the image being reflected and projected. The dope pusher, superstud, superspade formula worried many black leaders and they called for an effort to balance the image. This came soon with such films as *Sounder, Black Girl,* and *Lady Sings the Blues,* and the black film began to settle down and round out. The blatant exploitation accomplished through cheap formulas seemed to have run its course by 1974. James Murray wrote in his book *To Find an Image* that there are three goals of black cinema; (1) the correction of white distortions, (2) the reflection of black society, and (3) the creation of a positive black image.

The accomplishment of these goals requires exploration, not exploitation. It requires a sense of purpose in those making black films other than making money. Above all, it requires time and thought. Quickie productions designed to simply "take the money and run" are ultimately self-defeating and accomplish none of Murray's goals.

The development of a black cinema, unfortunately, has not been duplicated or even attempted with other races, most significantly the American Indian. Some individual attempts have been made to reflect a more honest reality in such films as *Tell Them Willie Boy is Here* (1970), *Soldier Blue* (1970) and *Little Big Man* (1971). However, the key here, as it was in the development of a black cinema, is economics. The black cinema developed primarily out of the opportunity to make money. The population was there, the theaters were there, the only thing missing was the films. With the Indian, the population is not only considerably smaller, it is widely scattered and predominantly rural. The economic potential is not there and until it is, the development of an Indian or other racial cinema will have to wait.

Film and TV

We pick up this story again and see that by the mid-Seventies, the patterns begun in the Fifties intensified and solidified. Motion picture attendance had gone steadily down while the number of TV sets increased. What started out as competition moved to cooperation and ultimately coexistence. What looked like a destroyer at one time, has turned out to be a savior. Without TV, Hollywood would not have survived, even in its diminished existence. Of the 20,000 odd jobs in Hollywood today, 50% of them are in TV. Ninety percent of all prime time TV (8–11 EST) is on film. More importantly, motion pictures make up a significant part of this prime time programming. As William Fadiman noted in *Hollywood Now:* "More people than ever before are seeing Hollywood films, but most of them are not paying Hollywood for the privilege." Motion pictures account for more than half of all network prime time programming and up to 80% of the air time on non-affiliated independent stations. Universal Studios turned out 80 feature films in 1972, breaking an industry record set back in 1927. Fewer than 25, however, were for theatrical release. MGM stopped theatrical production altogether in 1973, concentrating its efforts exclusively on television.

Television has become the "B" movie and as such provides the same function for the industry that "B" movies have always provided—a substantial, reliable, steady income. New markets in the area of cable and pay TV hold great potential and it is quite clear that TV and motion pictures are firmly and permanently linked together.

The 1974 television season had six series taken directly from motion pictures *(Born Free, Paper Moon, Planet of the Apes, The New Land, M.A.S.H., The Odd Couple)*. More importantly, however, was the trend indicated by Les Brown in *The New York Times:* "For all the new program series that make up a television season, the heavy ammunition for mass audience at the networks remains a product created for another medium, the box-office movie." 1974 saw NBC-TV pay $10,000,000 for *The Godfather*, $5,000,000 for *Gone With the Wind*, and another $3,000,000 for *Dr. Zhivago*. ABC-TV paid $3.3 million for *The Poseidon Adventure*. These blockbuster movies and equally blockbuster prices were clear evidence of the tremendous appeal and commercial clout a single movie can have for a network. *The Godfather* completely dominated two evenings and won the ratings war for NBC-TV on those evenings.

Regulation and Control

The big story in this area of the past decade was, of course, the rating system introduced in 1968. When the old Production

Code gave a "Seal of Approval" to *Who's Afraid of Virginia Woolf?*, in 1966 granting an exception to the language used, it effectively killed what power it had left. It simply could no longer stand as a moral guardian against the onslaught of increasingly sophisticated films. There were, of course, economic reasons for the change as well. The industry was fighting to keep its head above water and the chief culprit was still TV. Technology had not really worked and now that color TV was a reality the only area left seemed to be more adult themes. So, on November 1, 1968, the G, M, R, X rating system went into effect. The labels have changed since then to G, PG, R, X, but the distinctions remain the same. G is for general audiences; PG suggests parental guidance may be necessary; R means the film is restricted to those over 17 or accompanied by an adult; and X means that the film is banned for everyone under 17.

The industry intended it primarily as a labeling system, but quite clearly it has not been that. Decisions and judgments must, of course, be made concerning content, particularly in the R and X categories. Therefore, the industry still attempts to regulate content, especially when the difference between an R and an X carries heavy economic weight. Banning a large portion of the population from a film is taking a big risk. Consequently, most filmmakers using strong sexual themes seek the R or even a PG rating and will tailor their films to the industry's board of review in order to obtain it. Industry statistics reveal that the vast majority of films in the years 1972–1974 received either PG or R ratings.

As a result, industry self-regulation still exists. There are still complaints about the power wielded by boards of review, but as a device to offset outside regulation the rating system has for the most part worked well.

In the area of the courts and their ongoing battle with obscenity, the Sixties and Seventies have seen continued progress made in the positive direction of freeing the screen of unnecessary and illegal restrictions. In 1965, the U. S. Supreme Court struck down the Maryland censorship law as unconstitutional and effectively eliminated all state regulation. Local regulations were another matter, however. Two decisions, one in 1973 and the other a year later, did not really clarify the matter much. In June, 1973, in Miller vs California, the Supreme Court stated that in deciding what was obscene, "Community standards should apply." Many thought that this would open the way for an all-out war against obscene films by local juries. One year

later, however, in the *Carnal Knowledge* decision, the Supreme
Court affirmed that it was only talking about hard-core pornography, not anything people happened to consider obscene. This,
of course, still leaves open the whole question of what is obscene
and has perpetuated the picture by picture method of reviewing
obscenity cases. There was a defining of terms in "Miller" which
provided some help. The court stated obscenity included "representations or descriptions of ultimate sexual acts, normal or
perverted, actual or simulated, representations or descriptions of
masturbation, excretory functions and lewd exhibition of the
genitals." The judges applied this definition in the *Carnal
Knowledge* case, declaring the film not obscene.

Conclusions

Well, where have we come since the mid-Sixties? What is
a NOW movie? Where will violence and sex take the American
film?

Few overall generalizations can be offered. One concept,
however, stands out, valid today, as it has been for the past 50
years. Ninety percent of the motion pictures made during the
past 10 years are products of an industry. Films, in order to
survive in this country, must still make their way in the open
marketplace. That is why, despite new audiences, new filmmakers, new films, and a new industry, the same concepts of cycles
and trends and market appeal dominate. Films are mass communication. Their creators will continue to make films and will
continue to make certain films as long as their audiences are
willing to respond to their product.

In 1967, *Time* magazine, in an analysis of the new trend in
motion pictures supposedly begun by *Bonnie and Clyde* and *The
Graduate*, issued what turned out to be a prophetic statement
about the direction of the New American Cinema:

> For all the new talent, new money and new freedom available it
> is not certain that Hollywood can or will sustain the burden of
> living in a renaissance. Technical innovation does not in itself
> guarantee quality. There is some evidence already that the relaxa-
> tion of censorship, for example, only replaces euphemistic clichés
> with crass clichés. Love scenes are not necessarily better because
> they are nuder. By getting closer to graffiti, movie dialogue does
> not necessarily get closer to truth.

The ten years up to the mid-Seventies may not, therefore, have been a true renaissance. They may have been just a shifting of the sands, covering up some old structures, and uncovering some new ones. Robert Taylor perhaps summed it up best when he said:

> If today is still the 20th Century, the Hollywood of the 1930s and early 1940s was 200 years ago. In a sense it was baroque. There was a style of living and making motion pictures which no longer exists. It has been coldly modernized into something very factual, very efficient—and I'm afraid, not very much fun.
>
> It ended in the late 1940s with the unexplained but seemingly premeditated murder of glamour. Television, taxes, actors pricing themselves to the skies . . .
>
> I can't explain the demise. Perhaps if someone could correctly explain the phenomenen of rock 'n' roll, Beatle haircuts and the beatnik wardrobe, we will start to understand. In any case, it was 200 years ago. . ."

16
New Directions

Any summary or stocktaking of the directions in which the motion picture may be running today remains bound to those same forces which made it a unique blending of art, industry, technology, and social phenomenon from its beginnings. Born of science, nurtured by both art and industry, film has continued in the last quarter of its first century to be guided by both scientific and aesthetic invention, and to the requirements of society as well as those within its own industry. And today, film as art comes under the purview of the scholar in fields far beyond the traditional arts that gave it birth and early sustenance. Movies have become a variety of things for an increasing number of people in diverse areas of production, consumption, and inquiry. Not only the form and function of films themselves have been affected. The very nature of the film viewing experience today will be a significant part of the study of film history in the future.

Studios, Stars and Systems

The most direct influences on film form and function are tied today, as they have been in the past, to the complexion and requirements of the producing industry and to the conceptual and stylistic mode of its artisans and artists. The still pervasive American film in particular finds itself strongly affected by an

487

industrial system that has undergone dramatic changes since the halcyon days of Hollywood and the stars. No longer is American feature film production centered in the extravagances of the big studios and the glamour of personalities both before and behind the camera. The advent of television and the court's divorcement ruling had resulted in uncertainty and loss of control at the box office. With corporate officers more and more replacing the pioneer showmen, control in production involved cost accounting and other austerity measures which were consonant with the new corporate image and which would afford individual films a better chance at a profit margin in a period of dwindling market and sharply rising costs.

The most heralded change has probably been the dissolution of the huge studio physical plants and the army of studio personnel that kept them running. The publicized auction in 1970 of Metro Goldwyn Mayer's props, costumes, and set pieces from a host of past productions was only one of many such divestments in Hollywood which have put the backlots and the sound stages on the real estate market (some have been retained by television subsidiaries and syndicates) and left the film companies to provide financial backing and distribution channels for independent production companies and packaging agencies. The so-called "collapse of Hollywood" brought to an end the big studio production system and a good deal of the physical part of what was Hollywood. What remains today is a financing and distribution system which has made room for the independent producer and moved production out of Los Angeles and into the home-town streets and country lanes where the action is said to be. By 1971 two-thirds of American features were being made by independent producers. About the same percentage (70%) were produced outside of Hollywood, although something of a migration back to studio lots has been underway more recently.

With the decline of the big studios as production centers have gone the stables of stars under long-term contract to big companies. No longer are the studios in the business of luring favorites to multi-film commitments and the launching of promotional campaigns to assure their ascendancy. Today popular film personalities are still sought as a hedge against obscurity, but by no means a guarantee of success. They are signed on a single film basis, often working for a percentage rather than a salary. With the opening up to independent production, some top stars like Sidney Poitier, Paul Newman, and Barbra Streisand have set up their own independent production and distribution companies.

Several studio heads had also long enjoyed the status of stardom—Harry Cohn, Jack Warner, Sam Goldwyn, Louis B. Mayer. But the new corporate image of the film industry was the result of a takeover of the major studios by large conglomerate corporations. As mentioned previously, Warner Brothers has been absorbed by Kinney National Service Inc., Paramount by Gulf and Western, and United Artists by Transamerica Corporation. The studio bosses, kept on for a while in figurehead positions, are now virtually all in retirement.

Many star directors with long associations with the major studios are also gone from the scene or are sharing billing with new talents, many of them from theatre and television. Billy Wilder, John Huston, Fred Zinneman, William Wyler, Alfred Hitchcock, Orson Welles are all either gone or are in semi-retirement. John Frankenheimer, Sidney Lumet, Martin Ritt, and Delbert Mann, the new television breed of directors who began to make their mark on the big screen by the early Sixties, have now been joined by the stage directors—Mike Nichols, Francis Ford Coppola, and the stars themselves, Paul Newman, Burt Lancaster.

If the American industry has been marked by dissolution of the old studio system, the foreign industry, particularly in Europe, has been marked by retrenchment and consolidation. Of the major industries of Western Europe all have now faced the television onslaught which has resulted in dwindling patronage. The exceptions are in France, where vigorous independence in production continues to lure audiences and in Italy, a latecomer in use of color and television film. Despite the French flare for independence, an era of co-production has been firmly established between Italy and France and in its wake, a new international cinema with less easily definable national character. Co-production between these two nations has been especially successful in recent years and has spurred the exploration of a European Film Community or Common Market in financing, marketing, and exhibition of films which has been in progress since the early Sixties. The designs for a consolidated European film industry have included multilateral financial co-production and distribution networks covering member nations. How such integration would be attained is still open to speculation. Even less clear is the direction such co-production would lead in the nature and quality of films themselves or the effect it might have on the American and European markets. An interest of many which is articulated by an official of the National Center of

French Cinema is in "refusing to play into the hands of the Americans without becoming anti-American." This "Défi Américain" posture is calculated to break the dominance of the American film interests in Europe, particularly in distribution, without jeopardizing the European-American co-production, which inevitably means European settings and talent and American financing.

Film Styles and Audience Disposition

The causal relationship (and indeed the direction of influence) between changing styles in film and the shifts in mood and complexion of movie audiences is speculative at best. Nevertheless, the new look or renaissance in European and subsequently in the American film has been accompanied by changes in audience make-up and expectations that are obviously more than coincidental. By the late Sixties the family audience had deserted movies. Filmgoers were fewer, but they were also younger, better educated, more affluent, and more inclined to return to the movie theatre on a frequent basis.*

The nature of the new audience is easier to define than its mood and expectations, but some trends are clearly established. The new generation of filmgoers is no longer enamored by big budget spectacle and stars. It bypassed *Star* (Julie Andrews), *Paint Your Wagon* (Lee Marvin), and *Boom* (Elizabeth Taylor) in favor of *Medium Cool, Goodbye Columbus,* and *Alice's Restaurant,* all produced for less than $2,000,000 and were stampeding to see *Easy Rider,* which cost its producer-stars Dennis Hopper and Peter Fonda less than $500,000 to make. The producers of such shoestring bonanzas had not found the secret formula in low-budget verisimilitude on the subject of alienated youth. Attempts by other producers to capitalize on the popularity of what seems to be emerging as a hardy new genre are often frustrated. The youth audience is discriminating, and what they are rejecting is clearer than what they are willing to embrace.

*Opinion Research Corporation, in a survey conducted for the Motion Picture Association of America, shows that 73% of admissions are between the ages of twelve and twenty-nine (40% of the U. S. population). The survey also indicates that frequent moviegoers, which account for 86% of admissions, represent only 23% of film age population (over twelve). Two-thirds of those with some college education are frequent or occasional moviegoers, while 60% of families with annual income of $15,000 are in this category.

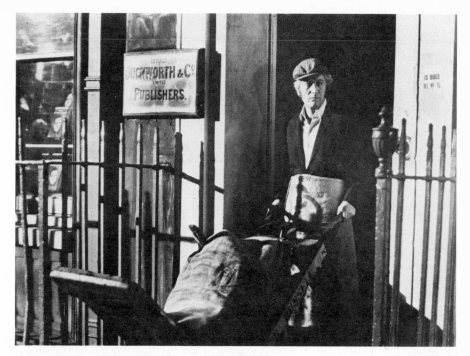

Frenzy. Hitchcock uses the bustle of contemporary London and its Covent Garden Market as settings for murderous intrigue.

They have on occasion been caught up, along with their elders, in nostalgia tripping, but have nevertheless been saying no to the sugar-coated dreams and neatly contrived dramas of past movie generations.

What is clearly being accepted as part of film's new image is both thematic and stylistic freedom for the exploration of attitudes, value systems, and the mental landscape. Cinematic storytelling, which started the medium on an aesthetic course, has today become less an end in itself and more a means of conveying a proposition or even a question related to human values and philosophic thought. *Love Story,* which may seem pedestrian as a screenplay, is found to be effective as mood building and a definition of attitudes. *Slaughterhouse Five* (1970), like *Hiroshima, Mon Amour* (1959), is largly a diagram of thought patterns. Even Hitchcock, a master of the screenplay who provides the delights of clue hunting and the rude surprises of plot twists in such early gems as *The Thirty-Nine Steps* (1935), and *The Lady Vanishes* (1938), seems more interested in allowing us to savor the bizarre variations on atmosphere for terror and voyeuristic indulgences in *Frenzy* (1972).

A pioneer in unconventional storytelling, Luis Buñuel, takes us even further today in the direction of free association and film dialectics. He is joined by a new generation of directors, many from Eastern Europe, who shun conventional narrative techniques, particularly the conventions of time and place. Free movement in time and space has allowed easier access to the future as well as past and present tenses. Stanley Kubrick takes us on a journey in *2001* (1968) which is supposed to suggest at least a half way point to infinity. Lindsay Anderson in *If* (1968) draws us into the future conditional as does Kubrick himself in *A Clockwork Orange* (1972). Many other filmmakers as well seem to be at least attempting an answer to the question posed back in 1930 by a writer for an early film journal:

> To what extent is cinema capable of penetrating into the various tenses? The thought consciousness roves freely from past to future, present to conditional. . . . I wander often in the subjunctive . . . the future "if" . . . would, should, might . . . *provided.* Present tense is easy. There is the "cast back" to the past. Where is the subjunctive, conditional?*

The new freedom found in the design of dramatic films today often leads to the more contemplative approach to subject matter. Roemer's *Claire's Knee* (1971), Visconti's *Death in Venice* (1971), as well as the aforementioned Kubrick and Anderson films, are aural-visual constructs of a premise. They are still stories, but instead of beginning "Once upon a time," they start by asking "What might happen if . . . ? ," and then proceed to illustrate.

In the wake of an undistinguished record by European films in the early Sixties, the critical and popular acclaim of such American films as *The Graduate, Bonnie and Clyde, Easy Rider* and *Midnight Cowboy* were being interpreted as America's own new wave or renaissance. The filmmakers Penn, Nichols, Coppola, Schlesinger, Bogdanovich, and Kubrick were rising to star status among directors, with only Bergman, Fellini, and Truffaut escaping at least partial eclipse among the Europeans.

New themes were varied but were liberally represented by some variation on the open road that is closed. *Bonnie and Clyde* (1967), *Butch Cassidy and the Sundance Kid* (1969), *Easy Rider* (1969), and *Five Easy Pieces* (1971) set the tone. With the road pictures and rock documentaries running their course, the Seven-

---

*L. Saalchutz, "Present Tense," *Close Up*, Volume VI, Number 3, March 1930, pp. 204–210.

ties have not produced any easily distinguishable genre trends, save a flurry of works using the city setting as asphalt jungle, a flirtation with the occult, and the paying homage to styles and stories of the recent past. Pauline Kael has suggested that young movie audiences are "going to movies looking for feelings that will help synthesize their experience." A broad range of films from socially conscious cartoons (Bakshi's *Heavy Traffic*) to cinéma vérité of narrative documentaries would seem to be helping to satisfy such audience needs.

But contemplative cinema notwithstanding, a large proportion of today's features seem to depend heavily on the immediate sensations derived from scenes of violence and sexual stimulation. Screen violence, given the mark of aesthetic responsibility (and respectability) by *Bonnie and Clyde* and *The Wild Bunch* in the Sixties, continues unabated in the Seventies with *The French Connection, Dirty Harry, Straw Dogs, A Clockwork Orange, Walking Tall,* and *Death Wish.* The controversy over dramatic necessity versus gratuitousness, which goes back to the earliest critical examination of movies, comes no closer to resolution. Sudden, turbulent, and often deathdealing action has been part and parcel of screen storytelling from the beginning, but in recent years has become more graphic, more pervasive, and simply a cinematic way of life.

The sweeping away of many sexual taboos in film in the past decade has raised the challenge of dealing with even further taboo subects with candor. Homosexuality and incest, probably the most sensitive topics for public exposure and surely the most forbidden in film history, have not only received candid treatment, but have been handled in such morally ambiguous or neutral tone that they have been rendered unobjectionable if not downright appealing. Louis Malle manages to make the lovemaking between a fifteen-year-old boy and his mother in *Murmur of the Heart* (1971) seem natural and even poetic. Our surprise comes not from the activity portrayed, but, belatedly, from our own benign reaction to it.

Violence and sexual candor in film are today as much a matter of style and structure of the film as they are of content. The films may or may not address themselves to these subjects, yet are often pervaded by an atmosphere or mood of violence or eroticism. More than ever before, any attempt to separate the subject matter of a film from its style is self-defeating. *Mise-en-scène,* used by film theorists to describe what the Soviet filmmaker Pudovkin had described as the "total atmosphere of the

film," is often a critical link. It has been strongly reestablished
as a key element in film today, not simply tying together the
scenery and the action, but allowing the action to flow as a
natural extension of the total mood or atmosphere of the film.
Bergman, Fellini, Godard, and more recently Peckinpah, Altman, and even Bakshi have been showing characters in their
films as part of their environment. The aesthetic *raison d'être* for
mise-en-scène goes back as far as some of the Biograph one-
reelers and was reinforced through the "Kino Eye" spirit of
cinematography in the Twenties and the postwar neorealist movement in Italy. Today, technological developments and economic
pressures as well as aesthetic tenets have given a new look to the
concept of *mise-en-scène*. The demise of the backlots and availability of more portable and flexible equipment have tended to
put the camera where the action is, or is purported to be; and the
action is shown to be part and parcel of the milieu.

But refinement in the total atmosphere of the film has been
taken beyond faithful recording or representation of physical
detail, and free association styles, identified by their jump cuts,
slow motion, flash forward, and pop focus suggest a new dimension in realism which acknowledges the presence of the camera.

Murmur of the Heart. Louis Malle's gentle satire on
family life and the growing up of privileged youth.
MUSEUM OF MODERN ART/FILM STILLS ARCHIVE

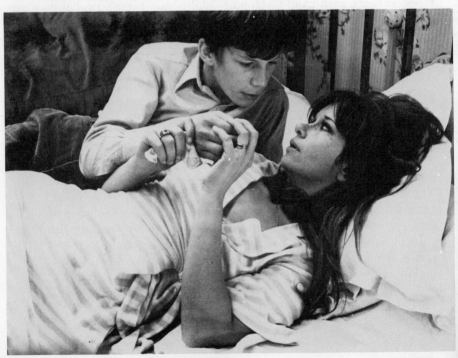

Day for Night. Truffaut is director, both on and off camera, in this
celebration of movie-making fantasy and the real-life drives and
anxieties of the people who make the movies.
MUSEUM OF MODERN ART/FILM STILLS ARCHIVE

In several films—*8½* (1963), *Blow-Up* (1966), *Medium Cool*
(1969), and *Day for Night* (1973)—the media have become at
least a part of the message. More important than the self-portrait
(or self-indulgence of such McLuhanesque approaches) is the
tendency to make use of the affinities peculiar to film for suggesting mental reality or psychological truth. For better or worse,
more films today are providing immediate experience rather
than a "by-the-numbers" exercise in plot construction.

The non-narrative genres of documentary and experimental
films have often led the way in suggesting new directions in form
and function. The postwar experimentalists have moved toward
more personal and subjective statements, revealing an emotional
rather than a pictorial landscape. Directors like Gregory Markop-
oulos, Kenneth Anger, and Stan Brakhage are film poets who
set aside accepted concepts in cinematic technique and subject
matter in treatments ranging from the film journal of the New
York subway (Carson Davidson's *Third Avenue El,* 1955) to the

495

surreal sexual imagery of Kenneth Anger's *Fireworks* (1946) and
Brakhage's *Flesh of Morning* (1956). Stylistic experimentation,
which has run the gamut of Vanderbeek's collages, nonedited
marathons of Andy Warhol, and the non-photographed images of
Brakhage turn now to the electronic and computer age for new
possibilities. Stan Vanderbeek has produced a series of "poem-
fields" which are films produced through computer programming.
Electronic effects from television, such as chromakey images, are
being explored by the filmmaker.

As with earlier experimental movements, most films of the
genre have limited exposure. With the exception of Warhol, who
has reached a commercial market, most experimentalists remain
"underground" or limited to noncommercial distribution and
exhibition patterns. The assimilation of experimental styles by
commercial cinema is continually demonstrated by such films as
Kubrick's *2001* (1968), Hill's *Slaughterhouse Five* (1972), and
more recently by Friedkin's *The Exorcist* (1974).

The documentary tradition of "recording and interpreting
the real world" has also shown new approaches to form and
function, if abandoning some of its traditional functions. John
Grierson, in "The Last Interview," which was published in
1972,* says that nobody has taken up the poetic line in documentary begun in the Thirties. He does, however, recognize four
distinct documentary forms today: the travelogue, the "on the
spot with living people" form explored by Flaherty, a "drama on
the doorstep" approach, which seems to follow Grierson's own
tradition of discovery of the working people, and finally the
cinéma vérité, which he designates as internal communication of
the local community. Though cinéma vérité is today seldom the
self-portrait that Grierson describes, it has become central to a
great deal of what is produced in the name of documentary.
Something more than style and short of religion, it describes the
audio-visual journalism that has taken film reporting past the
newsreel and into what is variously referred to as narrative
documentary, feature documentary, or the cinematic equivalent
to the nonfiction novel. Its more notable practitioners include
Richard Leacock and D.A. Pennebaker *(Monterey Pop,* 1969),
who pioneered and continue to explore the form, Frederick
Wiseman, whose *Titicut Follies* (1967), *High School* (1968), *Law
and Order* (1969), and *Hospital* (1970) settle on the functioning
and misfunctioning of traditional social institutions, and the

*Film Quarterly, Volume XXVI, Number 1, Fall 1972, pp. 24–30.

Maysles brothers, David and Albert, who in *Salesman* (1969) continue an examination of somewhat less than traditional life styles begun with their studies of the Beatles and film producer Joseph E. Levine. Here the cinéma vérité camera records eight weeks in the life of four salesman from the Mid-American Bible Company on the road in Massachusetts, Illinois, and Florida.

The vitality in cinéma vérité filmmaking today is no accident. Lightweight and flexible equipment have made it physically feasible to move into and around with a subject; television, with its special affinity for intimacy, has given it a home. A shift in attitude concerning documentary realism is also important—that it is not so much how people behave once they have forgotten the camera's presence that is so interesting as what people choose to reveal about themselves, once they feel that the camera is no longer affecting their behavior.

A school of documentary which now emerges to further illustrate how the medium's style can do the lion's share in conveying the message is one called simply "Newsreel." Composed of young radicals on the East and West coasts, it strives to use film as a revolutionary weapon by turning to purposely disjointed, unsynchronized and otherwise abrasive technique to stir complacent viewers into an awareness of political issues. Although this, like other documentary approaches today, may lack the poetic refinement of Flaherty, they show a healthy respect by filmmakers and viewers alike for film's potential in direct social engagement.

Technology and Exhibition

What wonderful dimensions the idea may arrive at by the commencement of the next century I am not prepared even to hint at. Whether the canvas will be done away with and the figures will be seen flitting about, spirit fashion, propelled and reflected by some electrical or gaseous method, through the abstract space, we do not know. Whether by some trick of phonography or ventriloquism the figures will aid their pantomimic expression by deep sonorous tones of dramatic marvel, proceeding apparently from the life-like shadows of things that have been seen, is a secret locked away in the treasure troves of the future.*

*Margaret I. MacDonald, "Moving Pictures in the Year 2000," *The Moving Picture News*, April 22, 1911, Volume IV, Number 16, p. 7.

The importance of technology to the development of cinematic form has been repeatedly illustrated. Each time a major technological breakthrough has occurred, it has been preceded by a considerable period of anticipation and experimentation and followed by a period of exploitation and integration. Anticipation of sound is found in the piano accompaniment provided the earliest of films; color was more than a dream to silent filmmakers, as is illustrated by the use of hand-tinting and colored film stock in the works of Porter and Griffith. Curved and multi-screen projection go back to Hale's Tour and the triptych screen of Abel Gance for *Napoléon.* James Card, Curator of Motion Pictures at the George Eastman House in Rochester, New York, reports that at the Paris Exhibition in 1900, color, wide-screen, sound, and other special effects were displayed. The Lumiére brothers showed hand-tinted films on a 48×69 foot screen, and the *Cineorama* process using ten synchronized cameras and projectors was exhibited by its creator, Raoul Grimon-Sanson.

Though a receptive climate existed for such major innovations, it was the problems of technology that had to be solved before these could become accepted and viable embellishments. Sound awaited synchronization and amplification; color, the three-color process of photography; and wide-screen, the anamorphic lens.

Once the technological limitations were removed, such innovations moved into a period of exploitation in which the process was self-consciously worked and overworked for its own sake, with little regard for its contribution to total design. This period ultimately gave way to a period of integration, in which the process or device came under artistic control and through selective and otherwise creative uses became a part of the film's overall style and function. This shift from exploitation to integration was echoed by René Clair, when he said, "The talking film exists.... It is too late for those who love the art of moving pictures to deplore the effects of this barbaric invasion.... The talking film is not everything. There is also the sound film."

There is little question today that sound has become a creative element in film. With few attempts, until very recently, to use color to go beyond a faithful representation of actuality, the potential of using the color process in selective and controlled ways, beyond basic photographic realism, is open to debate. As for screen shapes and sizes, progress is still clearly in a formative period. Though basic wide-screen processes such as

CinemaScope have settled down to provide an unobtrusive and agreeably flexible aspect ratio, broader implications of film projection and the film viewing experience have not been fully realized and what has been termed "expanded cinema" is still in a period of anticipation and experimentation.

Multi-screen projection, as noted by James Card, had an unveiling at the Paris Exposition in 1900, twenty-seven years before Abel Gance's *Napoléon* was shown in "Polyvision" on a triple screen at the Paris Opéra. It was not until the arrival of television, however, that multi-image became more than passing fancy. It was probably that medium's tendency to cultivate our appetite for simultaneous action—the split screen award shows originating from both East and West coasts—that helped spur exploration. It is even more likely that the search for visual-aural experiences *not* available on the small screen brought about the flurry of multi-projections in the Sixties. The 1964–65 New York World's Fair became a major showcase for multi-screen projection. Eastman Kodak's *The Searching Eye,* Disney's *Circarama* transplanted from Disneyland in Anaheim, and IBM's computer style show were fair favorites. The Johnson's Wax Pavilion offering *To Be Alive,* a documentary short by Francis Thompson and Alexander Hammid, which utilized a triple screen, became a feature attraction of the entire exposition.

With the opening of Expo '67 in Montreal came an explosion in film exhibition techniques. With the aid of refined optics, electronics, and computer programming, these included not only multi-screen projection but multi-media and multi-dimension programs as well. It was the less bizarre variations of multi-image, utilizing a flat or slightly curved single viewing surface, that showed the greatest flexibility and potential for more conventional film functions. Multiple image, single composite image, simultaneous repetition of an image, contrasting of images, and even the variable masking or framing of images by allowing sections of the overall viewing surface to remain dark, were all demonstrated with varying degrees of success. *We Are Young,* a twenty-minute presentation of the Canadian Pacific Cominco Pavilion, used six screens in two rows of three to examine the dilemmas of youth in the modern world. The most ambitious and popular exhibit of the fair was a multi-part show by the National Film Board of Canada called *Labyrinthe.* It featured a double triptych or five screen cross at one point and a huge well ringed by balconies for viewing at another. In the latter presentation, images of the challenge of "Man and His

World" were projected on a screen extending the forty-five foot height of the well, and also on a screen at the bottom of the well, which allowed for interaction.

Adoption by the film industry of Expo's multi-image experiments began the following year with Norman Jewison's *The Thomas Crown Affair* (1968) and Richard Fleischer's *The Boston Strangler* (1968). Jewison used multi-screen images to create the kind of simultaneity that Pudovkin described in his montage theory and revealed in his films—the cross-cutting between simultaneous actions that goes back to *The Great Train Robbery* (1903). With the Jewison film it was showing simultaneously, rather than sequentially, two or more actions representing the complex preparations and execution of a modern-day robbery. John Frankenheimer made further use of multi-image in the racing scenes of *Grand Prix* (1968). But these can hardly be pegged as trend-setters and the use of multi-image in feature films has since been scarce. On the home screen, however, it has become a standard device in telecasting sporting events, variety specials, and many other types of program.

Margaret MacDonald's speculation about movies in the year 2000 included the vision of figures seen "flitting about, spirit fashion, propelled and reflected by some electrical or gaseous method, through the abstract space." Though film images continue to be two-dimensional, a number of ways have been found to give the the impression of in-depth viewing. These include a range of techniques employing curved and multi-screen forms such as Cinerama and CinemaScope. More conventional techniques of composition and deep focus, which give the impression of depth to the standard 35mm flat image, are also prevalent. True stereoscopy came with 3-D movies, which went commercial in 1952. *B'wana Devil,* the first feature-length stereoscopic film—"A lion in your lap! A lover in your arms!" the ads read—was followed by several horror and adventure tales in 1953, all of which exploited the stereo effect by having objects pop out of the screen and into the laps or past the ears of spectators. The craze was already on the wane by the following year and Hitchcock's *Dial M for Murder,* though photographed in 3-D, was released in a conventional print version. A revival attempt in 1972, which included the sexploitative *The Stewardesses* and Warner Brothers more durable offering from the original 3-D era, *House of Wax,* failed to make headway. Pedestrian and exploitative plots, plus the annoyance and eye fatigue from wearing the necessary polarizing glasses, left audiences unimpressed.

> Had the public thought it worthwhile to gaze at the screen through an apparatus, stereoscopic movies would have been here long ago. . . The Spoor-Berggren process, like the Vitascope process in sound, is only the first dislodgment of an avalanche.*

The future for stereoscopic film, scientists tell us, will most likely come by way of the holographic image, which employs a laser beam to produce an in-depth image in the form of the original object being projected. The fact that the hologram is a true stereoscopic image means that any change in perspective, such as moving from the left to the right of an object (or theoretically, through it) would reveal a new facet or angle of the object without the aid of moving camera or editing. Holographic motion pictures have already been produced, but these are at this point crude first steps which do not broach the problems of providing sufficient illumination of large objects or areas, reproduction for large audiences, reproduction in color, and a host of others. Still, an important first step has been made, and predictions for a viable holographic movie system run as early as ten years hence.

That the addition of a third dimension to film viewing can be absorbed by both filmmaker and audience seems in little doubt. Sergei Eisenstein, in writing on "The Future of Film," has observed that:

> Unlike sound, the application of colour and stereoscopy to the film will effect no radical departure: they involve no structural changes, but merely mark further stages in the evolution toward perfection. . . Stereoscopic films will at first give the onlooker a feeling of strangeness, but this will pass away after sixty feet of film have been shown.

There are, in addition to multi-projection and stereoscopy, a number of systems and devices which have at least the potential for modifying film's function, or at least the way we experience the medium. Shortly after the appearance of 3-D movies, two different systems promising the added realism of olfactory stimulation appeared in a few major cities of the U.S.—"Smellovision" and "Aromarama." Neither system caught on, nor has anything resembling George Orwell's futuristic vision of "the feelies" yet become a reality with the exception of the "multi-dimension feel of sensurround" which makes one a part of *Earthquake* (1974). Such systems might seem to have little

*Eric Elliot, "Stereoptimism," *Close Up*, Volume VI, Number 5, May, 1930, pp. 341–350.

chance of ever moving beyond the novelty stage, but with the serious interest today in multisensory experience and multimedia, the possibilities of broader sensory appeal involving film cannot be ignored. Under the influence of Marshall McLuhan's call for liberation from dominance of print media in favor of multisensory experience, museums, galleries, and exhibition and communication centers of all kinds are attempting to create media environment and kinetic experience by combining movies with a host of visual, aural, and tactile stimuli.

As an extension of the "happening" in which music, light show, and some form of performance (dance, poetry reading, mime) are in combination, the intermedia kinetic experience is becoming an electronic world in which multiple films are combined with other forms of projection, light orchestration, multitrack music and sound sources, kinetic sculpture, and live dance and acting. The discrete nature of the film viewing experience is being abandoned by showman and museum curator alike in an attempt to integrate movies with other sensory stimuli in providing mixed media show and exhibit.

The combination of film with live action goes back to the silent Japanese movie theatre, where the Hanashika—"the man who tells the story" or live narrator—was sometimes as popular with audiences as the stars themselves. Except where variety and vaudeville routines shared billing with movies, there has been little integration of film and live action in Western theatre. "Laterna Magika," a mixing of live action on the stage with screen action was devised in Czechoslovakia and first presented at the Brussels Worlds Fair in 1958, with repeat performances at both the New York and Montreal fairs. In an attempt to blend film sequences of exterior scope and spectacle with intimate live drama without interruption, other "living screen" processes have been devised, using a variety of screens in various combinations manipulated during performances by stagehands. Such homogenization of film and theatre has not developed beyond demonstrator models. What has been on the increase is the use of rear projection cinematography for scenebuilding or filmed interludes as part of stage productions.

The age of electronics has begun to touch on cinematic form in a variety of ways. Another Expo '67 attraction devised by the Czechs was *Kinoautomat*, an audience participation scheme which employed a computer to allow audiences to choose between plot developments at key intervals. The stars of the film would themselves come on stage to present the audience with the choice of plot alternatives and the audience members would then have their choice tallied by computer, which would then select the winning variation.

The long-range implications for such a system seem doubtful, but other uses of computer programming in cinematography go beyond gimmick and showy exploitation. In addition to the use of the computer in producing abstract films, such as the Vanderbeek works already mentioned, computer editing of films is now feasible and may soon revolutionize that process. It involves an electronic computerized system for editing visual material by using a sophisticated combination of video tape equipment and computer memory bank. The system makes it possible to call up a series of shots in a desired sequence, add, delete, reorder, and manipulate length of shots and even select special optical effects without ever touching the film itself. From both a practical and aesthetic point of view the possibilities here seem staggering.

Technology will without question have a critical role in the development of films of the future, probably more so than in the history of the medium to date. The mastery of scientific devices, however, will not alone assure meaningful application, and the challenge for future filmmakers will be, as it was for Porter, Méliès, Griffith, Clair, and other pioneers in revolutionary technique, to find means of using these creatively.

17
Film Enviroment and Experience

An Assessment

Film today is more than production methods, technology, and aesthetics. The functions that film serves and the nature of the film experience itself have undergone dramatic changes in the past two decades. The coming of television, shifts in exhibition patterns, and an increased awareness of "cinema" which extends beyond the actual viewing of a film are increasingly important to an understanding of the film experience. The more significant of these changes have to do with audience conditioning to the medium, the expanding role and changing stature of film in our society, and the variety of ways in which we experience movies today.

Looking first at the patterns of exhibition or, from the viewer's perspective, the nature of the film viewing experience, we discover an important part of the medium's evolution. We relate differently today to motion pictures, because we see them with much greater frequency and under more diverse conditions. Putting aside the special systems in multi-image and multi-media discussed in the previous chapter (which are not a part of our regular film diet), we find that the viewing of film has changed significantly over the years and is not the singular experience it was through the silent and most of the sound era.

Film viewing began with Edison's Kinetoscope, by which an individual peered through the eyepiece of a penny-arcade contraption for several seconds. Projection brought film to the theatre, first the makeshift storefront variety, then the nickelodeon, and later the grandiose palaces. By the Thirties the trend had already begun to reverse as streamlined, functional suburban or neighborhood theatres supplemented and gradually replaced the cavernous first-run houses. With the advent of television and dwindling audiences came the closing of many of the neighborhood theatres. These, together with the remaining palaces, were now being replaced by small, comfortable albeit utilitarian cinemas, often located in large shopping plaza complexes. Today the trend continues with multiple theatres designed to share a common lobby and other facilities, with individual auditoriums ranging from 150 to 500 seats. Some are cinema complexes incorporated into the grand design of enclosed malls where a full range of activities—shopping, professional consultation, dining—can be combined with a visit to the cinema without ever seeing the light of day. This fully climate controlled existence extends to fully automated theatres which provide, in addition to its film offerings, a sitter service or rendezvous point. With the institution of "dollar night," especially at these mall complex theatres, dropping in to a film becomes a casual experience, decided on short notice while engaged in consumer activities including various forms of "impulse buying."

At the other end of the spectrum, in contrast to the intimate and casual approach to filmgoing, major cities today offer film experience to rival the patronage of the other arts. Film theatres are often part of the civic or cultural center, where filmgoers mingle with symphony, opera, and ballet devotees. Lincoln Center in New York becomes the home of the New York Film Festival in September as well as other special film programs. In Shanghai, film showings, performances by the Peking Opera, and as many as twenty other arts activities may be going on simultaneously in one of the largest cultural centers in the world. The National Film Theatre in London, part of the complex on the south bank of the Thames which began with Festival Hall, has regular contemporary and retrospective screenings and film lectures. More recently, the American Film Institute Theatre has been established as part of the John F. Kennedy Center along the Potomac. Like other civic centers, it serves as a repertory film theatre which gives special, though by no means exclusive, attention to director and genre retrospectives.

Whether as part of such cultural center offerings in large metropolitan areas, or local art house fare, more film from a greater variety of genres and periods is available today in an ever increasing range of settings. With the advent of in-flight movies on commercial airlines, the range of settings is further extended if not improved. But what has happened in regular commercial circuits is minuscule compared to the effect that the 16mm film field and television have had on the nature of film viewing today. With the coming of more portable and flexible 16mm projection equipment, virtually any room or hall that can be darkened becomes a movie theatre. The rapid expansion in 16mm distribution through the Sixties, coupled with the rise in film societies, particularly on college campuses, has made an even greater variety of film available in even more casual surroundings.

Television has already extended the availability of a wide range of film material, including a good deal that was intended originally for theatrical distribution. With the prospect of film packaging by way of cartridge and cassette systems, the supply of film fare would seem to approximate infinity. Research and development on video cartridge systems has been underway since the introduction of video tape. Systems now becoming available for home use and being promoted as "complete home entertainment centers" provide for home video recording in black and white with instant playback, as well as full-color off-the-air recording and cassette playback. Among cassette tapes now available for rent are a range of American and foreign features from *Casablanca* to *Claire's Knee*. Though purchase of film favorites is not possible, one can record these off the air.

Lack of standardization among several cassette systems and the high cost have been limiting factors in mass production and sales. At the same time it has allowed experimentation to progress in other directions. Less developed but holding greater promise in initial cost, durability, and flexibility is the video disc. In addition to providing variable speed, reverse, and frame by frame replay, the system will permit instant access to a desired scene, just as one can select a band on an LP record. Such flexibility not only surpasses that of video tape, but makes the motion picture projector and sprocketed film seem archaic by comparison.

Coupled with accessibility and range in viewing conditions, the conditioning that occurs in audiences strongly influences the quality of the film viewing experience today. The pervasiveness of exposure to film serving a variety of functions in an ever increasing array of settings has resulted in an increased familiarity with and understanding of "film form" and "film sense," sometimes referred to as "cinema literacy." The training began with the moving camera and the close-up, which, in spite of some early anxiety about showing only half an actor, was quickly understood and accepted by viewers. Since then, a wide variety of cinematic techniques involving camera, editing, decor, sound, and a combination of these has been assimilated by viewers, particularly through television exposure. The flashforward, slow motion, and jump-cut are accepted by viewers who have given little thought to the theory behind their use. In the same way, viewers have gradually accepted the deemphasis of plot intricacies in favor of *mise-en-scène* and character analysis. Though still interested in story, most viewers are satisfied with less elaborate synopses and have learned to adjust to "closet drama" and other less expansive and fluid forms which had always been considered so much a part and parcel of cinema.

We relate differently to motion pictures today because of conditioning to a wide range of cinematic technique in the service of a broader range of functions. But the conditioning extends beyond the viewing experience itself. Among literate and culturally enriched social levels, which make up the majority of movie house patrons, film literature, including both serious conceptual writings and promotional material, is coloring attitudes toward the medium and specific films. To put it simply, film is written about and talked about more, and more seriously than ever before.

The explosion in film literature began in the mid-Sixties while movie attendance was still on the decline. Though fewer people were going to the movies, more were interested in reading about them, partly because television had made available a storehouse of past films, and partly because the paperback revolution made books about them and their directors cheaper to buy. The boom in film literature greatly expanded the scope of writings and basic format. Reprints of the established works of historians and theorists have been joined in the past several years by a wide assortment of both popular and esoteric works. Those which focus on a particular director are particularly popular in an age of auterism and cultism. These include biographies and film analyses as well as interviews with and essays by the filmmakers themselves. Film scripts, though still seeking a format that will more accurately convey what we see and hear on the screen, are in demand and both "modern" and "classic" films are being brought to print. New writings in history and theory are now appearing with increased frequency, both as discrete works and mixed with earlier essays in anthology form. Most popular are the coffee table tomes which use frame enlargements, production stills, an other photographic material to provide embellishment and documentation.

Writings in film criticism reflect an increased seriousness toward cinema and are keeping its wares before even the non-moviegoing public.* Today both popular weekly and monthly magazines and more literate journals have regular film reviews and essays. Large circulation magazines are giving more attention to serious analysis rather than the vital statistics and plot synopsis of a film. This abundance of critical writing in periodical literature has in turn opened an entire new area of film books. From the collection of reviews and comments written for *The Nation* and *Time* by James Agee came *Agee on Film* in 1958. Since then the compilation and reprinting of reviews and analytical essays by major critics and theorists have produced a legacy of literature on individual films and given the reading public a new kind of exposure to the wide world of film, even those who never see the movies. Fewer films, closer scrutiny by the critics, and elaborate advertising campaigns by producer and/or distributor combine to thrust a handful of pictures into the limelight. As a result, movies often become a part of our experience long before we get to the theatre—if we get there at all.

In addition to writings on film, the increase in exposure to film happenings helps to keep the medium and its product before the public eye. Festivals, televised awards presentations, personal and televised appearances of stars and directors, and even the increased presence of "on location" film crews help to keep audiences aware not just of moviemaking, but of the existence and progress of individual films.

Conditioning today extends in a subtle but pervasive way beyond publicity, criticism, and learning of film language. We relate differently to motion pictures today because of changes in the status of the medium.

More serious film fare and the more serious attitude toward it by critic and public are in themselves indicative of the new respectability of movies. But added to that is a kind of institutionalizing which puts "cinema" in a far different class than it was in the days of the Rialto, the Bijou, and the Dream. The rise of cultural standing of film by community and educational groups is supported by a dramatic increase in the past several years in film societies, academic offerings, and archival and research

*Vincent Canby, film critic for the *New York Times,* reports on being confronted by "I read all your reviews, even though I never go."

activities. The college film course has extended beyond those institutions like U.C.L.A. and New York University that pioneered in film scholarship, and today includes more than 3,000 courses at some 600 colleges and universities across the country; adult education and high school offerings further increase the number. Beyond the formal curriculum is an ever increasing number of community and college film societies dedicated to the study of motion pictures. There are nearly 2,000 of these which are affiliated with the American Federation of Film Societies, the majority having been in existence for less than five years.

Film research centers and archives represent a growing area of film activity today as well as an indicator of its new status as art and subject of serious inquiry. The Museum of Modern Art in New York, La Cinémathèque Francaise in Paris, and the National Film Archive in London pioneered the field of collection and preservation of film, film literature, and other related materials. The Museum of Modern Art is the home of a film library founded in 1935 by Iris Barry for the purpose of preserving a filmed record of the technical and aesthetic history of the art. The Museum collection today numbers over 4500 titles, many of which are part of a circulating program available to schools and film societies. The National Film Archive in London was also founded in 1935 and like the Museum in New York features viewing services as well as book library, still photograph collection, and film information service.

Today, these are joined by other national archives and institutes plus several independent and regional centers. In the U. S., these include the George Eastman House in Rochester, New York, the American Film Institute in Los Angeles and Washington, and Anthology Film Archives, also in New York.

The George Eastman House, since 1949 has been engaged in the collection and exhibition of films, photographs, and movie equipment and memorabilia. Under the direction of James Card, its curator, it today provides a special study collection and book library for film research.

Anthology Film Archives is unique in its attempt to present films in their original version and in refining the film viewing experience itself. Special projection facilities, auditorium design, and individual controls have been built into the ninety-seat theatre in order to provide optimum viewing conditions. Seat hoods and blinders between seats eliminate distractions, while remote sound and focus controls provide for individual viewer needs. Projectors are also equipped to show films in their original screen ratio and running speed.

The American Film Institute, established in 1967 under the National Foundation of the Arts and Humanities, is the newest national archive among the major film-producing countries. Since its foundation, it has continued its programs devoted to director training, film preservation, and what it calls its "scholarly and reference services." The preservation program has centered on a cooperative effort with the Library of Congress in transferring vintage films from decomposing nitrate to more stable acetate stock. Research and publication activities include a projected nineteen-volume catalogue of American films.

Institute and archive activities, of course, have only an indirect and limited effect on the average moviegoer. An innovation which may prove more significant to film's status as far as the average moviegoer is concerned is the launching of the American Film Theatre in 1973. It is also an event that might be looked on as bringing film full circle, or at least back to its 1908 venture in "canned theatre" via the Film d'Art movement. Heralded as "eight enchanted evenings" by its producers, it brought major actors, directors, and playwrights together in filmed versions of such prestigious stage works as Pinter's *The Homecoming*, Chekhov's *Three Sisters*, O'Neill's *The Iceman Cometh*, and Ionesco's *Rhinoceros*. Shown at only two matinee and two evening performances on a subscription basis, the eight films that made up the first season's offering were shown at 512 movie theatres throughout the United States and Canada. Ely Landau, who had brought famous plays to television on "Play of the Week," was once again providing audiences across the country with major works of the New York and London stage. Although the inevitable criticism followed most of these films—"plays aren't films and films aren't plays"—the new venture in filmed theatre managed to draw with some success upon the affinities of the two forms. Unlike the original Film d'Art movement, it brought aesthetic validity as well as prestige to the genre. In its second season, it brought additional quality theatre to film audiences in its screen versions of *Galileo, In Celebration, The Maids, Jacques Brel*, and *The Man in the Glass Booth*—an esoteric leaning, however, which may well leave the average moviegoer to other cinematic devices.

In 1925, when David Wark Griffith was invited by *Collier's* magazine to predict what moviegoing would be like one hundred years in the future, he proved to be remarkably prophetic. Although a national film theatre was not a part of his vision, he did foresee "a great deal more of the so-called intimate drama presented on the screen." In addition, he envisioned "actors appearing in twice the size you see them now," "film so sensitive that it will record the natural tints and colors as the picture is being photographed," and "motion-picture shows on regular schedule between New York and Chicago and between New York and London." Griffith also predicted that stereoscopic films by the year 2024 "will long since have been discovered and adopted." What can hardly be minimized as a flaw in Griffith's gift of prophecy was his prediction regarding sound: "I am quite positive that when a century has passed, all thought of our so-called speaking pictures will have been abandoned."

At the halfway point in the one-hundred-year span we find that most of the Griffith prophecy has already been fulfilled. In spite of his lapse regarding sound, he has led the way in opening new frontiers in filmic representation—both by deed and inspired declaration. The fact that no new prophet is at hand to extend the vision may itself be significant. It perhaps mirrors the uncertainty of the direction of the medium as both industry and art, at a time when it is becoming a pervasive communicative and aesthetic form. But the uncertainty is probably caused more by the multi-directional, multi-level opportunities now open to film rather than any question of its viability.

A Selected Bibliography

REFERENCE WORKS

Bukalski, Peter J. *Film Research; A Critical Bibliography With Annotations and Essay.* Boston: G.K. Hall, 1972.

Gottesman, Ronald and Harry Geduld. *Guidebook to Film: An Eleven-in-one Reference.* New York: Holt, Rinehart and Winston, 1972.

Manchel, Frank. *Film Study: A Resource Guide.* Rutherford, N.J.: Farleigh Dickinson University Press, 1973.

Michael, Paul (ed). *The American Movies Reference Book; The Sound Era.* Englewood Cliffs, N.J.: Prentice Hall, 1969.

——*New York Times Film Reviews 1913-1968.* New York: New York Times and Arno Press.

AMERICAN AND WORLD HISTORY

Balshofer, Fred J. and Arthur C. Miller. *One Reel a Week.* Berkeley and Los Angeles: University of California Press, 1967.

Bardeche, Maurice and Robert Brasillach. *A History of the Motion Pictures.* ed. Iris Barry. New York: W.W. Norton and Museum of Modern Art, 1938.

Baxter, John. *Hollywood in the Sixties.* New York and London: A.S. Barnes, 1972.

Baxter, John. *Hollywood in the Thirties.* London and New York: Zwemmer and Barnes, 1968.

Blum, Daniel. *A Pictorial History of the Silent Screen.* New York: C.P. Putnam's Sons, 1953.

Brownlow, Kevin. *The Parade's Gone By*. New York: Alfred Knopf, 1968.

Casty, Alan. *Development of the Film*. New York: Harcourt Brace Jovanovich, 1973.

Crowther, Bosley. *The Great Films*. New York: Putnam, 1967.

Dickinson, Thorold. *A Discovery of Cinema*. London: Oxford U. Press, 1971.

Fulton, A.R. *Motion Pictures: The Development of an Art From Silent Films to the Age of Television*. Norman, Oklahoma: University of Oklahoma Press, 1960.

Goodman, Ezra. *The Fifty Year Decline and Fall of Hollywood*. New York: Simon and Schuster, 1961.

Gow, Gordon. *Hollywood in the Fifties*. New York: A.S. Barnes, 1971.

Griffith, Richard and Arthur Mayer. *The Movies*. New York: Simon and Schuster, 1957.

Hampton, Benjamin Bowles. *A History of the Movies*. New York: Covici, Friede, 1931.

Hendricks, Gordon. *The Edison Motion Picture Myth*. Berkeley: University of California Press, 1961.

Hepworth, Cecil M. *Came the Dawn: Memories of a Film Pioneer*. London: Phoenix House, 1961.

Higham, Charles and Joel Greenberg. *Hollywood in the Forties*. New York and London: A.S. Barnes, 1968.

Houston, Penelope. *The Contemporary Cinema*. Baltimore: Penguin Books, 1963.

Jacobs, Lewis. *The Emergence of Film Art*. New York: Hopkinson and Blake, 1969.

Jacobs, Lewis. *The Rise of the American Film*. New York: Harcourt, Brace, 1939.

Knight, Arthur. *The Liveliest Art: A Panoramic History of the Movies*. New York: Macmillan, 1957.

MacCann, Richard Dyer. *Hollywood in Transition*. Boston: Houghton Mifflin, 1962.

MacGowan, Kenneth. *Behind the Screen*. New York: Delacorte Press, 1965.

Manvell, Roger. *New Cinema in Europe*. New York and London: Dutton/Vista, 1966.

Marek, Kurt W. (pseud. C.W. Ceram). *Archeology of the Cinema*. New York: Harcourt, Brace & World, 1965.

Mast, Gerald. *A Short History of the Movies*. New York: Bobbs Merrill, 1971.

Mayer, Arthur. *Merely Colossal*. New York: Simon and Schuster, 1953.

Pratt, George C. *Spellbound in Darkness: Readings in the History and Criticism of the Silent Film*. Rochester: N.Y.U. of Rochester Press, 1966.

Quigley, Martin. *Magic Shadows*. Washington: Georgetown University Press, 1948.

Ramsaye, Terry. *A Million and One Nights*. New York: Simon and Schuster, 1920.

Robinson, David. *The History of World Cinema*. New York: Stein and Day, 1973.

Rotha, Paul and Richard Griffith. *The Film Till Now.* New York: Funk and Wagnalls, 1950.

Sarris, Andrew. *The American Cinema.* New York: E.P. Dutton & Co., Inc., 1968.

Schickel, Richard. *Movies: The History of an Art and an Institution.* New York: Basic Books, 1964.

Taylor, Deems, Bryant Hale, and Marcelene Peterson. *A Pictorial History of the Movies.* New York: Simon and Schuster, 1950.

Tyler, Parker. *Classics of the Foreign Film.* New York: The Citadel Press, 1962.

Vardac, Nicholas. *Stage to Screen.* Cambridge: Harvard University Press, 1949.

Wagenknecht, Edward. *The Movies in the Age of Innocence.* Norman: University of Oklahoma Press, 1962.

NATIONAL HISTORY

Anderson, Joseph and Donald Richie. *The Japanese Film: Art and Industry.* New York: Grove Press, 1960.

Armes, Roy. *French Cinema Since 1946.* London and New York: Swemmer and Barnes, 1966. (2 vols.)

Barnouw, Erik and S. Krishnaswamy. *Indian Film.* New York: Columbia University Press, 1963.

Bergman, Andres. *We're In the Money.* New York: Harper and Row, 1971.

Cowie, Peter. *The Swedish Cinema.* New York: Barnes and Company, Inc., 1966.

Hull, David Stewart. *Film in the Third Reich.* Los Angeles: University of California Press, 1969.

Jarratt, Vernon. *The Italian Cinema.* (*The National Cinema Series*, ed. Roger Manvell). New York: Macmillan, 1951.

Kracauer, Siegfried. *From Caligari to Hitler.* Princeton: Princeton University Press, 1947.

Leyda, Jay. *Kino: A History of the Russian and Soviet Film.* New York: Macmillan, 1960.

Low, Rachel and Roger Manvell. *The History of the British Film.* 3 vols. London: Allen and Unwin, 1948-50.

Manvell, Roger. *New Cinema in Britain.* London and New York: Dutton/Vista, 1969.

Richie, Donald. *Japanese Movies.* Japan Travel Bureau, 1961.

Sadoul, Georges. *French Film.* (The National Cinema Series, ed. Roger Manvell.) London: Falcon, 1953.

BIOGRAPHIES

Barry, Iris. *D.W. Griffith: American Film Master.* New York: The Museum of Modern Art, 1965.

Behlmer, Rudy (ed). *Memo From David O. Selznick.* New York: The Viking Press, 1972.

Blesh, Rudi. *Keaton.* New York: The Macmillan Company, 1966.

Calder-Marshall, Arthur. *The Innocent Eye, The Life of Robert J. Flaherty.* W.H. Allen, 1963.

Capra, Frank. *The Name Above the Title.* New York: Macmillan, 1971.

Chaplin, Charlie. *My Autobiography.* New York: Simon & Schuster, 1964.

Cocteau, Jean. *Cocteau on the Film.* New York: Roy Publishers, 1954.

Donner, Jorn. *The Personal Vision of Ingmar Bergman.* Indiana University Press, 1964.

Griffith, Richard. *The World of Robert Flaherty.* New York: Sloan and Pearce, 1953.

Henderson, Robert M. *D.W. Griffith: The Years at Biograph.* New York: Farrar, Straus and Giroux, 1970.

Huff, Theodore. *Charlie Chaplin.* New York: Henry Schuman, Inc., 1951.

Richie, Donald. *The Films of Akira Kurosawa.* Berkeley: University of California Press, 1965.

Seton, Marie. *Sergei M. Eisenstein, The Definitive Biography.* New York: Grove Press, 1960.

Schickel, Richard. *The Disney Version.* New York: Simon and Schuster, 1968.

Thomas, Bob. *King Cohn: Life and Times of Harry Cohn.* New York: Doubleday, 1967.

Thomas, Bob. *Thalberg: Life and Legend.* New York: Doubleday, 1969.

Vidor, King. *A Tree is a Tree.* New York: Harcourt, Brace and Company, 1953.

Walker, Alexander. *Stardom.* New York: Stein and Day, 1970.

Weinberg, Herman G. *The Lubitsch Touch.* New York: E.P. Dutton, 1968.

GENRE STUDIES

Armes, Roy. *Film and Reality, An Historical Survey.* Hammondsworth: Penguin, 1974.

Barsam, Richard Meran. *Nonfiction Film: A Critical History.* New York: E.P. Dutton and Company, Inc., 1973.

Battcock, Gregory. *The New American Cinema.* New York: E.P. Dutton & Co., Inc., 1967.

Durgnat, Raymond. *The Crazy Mirror.* New York: Dell, 1969.

Fenin, George and William Everson. *The Western, from Silents to Cinerama.* New York: Orion Press, 1963.

Grierson, John. *Grierson on Documentary.* Edited and compiled by Forsyth Hardy. New York: Harcourt, Brace, 1947.

Jacobs, Lewis (ed). *The Documentary Tradition.* New York: Hopkinson and Blake, 1971.

Kobal, John. *Gotta Sing Gotta Dance: A Pictorial History of Film Musicals*. London and New York: Hamlyn, 1970.

Lahue, Kalton C. *Continued Next Week: A History of the Moving Picture Serial.* Norman: University of Oklahoma Press, 1964.

Lahue, Kalton C. *World of Laughter*. Norman: University of Oklahoma Press, 1966.

Manvell, Roger (editor). *Experiment in the Film*. London: Grey Walls Press, 1948.

Mast, Gerald. *The Comic Mind*. New York: Bobbs Merrill, 1973.

Mekas, Jonas. *Movie Journal; The Rise of the New American Cinema, 1959-1971*. New York: Collier Books, 1972.

Miller, Don. *"B" Movies*. New York: Curtis Books, 1973.

Renan, Sheldon. *An Introduction to the American Underground Film*. New York: E.P. Dutton and Company, Inc., 1967.

Rotha, Paul, Richard Griffith, and Sinclair Road. *Documentary Film*. London: Faber and Faber, 1952.

Stephenson, Ralph. *The Animated Film*. London: A.S. Barnes, 1973.

Tyler, Parker. *Underground Film: A Critical History*. New York: Grove Press, 1969.

INDUSTRY AND TECHNOLOGY

Beddeley, W. Hugh. *The Technique of Documentary Film Production*. New York: Hasting House, 1963.

Bluem, A. William and Jason Squire (ed). *The Movie Business*. New York: Hastings House, 1972.

Crowther, Bosley. *The Lion's Share*. New York: Dutton & Company, 1957.

Fielding, Raymond (ed). *A Technological History of Motion Pictures and Television*. Berkeley and Los Angeles: U. of California Press, 1967.

Guback, Thomas. *The International Film Industry: Western Europe and America Since 1945*. Bloomington, Ind.: Indiana U. Press, 1969.

Halas, John. *Art in Movement: New Directions in Animation*. London: Studio Vista, 1970.

Hall, Ben M. *The Best Remaining Seats*. New York: Bramhall House, 1961.

Hoffman, Charles. *Sounds for Silents*. New York: The Museum of Modern Art, 1970.

Jobes, Gertrude. *Motion Picture Empire*. Hamden, Conn. : Archon Books, 1966.

Limbacher, James (ed). *Film Music: From Violins to Video*. Metuchen, N.J.: Scarecrow Press, 1974.

Limbacher, James L. *Four Aspects of the Film*. New York: Russell & Russell, 1968.

FILM THEORY AND CRITICISM

Agee, James. *Agee on Film: Reviews and Comments*. New York: McDowell, Obolensky, 1958.

Alpert, Hollis. *The Dreams and the Dreamers*. New York: Macmillan, 1962.

Arnheim, Rudolph. *Film*. Translated by L.M. Sieveking and Ian Morrow. London: Faber and Faber, 1933.

Arnheim, Rudolph. *Film as Art*. Berkeley and Los Angeles: University of California Press, 1958.

Balazs, Bela. *Theory of the Film*. Translated by Edith Bone. New York: Roy, 1953.

Bluestone, George. *Novels into Film*. Baltimore: John Hopkins Press, 1957.

Clair, Rene. *Reflections on the Cinema*. London: Kimber, 1953.

Crist, Judith. *The Private Eye, the Cowboy, and the Very Naked Girl*. New York: Holt, Rinehart and Winston, 1968.

Eisenstein, Sergei M. *Film Form*. Translated and edited by Jay Leyda. New York: Harcourt, Brace, 1949.

Eisenstein, Sergei M. *The Film Sense*. Translated and edited by Jay Leyda. New York: Harcourt, Brace, 1942.

Farber, Manny. *Negative Space*. New York: Praeger, 1972.

Ferguson, Otis. *The Film Criticism of Otis Ferguson*. Philadelphia: Temple University Press, 1971.

Jacobs, Lewis. *Introduction to the Art of the Movies*. New York: Noonday, 1960.

Kael, Pauline. *I Lost it at the Movies*. New York: Atlantic, Little, Brown, 1965.

Kael, Pauline. *Kiss Kiss, Bang Bang*. New York: Atlantic, Little, Brown, 1968.

Kael, Pauline. *Going Steady*. Boston and Toronto: Little, Brown and Company, 1970.

Kael, Pauline. *Deeper into Movies*. Boston and Toronto: Little, Brown and Company, 1973.

Kauffmann, Stanley. *A World on Film*. New York: Harper & Row, 1966.

Kauffmann, Stanley. *Figures of Light*. New York: Harper & Row, 1971.

Kauffmann, Stanley. *American Film Criticism*. New York: Liveright, 1972.

Kauffmann, Stanley. *Living Images*. New York: Harper & Row, 1975.

Kracauer, Siegfried. *Theory of Film*. New York: Oxford University Press, 1960.

Lawson, John Howard. *Film: The Creative Process*. New York: Hill and Wang, 1964.

Lindgren, Ernest. *The Art of the Film*. New York: Macmillan, 1948.

MacDonald, Dwight. *On Movies*. New York: Berkley Publishing Corp., 1969.

Manoogian, Haig P. *The Film-maker's Art*. New York: Basic Books, Inc., 1966.

Manvell, Roger. *Film*. Harmondworth, Middlesex: Penguin, 1950.

Nicoll, Allardyce. *Film and Theatre*. New York: Thomas Crowell, 1936.

Pudovkin, V.I. *Film Technique and Film Acting.* Translated by Ivor Montague. London: Vision Press Ltd., 1958.

Rotha, Paul. *Rotha on the Film.* Fairlawn, New Jersey: Essential Books, 1958.

Sarris, Andrew. *Confessions of a Cultist.* New York: Simon and Schuster, 1971.

Simon, John. *Private Screenings.* New York: Berkley Publishing Corp., 1967.

Simon, John. *Movies into Film.* New York: Dell Publishing Company, 1971.

Spottiswoode, Raymond. *Film and its Techniques.* Berkeley: University of California Press, 1950.

Spottiswoode, Raymond. *Film and its Techniques.* Berkely: University of California Press, 1963.

Reisz, Karel. *The Technique of Film Editing.* London: Focal Press, 1953.

Talbot, Daniel (ed). *Film: An Anthology.* New York: Simon and Schuster, 1959.

Taylor, John Russell. *Cinema Eye, Cinema Ear.* New York: Hill and Wang, 1964.

Tyler, Parker. *Magic and Myth of the Movies.* New York: H. Holt and Company, 1947.

Tyler, Parker. *The Three Faces of the Film.* New York: Yoseloff, 1960.

Warshow, Robert. *The Immediate Experience.* Garden City, N.Y.: Doubleday, 1962.

Weinberg, Herman G. *Saint Cinema.* New York: Dover Publications, Inc., 1970.

Young, Vernon. *On Film.* New York: The New York Times Book Company, 1972.

SOCIAL FORCE

Carmen, Ira H. *Movies, Censorship and the Law.* Ann Arbor, Michigan: U. of Michigan Press, 1966.

Cogley, John. *Report on Blacklisting.* New York: Fund for the Republic, 1956.

Farber, Stephen. *The Movie Rating Game.* Washington, D.C.: Public Affairs Press, 1972.

Huaco, George. *The Sociology of Film Art.* New York: Basic Books, 1965.

Hughes, Robert. *Film: Book 2, Films of Peace and War.* New York: Grove Press, 1962.

Jervie, I.C. *Movies and Society.* New York: Basic Books, Inc., 1970.

MacCann, Richard Dyer (editor). *Film and Society.* New York: Charles Scribner's Sons, 1964.

Powdermaker, Hortense. *Hollywood, The Dream Factory.* New York: Little, Brown, 1950.

Randall, Richard S. *Censorship of the Movies*. Madison, Wisc.: U. of Wisconsin Press, 1968.

Schumach, Murray. *The Face on the Cutting Room Floor*. New York: William Morrow and Co., 1964.

Wolfenstein, Martha and Nathan Leites. *Movies: A Psychological Study*. Glencoe, Illinois: Free Press, 1950.

PERIODICALS, JOURNALS AND MAGAZINES

Action, 7950 Sunset Blvd., Hollywood, California 90046.

American Cinematographer, 1782 North Orange Drive, Hollywood, California 90028.

Business Screen, Harcourt, Brace, Jovanovich Publications, 757 Third Ave., New York, N.Y. 10017.

Cahiers Du Dinema, 635 Madison Ave., New York, N.Y. 10016.

Cinema Journal, 217 Flint Hall, University of Kansas, Lawrence, Kansas 66044.

Critic, 144 Bleeker Street, New York, N.Y. 10012.

Dialogue on Film, Center for Advanced Film Studies, 501 Doheny Road, Beverly Hills, California 90210.

Film, 4 St. Mary's Grove, London, Barnes, S.W. 13.

Film Comment, 214 E. 11 St., New York, N.Y. 10003.

Film Culture, G.P.O. Box 1449, New York, N.Y. 10001.

Film Heritage, Box 652, University of Dayton, Dayton, Ohio 54509.

Film Quarterly, University of California Press, 2223 Fulton Street, Berkeley, California 94720.

Films and Filming, 75 Victoria Street, London, S.W.1.

Films In Review, 210 E. 68 St., New York, N.Y. 10021.

The Journal of Popular Film, Bowling Green University, Bowling Green, Ohio 43402.

Journal of the University Film Association, 156 West 19th Avenue, Ohio State University, Columbus, Ohio 43210.

Motion Picture Daily, 1270 Avenue of the Americas, New York, N.Y. 10020.

Movie, 21 Ivor Place, London, N.W.1.

Sight and Sound, British Film Institute, 155 West 15 Street, New York, N.Y. 10011.

The Silent Picture, 613 Harrow Road, London, W. 10.

Take One, P.O. 1778, Station B, Montreal 110, Canada.

Variety, 154 West 46 Street, New York, N.Y. 10036.

Name Index

Film Index

526

General Index